MW01259038

THE KOREAN WAR REMEMBERED

For Mike & Donna Lennon,

With many fond memories

of good times.

Sincerely,

Michael Devine

7-3-2023

THE KOREAN WAR REMEMBERED

Contested Memories of an Unended Conflict

MICHAEL J. DEVINE

UNIVERSITY OF NEBRASKA PRESS | LINCOLN

The University of Nebraska Press is part of a land-grant institution with campuses and programs on the past, present, and future homelands of the Pawnee, Ponca, Otoe-Missouria, Omaha, Dakota, Lakota, Kaw, Cheyenne, and Arapaho Peoples, as well as those of the relocated Ho-Chunk, Sac and Fox, and Iowa Peoples.

Library of Congress Cataloging-in-Publication Data
Names: Devine, Michael J., 1945–, author.
Title: The Korean War remembered: contested memories of an unended conflict / by Michael J. Devine.
Other titles: Contested memories of an unended conflict
Description: Lincoln: University of Nebraska, 2023 | Series: Studies in war, society, and the military | Includes bibliographical references and index.
Identifiers: LCCN 2022049683
ISBN 9781496234698 (hardcover)
ISBN 9781496236036 (epub)
ISBN 9781496236043 (pdf)
Subjects: LCSH: Korean War, 1950–1953—Public opinion. | Korean War, 1950–1953—Monuments. | Korean War, 1950–1953—United States. | Memorialization—Korea (South) | Collective memory—East Asia. | Korea—Foreign relations—1945– | United States—Foreign relations—Korea. | Korea—Foreign relations—United States. | Korea—Politics and government—20th century. | BISAC: HISTORY / Asia / Korea | HISTORY / Wars & Conflicts / Korean War
Classification: LCC DS921.9 .D48 2023 | DDC 951.904/2—dc23/eng/20221129
LC record available at https://lccn.loc.gov/2022049683

Set in Minion Pro by A. Shahan.

For Maija
and
The Gang of Five: Bret, Chris, Mia, Lisa, and Brian

Contents

List of Illustrations		ix
Preface		xi
Acknowledgments		xix
List of Abbreviations		xxiii
Introduction		1
1.	The "Police Action"	19
2.	Forging Memories	49
3.	Lessons Learned	79
4.	Memorializing across America	105
5.	The Korean War Veterans Memorial	137
6.	Conflicted Memories of Allies and Foes	157
7.	Memory, Truth, and Reconciliation	185
	Conclusion	207
	Notes	219
	Bibliography	259
	Index	297

Illustrations

Following page 136

1. Gen. Douglas MacArthur's statue overlooks Incheon Harbor

2. Memorial on the grounds of the Hawai'i state capitol in Honolulu

3. The Korean War Veterans Memorial (kwvm) on the National Mall in Washington dc

4. The lonely kiosk adjacent to the kwvm on the National Mall

5. English-language guide to Victorious Fatherland Liberation War Museum in Pyongyang

6. The uss *Pueblo*

7. The War Memorial of Korea in Seoul

8. Statue of two brothers at the entrance to the grounds of the War Memorial of Korea

9. Plaques along the entrance to the War Memorial of Korea

10. The author meets with Gen. Paik Sun-yup in his office on June 8, 2011

11. The United Nations Cemetery in Pusan, South Korea

12. A quiet 2017 anti-American protest in Seoul, South Korea

13. An aging U.S. veteran of the Korean War on a 2016 revisit to South Korea

14. Purple Heart medal and letter from a grieving father, 1972

Preface

Fifty years ago the ancient port city of Incheon remained a dusty and shabby place. Neglected buildings stood unsteady along unpaved streets, and local farmers moved their produce into crowded markets on overloaded bicycles or rickety carts pulled by scrawny animals. Today gleaming office towers of steel and glass rise above a modern city of three million souls. Located just twenty miles south of the demilitarized zone and just west of Seoul, the South Korean capital, Incheon bustles with all manner of traffic along crowded highways and high-speed rail and subway lines. Huge oceangoing vessels fill the busy seaways, and the world's major airlines fly in and out of a spectacular facility that experienced travelers consider the most modern international airport anywhere on the planet. Thousands of metal containers are loaded and unloaded from ships each day, while fleets of shiny new Hyundai and Kia autos, pickup trucks, and suvs await shipment to enthusiastic buyers throughout the world. However one aspect of the city remains the same as it did fifty years ago: the giant, heroic statue of Gen. Douglas MacArthur overlooking the harbor where the dramatic amphibious landing he led in September 1950 briefly altered the course of the Korean War.

As a young Peace Corps Volunteer newly arrived "in country" during the winter of 1970, I was assigned to teach English at Sogang Jesuit University in Seoul. Even before landing with my young Peace Corps colleagues at Seoul's then grim and outdated Kimpo Airport, I was eager to visit the Korean War sites and battlefields, including Incheon. I had already earned a master's degree in American history and envisioned a career teaching U.S. history after leaving the Peace Corps. Beyond my interest in history, as a son of the flat lands of the vast American Midwest, I was anxious to view the port of Incheon and explore the thirty-feet-high seawalls and watch for myself the movement of the harbor's powerful, treacherous tides. Once settled in at Sogang Jesuit University, I persuaded a few students to accompany me to visit Incheon by way of a rickety and rusted train. On the trip we passed aging steam locomotives still in wide use on Korea's rail lines. My tour of the old port city ended with a visit to Freedom Park overlooking the harbor and the numerous small islands far out in the bay (where the great Incheon International Airport is now located). The park commemorates the September 1950 Battle of Incheon, where forces led by MacArthur turned the course of the Korean War. And there, at the center of the park's open space, stood a statue of the general, nearly twenty feet tall. I remarked on the imposing and massive bronze statue, and I casually noted that there was no monument to Pres. Harry S. Truman.

My students were shocked that I would even mention such a villainous character. "Truman was bad: he caused Korea to be divided because he fired MacArthur," they said, almost in unison. "MacArthur wanted to unify Korea, and that's why Truman fired him," they all agreed. "General MacArthur was number one," they insisted, "and President Truman was number ten." In response I observed that, because of Truman's decisive decision in June 1950, MacArthur was ordered by his commander in chief to defend the Republic of Korea when the North Koreans invaded. I also pointed out that, if not for Truman, Korea would almost certainly be united—but under the Communist regime in the north. But the students remained adamant: Truman was responsible for the division of their homeland because he fired General MacArthur. This incident would be just my first experience in a long career of encountering public memory completely at odds with my own understanding of history.

Actually my young Korean students were not wrong. Truman was responsible for the division of Korea—twice. On two critical occasions Truman's actions led to a division that saved South Korea and allowed for the eventual rise of a free society, democratic government, and vibrant economy in the southern half of the Korean Peninsula. Truman's agreement following the Potsdam Conference of July 1945, which established what was intended to be a temporary military division along the 38th parallel, decisively prevented Soviet (Union of Soviet Socialist Republics, or USSR) domination over all of Korea at that time. Then in 1950 Truman's determined U.S.-led resistance to the North Korean invasion of June 1950 again saved the south and its fledging republic from a repressive Communist dictatorship. Indeed Korea is divided, but the situation could be worse, much worse.

At this time I had no way of knowing that Korea would be central to my life for the next half century and that my career as a historian engaged in the management of museums and historical institutions would lead to the writing of this book. A few months after my visit to Incheon, I met a special Korean woman. She was an instructor of English at a women's teachers college in Seoul, and we soon began an intimate affair that has now lasted for more than fifty years. Maija grew up as a Korean War survivor, having fled Seoul with her mother in the cold and ice of December 1950 as a huge army of Chinese "volunteers" supporting a small, reorganized North Korean military force approached the city. Along with tens of thousands of terrified refugees, she and her mother journeyed south by freight train and on foot. Separated from her father and his second wife, brought into the family in the months before the war started to produce a boy baby, the distraught mother and her daughter found refuge in Masan, a small city at the southernmost end of the Korean Peninsula. As I began to listen to her stories of a childhood so unlike my own in a comfortable and secure middle-class neighborhood in Joliet, Illinois, my interest in the contemporary history of Korea grew—along with my fascination with the storyteller herself. At the conclusion of my Peace Corps experience, Maija accompanied me as my wife back to the United States, where I completed my studies for a doctorate in U.S. history.

At the end of my graduate studies, I had every intention of embarking on a career in teaching at a college or university. However, my career suddenly turned in an unexpected direction, and I set off on a long journey through public history with leadership positions in state and federal historical institutions. Through a variety of unplanned and unexpected developments, I found myself in 1974 at age twenty-nine taking over as the director of a little-known and underfunded state commission in Ohio charged with planning and implementing programs to commemorate the bicentennial of the American Revolution. This position would lead to a forty-year career as a public historian managing major museums and historical organizations in Ohio, Maryland, Illinois, and Wyoming, along with frequent consultations with the National Endowment for the Humanities and various historical programs throughout the country. Eventually my peripatetic career would circle back to involvement with international affairs and Korean issues with my appointment in 2001 as director of the Harry S. Truman Presidential Library.

In my administration of museums, memorials, monuments, commemorative events, publications, and video productions, I became involved in practical and pragmatic concerns for which my graduate training had left me unprepared. Among them were the political challenges of collaborating with governors and their staffs, securing legislative funding, acquiring corporate and foundation support, and developing cooperative relationships with local governments and various educational institutions. On the job I learned the art of dealing with a staggering array of local, state, and federal bureaucracies and regulators, along with university administrators, religious leaders, and an endless range of civic, ethnic, and patriotic organizations. Moreover, I confronted the challenges created by disgruntled employees, patronage appointees, and incompetent, unsupportive, or inattentive board members—often appointed to bodies governing historical agencies because someone thought they had to be placed somewhere as a reward, and it seemed to be thought that they could not do too much harm with a historical organization (as opposed to highways, public safety, or the Department of Corrections). And then came lessons in crisis management—brought on by nature's wrath, public-relations disasters, and violent and destructive elements within society.

These challenges all had to be addressed while enabling teams of curators, archivists, exhibit designers, editors, event planners, and education specialists to engage in the process of preserving the past and telling the public important stories about that past in a concise, factual, and compelling manner. A colleague once told me that producing public history with both truth and integrity for hundreds of thousands of individuals while also satisfying elected officials, educators, regulators, and all sorts of advocates for diverse interests required the craftiness of a fox, the strength of a lion, and the gut of a goat. But it all proved to be exciting and rewarding work.[1] In response to my children's questions about what their father did in his office, I told them my job was to engage in combat every day with the forces of historical ignorance.

After a twenty-five-year absence from Korea while directing statewide history programs, the good fortune to return to Seoul came in 1995 with a Senior Fulbright Lectureship to teach U.S. history at Yonsei University. Maija was horrified by this prospect. Bitter memories of her troubled childhood and the severe restrictions on women still imposed by Korea's ancient Confucian customs left her with no interest in reconnecting to the land of her birth. Nevertheless, we both experienced a highly productive, positive, and enjoyable six-month tenure in Korea, accompanied by our two youngest children; and Maija began a writing career that led to the publication of short stories and an award-winning novel about survival during the Korean War and its impact on divided families.[2] Meanwhile, I developed associations with Korean War veterans and survivors, as well as numerous scholars of recent Korean history. Most importantly the Yonsei University assignment by the Fulbright commission also put me in contact with Horace G. Underwood (1917–2004), a prominent educator and member of a third-generation missionary family who had founded Yonsei University in the 1880s. Along with his younger brother Richard, Horace had served as a translator for the United Nations Command at the armistice negotiations in Panmunjom from 1951 through 1953 and later worked to build South Korea's modern system of higher education. I developed a close friendship with Dr. Underwood and began working with him to produce a memoir of his long involvement with the Korean people.[3]

A few years following my first Fulbright experience in Korea, I returned to East Asia for the 1998–99 academic year as the Houghton Freeman Professor of United States History at the Johns Hopkins University–Nanjing University Graduate Center for Chinese and American Studies in Nanjing, China. In many ways this was the most fascinating and rewarding twelve months of my career. While traveling widely throughout China, Korea, and East Asia at a time of unparalleled transition in that region, I had the experience of teaching exceptionally talented and enthusiastic Chinese graduate students preparing for careers in varied international endeavors. In addition, among my new and significant international associations was a friendship with the brilliant young scholar of U.S.-China relations Ren Dong Lai, whose inquisitive mind, knowledge of diplomatic history, and awareness of multicultural sensitives was unsurpassed. Sadly the ravages of cancer cut short his life and his time in the history profession, and I miss his thoughtful guidance, friendship, and unfailing sense of humor.

Upon the completion of my year in China, it became clear that my career was drifting away from American state and regional history and back toward diplomatic history and international affairs—graduate school specializations I had never abandoned while engaged in historical agency management. A position combining management of historical programs with my interest in Korean issues and international relations came with my appointment in September 2001 as the director of the Truman library in Independence, Missouri. Truman's presidency, unlike any of its predecessors, was from its very first day immersed in international issues, and Korea played a major part in establishing Truman's legacy. Over thirteen years my work at the Truman library placed me into close associations with many aspects of U.S.-Korea relations through sponsorship and participation in conferences, publishing ventures, archival projects, and exhibits. I made several trips to Korea in my capacity as the director while I renewed old friendships with prominent historians and leaders of the American Studies Association of Korea. My official role put me in the company of such prominent South Koreans as Gen. Paik Sun-yup, former South Korean president Kim Dae-jung, opinion writer and columnist Cho Gab Jae, and the trustees of the Park Chung Hee Presidential Museum. I also enjoyed the acquaintance of President Truman's daughter, Margaret, and her surviving sons, senior staff and retirees of the library, and several aides who served in the Truman White House. All remembered the former president with fondness. In particular, for fourteen years I benefited from a relationship with George Elsey, who served in the White House for both FDR and Truman. Elsey's sharp mind and generous spirit proved to be of assistance to me in many ways, and I remember him as a valued resource, friend, and mentor.

Needless to add here, the following chapters on public memory and memorialization are profoundly influenced by both my four decades of labor in the arena of public history and my personal memories acquired over more than a half century of interactions with Korean affairs and Korean people of many professions, socioeconomic backgrounds, and political affiliations.

In examining the record of the public memory of the Korean War, I have focused my study on the United States, while placing this nation's remembrance in the wider international context. I have sought to explore the war as a public memory in the two Koreas and the People's Republic of China. In examining those cultural auditoriums where memories are found, I have endeavored to include a wide sampling of memoirs, movies, museums, memorials, and monuments, while stopping well short of seeking to identify every known artifact related to memory of the Korean War. In addition, the literature on the Korean War is vast, expanding, and published in several languages. It is impossible to include every item written over a period of seven decades. Nevertheless, within the limits posed by travel, language, and access to sites and archival records, my research is sufficient, I believe, to draw conclusions that present an accurate comprehension of the subject and insightful assessments of a conflict and its contested public memories ongoing for seventy years.

Acknowledgments

Over the years I have worked on this project, many individuals and institutions have provided support and assistance. Foremost among them are the Woodrow Wilson Center in Washington DC, and its director of the History and Public Policy Program, Christian Ostermann. The Center for the Study of the Korean War (now a collection of the Harry S. Truman Library) and its director, Korean War veteran Paul Edwards, provided valuable assistance and a welcome place to work early on in this endeavor. His son Greg aided early drafts of chapter outlines. The staffs of two institutions with which I have a special relationship, the Truman library and the American Heritage Center at the University of Wyoming, gave me the excellent service they are famous for providing all their researchers. Moreover, the University of Wyoming Department of History, where I am an adjunct professor, made special accommodations for me during my trips to Laramie, and I am especially grateful for the interest and support of Dr. Isa Anderson Helfgott, the department's chair.

A Fulbright award to serve as a senior lecturer in American History at Sogang University in Seoul, Korea, during the 2017–18 academic year allowed for an extended period to visit and revisit familiar Korean War sites and memorials, renew and enrich old friendships, and establish new relationships. I am particularly grateful to Ms. Shim Jae-ok, director of the Fulbright Commission in Korea. Prominent Korean journalist Cho Gab Jae and his associates offered important assistance and support— moral, logistical, and financial. Among the Korean scholars who assisted me during my time in Seoul during my two Fulbright appointments was Prof. Lee Boh-hyung, the former chair of the history department at

Sogang University and founder of the American Studies Association of Korea. A great friend and mentor since my Peace Corps days, Professor Lee is a Korean War veteran whose memory remains sharp in his ninth decade. Also providing aid were professors Nam Si Uk and Pak Jin bin of Kyung Hee University and Park Dam of Sogang. I also owe a special thank you to professors Min Kyoung-hyoun of Korea University along with Paul Tonks and John Delury of Yonsei University.

Over the course of my career in public history and during the years spent researching and writing this volume, I have met with many individuals holding vivid memories of the Korean War. These include veterans, survivors, government officials, and others with close connections to the war and its memorialization. Some I interviewed formally for this project, others told me their stories and shared opinions long before I envisioned writing this book. Foremost among them is my wife, Maija, a survivor of the war who fled Seoul as a child with her mother and lived as a refugee in Masan in the southernmost part of Korea as war raged on in other parts of the peninsula. Other members of her family who shared memories include her older brother, Rhee Sun Bak, her twin brother, Dr. Rhee Chun-joen, and cousin Im Sang Ho, who lived with Maija as a refugee. My uncle and godfather, Col. Alan Esser, served in the Korean War following his 1951 graduation from the U.S. Military Academy at West Point and visited me in Korea during my Peace Corps days while on assignments to the Republic of Korea. During my first Fulbright lectureship to Korea in 1995 I became well acquainted with Dr. Horace Underwood, a veteran of the war, and during that time, my family and I shared a guest house on the Yonsei University campus with Korean War veteran Dr. Mark Monahan (Lt. Chang Kil-yong). On a later visit to Korea I had the privilege of interviewing Gen. Paik Sun-yup at his office in the War Memorial of Korea in Seoul.

As director of the Harry S. Truman Library in Independence, Missouri, I met frequently with individuals who worked in the Truman White House. They appeared at public programs on the Truman presidency sponsored by the library, and I met with them individually on numerous visits. Most importantly was George Elsey, a prominent and influential White House aide, with whom I developed a close friendship. Others included Milton Kayle and Ken Hechler. On several occasions I had lengthy and pleasant meetings with President Truman's daughter, Margaret Truman

Daniel, who was never the least reluctant to share her candid opinions on Truman White House events and personalities. Additional perspective on the Korean War and its memory came from my acquaintance of nearly two decades with Dr. Paul Edwards, a Korean War veteran and founder and director of the Center for the Study of the Korean War. I am also appreciative of the time and informative views provided by Tom Stevens of Overland Park, Kansas, a founder and past president of the Korean War Veterans Association; Tressa Park, a driving force behind the Kansas Korean War Memorial; Hal Barker of the Korean War Project; Gen. Richard G. Stilwell of the Korean War Veterans Memorial Advisory Board; and Col. James Fisher and Michel Au Buchon of the Korean War Veterans Memorial Foundation.

Of course any project of this nature builds on the work of earlier scholars, and I am deeply indebted to the significant contributions to the understanding of the Korean War and its legacy to the work of Allan R. Millett, James I. Matray, Sheila Miyoshi Jager, Melinda Pash, Judith Keene, Paul Edwards, Steven Casey, William Stueck, and Kangdan Oh.

Several talented and skilled young graduate students in the United States and Korea assisted me with their excellent computer skills. They include Marcin Jerzewski at the Wilson Center, Abaigail Eagan of the University of Wyoming, Elise Schuster, an international student at Korea University, and Eom Taegyung, my assistant at Sogang University. While working in Seattle, Washington, my project was aided by Kelli Yakabu and Karen Wang, both outstanding graduate students in the school of Library and Information Science at the University of Washington. Several scholars read my manuscript, in part or in whole, and offered numerous helpful comments and suggestions: Kangdon Oh, Kathryn Weatherby, Raymond Geselbracht, James Matray, Robert Beatty, and Heather Miller. Marla Miller of the University of Massachusetts Department of History guided my work on early drafts of the manuscript, and she provided thoughtful and informed recommendations on public history issues.

In spite of all the expert assistance and advice I have benefited from, readers will discover errors of omission and commission that must be attributed entirely to me.

Maija Rhee, my partner and collaborator on everything in my life for more than half a century, deserves a special mention. She is in many ways responsible for my continuing fascination in all things Korean and a source of endless observations and explanations regarding the mysteries I still encounter in Korean culture. And she is a provider of sound advice that has kept my life and career focused, rewarding, and enjoyable, while at the same time serving as the loving center of our family.

Abbreviations

ABMC	American Battle Monuments Commission
CIA	Central Intelligence Agency
CVID	complete, verifiable, irreversible denuclearization
CWIHP	Cold War International History Project
DMZ	Demilitarized Zone
DPRK	Democratic People's Republic of Korea (North Korea)
HSTL	Harry S. Truman Library
IAEA	International Atomic Energy Agency
JCS	Joint Chiefs of Staff
KATUSA	Korean Augmentation to the United States Army
KMAG	Korean Military Advisory Group
KPA	Korean People's Army (North Korea)
KWNM	Korean War National Museum
KWVA	Korean War Veterans Association, Inc.
KWVAB	Korean War Veterans Advisory Board
KWVM	Korean War Veterans Memorial
KWVMAB	Korean War Veterans Memorial Advisory Board
KWVMF	Korean War Veterans Memorial Foundation
MIA	missing in action
NATO	North Atlantic Treaty Organization
NPS	National Park Service
OSS	Office of Strategic Services
PLA	People's Liberation Army (China)
POW	prisoner of war
PRC	People's Republic of China

ROK	Republic of Korea (South Korea)
ROKA	Republic of Korea Army
TRCK	Truth and Reconciliation Commission, Korea
UN	United Nations
UNC	United Nations Command
USAF	United States Air Force
USDS	United States Department of State
USFK	United States Forces, Korea
USSR	Union of Soviet Socialist Republics (Soviet Union)

THE KOREAN WAR REMEMBERED

Introduction

This book is intended to fill a gap in the study of the Korean War and enhance the expanding literature in the field of public history. The focus is the evolution over seven decades of an unsettled American public memory of the Korean War as expressed in monuments, memorials, museums, and commemorative events. Two central themes course through the chapters of this study. First, the public memory of the war in the United States and other parts of the world has evolved significantly over the second half of the twentieth century and into the twenty-first. This evolution will undoubtedly continue to transform as ever-changing domestic culture and perceptions of international developments and relationships shape our appreciation of the brutal warfare held in check to this day on a divided peninsula by a fragile armistice. Second, the evolving and conflicted memory of the Korean War in the United States can only be understood and appreciated in a broad international context. To understand and fully appreciate the mnemonic sites of remembrance in the United States, it is necessary to look abroad, as many of the memorials dedicated to the service of U.S. soldiers and those of the United Nations Command (UNC) are located in South Korea. Furthermore, most of the scores of monuments recognizing Korean War veterans in the United States came about with significant support from the local Korean-American community, and the Korean War Veterans Memorial on the National Mall in Washington DC, would not exist had advocates and planners not received critical financial support from Korean corporations and the government of the Republic of Korea. Likewise, understanding the war and its troubled legacy requires an examination of the conflicting public memories of the unfinished war that exist in the two Koreas and the People's Republic of China (PRC) and hinder international efforts to achieve peace and reconciliation.

While my primary interest is the United States, in any effort to understand the contested memory of the Korean War, attention must be given to the contentious and conflicting public memories elsewhere, especially in the two Koreas and the PRC. In addition to assessing "theaters" of public memory, this study will explore nearly seven decades of contentious international scholarship and the extent to which public policy, international affairs, and efforts at peace and reconciliation remain influenced by the troubled memories of the Korean War experience.

Commonly held interpretations of past events define a nation's existence and legitimacy, and how the past is understood influences contemporary society. Indeed, collective memory is as much about the needs of the present as it is about the past. Memory interprets the past and holds symbolic power capable of energizing and empowering a people, and public representations of history in popular culture, museums, and memorials can provide convincing messages to a population. Both memory and history overlap and share common spaces. Yet memory is not history and cannot be substituted for historical analysis. While history strives for rational and objective, evidence-based search for truth, collective memory is emotional, selective, and highly subjective. It can be employed in forgetting horrific incidents, details, or even crimes, and especially troubling memories can be suppressed through a generally held communal forgetfulness.[1]

In spite of their limitations, both history and memory are employed relentlessly by all societies in efforts to reconstruct their past while attempting to shape their present. No binary exists between history and memory. History, like memory, is never fixed in place or static. As new documentation and other forms of solid evidence become available, historical analysis is constantly rewritten. In addition, the passage of time, changes in societal norms, and altered geopolitical circumstances lead to fundamental reevaluations of past events. Of course history is also subjected to deliberate misuse; and, under pressure from powerful interest groups or government impositions, interpretations of the past can become nothing more than propaganda. Likewise, public memories can be imposed from above by an authoritarian regime or a governing class in control of popular culture. Furthermore, because a nation's commonly held public memory can be mistaken for history, there exists a danger of memory altogether replacing the necessary quest for historical truth. Whenever this happens the highly subjective nature of public memory can be particularly problematic in international relations, domestic good will, and the formation of sound government policy.

Over the past thirty years, the remembrance of wars has increasingly attracted the attention of American scholars. Historian Jay Winter has observed a "memory boom" among academics, as well as the public, and has noted "the efflorescence of interest in the subject of memory inside the academy and beyond it—in terms of a wide array of collective meditations on the war and the victims of war." Winter states that, in recent decades, the need to acknowledge the victims of war and its ravages has become central to contemporary cultures in many countries; and while the focus of Winter's study is World War I and its legacy, he sees a common pattern in the public remembrance of all twentieth-century wars. He writes that "whether we are dealing with the international warfare of the early twentieth century or the fragmentation of warfare since 1945, remembrance follows armed conflict as night follows day."[2]

Both victors and the vanquished seek for themselves a common memory of war. The Korean War is no exception. As remembrance of warfare contributes mightily to the creation of national identities, governmental appropriations and private funding are aimed at establishing an orthodox or officially sanctioned interpretation of a war. Examining how a nation remembers those who died in warfare further allows for the analysis of a nation's policies, racial and gender attitudes, and class structure. Nevertheless, differing memories of wars still find expression, although a general consensus, or "homogenization," of national memories tends to emerge eventually about the nature of a war and its impact on the national psyche.[3] However, after seven decades, the public memory of the Korean War of 1950–53 appears as yet unresolved in the United States and elsewhere—particularly in the two Korean states where the devastating warfare took place. Furthermore, because the conflict (not officially declared a "war" in the United States until 1999) was not ended by the 1953 armistice but only placed on hold, it may be some time before the war's ultimate impact on the souls of the various participants is fully known.

This study will center on the memories of war held in the United States and nations whose leadership expended blood and treasure in the violent Korean conflict of 1950–53. In the United States and elsewhere, all parties to the warfare have learned to recast the memory of war to serve their needs. In the case of the Korean conflict, as soon as the armistice quieted major military operations, diverse national memories among the participants began to emerge. While more than sixty nations were involved in the Korean War in some manner, the two Koreas, China, and the United States paid the highest price and maintain the most vivid public memories.[4] These states each advanced radically differing public histories of the ongoing conflict and its results, and each has employed the memories of the war to advance social and political agendas. Because the war remains unfinished business, public memories of the warfare and its aftermath will continue to evolve in order to align with changing international realities.

It appears most Americans only vaguely remember the Korean War, if at all. It is recalled as a conflict that occurred in the distant past and left the world with a volatile and dangerous situation in East Asia. Few Americans appear familiar with the specific causes or consequences of this war, suspended by an uneasy armistice that has survived nearly seven decades. While considered a "forgotten" war in the pantheon of the armed conflicts of the United States, ironically the Korean War appears to be increasingly remembered among aging veterans of the war in monuments and memorials and in public concern for national security when North Korea tests nuclear weapons. For Koreans living either north or south of the demilitarized zone (DMZ) that divides their nation, the war of 1950-53 is a central fact of everyday life. The impact of the war shapes their daily existence, as the Republic of Korea (South) and the Democratic People's Republic of Korea (North) both adhere to conflicting official memories of the Cold War confrontation that separated their ancient civilization into heavily armed and ideologically opposed regimes.

In this examination of the contested memories of the Korean War, the first chapter seeks to review the Korean conflict of 1950–53 in the context of the worldwide Cold War that emerged following World War II and a bitter rivalry on the divided Korean Peninsula for dominance between two opposing foreign philosophies. Communism as a form of governance arrived in the north during autumn 1945 with cadres of exiled Koreans reentering their homeland from the Soviet Union (USSR), China, and elsewhere accompanied by Soviet military units. At the same time, Korean supporters of Western-style democracy and a capitalistic economic system returned to Korea following decades of advocacy for their nation's independence in the United States, China, and Western nations. The artificial division of Korea along the 38th parallel—a decision made at the 1945 Potsdam Conference without serious analysis of the potential effects or input from Koreans themselves—became permanent by 1948. The resulting establishment of two regimes—the Soviet-backed Democratic People's Republic of Korea (DPRK) in the north and the U.S.- and UN-backed Republic of Korea (ROK) in the south—led to a nasty rivalry over who would dominate the country. Inevitable skirmishes along the border and guerilla fighting in the south led to a full-scale attack by the north on June 25, 1950. This sudden invasion came with the approval and support of the USSR and China's new Communist government. In the United States, Pres. Harry S. Truman and members of his administration, who viewed the invasion as a brutal effort to expand Soviet influence in East Asia, immediately responded to the North Korean attack, committing military forces under a UN mandate to rescue the fledgling Republic of Korea. In the eyes of many Americans and American allies alike, the manner in which the thirty-seven-month-long war was fought, the limited use of military power on both sides of the conflict, and the ill-defined objectives of the conflict overall made this a different war from any other wars that had been fought thus far in the twentieth century. For Americans, whose memories were dominated by the recently and victoriously concluded Second World War, Korea appeared unique in the annals of U.S. warfare.

The Korean conflict established lasting memories in the United States during the fighting and immediately thereafter, a process explored in chapters 2 and 3. Even as warfare raged across the Korean Peninsula, memories began to form of columns of soldiers retreating across frozen, snow-covered fields to avoid capture by "hordes" of Chinese; devastated landscapes; stranded orphans and civilian carnage; mistreated prisoners of war (POWs); and "brainwashed" U.S. and UNC captives confessing to bogus war crimes. These early memories (more like nightmares) had an impact on the treatment of U.S. and allied veterans, who many people viewed as less successful and less heroic than those who had fought in World War II. Misconceptions about the war were vividly portrayed in popular culture, while Republican critics of the Truman administration turned against the war, denounced Truman's refusal to expand the war beyond Korea, called for the use of nuclear weapons, and railed against the abrupt dismissal of their popular hero Gen. Douglas MacArthur. Yet as images of war seared the public memory, the war had little or no impact on most Americans' daily lives; and UNC allies, most of whom had provided only token support for the far-off war effort in Korea, remained focused on their own economic and political issues. In spite of the conflict's limited use of weapons and its confinement to a small, mountainous stretch of land in East Asia, the unfinished war in Korea would permanently change the geopolitics of the region and the course of world affairs. This reality would soon be recognized by world leaders, whose conflicting memories of the war would influence policy throughout the Cold War and into its aftermath.

By the mid-1980s, international developments in East Asia brought about a profound evolution in the public memory of the war in the United States and the nations of the UNC alliance. Chapters 4 and 5 examine how South Korea's unexpected emergence as a genuine democracy with a surging economy coincided with the hosting of the successful 1988 Summer Olympics in Seoul and presented the world with a dramatically changed view of the Republic of Korea. As the ROK thrived and received diplomatic recognition from both the USSR and China, the DPRK became more isolated than ever and sank further into economic stagnation, famine, and despotism. There now seemed justification for commemorating those who fought decades earlier to save the nascent but still impoverished democracy in South Korea from Communism. Across the United States, grassroots efforts by veterans, their families, and Korean immigrants led the way in creating a new memory of the Korean War.

The focus of chapter 6 is the conflicting nature of memories of the two Koreas and China, as well as other nations involved in the war. The memories of these nations appear only in the background of earlier chapters, but the understanding of our continuing war in Korea requires an exploration of the conflicted public memories that hinder peace and reconciliation. In both North Korea and China, the United States is remembered as the callous and inhumane aggressor and instigator of the conflict. Perhaps not surprisingly, these dictatorial regimes have retained tight control over officially sanctioned memories and narratives about the past. These two wartime allies differ, however, on the critical role played by the hundreds of thousands of "volunteers" from the PRC. China sees its support of North Korea as a selfless act of support for a Communist neighbor in mortal peril, while North Korean leaders maintain that the DPRK's survival resulted from the brilliant and courageous leadership of Kim Il-sung and his ingenious philosophy of Juche, or self-reliance. South Korea, in contrast to its Communist neighbors, generally ignored the history of the war and sought to suppress its memory throughout three decades of military dictatorship that followed the 1953 armistice. Only a heroic statue of General MacArthur overlooking the harbor at Incheon and a vast cemetery for UNC soldiers killed during the conflict marked the war's remembrance. This changed with the arrival of democracy in the late 1980s, when the ROK began to commemorate the war as a successful effort by the Korean people and their UN allies to fight off an invasion of Communist forces seeking to destroy the new republic. Chapter 7 and the conclusion bring the story of conflicting memories and contested historical narratives up to date, even as the contest for dominance on the Korean Peninsula continues.

The North Korean invasion across the 38th parallel on Sunday, June 25, 1950, shocked the United States and its allies, bringing back memories of the Sunday morning when Japanese bombers struck Pearl Harbor just a decade earlier. Once again a surprise attack disrupted a peace that proved to be far more fragile than it appeared. Unlike previous wars, the Korean conflict came without prologue, as Americans were concentrating on rebuilding their lives, growing their businesses, and buying homes and cars while feeling secure behind their arsenal of nuclear weapons. President Truman and his key advisors correctly understood the North Korean attack as Soviet-inspired, an attempt to advance Communism in East Asia through force. They worried that the Soviets might, if successful in Korea, threaten Berlin, Western European stability, and the new North Atlantic Treaty Organization alliance. Truman also saw the attack on the Republic of Korea as a direct assault by the Soviets on the United Nations (UN) and believed that standing up to aggression was the only course that could spare the UN from the fate that befell the League of Nations in the 1930s.[5]

The nature of the Korean War and U.S. involvement in an international conflict that did not directly threaten U.S. security proved to be difficult for the public to embrace or understand. Initially the war had wide public support in the United States. The roles of the Soviet Union and the new PRC as U.S. Cold War adversaries immediately became apparent. Republicans on the political right, as well as leftist critics of President Truman's Cold War policies toward the Soviets, expressed support early on for the "police action" to save the Republic of Korea. Although a significant antiwar movement never emerged, support for the war diminished over the next three years as casualties increased and as the United States expanded its goal of saving the south to unifying all of Korea. China's unexpected entry into the war caused alarm, and the war's brutality—with images of lightly armed Chinese forcing a retreat of the U.S. military, soldiers huddled in the bitter cold, long lines of terrified refugees, and starving orphans abandoned on the deserted streets—shocked the U.S. public and left lasting memories. Many people in the United States soon came to view the limited war in Korea as a conflict that did not conform to broadly held memories of prior conflicts, especially the decisive end of World War II. Furthermore, President Truman's seemingly abrupt dismissal of General MacArthur, a popular hero of World War II, who had publicly argued that in Korea there was "no substitute for victory," caused the president's public approval rating to crash. Finally the long, protracted, and inconclusive nature of the peace negotiations, begun at Kaesong in July 1951 and continued in Panmunjom, were complicated by the thorny issue of repatriation of POWs, bewildering the American public. Growing dissatisfaction with the conduct of the war in Korea became a major factor in the presidential campaign of 1952.[6]

Americans turned away from a war that was not formally declared, where the real enemy—the Soviet Union—was never directly confronted, and in which the aim was not a lasting peace, or even the complete eradication of the Communist North Korean regime and expulsion of the Chinese from the northern half of the peninsula. People of the United States considered themselves a citizenry reluctant to use force except to protect their national existence or advance some noble or altruistic purpose, and a limited war headed toward a messy settlement and unpopular compromises did not fit the image they had for their nation. When the U.S. government refused to commit itself to an outright military victory, disillusionment took over.[7] Of course the allies of North Korea, the Soviet Union, and the PRC also restrained themselves from an all-out commitment of their military forces and proved willing to settle for a negotiated armistice, short their goal of reunification, but Americans did not seem to notice.

Popular new mythologies about the Korean conflict entered the public memory during the war and in the years immediately following the 1953 armistice, and the initial memories many people in the United States were forming were based on the most unpleasant aspects of the Korean War. The fact that many Americans believed the United States had never participated in a "limited war" where the objective was something less than total victory, rendered the armistice to many Americans (and their allies) a disgraceful capitulation to Communist aggression that allowed a propaganda victory to the enemies of democracy. Additionally, at the end of combat in Korea, the supposedly unpatriotic behavior by many of the nearly 7,200 U.S. soldiers, sailors, and airmen held captive in brutal conditions by the North Koreans and their Chinese allies became an issue of national concern. At least 2,730 American POWs (nearly 40 percent, an astonishingly high rate) died under horrific conditions in captivity, and most who survived behaved honorably and loyally; however, the lingering POW issue would mean that, unlike veterans of all other U.S. wars in the twentieth century, Korean War POWs were stigmatized for decades. The American public was led to believe that never before (or since) in American history had the nation's POWs behaved in such an atrocious and cowardly manner. Even worse, when twenty-one U.S. POWs refused to return home at the end of the war, the news landed like a punch in the gut. The term *brainwashing* entered the American lexicon, and an entire body of literature emerged questioning the toughness, patriotism, and courage of the post–World War II generation of soldiers. Social scientists even advanced theories for this apparent weakness and put forth recommendations for how to strengthen the wimpy, overly protected "mama's boys" reared by domineering mothers.[8] Peace in Korea, when it finally arrived, left the U.S. populace feeling less secure and in no mood to remember or memorialize the unpopular conflict.

In East Asia the Korean War drastically altered geopolitical alignments and resulted in the formation of new public memories among the war's participants. Within the two Koreas, differing public memories soon emerged, shaped by authoritarian regimes with political agendas. In the south, Pres. Syngman Rhee expressed his nation's frustration that their primary patron and ally would not expand fighting to bring about Korean unification after China entered the conflict. This sense of disappointment was expressed in Rhee's public praise and memorialization of General MacArthur. Rhee's frustration coexisted with an acknowledgment of dependence on the United States for continued security and feelings of gratitude toward the United States and UNC nations for having saved the fledgling Republic of Korea. As an evolving democracy, a significant measure of dissent from the official ROK orthodoxy and dictatorial policies remained, periodically boiling over in antigovernment demonstrations. Finally in 1960 a huge student-led protest forced the aged Rhee into exile in Hawai'i. By contrast, in the north absolutely no opposition was permitted, and the myth soon emerged that their nation had almost single-handedly stood up to the most powerful nation on earth and prevailed under the brilliant leadership of Kim Il-sung. This narrative became the national creed, and following the 1953 armistice, Kim immediately began to consolidate his power, purge his Communist rivals, and memorialize his wartime leadership. By 1960 he had developed a cult of personality unknown anywhere on earth for its intensity and longevity. At the same time, China officially formed a public memory that painted the war as a glorious victory, which ensured the independence of a client Communist state (albeit one that never publicly expressed much gratitude to its sponsors). Although frustrated that their nation, like Korea, remained divided, with a U.S.-sponsored regime in Taiwan, Chinese Communist leaders were emboldened at having fought the United States to a draw. Mao gained recognition as the leader of a new China that rivaled the Soviet Union in prestige among Communist states. Meanwhile, the Soviet Union, in de-Stalinization mode following the armistice, had little it wanted to remember or memorialize—or even publicly acknowledge.[9] These differing memories of the Korean War shaped the course of international affairs in East Asia for decades to come.

In the United States, memory of the Korean War profoundly influenced foreign policy in East Asia and beyond. Korea expanded the Cold War into a global military confrontation and drastically increased the presence of the United States in East Asia. The war in Korea also led directly to involvement in the Vietnam conflict. Already supporting the French government's desperate attempt to hold on to its colony at the time the Korean War broke out, the Truman administration quickly increased aid to the French in the belief that the struggle in Indochina was, like the war in Korea, a test of the American will against Soviet-sponsored aggressors. A decade later, with the French gone, American leaders tied themselves to a series of ineffective anti-Communist regimes in South Vietnam. In the 1960s the Democratic administrations of presidents John F. Kennedy and Lyndon B. Johnson were concerned that any sign of weakness in the face of Communist threats would lead to a repeat of Republican attacks on their leadership, like those charging the Truman administration with the "loss of China" and Sen. Joe McCarthy's witch hunts in the early 1950s for Communist traitors lurking within the federal government and elsewhere in American society. Neither Kennedy nor Johnson were willing to risk the pursuit of any policy in Vietnam other than the escalation of support for the weak, anti-Communist regimes existing in the southern half of the country. Korea seemed to make the case for limited war as a means of successfully enforcing containment.[10] Eventually U.S. leaders would see that the historical comparison of Vietnam as another Korea was a false analogy, but not until the Vietnam War had ended in disaster. At the same time, lingering Korean War-era hatred and fear of China prevented full normalization of relations with the United States until five years after the U.S. exit from Saigon. This was also well after a clear deterioration of Sino-Soviet relations had become apparent to all, and most other nations of the wartime UNC had established full diplomatic relations with the PRC.

Following the 1953 armistice, both North and South Korea appeared to be competing dictatorships locked in a struggle for legitimacy and dominance on the peninsula, all while abusing their own citizens and threatening regional stability, if not world peace. Yet the public memory of the Korean War in the United States and other nations changed little over three decades, even as world events altered international relationships and new political realities emerged. At the same time, the uncertain peace along the jagged DMZ separating the two Koreas remained problematic. Although the attention of the United States and the world would soon be overshadowed by the war in Vietnam and other Cold War crises, troublesome incidents along the DMZ occurred almost as soon as the signatures were affixed to the truce documents. Violent acts in different locations continued to puncture the fragile truce put in place by the 1953 armistice. These included commando raids and intrusions into each other's boundaries by both North and South, the unsuccessful January 1968 attempt by thirty North Korean infiltrators to assassinate South Korean president Park Chung-hee in Seoul, and the capture two days later of the USS *Pueblo*, an American spy ship that had approached North Korean waters. In the 1970s North Koreans dug a series of tunnels under the DMZ as part of a plan to allow thousands of troops to secretly enter the south, and in 1978 terrorists from the DPRK murdered seventeen high-ranking members of the South Korean government by detonating a bomb at a public ceremony in the capital of Burma (now Myanmar). By the mid-1980s it appeared that the two Koreas were roughly equal in military strength while still dependent on their much stronger allies.[11]

However, the 1988 Summer Olympics in Seoul served as a watershed in the world's opinion of the Republic of Korea. The spectacularly staged event showcased the ROK's economic and social advances and signaled the rising confidence of the South Korean population. Within a few years of the Seoul Olympics, the south held its first truly democratic elections and enjoyed universal status as a rising Asian "economic tiger." Changing international dynamics soon led to the normalization of relations between South Korea and both of the North's wartime sponsors—the Soviet Union and China. Then, with the implosion of the Soviet Union on December 26, 1991, the DPRK was suddenly more isolated than ever; its economic collapse demonstrated North Korea's dependence on the financial aid once provided by its longtime sponsor.[12]

All these unexpected developments had a profound impact on public remembrances of the war and led to reassessment of its consequences. In recent decades both the people of the Republic of Korea and the United States have witnessed a rising recognition of the war's strategic importance. By the 1990s Americans began to see the war as both a necessary and successful endeavor. A dominant public narrative in both nations now understands the war as a conflict in which U.S. and UN intervention saved the ROK. In spite of lingering anti-American sentiments in some sectors of the South Korean population, five decades after the North Korean invasion the vast majority of those living in the ROK look favorably upon the United States.[13] Coinciding with this new, positive view of South Korea, the American public's appraisal of President Truman, whose approval ratings had dropped to less than 30 percent in 1952, had risen to the point where he came to be remembered among the nation's six or eight greatest presidents.[14]

Among a considerable number of South Koreans, and within the United States and its UN allies in the Korean War, there exist those who remember the war as something other than the rescue of a fledgling and imperfect democracy from Communist aggression. South Korean critics of U.S. policies rail against the undeniable wartime atrocities committed by U.S. forces, American support for the harsh and cruel dictatorships of Syngman Rhee and the generals who succeeded him, and the profiteering and corruption in a series of South Korean regimes. These South Koreans, along with American scholars of a "revisionist" school, condemn the failures of South Korea's leaders to address the myriad social and economic needs of the South Korean people and view the Korean War and its unpleasant aftermath as evils brought about primarily because of U.S. interference in Korea's civil dispute.[15] In their admirable idealism, they believe that somehow the Korean people, if only left to themselves, would have long since resolved all their internal differences, unified the peninsula, and created the world's most peaceful, prosperous, and egalitarian state. This simplistic view is frequently shared by certain American and South Korean academics, radical labor unions, and leftist political groups—at times infiltrated, funded, and supported by Communist North Korea.[16]

More radical and activist South Korean critics of the United States have organized violent demonstrations in recent years to protest U.S. military involvement in the massacre of more than two hundred South Korean civilians at No Gun Ri in 1950 and to remove the statue of General MacArthur from its place of honor in Incheon—only to be repelled by countermeasures by patriotic and pro-American ROK veterans. Leftist demonstrations in the past few years have also challenged the rewriting of school textbooks to include an anti-Communist consensus on the war and its aftermath.[17]

Contested public memories of the Korean War in the Republic of Korea, where it is possible to both hold and express memories counter to the official narratives, are currently examined in government investigations and peace and reconciliation commissions in an effort to merge truth with memory. While issues remain contentious and unresolved, the efforts at reconciliation have, in South Korea at least, led to a greater understanding of the war and its legacy. No similar effort at seeking truth and reconciliation exists in the north.

While the memory of the Korean War remains unsettled and conflicted, the Korean War's importance as a critical turning point in post–World War II international relations cannot be ignored. Scholars and policy makers have not overlooked the significance of the first armed confrontation of the Cold War, and the international literature on the war is vast, contentious, and expanding.[18] In his study of the Korean War in its international context, historian William Stueck has concluded, "The Korean War is too complex an event, its terrain too ideologically charged and the documentation of many of its parts too incomplete to lend itself to scholarly consensus."[19] While World War II brought about monumental changes in world affairs, historians have come to understand that the "limited" Korean War prevented drastic changes that would have destabilized East Asia. The Korean War maintained a Cold War status quo and established the Soviet-American competition as something less than an unrestricted conflict. Indeed, the definitive assessment of the Korean War continues as a work in progress, and it appears to be too early to place the Korean War in the pantheon of twentieth-century warfare.

The outcome of the three-year-long conflict, placed on hold by the uneasy armistice of July 1953, has resulted in seven decades of unprecedented peace and prosperity for the nations of East Asia with the notable exception of the self-isolated North Koreans.

Because of the lingering dissatisfaction with the way the war was fought and its inconclusive ending, memorializing the Korean War and publicly honoring its veterans came about with remarkable slowness in the United States. It seemed the war was easy to ignore. Most who served in the U.S. Armed Forces during the war years never saw Korea, and young men often avoided the wartime draft altogether with college deferments. Unlike the years of World War II, most American families experienced little or no changes in their daily lives during the Korean conflict. There was no rationing, shortages of any kind were few, and there existed little sense of immediate threat to national security—or even the continuing economic prosperity.

By 1953 news of the war no longer appeared on the front pages of U.S. newspapers. For the most part, Korean War veterans arrived home one by one from an unpopular conflict following staged rotations based on a point system. They frequently returned to a public largely unaware or unappreciative of their service. Korean War veterans came home at a time when American memories of the victorious World War II were still fresh, and the war from which they returned had grown increasingly unpopular. Furthermore, the misrepresentation of issues related to possible collaboration with their Communist captors by American POWS tainted all veterans. To a large extent, Korean War veterans were ignored or treated with indifference rather than forgotten.[20] For decades veterans of the Korean War tended to keep to themselves, except for occasional reunions with fellow veterans.

The approach of the war's fiftieth anniversary brought Korean War veterans a new appreciation from the public. Beginning in the 1980s, veterans and their families came to realize that, unlike veterans of the recently concluded Vietnam War, American society had never appropriately recognized them, and they actively sought to create what they considered a new memory of the war and a proper awareness of their service and sacrifice. Along with their families, veterans themselves have been at the forefront of the memorialization efforts, often assisted by local Korean American communities and South Korean corporations. After the Vietnam Memorial had been completed and unveiled in the early 1980s on the National Mall in Washington DC, efforts to create a Korean War memorial took on a new urgency. Following almost a decade of controversy and poor planning, a memorial consisting of eighteen oversized military figures moving somberly across an uncertain terrain was dedicated in 1993. It had to be rededicated four years later because shoddy construction had quickly turned the memorial into an eyesore. In the National Defense Authorization Act for Fiscal Year 1999 (Section 1067), the U.S. Congress officially changed the "Korean Conflict" to the "Korean War." By 2000 almost every state, along with numerous local governments and institutions, had erected memorials honoring their Korean War veterans. After more than a half century, the long-delayed attention has given Korean War veterans a sense of pride and camaraderie. One veteran noted the change, saying, "You go to reunions and you find yourself trying to remember what you spent the last fifty years trying to forget."[21]

To some extent the long period of forgetfulness in the United States was shared by other countries that participated in the UNC. However, all the participants in the Korean War have now memorialized their nation's involvement in the first armed conflict of the Cold War era. Numerous memorials to the veterans of UNC nations can be found along the southern side of Korea's DMZ and in the veterans' home countries. In Korea, where the war was anything but limited, both North and South have constructed museums and memorials to the world telling vastly different stories about its origins, conduct, and outcome. A particularly stark contrast in the competing narratives of their war museums concerns the roles of foreign powers in the Korean War. In North Korea the story is all about the brilliant Kim Il-sung leading his courageous followers who, with no outside assistance, defeated the "U.S. imperialist invaders [who] . . . on July 27, 1953, fell on their knees before the Korean people and signed the Armistice Agreement."[22] Little notice is given to the DPRK's essential Chinese allies and none at all to the Soviet role in authorizing the war and providing critical military assistance—including jet aircraft and pilots. Memorials are a more recent development in South Korea, where emphasis in the Korean National War Museum focuses on the government's legitimacy by proudly exhibiting the ROK's UN recognition, support, and critical wartime assistance from more than sixty member nations during the war and in postwar reconstruction. China's memorials stress its heroic aid to a weak and threatened Communist neighbor and the war's significance in establishing the People's Republic as a world power.

Any understanding of contemporary East Asian affairs requires an understanding of the multinational nature of the Korean War, its contested and conflicted memories, and its unresolved outcome. The 155-mile-long DMZ that separates the two Koreas remains one of the most heavily fortified (and potentially the most volatile) borders in the world. Because of this unfinished legacy, the Korean War holds a place at the forefront of the diplomacy with East Asian nations and in the crafting of international policies in the Pacific region. The tense situation along the DMZ is exacerbated by North Korea's development of a significant and dangerous nuclear arsenal. Moreover, the recent emergence of the PRC as an economic and military superpower has complicated international relations in the region. Both South Korea and Japan, for nearly three quarters of a century dependent for their security on alliances with the United States, appear nervous as they reassess their own independent defense capabilities. Meanwhile, as those who participated in or endured the Korean War are passing from the scene, nations strive belatedly to remember and memorialize their deeds. These developments all indicate that it will not be easy to forget, or even assign to a shared public memory, a war that is not yet over.

1 | The "Police Action"

In June 1950 an America hardly aware of Korea suddenly found itself involved in a bloody overseas conflict, and the public began to shape an understanding of the war based on its commonly held memory of World War II. But the Korean conflict was not at all like World War II. Initial support for U.S. effort in the Korean conflict evaporated as the costly struggle staggered toward an inconclusive armistice. Even as the fighting continued, the various combatant states began to shape conflicting narratives about the war's cause and its meaning.

Phil Lagerquist was a local celebrity in Independence, Missouri, when I became director of the Harry S. Truman Library in 2001. The popular octogenarian had retired years earlier from his position as an archivist at the library, where he had worked for many years, beginning his service even before the facility officially opened. Now he walked about the town every day, and Phil could be spotted traversing the streets and sidewalks Mr. Truman had known. Like most of the first members of the library's staff, Phil had come to know the former president well, and fondly recalled that, until the late 1960s, when old age and health problems took a toll on his energy, former president Truman worked almost every day in his presidential library. There he would meet with visiting foreign dignitaries, local and national politicians, old friends, tourists, and school groups. The former president loved to share memories of his White House years with students, and he took questions from his young audience. According to Phil, Truman was often asked what his most difficult decision as U.S. president had been. His answer was always the same: "The decision to enter the Korean War."[1] The young students could not have understood the full meaning of the former president's decisive decision of June 1950. Perhaps even Truman never completely appreciated during his lifetime how profoundly and permanently his actions during the Korean conflict would change American society and the course of East Asian history.

Understanding the conflicted memories of the Korean War in the psyches of the participants requires a careful assessment of the conflict's causes, conduct, and lasting consequences on the international world order. The war erupted suddenly and shattered the peace brought about by the end of World War II—a peace that proved more fragile than it had appeared. During the second half of 1950, the two Koreas, the Soviet Union, the People's Republic of China, and fifteen allied countries hastily assembled into a United Nations Command (UNC) under U.S. leadership, all found themselves drawn into a war larger and far more prolonged than any had anticipated. The warfare on the Korean Peninsula raged with savagery for thirty-seven months, devastating the civilian population both north and south of an artificially drawn dividing line, and brought the world to the brink of a nuclear holocaust. Just five years before the war, Korea was a land that had appeared on world maps as nothing more than a province of Japan. It now became, in the early years of the Cold War, the battleground for a clash of the major world powers. Remarkably the war did not expand beyond the mountains and valleys of Korea, and great powers, while destroying Korea, limited their expenditure of treasure and deployment of weaponry on this mountainous region to achieve nothing more than a return to the status quo ante bellum. The war came to an end with an armistice that left all sides dissatisfied. Yet the war changed East Asia and the world in ways both consequential and lasting, leaving the combatants with memories that remain a hindrance to achieving the war's final resolution.

The Korean War came about because the leader of North Korea wanted it, and he successfully secured the authorization and support of his Communist allies. A full-scale war erupted in Korea on June 25, 1950, when a heavily armed force from North Korea, backed by the Soviet Union with the PRC, crossed the 38th parallel with the intention of conquering South Korea. While caught off guard, President Truman reacted quickly and in a forceful manner not expected by Communist leaders in Moscow, Beijing, and Pyongyang. For months Joseph Stalin, premier of the Soviet Union, and Mao Zedong, chairman of a new Communist regime in China, had been planning an invasion of South Korea. They had both met secretly with the young, ambitious Kim Il-sung of the recently created Democratic People's Republic of Korea (DPRK) to plot a strategy and pledge assistance for his plan to seize control of South Korea. The Communist leadership anticipated a sudden and decisive victory in just a matter of days over the south's fledgling Republic of Korea. They anticipated that the United States would do nothing more than stand by while providing asylum to Syngman Rhee and his cohorts. After all, the United States had not intervened with military force a year earlier to rescue its long-time ally Chiang Kai-shek and his Republic of China from Communist takeover in 1949. However, the Communist leadership had misjudged Truman's determination to save South Korea. Truman saw the invasion by the North Koreans as an effort by Communist rulers in Moscow and Beijing to extend Communism in East Asia, threaten the security of Japan, and disrupt, if not destroy, the credibility of the United Nations (UN).[2] Following thirty-seven months of bitter conflict and nearly five million deaths, it appeared nothing more than the status quo ante bellum was achieved. All involved in the conflict reluctantly settled for an uneasy truce. While it may have seemed that the conflict had left the situation on the Korean Peninsula unchanged, the warfare had in fact altered East Asia and the world in ways unimaginable just a few years earlier.

In the aftermath of World War II, President Truman's decisions led to the establishment of the ROK in the southern half of the Korean Peninsula. However, during the first five years of his presidency, the primary focus of his foreign policy was directed elsewhere. Hastily sworn in as president on April 12, 1945, just hours after Pres. Franklin D. Roosevelt (FDR) died of a massive stroke, Truman faced immediate daunting challenges throughout the war-torn world. During his first months in office, the untested and largely unknown new president confronted myriad complex challenges, including an unfinished world war that had already left fifty-five million dead and millions displaced through Europe and Asia. In addition the world was about to enter the nuclear age, and Truman would be called upon to decide how America's frightening, new atomic weapons would be deployed. Meanwhile, the infrastructure and the economies of the world's great powers, with the exception of the United States, lay in ruins. At home the American public had grown weary of the human and financial costs of war. Political and business leaders expressed concerns about the return of the Great Depression. Organized labor seethed with unrest and growing tensions around civil rights for African Americans and other minorities threatened domestic stability.[3] Maintaining harmonious relations with principal allies had proved difficult even for the experienced and clever FDR; and now with victory against the Axis powers in sight, fractures in the Grand Alliance became apparent on many fronts. It seemed that the enormity and complexity of the emerging new world might be more than any American leader could possibly manage.

At first President Truman struggled to determine the course of American foreign policy set by his predecessor. However, it soon became apparent that FDR had bequeathed no master plan. Truman had to determine on his own how to bridge the gap between harsh diplomatic realities and the lofty wartime rhetoric expressed in the Atlantic Charter and other idealistic wartime pronouncements and agreements. He had served as vice president for only eighty-two days, had never attended a cabinet meeting, and had only two brief meetings with the president, during which there was no substantial conversation.[4] Briefing himself as best as he could, with conflicting advice from FDR's aides and cabinet members, Truman arrived in Potsdam in July 1945 to meet with Winston Churchill and Joseph Stalin with an overriding priority—end the war against Japan as quickly as possible. To accomplish this, he believed, the allies required the aid of the Soviet Union. The future of Korea, along with other issues of less urgency, would be addressed by the staff members. Following his first and only face-to-face meetings with the Soviet premier, President Truman believed he had achieved his goal. On July 17 Truman privately wrote, "Most of the big points are settled. He'll [Stalin] be in the war on August 15. Fini Japs when that comes about."[5] The anticipated acquisition of a nuclear weapon did not appear to change Truman's belief in the need for massive Soviet support to defeat Japan. Two days after the successful test of an atomic bomb at the Alamogordo Bombing Range in New Mexico, Truman confided to his wife, Bess, "I've gotten what I came for—Stalin goes to War August 15 with no strings on it. . . . We'll end the war sooner now, and think of the kids who won't be killed! That's the important thing."[6]

A few weeks later, Japan surrendered, following the use of two atomic weapons by the United States and the Soviet declaration of war against Japan on August 8 (a week earlier than Truman had expected).[7] With the war suddenly ended, Truman's attention understandably turned to reconstruction of the devastated societies and economies in Europe and Asia. At the same time, he focused his energies on creating a world order that would eliminate the possibility of what he feared the most throughout his entire presidency—a third world war.

Korea never ranked highly in Truman's agenda as he planned for the post–World War II world order. Truman was aware of the Allies' agreements regarding the Far East made at Cairo, Tehran, and Yalta, and he had been briefed by FDR advisor Harry Hopkins that Stalin favored and was committed to a four-party trusteeship in Korea. However, at Potsdam the leaders left to their aides the discussion of Korea and what Truman considered the minor but related matter: a temporary demarcation line to separate U.S. and Soviet military forces entering the peninsula as the Japanese military personnel and colonial administrators were evacuated. Without much attention to this issue, all parties later agreed to a proposal made by U.S. military officers to separate American and Soviet zones along the 38th parallel, dividing Korea into roughly equally sized halves. As Truman recalled in his *Memoirs*, "The division of the country would be solely for the purpose of accepting the Japanese surrender and that joint control would extend throughout the peninsula."[8]

Yet early on Truman had serious reservations about Soviet cooperation in the Far East. Henry L. Stimson, secretary of war, had warned Truman in the weeks prior to the Potsdam Conference that the Soviets were seeking to advance their influence in East Asia by installing a Communist government in Korea, making "Korea the Polish question transplanted to the Far East." Meanwhile rival political factions were already emerging in Seoul that soon would confound an unprepared U.S. military occupation force upon its arrival early in September. Adding to the concerns, Chinese diplomat T. V. Song warned the U.S. ambassador to Moscow, W. Averell Harriman, that Stalin wanted no foreign troops in Korea because the Soviets already had stationed in eastern Russia two armed divisions of ethnic Koreans and numerous highly trained Korean political cadres ready to pour into the country to assure that the Soviets would dominate any four-power trusteeship.[9]

The first signs that the creation of the 38th parallel would become problematic came within weeks of the Potsdam meeting. When the Soviets launched military strikes against Japanese-held territories in Manchuria,

Ambassadors Harriman and Edwin Pauley both urged President Truman to secure industrial sites in Korea and China.[10] Pauley was a wealthy California oil tycoon, Democratic Party stalwart, and manager of the 1944 Democratic National Convention in Chicago where Truman was nominated for the vice presidency. Truman appointed Pauley as the president's special ambassador on reparations, an issue Truman understood to be of the highest importance for the Soviet leadership. Truman understood that there was little he could do to restrain the Soviets in North China and North Korea. And when the Soviets began to treat the 38th parallel as a permanent border, Truman was preoccupied with matters he viewed as more pressing. In private Truman expressed his true feelings about the Soviet approach to reparations, writing that "the Russians are naturally looters and they have been thoroughly looted by the Germans over and over again and you can hardly blame them for their attitude."[11] As it turned out, because they intended to occupy Korea, the Soviets, while treating the Koreans poorly, did not dismantle the Japanese-built industrial infrastructure.

In the months following the Japanese surrender, U.S.-Soviet cooperation deteriorated on the Korean Peninsula. A report of June 22, 1946, from Ambassador Pauley confirmed Truman's concerns over Soviet intentions in Korea. Hoping to avoid the kind of drastic postwar reparations that had devastated Germany at the end of World War I and helped lead to another world war, Truman appointed Pauley to serve as his special representative on reparations, because the position required, in Truman's words, "a tough bargainer, someone who could be as tough as [Soviet foreign minister Vyacheslav] Molotov."[12] During a six-day visit with his inspection team to North Korea from May 29 to June 3, 1946, Pauley received little cooperation from the Soviets, who appeared to be in complete control of the northern half of Korea. Russian officers placed restrictions on the movements of Pauley's team and denied access to important sites. The Soviets were "stalling," Pauley reported to Truman, while at the same time "entrenching themselves more firmly in North Korea." Pauley viewed the situation in Korea as "an ideological battle ground upon which our entire success in Asia many depend."[13]

While Pauley urged the president to confront the Soviets in Korea, Truman was determined to follow a more cautious policy. Pauley persisted, nevertheless. In a public statement prepared for June 23, Pauley noted that "the iron barrier at the 38th Parallel must be removed and free commerce reestablished between the Northern and Southern parts of the country."[14] A few weeks later, in a response to Pauley's report, Truman stated that he considered "one of the principal objectives of our policy there to be to prevent Korea from again becoming the source of future conflict." Truman was well aware that both the Sino-Japanese War of 1895 and the Russo-Japanese War of 1904–05 had arisen from conflicts in which major powers struggled over control of the Korean Peninsula. Despite his apprehensions and apparently more concerned about the current confrontations with the Soviets in Europe, Truman informed Pauley that he would continue efforts to persuade the Soviets to comply with the wartime agreements made with regard to Korea.[15] While problems on the Korean Peninsula caused concern to Truman and his administration, other troubling issues, including the civil war in China and the Soviet threat to West Berlin, appeared more urgent.

With American attention focused elsewhere, Koreans themselves were in the process of addressing their nation's fate. In the autumn of 1945, two ambitious political leaders with conflicting visions for an independent Korea arrived at opposite ends of the peninsula. Although both were returning from exile as heroes, Syngman Rhee and Kim Il-sung were polar opposites, and early hopes for a united Korea soon vanished. Initially the *Hyongmyon Sinmun*, a leftist newspaper, openly welcomed the return of both Rhee and Kim: "Great leaders of the entire nation whom 30 million people admire and longed for have returned at the same time. Great joy and emotional stirring of the entire people for welcoming Dr. Syngman Rhee and General Kim Il-sung."[16] However, conflict along the 38th parallel began as soon as the Japanese colonial masters withdrew. With Rhee and Kim, many other long-exiled Korean political leaders returned from the United States, China, the Soviet Union, and elsewhere. They brought with them competing ideas for the formation of an independent and united Korea based on democracy and capitalism or a form of Soviet-style Communist dictatorship.[17] The notion of a trusteeship in Korea (as agreed to by the major powers at the Yalta Conference) was abandoned, along with initial hopes of a unified government on the Korean Peninsula.

Complicating matters for the American military and diplomats was the brutal suppression of political liberties by South Korea's rightist groups who had taken control of the political process. Assassinations of popular South Korean opposition figures, and the prickly, obstinate, and head-strong personality of emerging South Korean leader Syngman Rhee, caused concern in Seoul and Washington DC. Once a student radical who opposed both Korea's decadent five-hundred-year-old Choson dynasty and the Japanese colonizers in the first decade of the twentieth century, Rhee had returned to his native land after a forty-year exile in the United States, where he earned a doctorate from Princeton, advocated for Korean independence, and ministered to the Korean Christian community in Hawai'i. He quickly attached himself to the most anti-Communist elements in Korean society, including landowners and the many wealthy Koreans who had served the Japanese business and government interests during the harsh colonial rule. He also attracted the support of the south's sizable Christian minority—many thousands of whom had fled the regime in the north. Truman considered Rhee to be stubborn, dictatorial, and inattentive to deteriorating economic conditions in his country. Furthermore, Truman viewed Rhee as arbitrary and excessively harsh in his dealings with political opponents, a leader who "attached himself to men of extreme right-wing attitudes."[18] Nevertheless, in 1948 Truman extended diplomatic recognition to the Republic of Korea, with Rhee as president, following UN-sponsored elections on May 10, 1948, south of the 38th parallel. The previous year a United Nations Temporary Committee on Korea (UNTCOK) had been established to hold elections throughout the peninsula. The Soviets and their North Korean operatives would not allow elections under UN supervision and responded to the UN's recognition of the Republic of Korea by proclaiming their own Democratic People's Republic of Korea under the leadership of the ambitious young Communist who had renamed himself Kim Il-sung after a highly regarded independence fighter of an earlier era. In effect the Korean people were now divided into two ideologically opposed countries, each dependent on considerable support from sponsors beyond its borders.[19]

The leaders of the two Koreas held opposing and irreconcilable political philosophies acquired during their years in exile. The elderly, determined, and nationalistic Rhee maintained decidedly pro-American views, honed during his studies at Princeton University and his decades as a Christian church leader among Korean expatriates in the United States. In exile Rhee had been involved in diplomatic efforts for an independent Korea longer than Kim Il-sung had been alive. Imprisoned by the Japanese as a young advocate of independence, Rhee developed relationships with prominent Americans, including Woodrow Wilson, Eleanor Roosevelt, and Pearl Buck. When he returned to Korea in 1945, his work abroad with the Korean Provisional Government had made him the most widely known Korean in the world. On the other side of the 38th parallel, Kim, still in his thirties as he rose to power in North Korea, had earned a modest reputation during World War II as a leader of small guerilla forces in Manchuria, attacking remote Japanese outposts. He arrived in Pyongyang wearing a Soviet military uniform displaying the rank of captain. Despite his youth, the Russian-speaking Kim attracted the attention of the Soviet military. Although one Soviet observer stated that Kim "reminded me of a fat delivery boy from a neighborhood Chinese food stall," the young North Korean proved to be capable and ambitious.[20] At least in the early period of Soviet governance in North Korea, Kim proved to be popular with reform-minded North Koreans, and he even enjoyed a degree of genuine support among South Korean leftists. As the Soviets tightened their hold on the northern half of Korea, they saw the clever, energetic, and ruthless Kim as a useful and dependable Korean national who could put a popular face on the Soviet-style regime they intended to impose.[21]

Radical political elements soon dominated both sides of the 38th parallel. In the north, where the Japanese colonial government had developed the most industrialized region in Asia except for the Japanese home islands, Kim and his Soviet mentors quickly set about installing a Communist system of governance. Soon Communist political "reforms"— confiscation of property and suppression of religions, in particular Christianity—caused more than one million refugees from the north to flee south into the American zone. There these refugees tended to join the most ardent anti-Communist elements in South Korean society. At the same time, the Soviet-backed regime in the north infiltrated labor groups and leftist political organizations in the south, frustrating the poorly organized American military efforts to establish a stable government and turning many Korean moderates into rightists. With the creation of the Republic of Korea, Rhee, whose political support came from wealthy landowners, Christian leaders, the police and military (trained largely during the Japanese occupation), and more than one million North Korean refugees, unleashed brutal campaigns to destroy the Communists, often attacking legitimate leftist political organizations and any democratic groups that posed even the slightest threat to his authoritarian rule. "There are no moderate groups in Korea anymore. There are only Rightists and Communists," Rhee's Austrian-born wife, Francesca, confided to a friend.[22] By spring 1950 Rhee's ruthless policies had nearly wiped out the North Korean cadres, along with many liberal leaders who had expressed legitimate opposition to Rhee and his policies. Nevertheless, his opponents won a majority of seats in the assembly in the May 1950 elections. Rhee now began to turn up his rhetoric against the north and, much to the annoyance of the United States, talked openly of reunifying Korea by force. At the same time, in the north Kim realized that any possibility of reunifying Korea under his authority was slipping away. So he turned once again to his sponsor, Joseph Stalin.

Meeting with the Soviet leader in early 1950, Kim pleaded for authorization and support for an attack across the 38th parallel. Stalin had refused earlier requests, but this time he signaled a willingness to discuss the matter. The United States had now withdrawn all but a token military presence in South Korea, China had a new Communist government under Mao Zedong, and the Soviet Union now possessed a few nuclear weapons of its own. Although there exists no evidence of this, Stalin may have also assumed that, because secretary of state Dean Acheson had left Korea outside the U.S. "defensive perimeter" in a January speech before the Washington Press Corps, the Americans would not come to the aid of Rhee's fledgling government. Whatever factors led to Stalin's decision, the Soviet leader remained cautious and, during a second meeting in March in Moscow, told Kim to seek assurances of support from China. He warned Kim, "If you get kicked in the teeth, I shall not lift a finger. You have to ask Mao for all the help."[23]

The situation in Korea was a security concern to the Truman administration—one of many across the globe. Clearly the new Republic of Korea was seriously threatened by the Soviet-sponsored north. In September 1949 the newly created Central Intelligence Agency (CIA) noted that there existed "no prospect . . . that the northern regime can be deposed by the forces of the Republic, while the Republic itself is highly vulnerable to hostile action from the north." The report continued with an assessment of northern weaknesses, noting that most Koreans had come to realize that the Communist regime could not bring about unification, a just distribution of land, and an efficient production of food. "Although Koreans attribute some of the responsibility for the partition of Korea to the U.S.," the report stated, "they place most of the onus for the continued separation on the policies of the Soviet Union and generally realize that communist-sponsored 'unification' would result in a complete extinction of Korean nationalist aspirations."[24] A few months earlier, the CIA had warned that a withdrawal of U.S. forces from Korea "would probably in time be followed by an invasion to coincide with communist-led South Korean revolts." With support possibly from the People's Republic of China, the report predicted a collapse of the Republic of Korea and recommended the "continued presence of a moderate U.S. force . . . [to] assist in sustaining the will and ability of the Koreans themselves." Meanwhile, Col. Gen. Terentii F. Shtykov, the principal Soviet official in North Korea, received reports from Moscow about weaknesses in the north in which Stalin expressed his concerns that "the 38th parallel must be peaceful. It is very important."[25]

While Truman and Secretary Acheson agreed with the CIA assessments, the United States was now committed to a policy of "containment" in Europe and faced severe budgetary constraints in the implementation of widening commitments to defend the security of Western Europe through a new defense alliance, the North Atlantic Treaty Organization (NATO).[26] President Truman, a fiscal conservative, knew Congress was stunned by the enormous budget deficits of the World War II years and even more determined than he to balance the federal budget. Therefore it was no great surprise, but a serious concern, when the U.S. House of Representatives voted to deny an administration request for economic assistance to Korea in early 1950. The government of the Republic of Korea was dismayed by this congressional action and President Rhee immediately dispatched diplomats to meet with Secretary Acheson. The American secretary of state was sympathetic and pledged continued administration efforts to secure funding. However, in a meeting with ROK ambassador John M. Chang and Rhee's special representative Pyung Ok Chough, Acheson responded coldly to a request that the United States assist ROK's increase to 100,000 troops, stating that the U.S. military felt 65,000 was the "optimum effective strength for the Korean Army." When asked for a public assurance that the United States would "stand by the Republic of Korea in the event of trouble," Acheson stated that "such a specific military commitment by the United States was out of the question." Finally, in response to the suggestion that a Pacific pact, analogous to NATO, be created in East Asia with ROK as a member, Acheson replied that the United States "did not at this time contemplate any further extension of the North Atlantic Pact."[27]

The South Koreans continued to press for military assistance. Ambassador Chang met with Acheson shortly after the secretary's notorious National Press Club speech on January 12, 1950, in which Acheson drew a U.S. defensive perimeter that excluded the ROK. In Acheson's telling the Korean ambassador "expressed the appreciation of President Rhee and the National Assembly for the Secretary's remarks regarding Korea at the Press Club." In retrospect it seems unlikely that Acheson's drawing a U.S. defensive perimeter that excluded the ROK was decisive in influencing Premier Stalin at that point, as there were already other more obvious indications that the United States intended to reduce its commitments on the Asian continent. These included the refusal to rescue the Nationalist regime in China the previous year and the reluctance to provide the Republic of Korea with additional military aid. Possibly the Korean ambassador appeared satisfied with Acheson after the National Press Club speech just to be polite and concentrated instead on the issue of much needed reconsideration by Congress on economic and military aid to his country. But South Korean leaders remained anxious about U.S. intentions and public statements. A couple of weeks later, when Icky Shin, chairman of the Korean National Assembly, met with Secretary Acheson on March 22, the anxious Korean legislator stated that he "hoped the American defense line in the Far East could be stretched to include Korea."[28]

A number of factors kept the Truman administration from providing the Republic of Korea with the aid requested. In part the administration was stymied by a reluctant and fiscally conservative U.S. Congress. Dissatisfaction with President Rhee was an issue as well. The arrogant and authoritarian Rhee damaged his own cause by using dictatorial methods against all political opposition and threatening to invade the north. However, concerns in other parts of the world seemed to override all. While caught between Soviet intransigence and a South Korean regime not to its liking, an invasion of Taiwan by the People's Republic of China appeared imminent. "We knew that this [Korea] was one of the places where the Soviet-controlled Communist world might choose to attack," Truman noted in his memoir. "But we could say the same thing for every point of contact between East and West, from Norway through Berlin and Trieste to Greece, Turkey and Iran; from the Kuriles in the North Pacific to Indo-China and Malaya . . . each commander believed that his area was in the greatest danger."[29]

When the North Korean attack did come on June 25, 1950, Truman's reaction was quick and decisive. He recalled how prior to World War II, Western democracies and the League of Nations had failed to address foreign aggression in Ethiopia, Manchuria, Austria, and Czechoslovakia. He saw the United Nations, along with the Republic of Korea, threatened with destruction. Yet even as his advisors and key cabinet secretaries met at Blair House in Washington DC, on the evening of June 25 to map out an immediate response to the Soviet-sponsored invasion of the Republic of Korea, Truman's thoughts remained elsewhere. Truman was concerned that the attack on Korea might be Stalin's effort to get the United States bogged down in a war in East Asia in order to strengthen a Soviet position elsewhere in the world more important to them than the impoverished southern half of the Korean Peninsula. As the Blair House meeting ended, Truman stood quietly in a corner of the room intently studying a large globe. As young White House aide George Elsey approached, the president turned to him and said, "This is what the Russians are really after." Truman was pointing to Iran.[30]

The North Korean invasion quickly changed the nature of the Cold War into a worldwide military confrontation. Even as he ordered Gen. Douglas MacArthur to command U.S. and UN forces to assist the stricken Republic of Korea, Truman remained preoccupied with denying the Soviets what he viewed as their true objectives in Europe and the Middle East. To address the Soviet aggression, Truman implemented lasting changes in U.S. foreign policy. In East Asia his defense policies now reached far beyond Korea. Yet Truman remained cautious, hoping to confine the military conflict to the Korean Peninsula. Believing Premier Stalin had a more ambitious agenda than unifying the Korean Peninsula under a Communist regime, the president wrote in his personal diary, "Must be careful not to cause a general Asiatic war. Russia is figuring on an attack in the Black Sea and toward the Persian Gulf. Both prizes Moscow has wanted since Ivan the Terrible."[31]

The North Korean attack changed American foreign policy and the dynamics of East Asian relations both immediately and in the long-term. Within days of the June 25, 1950, North Korean attack, the United States was at war with the backing of a UN Security Council resolution, approved because the Soviet Union was absent in protest to the Nationalist government of Chiang Kai-shek still representing China at the world body. In their initial responses European allies appeared pleased that the United States had confronted Soviet aggression in support of collective security. While charged with a UN resolution, Truman sought no authorization from Congress—a mistake that would damage him politically when the war dragged on for three years. Insisting that military intervention in Korea was merely a "police action," a term suggested to the president by a reporter during a press conference, Truman maintained that he needed no congressional approval.[32] In addition to ordering General MacArthur, then supervising the postwar occupation of Japan, to take command of U.S.-UNC forces in Korea, Truman immediately deployed the U.S. Seventh Fleet to the Taiwan Strait, dashing any possibility of a U.S. reconciliation with Mao's new People's Republic of China. Furthermore, the United States increased aid to the French effort to hold on to Indochina as it confronted Communists leading an independence effort there. Finally the North Korean attack drove the Truman administration to adopt a radical plan for an expensive and massive rearmament plan labeled NSC-68, creating the national security state and in effect extending the containment policy already in place in Europe.[33]

Early combat in Korea was characterized by dramatic reversals of fortune on both sides. In the first months of combat, the United States and the UNC encountered unexpected strength on the part of the North Korean aggressors. A staggering number of civilian causalities shocked the world as South Koreans were caught up in warfare that on the Korean Peninsula was anything but limited. The North Koreans came close to driving the South Korean forces and UNC off the peninsula in the summer of 1950. However, a stiff resistance along the "Pusan Perimeter" in the southeastern corner of the country held off the invaders until a U.S. landing on September 15 at the port of Incheon. That invasion led by General MacArthur put the forces of Kim Il-sung into full retreat. The general soon received authorization to advance beyond the 38th parallel into North Korea. "We want you to feel unhampered tactically and strategically to proceed north of the 38th parallel," wrote U.S. secretary of defense George Marshall.[34] Pyongyang, North Korea's capital, was captured, and Kim Il-sung hastily fled to the mountains to await rescue from his Communist allies. The UNC forces advanced to the Yalu River at the border with China, while Kim Il-sung and the remnants of his military took refuge in the rugged terrain in the country's northeastern regions. Meeting with Truman at Wake Island in October, a confident General MacArthur assured his commander-in-chief that military operations against the Korean Communists were wrapping up and that American troops would be home for Christmas. MacArthur told Truman that Chinese threats to intervene if American forces advanced to its frontier could be ignored.[35] But the Chinese did enter the war, and in late November UNC forces were soon in full retreat.

Even as MacArthur was meeting with President Truman at Wake Island, Chinese forces began to cross the Yalu in great numbers. China's decision to enter the Korean War came following a series of events that shaped the thinking of the new regime that had seized power under the leadership of Communist Party chairman Mao Zedong in the fall of 1949. Mao, informed by Kim Il-sung of his meetings with Stalin, had received assurances of Soviet support if China entered the war to assist the North Koreans. Mao and his advisors became concerned soon after Kim's attack on the south, observing that his rapid advance had left the North Korean lines of supply exposed. Weeks before the Incheon landing, Mao began moving troops from China's southern coast, where they were preparing to invade Taiwan, as well as to outposts along the Yalu River, which borders North Korea. Meanwhile, Chinese premier Chou Enlai sent a warning to the United States that China would not tolerate U.S. Armed Forces crossing the 38th parallel and advancing toward its border with North Korea. Because the United States did not have diplomatic relations with the PRC, these warnings were sent through Indian diplomats, who were not trusted by their American counterparts. As MacArthur's forces moved toward the Yalu, Mao felt compelled to defend his regime by assisting his faltering Communist neighbor.[36]

Chinese intervention altered the course of the war. Traveling in small groups at night, and under the cover of low clouds and heavy snowfall, at least 250,000 Chinese volunteers confronted MacArthur's UNC forces by complete surprise. Having ignored intelligence reports of Chinese intervention, the UNC was overwhelmed and soon in full retreat from Pyongyang and the Chosin Reservoir in early December. Humiliated by this military fiasco, MacArthur now called for an expanded war against China. The UNC forces were driven back south of the 38th parallel, and the Chinese, along with a much-weakened North Korean force, retook Seoul, forcing the flight of hundreds of thousands of South Koreans, who remembered the horrible atrocities the Communists had perpetuated just a few months earlier. In the hasty retreat from Pyongyang, U.S. Eighth Army commander Walton Walker died when his jeep overturned. General Matthew Ridgway replaced Walker and took command of the U.S. Eighth Army and UNC ground forces. In January 1951 Ridgway's assertive leadership halted the retreat, and his counterattacks drove the overextended Chinese back across the 38th parallel. By early summer 1951, the fighting had bogged down into trench warfare. This line of battle morphed into a vicious and frustrating stalemate, roughly along the artificial separation that had existed before the North Korean invasion. As brutal fighting continued for another two years, neither side advanced despite heavy causalities. Meanwhile, U.S. and UNC air power mercilessly pounded military and civilian targets in North Korea.[37]

From the opening days of the war, Korea's civilian population suffered both as collateral damage and from deliberate atrocities. The northern invaders murdered South Korean political leaders and other prominent individuals who were captured before they could flee from Seoul and other cities. South Korean men were pressed into North Korea's military and often forced to advance on South Korean and UNC positions without weapons. In many recorded instances, the heavily armed soldiers of Kim Il-sung disguised themselves as civilian refugees to sneak through UNC lines and cause mayhem. The North Koreans also executed UNC and South Korean prisoners of war (POWs) and imprisoned both military and civilian captives. These prisoners, including foreign missionaries and aid workers, were held in deplorable conditions where they experienced inhumane suffering and a high death rate. Aware of North Korean tactics, South Korean and UNC forces forcefully halted the refugees or mistook them for DPRK military units. Influential military strategist and author, Col. Harry G. Summers Jr., remembered his experience as a young infantry squad leader in Korea during the initial months of the fighting and the Eighth Army's retreat as North Korean and Chinese forces advanced.

"There were hundreds of thousands of refugees streaming south," he recalled. "It was the most pitiful thing I had ever seen. If they got within a hundred yards of the road, they were shot. There was only one road to move the Eighth Army on, and that road had to be kept open."[38]

It is not possible to adequately assess the toll of the atrocities perpetuated throughout the war by the opposing forces. Due to strict wartime censorship, only in recent years have many U.S. and UNC incidents come to light. It is clear, however, that Koreans both north and south of the 38th parallel suffered unspeakable horrors and were scarred for life with memories of this brutal fighting. It was in the first months of the war, as the combatants moved up and down the ravaged Korean Peninsula and crossed the 38th parallel several times, that most of the outrageous incidents took place. The Western press reported on North Korea's inhumane treatment of civilians and POWs, but atrocious behavior by the South Korean military and civilian gangs along with the U.S. military was seldom acknowledged and often overlooked. As historian Sheila Miyoshi Jager has noted, "Already in the opening weeks of the war, a subtle yet distinct process of 'forgetting' was beginning to take place."[39]

Perhaps the most devastating aspect of the war on the civilian population was conducted by U.S. air power. American political leaders and military analysts believed initially that UNC air power would be decisive in bringing the war to a rapid conclusion. Military advocates were convinced that heavy and continual bombardment from above, along with the indiscriminate use of napalm, would reduce the North Korean and Chinese will to continue the fight. By mid-1951 they realized they had been wrong. Nevertheless, the bombing of North Korea continued, destroying every city and town in North Korea and reducing the infrastructure of North Korea to rubble. Napalm scorched both civilian and military installations, blackening the countryside as the air campaign continued relentlessly. In fact the U.S. Air Force, now a separate branch of the armed services, had doubled in size, and new technologies continued to inflate expectations. In spite of its limited success in Korea, the Eisenhower administration adopted air power as the cornerstone of its "New Look" defense policy.[40]

The Korean War would be remembered, among other things, as the first modern war when U.S. forces fought in racially integrated units. Following President Truman's executive order of 1948, the U.S. Armed

Forces gradually began a process of integration. African Americans fought together with Asian Americans, Native Americans, Hispanics, and Caucasians. Because of long-standing, entrenched racial bias, Black soldiers had traditionally fought in segregated units led by white officers. In Korea the process of racial integration, unofficially begun out of necessity during World War II, accelerated. Although the U.S. Army implemented integration more slowly than the U.S. Navy or U.S. Air Force, the experience often served as the first interaction many whites had with their fellow citizens of different racial backgrounds. General Ridgway, inclined toward integration from the start, convinced his commanders in the field to implement integration. While all did not proceed smoothly, the pressure of warfare, including troop shortages, forced senior military leaders to view integration as an improvement in the U.S. Army's effectiveness.[41]

Nonetheless, controversy regarding the combat readiness and courage of Black soldiers remained. The record of the nation's last all-Black 24th Infantry Regiment became a particular target of criticism from military officials. Writing in the early 1960s, historian Roy Appleman singled out the 24th for criticism in the first weeks of the war. Appleman, who was the U.S. military's official historian of the Korean conflict, viewed the 24th Regiment as "frightened and demoralized" with "a tendency to panic" or "bug out" in his early account of the fighting near Yechon. However, as U.S. forces withdrew from the onslaught of heavily armed North Koreans, numerous units, both white and Black, "bugged out" or "broke and ran" in the face of superior enemy numbers and firepower. Not until the 1980s would the record of the 24th be set straight.[42] The participation of Black soldiers in combat fighting in integrated units drastically changed the face of the American military in subsequent conflicts. The experiences and memories of Black soldiers, sailors, marines, and airmen in the Korean War would prove to be a significant factor in how African Americans viewed military service. In addition, Black veterans returned to their homeland prepared to engage actively in the struggle for equal rights.

The Truman administration sought to limit the "police action" to the Korean Peninsula, although options to expand the war received consideration. The idea that nuclear weapons might be deployed was evaluated early on and remained a factor in the Truman administration's strategic planning. Military planners in the United States had placed the nuclear option on the table from the first months of the conflict.[43] In response to a reporter's question in a press conference on November 30, 1950, President Truman responded undiplomatically—but honestly—that the U.S. military in Korea would take "whatever steps are necessary to meet the military situation." The reporter persisted by asking, "Will that include the atomic bomb?" Truman replied, "That includes every weapon we have. There has always been active consideration of its use." Unfortunately the president left the impression that the commander in the field, General MacArthur, would make the final decision on the use of all weapons, including nuclear bombs. Clarifications from the White House were quickly issued, but much damage had already been done. British prime minister Clement Attlee immediately arranged to visit the United States to meet with the president and express concerns of the British and NATO allies about the possible escalation of the war in Korea.[44]

After the Chinese entered the conflict in Korea, Truman announced a state of emergency. Yet the president, his top advisors, and the Joint Chiefs of Staff agreed that an all-out war with the PRC had to be avoided. Truman understood the fears of the NATO allies that attacks on military installations within China could bring the Soviet Union into the conflict; that country was now armed with their own small but lethal arsenal of atomic bombs. The Truman administration also saw the real possibility for the war spreading to the Middle East and Western Europe—where Soviet conventional forces held an overwhelming advantage. Focused narrowly on Korea, MacArthur did not share Truman's wider concerns or those of U.S.-NATO allies. Nuclear weapons remained an option nevertheless.

In the spring of 1951, the tide of battle in Korea turned in favor of the UNC and South Korean forces. With success on the battlefield, diplomatic channels had opened the possibility of peace negotiations that would restore the two Koreas to roughly the status quo ante bellum, a resolution of the conflict Truman was now willing to accept. To keep MacArthur (and to a lesser extent, other U.S. commanders) from making unhelpful public statements while sensitive diplomatic efforts were underway, President Truman had issued an order in December 1950 to all theatre commanders calling for "extreme caution" in public statements, which were to be cleared in advance by both the State and Defense Departments. Believing this directive did not apply to him, MacArthur famously and blatantly ignored the president's order. By the spring of 1951, it had become clear to the American public and allied leaders that General

MacArthur's views on the conduct of the war in Korea differed from those of the administration in Washington. The general publicly argued for a wider war and the authority to attack targets in China. MacArthur's letter to Republican House leader Joseph W. Martin was the final straw, when on April 5, 1951, from the floor of the U.S. House, Representative Martin read the general's missive critical of administration policy, concluding, "There is no substitute for victory." Truman relieved General MacArthur of his command on April 11 and replaced him with General Ridgway—who was in effect already leading the UNC and ROK military effort on the Korean Peninsula with little direction from MacArthur.[45]

Many Americans supported MacArthur's calls for an expanded war, and the old general returned to the United States to a hero's welcome. Still remembered for the victory in World War II, MacArthur enjoyed one of the greatest ticker-tape parades ever seen in New York City, and in Washington DC, he delivered a farewell speech in his typically dramatic style. Following the speech, senator from Missouri Dewey Short exclaimed, "We have heard the voice of God." Rather than fade away, as he had indicated he would in his address to Congress, MacArthur launched a speaking tour during which he called for an expanded war in East Asia and seemed to be positioning himself as the Republican Party's nominee for president in 1952. But the American public proved to be less than enthusiastic about a greater military involvement in Korea.[46] In addition, a leak from the White House of transcripts recording the general's insistence that the war was all but finished and there existed little likelihood of Chinese intervention during his October 1950 meeting with President Truman on Wake Island further damaged MacArthur's reputation.[47] It would be General MacArthur's erstwhile pre–World War II aide, Dwight D. Eisenhower, who would secure the Republican Party's nomination and the presidency of the United States in the 1952 election.

While the fighting in Korea raged, peace talks sought to end the conflict. Negotiations began on July 10, 1951, at the village of Kaesong near the front lines. The negotiations, conducted by senior military officers rather than diplomats, soon moved to Panmunjom and dragged on for two years, complicated after December 1951 by the thorny issue of repatriation of POWs. Through 575 often rancorous meetings, the American, Chinese, and North Korean generals grappled with the POW issue while trying to score propaganda victories. The Chinese and North Koreans held to the position established by the 1949 Geneva Convention that all prisoners must be repatriated to their homeland. The Truman administration understood that many Chinese and North Korean POWs did not want to be repatriated and feared for their safety if returned to the DPRK or PRC. Furthermore, a large number of the Chinese were former Nationalists and had loyalties or family ties in the exiled regime in Taiwan. Also among the UNC-held North Korean prisoners were Korean conscripts from both sides of the DMZ. Many northerners had no desire to be returned to the harsh rule of Kim Il-sung, and of course southern conscripts forced to bear arms for the DPRK had no ties at all to the north.[48]

The Truman administration and the American allies (with the notable exception of Syngman Rhee) were prepared to settle for a continuation of the two regimes on a divided peninsula and end the conflict on the Korean Peninsula. In fact, the Chinese and North Koreans desired a settlement as well—especially since the Soviet Union had failed to provide much of the military support that had been promised.[49] As peace talks stalled, fighting continued more or less along the 38th parallel where the peninsula had been divided when the war was started. Meanwhile, thousands of Americans and UNC POWs languished and suffered unbearable conditions in North Korean camps. At the same time, in the UNC camps Chinese and North Korean POWs fought viciously among themselves over political ideologies and loyalties as both sides saw the POW issue as a potential propaganda matter supporting their claims of legitimacy. Within the wretched, poorly managed UNC camps, groups of prisoners sought to win converts to their cause, often using brutal tactics. Tensions within the camps exploded in violent uprisings, most notably in early May 1952 on Koje Island, where Communist cadres briefly took over a section of the prison and held the camp's commanding officer, Brigadier General Francis Dodd, hostage for several days. UNC and ROK troops soon took back control of the Koje Island camps, but the incident was a huge embarrassment to the UNC and a propaganda coup for the North Koreans and Chinese.[50] Throughout the fighting and negotiating, millions of Korean civilians, both North and South, suffered and died from the unrelenting violence. Amid this the American public tired of the seemingly unending conflict that their leaders appeared unwilling to pursue to an outright victory.

The election of Republican Dwight D. Eisenhower to the U.S. presidency in 1952 did not alter the course of the war, although in his presidential campaign he implied his extensive military experience would enable him to find a victory in Korea. Following his election in November 1952, President-elect Eisenhower made good on his campaign promise: "I shall go to Korea." The renowned general's quick visit to the front lines to meet with and share a hilltop lunch of sandwiches, soft drinks, and beer with Mark Clark, then UNC commander general, and other U.S. officers had little to do with a change in strategy. As a diplomatic exercise, his brief time in Korea was nearly disastrous for the American relationship with its difficult but much-needed South Korean ally, Syngman Rhee. Eisenhower was reluctant to meet with Rhee, and snubbed a well-orchestrated welcoming ceremony in which the South Korean leader had turned out a hundred thousand enthusiastic residents of Seoul on a bitterly cold December morning. Following pleas from ROK's general Paik Sun-yup, the staff of General Clark, who was now in command of UNC forces, and U.S. diplomatic staff arranged a face-saving event in Rhee's office where numerous public relations photos were taken so that the ROK's president could overcome the embarrassment of being stood up a day earlier. The meeting still proved to be something of a disappointment, as Eisenhower made it clear to Rhee that under a new Republican administration there would be no renewal of U.S. offensive operations into North Korea.[51]

Upon his return to the United States, the president-elect announced no new strategy, but he quietly agreed to consider a plan for a military victory in Korea drafted by MacArthur. Eisenhower met privately with his former commanding officer on December 17, 1952, at MacArthur's Waldorf Astoria apartment. The elderly general's *Memorandum for Ending the Korean War* called for the United States to use nuclear weapons if the Chinese and Soviet leaders did not respond to a U.S. ultimatum for ending the conflict.[52] Disregarding MacArthur's plan, which the old general eventually published in his memoirs a decade later, Eisenhower kept the details of their meeting to himself. At the time of his inauguration in January 1953, Eisenhower appeared committed to no policy in Korea beyond that of his predecessor. Within six weeks of Eisenhower's inauguration, however, the savage combat on the Korean Peninsula moved to a swift conclusion.

This sudden change resulted from the death of Premier Stalin. Following the Soviet dictator's unanticipated demise on March 5, 1953, the Soviet Council of Ministers adopted a resolution on the stalemated war in Korea and sent letters to Mao Zedong and Kim Il-sung with statements indicating a willingness to reach an armistice. Exhausted from the bloody conflict, Mao and Kim were already prepared to settle. At Stalin's funeral China's Zhou Enlai proposed advancing peace negotiations with great urgency. Two months later President Eisenhower's administration publicly hinted that it would use nuclear weapons against China if the issue of POW repatriation remained unresolved. However, by this time, Moscow and Beijing had already decided to find a resolution. Between April 20 and May 3, seven hundred UNC POWs and more than seven thousand sick and wounded from the Communist forces were voluntarily repatriated in an exchange called "Little Switch." Over the next two months, remaining issues were settled, and an armistice was signed on July 27 between the United States, the DPRK, and the PRC. Rhee, disappointed that his principal ally, the United States, would not fight to bring about reunification, refused to sign the armistice agreement. Only the pledge of a mutual defense pact by President Eisenhower secured Rhee's reluctant cooperation in ending the fighting.[53]

Contentious issues remained, but the armistice brought the combat in Korea to a halt. Further negotiations on reunification were planned to take place in Geneva, Switzerland. But these talks held in 1954 were sidetracked by events in Indochina, where the French had lost control of their colony to Communist forces. Korean matters were set aside and remained unresolved.[54] The Korean Peninsula was left divided, with two regimes competing for legitimacy. An unknown number of Korean families were separated at the time of the armistice, and most would never see their loved ones again—or even know if they were alive or dead. There were also thousands of South Korean, American, and UNC POWs unaccounted for, and the fates of most remain unknown to this day. Nevertheless, a fragile peace was in place and major combat operations had ceased.

The inconclusive armistice of July 1953 left all combatants dissatisfied. South Korea's Syngman Rhee attempted to sabotage the peace negotiations at the last minute by releasing from ROK camps thousands of Korean POWs who did not want to be returned to the north and were awaiting evaluation of their status. Confident of their true loyalties, Rhee allowed these prisoners to melt into southern society before investigators from neutral nations could thoroughly interview them and confirm their real intentions. This action infuriated the Chinese and North Korean negotiators, who suffered a significant propaganda defeat at the hands of their truculent South Korean foe. At this point the Eisenhower administration became so upset with the troublesome Rhee that serious consideration was given to a secret project named "Operation Everready" that would have replaced Korea's stubborn and aging leader with someone more cooperative and better prepared to address South Korea's military and economic challenges.[55] On the other side of the DMZ, the North Koreans had to settle for pretty much the status quo that had existed before they launched their fateful attack on the south. They had gained nothing after three years of war except millions of deaths and the destruction of their country. Frustrated by their failure to drive the Americans and their UNC allies off the Korean Peninsula, the Chinese had to console themselves with having at least held the United States to a draw while preserving a weak and needy Communist neighbor along its northeastern border. Nevertheless, Mao claimed a victory for his new regime in fighting the United States to a stalemate. The Soviets meanwhile appeared relieved that Stalin's adventure on the Korean Peninsula had come to an end with little damage to their own nation.

Amid the devastation throughout Korea, both Kim Il-sung and Syngman Rhee emerged from the ashes and rubble in their respective capitals. Both felt strengthened and emboldened. Given his disastrous blunders and miscalculations, it is amazing that Kim's regime survived at all. Yet in the years following the armistice, Kim set about instituting a cult of personality unrivaled anywhere on earth. He also systematically purged Communist elements in the north that he suspected might be a threat to his power. These most notably included southern Communists who had taken refuge in the north and Communists who had returned to Korea from China following World War II. In addition, in the aftermath of the war, Kim cleverly played the Soviet Union and China against each other in seeking aid to rebuild his nation's infrastructure and damaged military. In the south Rhee secured military and economic assistance from the United States and humanitarian aid from numerous religious and charitable organizations. Like Kim, Rhee dealt with his domestic political rivals in his accustomed heavy-handed manner. In China, Mao enjoyed a new status among world leaders, gaining a significant measure of prestige at home and abroad as a Communist leader whose influence appeared to match that of the Soviets—especially with Joseph Stalin's passing from the world stage.[56] Tragically, with his new authority confirmed, Mao initiated a series of horribly misguided programs over the next two decades, including the Great Leap Forward and the Cultural Revolution. These resulted in the deaths of tens of millions of his citizens.

Of the East Asian nations, Japan found itself in the most fortunate position at the war's end. Not directly a party to the combat in neighboring Korea, Japan benefited by serving as a supply base and staging area for the massive military operations taking place in its former colony. The outbreak of the war brought about a conclusion of negotiations with the United States to officially end World War II with a treaty along with a security arrangement and a plethora of trade and economic partnerships with the United States. The Japanese prime minister Shigeru Yoshida even stated, undiplomatically, that the war had been "a gift from the Gods."[57] The obvious prosperity that came to Japan as it supported the UNC during the war years only caused further resentment toward that nation from China and both North and South Korea. And this ill-will would never fade, as it joined the existing anti-Japanese feelings generated by Tokyo's colonial policies and war crimes of World War II.

The Americans, unaccustomed after World War II to fighting for anything less than a total victory, reluctantly accepted the stalemate along the DMZ, a troublesome ally in Syngman Rhee, and a new burden for maintaining peace throughout East Asia and the Pacific. By the end of the warfare in Korea, the United States had—without previously planning to do so—expanded its "containment policy." That policy had initially been targeted against the Soviet Union's threat to Western Europe; now it included all of East Asia. In effect the United States had forever abandoned its "Fortress America" mentality and became the de facto policeman for much of the world. In addition, the United States had adopted a radical expansion of its military—defense spending tripled, the hydrogen bomb was successfully tested and added to the American arsenal, and the ambitious and costly policies for a massive expansion of atomic, conventional, and psychological warfare outlined in the National Security Council's document NSC-68 were already in full implementation.[58]

No one could have possibly foretold in 1953 that the unresolved "police action" in Korea that left the peninsula divided between two bitter foes would lead to an unprecedented era of peace and stability as well as amazing economic prosperity for all but the unfortunate people held in

North Korea's brutal dictatorship under three generations of the Kim dynasty. Indeed, in an unanticipated way, the Korean War stabilized the Cold War, as both the United States and the Soviet Union came to understand that heated conflicts could remain limited while fought on soil that belonged to neither superpower. In the decades following the 1953 armistice, grim conflicts in Asia and the Middle East tested the wills of the rival superpowers but did not lead to direct confrontation. Historian William Stueck has noted, "In its timing, its course, and its outcome, the Korean War served as a substitute for World War III."[59]

Miscalculations on all sides had led to a war that produced outcomes with lasting consequences and altered the character of the Cold War. The 1953 armistice meant that both North and South Korea would endure, and the Eisenhower administration and the Soviet leadership were left supporting needy, troublesome, and frequently embarrassing Korean allies. The Soviets would soon be displeased with Kim's purge of distrusted Communist elements not loyal to his every whim. Meanwhile, the Chinese were forced to accept the loss of Taiwan and a long exclusion from a rightful leadership role in the United Nations. At the war's end, the United States and the Soviet Union both rushed to build their vast military might and engaged in a costly nuclear arms race that soon added long-range aircraft and hydrogen bombs to their arsenal. Additionally NATO became a formidable military alliance, and the containment policy the United States had adopted to check Soviet influence in Europe now included East Asia. The Soviet Union responded by creating the Warsaw Pact with central and eastern European Communist states; however, relations with China, damaged by Soviet failures to provide the assistance promised during the Korean War, continued to deteriorate. The hastily made, crucial decisions of the leaders in Washington, Moscow, and Peking in the first six months of warfare on the Korean Peninsula had altered world history.[60]

While most Americans appeared anxious to forget about Korea, the war had already seared the memory of the public in ways that altered the national character. Although victory was achieved in October 1950 with the saving of the ROK and the crushing defeat of the North Korean aggressors, the Chinese intervention forced the UNC forces into a retreat and the abandonment of the expanded mission to unify the Korean Peninsula under Syngman Rhee's government. In 1950 a nation enjoying peace and post–World War II prosperity had suddenly encountered a war that came without prologue and was not fought to totally vanquish an aggressive foe, or even the real foe, the Soviet Union. Instead Americans initially viewed the conflict as fought to maintain a status quo and leave in place a weak, autocratic regime. That the violence was halted by a seemingly shameful compromise with Communists only exacerbated the disillusionment.

The end of the fighting in Korea appeared to do nothing to make the world safer and led to a vast expansion of the U.S. military and the huge budget appropriations needed to support new, burdensome commitments abroad. Meanwhile, new concerns arose over the threats posed by the possibility of Communist spies embedded in U.S. government offices, university campuses, labor unions, and influential institutions. Other threats to the republic seemed to come from returning POWs, who may have cooperated with their Communist captors, suggesting to some a general weakening of the character of the American male who no longer seemed to measure up to the standards set by the heroic generation of World War II. The war in Korea devastated President Truman's second term. As his public approval ratings dropped, domestic reforms outlined in his 1948 presidential campaign for a "Fair Deal," including improved civil rights legislation and expanded social welfare programs, were placed on hold. Budget deficits rose precipitously even as taxes increased. As a result of these developments in the 1950s, the nation grew more cautious, conservative, and fearful of change. The culture of the United States seemed to become more inward looking, even as its nation's foreign policies, interests, and commitments abroad vastly expanded.

The conflict in Korea altered the way the United States fights wars, although the nation's public memory seems to be largely unaware that it was the Korean War that brought about this fundamental change. From 1953 onward—in Vietnam and the wars in the Middle East—wars have been undeclared by Congress, although presidents, remembering Truman's neglect of congressional authority, have sought some form of authorization or approval, short of a declaration of war, for overseas military actions. Undeclared wars fought since Korea employed limited use of weaponry, have been confined to specific geographical locations, and waged against enemies that pose no direct threat to U.S. survival. Moreover, recent wars have caused little disruption of economic or social life within the United States, except for antiwar protests, usually confined to certain distinct elements in society. Wars since Korea are fought by racially integrated armed forces with personnel increasingly drawn from the least affluent elements of the population and rotated in and out, and sometimes back into, warfare. Extensive bombing campaigns launched from safe, secure bases or aircraft carriers devastate the civilian populations in the war zones, usually with little impact on the war's ultimate settlement, which tends to be a return to a stalemate or political status quo ante bellum achieved only after a long, protracted period of negotiation that continued as seemingly interminable fighting raged on and on. As in Korea, by the time limited wars in Vietnam, Iraq, and Afghanistan staggered to unsatisfactory ends, the public's attention to the warfare had focused on other matters.

Ultimately public memory in the United States, as well as the judgment of history, would turn in Truman's favor while the public admiration of his principal wartime nemesis, General MacArthur, would fade away. After MacArthur failed to secure the Republican Party's nomination for the presidency in 1952, the aging general's speeches reached ever-diminishing audiences, and he never moved the American public to call upon their elected leaders for an expansion of the war in Korea or an engagement in a military confrontation with China or the Soviet Union. Criticism of President Truman's leadership during the Korean conflict seemed hollow in light of MacArthur's Republican Party allies' failure to offer any alternative to the course followed by the Truman administration. The general's legacy declined, although he remained a popular icon for conservative elements in the American political spectrum, received a state funeral befitting a president, was awarded with a library and museum in Norfolk, Virginia, that rivaled the federal presidential libraries, and enjoyed a place of honor in the memory of many South Koreans, where many female shamans (mudangs) often practiced MacArthur worship—even smoking pipes and wearing sunglasses. Historians began writing critically of his failures during World War II, particularly the neglect to protect his air force in the Philippines from Japanese attack in December 1941 and his unnecessary effort to liberate Manila from Japanese forces in 1945, which left that city in ruins. And above all his critics pointed to his lack of any preparation for the possibility of the Chinese crossing the Yalu River and entering the Korean War in the winter of 1950. Military historians denounced his insubordination to presidential authority. Moreover his arrogance, imperious style, and obvious self-aggrandizement drew the attention of both his admirers and adversaries.[61] David Halberstram, a keen observer of American society, has noted, "In an odd way, MacArthur, who so looked down on Truman as a little man, had enhanced Truman's reputation for courage and integrity, and made him a bigger man."[62] Indeed, over time Truman's own place in public memory was enhanced by comparison to his most ardent political opponents, especially MacArthur and Pres. Richard M. Nixon. Truman's honesty, humility, and down-to-earth lifestyle also appealed to a public that saw their former president return to his modest home in middle America and settle into his familiar old neighborhood as "Mr. Citizen." Truman's two-volume memoirs and the best-selling *Plain Speaking*—a quasi-autobiographical account of his life and times by Merle Miller, based on clearly exaggerated and spiced-up taped interviews with Truman—helped cement the former president's reputation as a "man of the people." A popular movie also aided Truman's image. Going beyond the amped-up rhetoric of *Plain Speaking*, in 1975 actor James Whitman presented a one-man performance as a feisty Harry Truman in *Give 'em Hell, Harry!* that garnered an Academy Award nomination.[63] In the 1970s far more lasting and substantial support for Truman's reputation resulted from the declassification of presidential records and government documents held in the Truman Presidential Library in Independence, Missouri, and in other archives. In addition, hundreds of private papers were discovered in the attic of the Truman home following the death of the president's widow in 1982. This material contained Truman's candid assessments of world affairs, foreign leaders, domestic policies, and family issues. The enhanced documentary record humanized the former president, placed his steady leadership in the context of the political vortex in which his administration coped with a changing world. The archived records solidified Truman's public image and allowed for the writing of David McCullough's popular, Pulitzer Prize-winning biography *Truman*. The wealth of solid documentation also led to superb analysis of the Truman era and the president's achievements, flaws, and failures by scholars Alonzo Hamby, Robert Ferrell, and many others.[64] At the dawn of the twenty-first century, as General MacArthur's place in history continued its decline, the one-time farmer, infantry captain, haberdasher, county politician, little-known U.S. senator, and overlooked vice president was held in the memory of Americans as one of the nation's greatest leaders.

President Truman's legacy will forever be tied to the Korean War and the most difficult decision of his presidency. However, at the time of his death, on the day after Christmas 1972, the significance of the war in reshaping the Far East and the international world order had not yet become apparent. The war in Korea was not what Truman wanted, and its results were not at all what he expected. The war's results were not what Joseph Stalin, Kim Il-sung, or Mao Zedong expected either.

2 | Forging Memories

Public perceptions of the Korean War in the United States were influenced by partisan rhetoric, misinformation about the conduct of American prisoners of war (POWs) and the effects of "brainwashing" on returning veterans, exaggerated concerns over national security, and paranoia about the possibility of Communist agents infiltrating the U.S. government. Partisan political rhetoric, the news media, popular fiction, and motion pictures, such as *The Manchurian Candidate* and M*A*S*H, shaped early American public understanding of the Korean War as less heroic than all other wars in which the United States had participated. Meanwhile, the memories of political leaders, military commanders, and journalists sought to record the war and justify key decisions.

In the autumn of 1955, a young soldier returning from service in Korea and wearing his uniform stopped a man on a Chicago street to ask for directions. "Are you a soldier?" the man inquired. "Where have you been?" When the soldier replied that he had been in Korea, the man seemed stunned. "Where's that?" he asked.[1] Clearly Americans were eager to place the Korean War on a back shelf in the warehouse of public memory. Unaccustomed to the political realities of a "limited war," sheltered by military censorship from press accounts of the war's horrifying realities, unbothered by significant or prolonged antiwar protests, and seldom inconvenienced by wartime shortages or rationing, most Americans could simply ignore the war and let the entire unpleasantness fade from memory.

Lasting memories of the Korean War were being formed even as the realities of the conflict were being overlooked or forgotten. How the past is understood and remembered always influences the present, even if historical narratives and memories are vague, clouded, or false. Interpretations of past events, especially wars, are used by nations to define their existence. Popular narratives, even if false, can provide widely held remembrance. At the same time, troubling and unpleasant memories can be suppressed through communal forgetfulness.

Despite this trend toward public forgetfulness, conflicting narratives of the Korean War were already being forged in the United States and among allies and foes. These would create lasting memories, shaping the national psyches of all involved. However, over the decades, these memories would evolve and transform as a result of international realignments and changing economic and political realities. But the contested and conflicting narratives and memories of the war and its uncertain lessons were never truly forgotten. Veterans of the Korean War returned to an American society that had already begun to forget the conflict. Even as savage warfare raged across the divided Korean Peninsula, news of the conflict and the protracted peace negotiations began to disappear from the front pages of U.S. newspapers. The grim signing of documents in the demilitarized zone (DMZ) at Panmunjom for the July 1953 armistice may have ended the combat, but the event generated no parades or celebrations. Unlike returning veterans of World War II, Korean War veterans believed their service was forgotten, misunderstood, or at least overlooked. Even among historians who studied the record of the war in Korea labeled it the "forgotten war."[2] Locked between the war of the "Greatest Generation" and the long, agonizing catastrophe in Vietnam, the conflict in Korea was easy to overlook.

Nevertheless, the vast majority of the American veterans of the Korean War returned home and resumed their earlier lives in a manner similar to veterans of previous wars. While savage fighting raged along the front lines, most never heard a shot fired in anger. Nearly 5.7 million men and women were Korean War-era veterans, and only 1,789,000 served "in theater." While lacking the heroic designation of the "Greatest Generation," most Korean War veterans sought to put their experience behind them and return to normal civilian life. They made that transition successfully. Even though Pres. Dwight D. Eisenhower and the Republican Congress cut veterans' benefits, made the GI Bill more restrictive, and limited access to some government-funded opportunities for Black veterans,

Korean War veterans took advantage of government assistance at a high rate. Veterans of the Korean War earned 17 percent or more income than their peers who had not served in the armed services, and Korean War veterans had a higher rate of home ownership than nonveterans. They were also more likely than veterans of World War II, Vietnam, and the wars in the Persian Gulf to have earned a college degree. Furthermore, African American and Hispanic veterans of Korea exceeded by far their nonveteran counterparts in income in the decade following the war.[3] Many veterans of the Korean War went on to have distinguished professional careers in civilian life: Neil Armstrong, Edwin "Buzz" Aldrin, and several of their fellow astronauts in the Mercury Program; actor James Garner (*Maverick* and *Rockford files*); U.S. representative Charles Rangel (awarded both the Bronze Star and Purple Heart); U.S. senator John Warner of Virginia; and television personality Ed McMahon. Hall of Fame baseball legend Ted Williams flew combat missions as the wingman for a squadron led by John Glenn, who would become the first American to orbit the earth, an extraordinarily popular national hero, and an influential U.S. senator from Ohio.[4]

Yet myths and falsehoods put forth by politicians, government officials, and critics in various professions created a legend that somehow soldiers who fought in Korea were of a lower caliber than those who had fought in earlier wars. A popular mythology emerged, claiming that the post–World War II generation of American males tended to lack a fighting spirit, yielded easily to their captors when taken prisoner, and failed to take advantage of opportunities to escape. This narrative of defeatism tarnished an entire generation and gave Americans additional cause to forget or ignore as much as possible the Korean War and its veterans. Meanwhile, throughout the war and in its immediate aftermath, veterans returned from their service alone, in a system of staged rotations based on a point system. There were few public welcoming ceremonies and no great parades, except for that received by Gen. Douglas MacArthur following his dismissal by Pres. Harry S. Truman. Soldiers came home to a United States where the celebratory memories of a great victory in World War II were still fresh.[5]

As the war in Korea expanded and failed to end in a quick and decisive victory, the American public became increasingly disillusioned with the rationale for war put forward by their leaders. Initially Truman's decision to enter the conflict drew wide public support in the United States. The decisive role of the Soviet Union in initiating the invasion of South Korea became immediately apparent to all but a few diehard apologists for the Soviets. Republicans on the political right, as well as critics of President Truman's Cold War policies toward the Soviets, almost universally expressed support for what President Truman called a U.S.-led action to save the Republic of Korea. Republican politicians, still upset with Truman over his alleged "loss of China," felt compelled to appear supportive of Truman's firm stand against further Communist advances in East Asia. But this approval came with warnings and continuing criticism of the administration's overall foreign policies. Major newspapers, with the notable exception of the *Chicago Tribune* and its affiliated *Washington Times-Herald*, backed Truman's decision to rescue South Korea; and two-thirds of Americans viewed military assistance to halt the North Korean invasion with approval in the summer of 1950.[6] A Gallup poll conducted just one month after the North Korean invasion found 78 percent of Americans in favor of Truman's actions, with only 15 percent expressing disapproval.[7] Unfortunately for President Truman, this public support would disappear over the winter of 1950–51 like pumpkin vines during a frosty January cold snap.

The reason was clear. The course of the conflict dramatically changed following China's massive intervention in November 1950, and as the number of casualties increased, support for the war quickly diminished. By the end of October 1950, the United States had succeeded in accomplishing the original and limited objective: saving South Korea from a Communist takeover by a North Korean force enabled by the Soviet Union. By crossing the 38th parallel, the U.S.-led Republic of Korea and United Nations Command (UNC) forces were engaged in an unanticipated and expanded mission: unification of the Korean Peninsula under the autocratic regime of Syngman Rhee. This larger mission seemed possible with limited military power, but the massive intervention of the Chinese in November made the new and enlarged mission impossible to accomplish with limited means, causing the costly military effort to bog down in uncertainty, frustration, and ultimately failure.

From the very start, the war in Korea had failed to generate anything like the patriotic fervor the nation witnessed following the Japanese attack on Pearl Harbor in 1941. Young men were not rushing to recruiting stations. Although a draft law, the Universal Military Training and Service Act, was in effect, most young men appeared to wait on the sidelines for this nation to call them for military service. Selective Service System director Lewis Hershey lamented, "Everyone wants out; no one wants in."[8] A wartime study of 4,585 American males at eleven U.S. universities found a willingness to serve if called upon, but noted the war in Korea lacked the "wholehearted support of public opinion that characterized the last war." While a widespread antiwar movement never emerged, the American public nevertheless came to view the war in Korea as a conflict that did not conform to commonly held memories of prior conflicts, especially the victorious and decisive end of World War II. In addition, President Truman's abrupt dismissal in early 1951 of the popular World War II commander General MacArthur, who famously argued for expansion of the warfare in Korea because there could be "no substitute for victory," caused the president's public approval rating to crash.[9] Finally the long protracted and inconclusive nature of the peace negotiations, begun in Kaesong in the summer of 1951 and complicated for a year and a half by the thorny issue of repatriation of Chinese and North Korean POWs, bewildered the American public. Within months half of Americans viewed the war as a mistake and nearly three-quarters felt the United Nations (UN) was not doing enough to support the war effort. Growing dissatisfaction with Truman's conduct of war in Korea would become the major factor in the presidential campaign of 1952.[10]

A limited war headed toward a messy settlement and unsatisfactory compromises did not fit the image Americans had of warfare. British historian Steven Casey has noted that "Americans recoiled from a war that never was declared formally, where the real enemy—the Soviet Union—was not the target, and in which the aim was not total peace, or even the eradication of the North Korean menace." Americans, he observed, liked to consider themselves reluctant to use force except to protect their own national existence or for some "noble purpose." Not fully understanding the conflict's causes and objectives, disillusionment took over when the U.S. government refused to conduct a total war.[11] Perhaps influenced by the powerful memories of the Civil War and the recent victory in World War II, the American public seemed to believe that all wars fought by the United States ended in a decisive victory or "unconditional surrender." This perception overlooked the historical reality that most of their nation's foreign conflicts, including those against Native Americans, ended in negotiated treaties and involved exchanges of money or territory. Outright conquest of a foreign power, followed by a military occupation, was never a goal—with the exception of World War II. Yet even in World War II, the United States settled for less than unconditional surrender from Japan, allowing that nation to keep its emperor. In reality the "limited war" in Korea was not unlike most American military engagements. The Soviet Union and the People's Republic of China also fought a limited war in Korea. The Soviets and Chinese restrained themselves from fighting beyond the Korean Peninsula, and Soviet pilots did not fly across the 38th parallel. Neither side made an all-out commitment of their military forces, but Americans, including the political and military leaders, did not seem to notice.

As the conflict continued, opposition to the war in the United States came in unequal measure from both the left and the right. Perhaps the most prominent of the early leftist critics was journalist I. F. Stone, who published *The Hidden History of the Korean War, 1950–1951* in 1952. Stone advanced, without any credible documentation, the remarkable notion that the United States had actually initiated the war in Korea. Stone saw the outbreak of war in Korea as a vast conspiracy of vicious capitalists, generals, and tyrants lurking about in Washington DC, Seoul, and Tokyo—everywhere but in Moscow, Beijing, and Pyongyang.[12] Prominent intellectuals, such as W. E. B. DuBois, and celebrities, including actor Paul Robeson, led noisy antiwar protests that resulted in federal authorities questioning their ties to the Soviet Union and the Communist Party. "Hands Off Korea" protest leaders at an antiwar rally in New York's Madison Square Garden drew thousands. But their efforts led to no widespread protests or change in Truman administration policy. DuBois became so disillusioned with the United States that he joined the Communist Party and moved to Ghana. A federal judge ultimately dismissed Robeson's indictment as an unregistered foreign agent, but his passport was confiscated. Michael Harrington, a writer for the *Catholic Worker* (a Christian, Socialist newsletter), was placed under surveillance. But overall, except for a few pacifist organizations and academic circles, Stone's radical views and those of other antiwar critics were not widely held. Moreover, the Korean War dealt a crushing blow to the American peace movement, which generally supported the concept of the United

Nations as a means to maintain world peace. With few exceptions, peace advocates viewed the Soviet Union as the instigator of the North Korean invasion. Even prominent peace advocate Henry Wallace, the 1948 presidential candidate of the Progressive Party and frequent critic of President Truman's Cold War policies, confided to a friend that "if our Left Wing friends were interested in peace they would write Stalin to end the Korean conflict."[13]

Unlike the Vietnam era, most of the war's criticism came not from the left but from politicians representing a divided political right. Many conservatives, the majority being Republican, argued against any American involvement in foreign conflicts that did not directly threaten the United States. But their argument was inconsistent. These isolationists, often "America First" advocates of the pre–World War II era, were bitter over the "loss of China" and believed the United States should have intervened to save the Nationalist regime before it collapsed in 1949. Most supported standing up to Communist aggression in Korea, at least initially. The conservatives' leader, Republican senator Robert Taft of Ohio, proved to be consistently incoherent and conflicted in his criticism of the Truman administration. While vilifying Truman, he could offer no alternative. The vacillating Taft had strongly advocated the unification of Korea until the Chinese intervened in the war. He then argued that the United States should withdraw from Korea altogether. When the war turned into a prolonged stalemate along what would become the DMZ, Taft termed the war pointless and costly. As the warfare in Korea bogged down and headed toward a stalemate, most Republicans followed Taft's erratic lead in expressing confusing and ever-changing views. Other Republican critics moved in an opposite direction and allied themselves with their popular hero, General MacArthur, who advocated an expanded war, including the use of nuclear weapons against North Korea's Soviet and Chinese allies. With Senator Taft offering no alternatives to Truman's policies, many Republicans abandoned the bipartisan foreign policy advanced during the first years of Truman's administration and joined in the reckless attacks of Wisconsin senator Joseph McCarthy, who claimed Communists had infiltrated the highest levels of the Truman administration. Republican criticisms sometimes included calls for secretary of state Dean Acheson to resign. Some Democrats from conservative states joined the administration's Republican critics. Lyndon Johnson, a first-term senator from

Texas, complained that the war was being fought "piecemeal" without the full use of American force, while his Texan colleague in the House of Representatives, Lloyd Bentsen, urged Truman to tell North Korea to withdraw or be "subject to nuclear attack."[14]

The political right was relentless and effective in attacking the Democrats in the White House and Congress over the war and how they were confronting Communism. Republicans maintained that anything Truman did in Korea was wrong. Senator Johnson headed a subcommittee to investigate the conduct of the war, similar to what President Truman had done as a U.S. senator from Missouri during World War II. When his committee investigated the defense industry, Johnson merely annoyed the Truman administration and clearly enjoyed the publicity he received questioning the actions of his president and the Joint Chiefs of Staff. The Republicans, however, were out for blood. They eagerly followed Senator McCarthy and sought to tarnish the Truman administration with charges of vast Communist conspiracies.[15]

Attacks on Truman's management of the war continued into the 1952 presidential election, and President Truman, damaged by the constant criticism of the war effort, announced at age sixty-eight that he would not seek another term in office. Gen. Dwight Eisenhower edged out both his former commanding officer, General MacArthur, as well as Ohio's Senator Taft to secure the presidential nomination of the Republican Party. Besides pledging on October 24, 1952, that if elected, "I will go to Korea," General Eisenhower asked voters how they could possibly expect Democrats "to repair what they had failed to prevent" in Korea. The unpopularity of the Korean War enabled Eisenhower's victory in the 1952 election, and memory of that unpopular war in Korea would remain the theme in coming elections. In his successful reelection campaign of 1956, Eisenhower claimed that it was his administration that had brought "peace with honor" in Korea, and in the second debate of the 1960 presidential election, which pitted the vice president, Richard Nixon, against Massachusetts senator John F. Kennedy, Nixon argued that Sec. Acheson's "wooly thinking" had led to "disaster for America in Korea."[16] Although Kennedy won the closely contested 1960 presidential election, he and his vice presidential running mate, Senator Johnson, were aware upon taking office that the Republican Party had come to believe the Democrats were vulnerable to criticism on Korea and any sign of weakness in confronting a perceived Communist threat in Asia. Both would shape their foreign policies accordingly.

The charges of weakness in the face of Communist aggression led to few public protests. Indeed, the vast majority of Americans were not directly impacted by the war. Although 1.5 million young men were drafted, deferments were common. Almost unnoticed, the Korean War started a wartime tradition, extending through Vietnam and the wars in the Middle East, in which a certain spectrum of the American population fought and died while most of the nation's population enjoyed life as usual. However, unlike the Vietnam War protestors a decade later, few in the United States considered the Korean War as a reason to make radical changes in their society. Of the conservative and isolationist nature of those opposed to the war, historian Alonzo Hamby has observed, "Korean War protestors waved the American flag, Vietnam protestors frequently burned it. Disapproval of Korea was encased in a lifestyle characterized by patriotism and conventional moral behavior."[17]

Early in the war, the supposedly weak and unpatriotic behavior of some of the more than 7,200 U.S. soldiers, sailors, and airmen held captive by the North Koreans and their Chinese allies became an issue of urgent national concern. Fears of a weakened United States quickly became themes for journalists, social critics, and self-proclaimed experts. Public outcry arose during the frigid December of 1950 with the hasty retreat of the U.S. Eighth Army from the North Korean capital and the U.S. Marines from the snow-covered mountains surrounding the Chosin Reservoir when faced with hundreds of thousands of fresh Chinese troops. Americans were shocked to the core. "There is something wrong with the American boy today," an opinion piece in the New York *Herald Tribune* proclaimed in December 1950. "He won't fight. He gladly takes a whipping, thinking only of running away. In my day he might have taken a whipping in a fight or a baseball game. But he always scrapped back. These boys are weak."[18] Concern was heightened later on by the conduct of some American POWs. Air Force Col. Frank Schwable, a highly decorated World War II veteran, along with others, created a global sensation when confessing, falsely, to using germ warfare against the North Koreans. More POW false confessions and anti-American statements from POWs followed.[19] Adding to the public outrage and confusion, U.S. servicemen seemed to have collaborated with their captors at a higher rate than POWs of other nations supporting the UNC. Moreover when 2,730 U.S. military POWs (nearly 40 percent, an astonishingly high rate) died from horrifying conditions in captivity, some claimed these soldiers lacked personal fortitude or the will to survive, suggesting they were responsible for their own deaths. The American public came to believe that never in U.S. history had so many of the nation's POWs behaved in such a pathetic and cowardly manner. The lingering POW issue would mean that, unlike veterans of all other U.S. wars in the twentieth century, Korean War POWs were stigmatized for decades. And there would be an even more shocking revelation—twenty-one American servicemen refused to return home at the end of the war. In the words of historian and Korean War veteran Paul Edwards, this news "hit Americans like a sledgehammer."[20]

The myths about the behavior of POWs were based on false information and a disregard or misreading of the facts. An outpouring of recent scholarship on the Korean War has addressed the numerous misconceptions related to POWs and placed the experience of U.S. and UNC soldiers in the historical contexts of modern warfare, especially the involvement of American and allied countries in Vietnam and seemingly endless Middle Eastern conflicts. Conditions in North Korean POW camps were cruel and inhumane by any standard. Since neither the North Koreans nor their Chinese allies had anticipated the entry of U.S. and UN troops into the war on the Korean Peninsula, they made no provisions for foreign prisoners. As a result, executions of U.S. and UNC prisoners by the North Korean People's Army occurred in the early months of the conflict, and those captives not shot to death were forced to march northward on more than 120 miles of rugged terrain under horrendous conditions. At the war's end, thousands of American and UNC personnel remained unaccounted for. At least 130 of 170 American prisoners died at the hands of their North Korean captors in the first weeks, some executed on the spot when injuries or fatigue kept them from keeping pace with their fellow prisoners. Once in POW camps, the captives suffered from the severe cold of North Korean winters and poor food and little medical attention. Conditions were particularly grim during the first years of the war. Even after the Chinese entered the conflict and physical conditions gradually improved, POWs were subjected to various forms of torture, including beatings, withholding of food and water, and severe sleep deprivation. In addition, prisoners were forced to stand while listening to long, repetitive lectures about the advantages of the Communist way of life. Using tactics known to police and prison officials since the days of the Spanish Inquisition, the Communist captors sought to extract confessions and admissions of war crimes. Black soldiers were singled out for special attention and asked by their captors why they would fight overseas in the armed forces for a country that treated them badly at home.[21]

U.S. military POWs, along with foreign nationals in South Korea taken into captivity in the early months of the war by the North Korean invaders, were treated most severely. Many died in the early months of the war on forced marches to the North Korean border with China, the Yalu River, if they were not immediately executed by their captors. Of the 7,245 U.S. military personnel taken captive during the war, 2,806 died in captivity and 4,418 were eventually returned to the U.S. military at the war's end. Nearly 700 escaped their North Korean or Chinese captors during the conflict, almost always while held near the front lines before being marched far to the north and placed in camps along the Yalu River. About fifty American POWs attempted escape from POW camps but were unsuccessful because of the harsh, unforgiving weather, long distances to freedom over rugged terrain, obvious foreign appearance, and insurmountable language barriers. Ultimately of the 3,746 returned American POWs, 565 were investigated for possible violations of the Uniform Code of Military Justice, including charges of murdering other POWs and collaborating with the enemy. Of these cases, 373 were dismissed on legal or administrative grounds. Of those remaining 6 U.S. Army officers were convicted, and 61 were discharged from the military for "unsuitability." One was reprimanded and 2 were given special assignments. One source estimates that only one-third of 1 percent of the surviving American POWs were even convicted of collaboration on treasonous offenses.[22]

Under political and ideological pressure, unknown to U.S. soldiers in previous wars, captured soldiers often proved unprepared to serve as pawns in a war of propaganda waged by competing ideologies. Nevertheless, many endured and behaved heroically. Wayne "Johnnie" Johnson, an eighteen-year-old private first class from Lima, Ohio, in a prisoner unit called the "Tiger Group," secretly kept a journal that chronicled the events of his captivity and the deaths of prisoners in his POW camp. Johnson would eventually receive a Silver Star in 1996. His documentation, hidden from his captors in an empty toothpaste tube, provides a haunting firsthand account of the horrific conditions in the North Korean POW camps and the brutality of those responsible. Johnson recorded a hundred deaths in the harsh November of 1950, including a nun, a teenage South Korean boy called "Johnny," and several international civilians caught up in the earliest months of the war. He described a particularly cruel North Korean officer called "Tiger" blowing off the head of an American officer as a lesson to the others on the death march to a POW camp near the Yalu River, as well as other acts by North Korean officers intended to terrorize the captives.[23]

Another POW, Dr. Alexander "Doc" Boysen, corroborated Johnson's story of the "Tiger's" extraordinary cruelty and provided a highly detailed description of life in the POW camps to the U.S. military authorities following his release from captivity. Like Johnson, Boysen was taken prisoner in the first weeks of the war. Upon his return Boysen described conditions in an official report as particularly harsh during the early months of the war when food, clothing, and shelter were inadequate to maintain prisoners' health. Proper attention to illnesses, battlefield wounds, and injuries resulting from the torture the North Korean guards inflicted was impossible. "Medical treatment was entirely lacking during this period," Boysen wrote. "Had we been allowed to operate our own camps, perhaps more of the men would have survived. . . . Malnutrition, complicated by dysentery and pneumonia, continued to take its toll. . . . The guards were allowed to do what they wanted to and continued to harass, beat, and cause prisoners unnecessary bruises and mental strain." In October 1951 the Chinese took over the camp where Boysen was held and conditions immediately improved with additional supplies of clothing and blankets. The physical maltreatment subsided, and Boysen reported that "our diet under the Chinese was sufficient in quantity though always insufficient in quality."[24]

Two years later Boysen coauthored an article with four other U.S. medical officers who had been POWs in Korea. Their work, published in the *Journal of the American Medical Association*, maintained that throughout their captivity, "Medical care never became adequate, although overall conditions improved and deaths were not as common after October 1951 when control of the POW camps was transferred to the Chinese." Nevertheless, deaths continued at an alarming rate due to starvation, exposure, and "harassment by the enemy." Deaths were so common, especially in the first year of the war, that prisoners felt that any illness would be a death sentence. In an effort to address this fatalistic attitude and encourage a fighting spirit, the American physicians coined the term *give-up-itis*. Unfortunately the doctors realized later on that their creation was misinterpreted by the press, where it was suggested that POWs in generally good conditions simply gave up and died. In fact, even with improved conditions, the majority of deaths were caused by prolonged respiratory infections and diarrhea. Far from giving up or lacking the will to survive, the doctors wrote, "It is amazing, not that there was a high death rate, but that there was a good rate of survival."[25] The doctors also addressed the Communists' efforts at indoctrination of the prisoners, who were informed by their captors that "we will correct the errors in your thinking." The Communists attempted to accomplish this by keeping prisoners cold, hungry, "and in a state of disorganized confusion until each person realized that resistance meant starvation or death." The indoctrination process included solitary confinement, withholding food and water, and months of "an intensive formal study program" lasting all day and emphasizing the evils of U.S. imperialism and the benefits of Communism. During the final year of the war, the "most intensive subject for special indoctrination was the bacterial warfare hoax," according to the authors, who concluded with dire warnings about the threat of Communist techniques to a free and open society.[26] The information provided by medical experts and others to the U.S. military and the public about dreadful conditions in POW camps under North Korean and Chinese control should have led Americans to welcome returning POWs as heroes for simply surviving. Sadly this was not the case, and a false understanding of the service of U.S. soldiers in the Korean war rooted itself into the national memory.

The ordeal of U.S. and UN prisoners of war did not end when hostilities ceased. Following the July 1953 armistice and their release from captivity, returning POWs endured intensive interrogation that lasted for weeks, months, and even years. Beginning on ships returning to the States, some POWs underwent eight hours a day of questioning by military psychologists and psychiatrists. Military intelligence officers were also on hand for the interrogation. Besides their experiences in the camps, these stressed and weakened former POWs were questioned about their personal histories and political beliefs, all in efforts to detect cases of "menticide," or deadening of pre-captivity values and an acceptance of Communist ideology. The Federal Bureau of Investigation collected and evaluated tens of thousands of pages of documents, and George Washington University (GWU) even secured a government contract to analyze the mountain of collected data, under the auspices of director Julius Segal. Under Segal's direction GWU issued a report in 1956 entitled *Factors Related to the Collaboration and Resistance Behaviors of U.S. Army POWs in Korea*, which looked at 579 POW returnees and found a lack of "esprit de corps" among them. The report concluded that 70 percent had "wittingly or unwittingly" aided Communist psychological war efforts. The report went on to state that one in ten had actively informed on fellow POWs and tagged 565 for further investigation. Yet after all the time and effort spent on the report, no one was ever tried for treason based on those interviews. The failure to find large numbers of returning POWs guilty of anything did not, however, alleviate the sense of shame and public embarrassment suffered by those who had already endured years of hideous confinement. The extensive interrogative process disrupted the POWs resettlement, as clearance was required from the U.S. Army Board of Prisoners of War Collaboration. Back pay was withheld, and frequent calls to hearings inconvenienced both witnesses and those being investigated as months, and sometimes years, went by.[27] Reputations were tarnished, lives blighted, and a cloud of suspicion tainted all Korean War POWs. The POW issue burned a lasting image in the American public memory of the Korean War.

Most U.S. veterans of the Korean War years never witnessed combat, crossed the Pacific, or experienced difficulties readjusting to civilian life. Furthermore, nearly all who survived the war in Korea behaved honorably and loyally. In spite of this, an entire literature emerged questioning the toughness, patriotism, and courage of the American male. In 1956 Maj. William Mayer, a U.S. Army neuropsychiatrist, interviewed many returning American POWs and became alarmed at what he perceived as a whole generation lacking in patriotism. He found the Korean War POWs to be weak and passive and wrote in *U.S. News & World Report* that "too many of our soldiers fell short of the American historical standings of honor, character, loyalty, courage, and personal integrity." He warned that the POW issue presented "a problem of fantastic proportion and should cause searching self-examination for all Americans, both in and out of uniform."[28]

Widely read authors on social trends in the United States added their assessments of the Korean War-era American male. Best-selling writer and pediatrician, Dr. Benjamin Spock, advanced notions for the apparent male weaknesses and put forth recommendations to strengthen the wimpy, overly protected "mama's boys" reared by domineering mothers.[29] A much less qualified authority, pulp fiction writer and self-proclaimed social critic Philip Wylie, added his unscientific and misogynistic diatribe to the discussion. In a 1955 reissue of *A Generation of Vipers*, Wylie went beyond his 1942 attack on American women that introduced the word *momism* to the American lexicon. He even suggested in a chapter entitled "Common Women" that "mom worship has gotten completely out of hand"; and he told his male readers, "Gentlemen, mom is a jerk." In their households filled with new electronic appliances, he claimed American women had little work to do and used their spare time for "rage, infantilism, weeping, sentimentality, peculiar appetite, and all the reticule of tricks, wooings, wiles, suborned fornications, slobby onanisms, indulgences, crochets, superstitions, phlegms, debilities, vapors, butterflies in the belly, plaints, connivings, cries, malingerings, deceptions, visions, hallucinations, needlings and weedlings which pop out every personality in the act of abandoning itself and humanity." Using their idle hours, made possible by labor-saving conveniences, he maintained women had weakened their sons. His vitriolic rhetoric found an accepting and wide readership. By the mid-1950s Wylie's ravings and unsubstantiated attacks had gone through twenty printings.[30] Even feminist author Betty Friedan claimed to see a clear decline in the American male. She wrote that "a deterioration of the human character" had been exposed by experts "who studied the behavior of the American GIS who were prisoners of war in Korea in the 1950's." Friedan saw give-up-itis as the cause of a high mortality rate in POW camps where American GIS became inert and withdrew into "little shells."[31]

Beyond weakness and momism, Americans needed an explanation for the perceived cowardice and weakness of U.S. POWS, and Edward Hunter, a journalist based in Miami, Florida, sought to provide it. He created the colorful and sensational term *brainwashing*. According to the House Un-American Activities Committee (HUAC), Hunter's credentials as an expert on human psychology and interrogation practices consisted of nothing more than a background as a foreign news correspondent, author, world traveler, and "specialist in propaganda warfare." In testimony before HUAC following the Korean War, Hunter ignored the already well-documented inhumane conditions in North Korean and Chinese POW camps and attributed the false confessions of American POWs and collaborations with their captors to frightening, new, Soviet-devised mind-altering techniques. Hunter claimed that specially trained interrogators sought "vulnerabilities" in their American and UNC captives and then "drilled away at weaknesses." He mistakenly charged that no American prisoners had escaped North Korean captivity and maintained that lack of will and character caused the extraordinarily high death rate among Americans in the POW camps. He further claimed that "discipline among Americans was almost non-existent. . . . It was dog eat dog."[32]

Early in the Korean conflict, the concept of brainwashing received official endorsement from the Central Intelligence Agency director Allen Dulles. In *U.S. News & World Report*, Dulles explained,

> The brain conditioning program of the Soviets is directed against the individual, case by case. Here they take selected human beings whom they wish to destroy and turn them into humble confessors of crimes they never committed or make them the mouthpiece of Soviet propaganda . . . new techniques wash the brain clean of thoughts and mental processes of the past, and possibly through the use of some "lie serum," create a new brain process and new thoughts which the victim, parrot-like, repeats.[33]

Following the Korean War, the notion of brainwashing became fixed in the American mind. The idea that brainwashing could turn U.S. POWs into mindless zombies was significantly advanced by Eugene Kinkead, a former U.S. Navy war correspondent and popular writer for *New Yorker* magazine's "Talk of the Town." His five-year study, assisted by the U.S. military, led to an award-winning book *In Every War but One* (1959), in which Kinkead concluded that brainwashing was a dangerous psychological weapon of the Soviet Union and a threat to every American.[34] Brainwashing became an enduring popular memory of the Korean War era, and its alleged techniques were suspected of infiltrating many aspects of American culture, from corporate politics to mass marketing to political campaigns.[35] By the 1960s the notion of brainwashing had taken on a life of its own, even though the scientific community had largely dismissed the concept.

Albert Biderman was among the first and most prominent academics to examine brainwashing from a social science perspective. He interviewed 235 U.S. Air Force POWs from the Korean War and concluded that brainwashing techniques used on American servicemen in the North Korean and Chinese POW camps were not at all new and succeeded only in eliciting false confessions. Indeed, Biderman and others found no prisoners who had been turned into robots with their minds washed clean. What had been responsible for the false confessions were various forms of torture well-known to inquisitors and police forces for centuries. These included starvation, dehydration, isolation, and sleep deprivation.[36] Biderman's work, along with that of others in the scientific community, thoroughly debunked the nonsensical brainwashing notions put forward by well-meaning professionals as well as misguided journalists and opportunistic frauds. Biderman concluded that the popular belief of wholesale collaboration by American prisoners with their Communist captors was a myth, and that there existed no evidence of unpredicted misbehavior or any sign of a "new weakness in our natural character." Singling out Kinkead and the military officials who had enabled his journalism, Biderman stated that their efforts "made prisoners of war, American society and, indirectly, persons with views I share the villains of their piece."[37] Nevertheless, the terrifying notion of Soviet-created zombies tarnished the images of all Korean War veterans, and the fiction of brainwashing became a lasting phenomenon in American culture.[38] In the case of brainwashing mythology, these false notions spread across the land much more swiftly and with more lasting impact than the truth.

When the armistice ended combat in Korea, heightened Cold War tensions left the nation feeling less secure than before the war started, and the United States was in no mood to memorialize an unpopular and unresolved conflict. Indeed, there appeared to be a desire to forget the war altogether. However, popular culture in the United States quickly reflected and interpreted the brutal conflict, focusing attention on both the realities and myths of the Korean War. Prominent script writers and major film studios crafted films that set in place early memories of the conflict that had taken the lives of nearly forty thousand U.S. soldiers and left millions of Koreans dead—most of them civilians. Even as the fighting and peace negotiations advanced slowly toward a stalemate, movies were already in production at Hollywood studios. *The Steel Helmet*, the first Korean War Hollywood film, appeared in 1951 and set a standard for realism that few other Korean War films achieved. It portrayed the chaotic early months of the war with shocking depictions of combat, confusion, and civilian casualties never surpassed in subsequent productions. The film accurately and realistically depicted American soldiers being captured and executed by the North Koreans and portrayed North Korean soldiers disguised as civilian refugees infiltrating the American units, creating chaos and panic. The film starred Gene Evans as a tough World War II veteran who tries to save "Short Round," an orphaned Korean boy. Released just eight months after the North Korean invasion, this low-budget production was directed by Sam Fuller, both a combat veteran and a Hollywood maverick. Although not a box-office hit, the film's stark realism and harsh message about the brutality of warfare in Korea made it a cult classic.[39]

In subsequent films the experiences of POWs, the notion of brainwashing, collaboration with Communist captors, and racial integration proved popular themes. In 1954's *Prisoner of War*, Ronald Reagan portrayed an American officer in a POW camp. Supposedly based on the experiences of Capt. Robert H. Wise (played by Reagan), the movie presents an American officer planted in a POW camp to make fake confessions in order to ingratiate himself to his captors and thereby acquire information on conditions in the POW camp for the U.S. military.[40] Collaboration again provided the theme in Rod Serling's *The Rack* (1956). Originally a TV play, the movie stars Paul Newman, whose character is a returned POW who initially finds himself welcomed home as a hero. However, he is soon facing court-martial for informing his Communist captors of a plot by fellow POWs to attempt an escape.[41] Military historian S. L. A. Marshall's book, *Pork Chop Hill* (1956), and the popular movie starring Gregory Peck that followed, presented a vivid depiction of the brutal and frustrating realities of the fighting in Korea for small plots of land during the final months of combat as the negotiations at Panmunjom wrangled over the contentious issue of the exact line of the proposed DMZ. Both the book and movie portray the heroic leadership of Capt. Joseph C. Clemons, played by Peck. The movie also introduces viewers to the troubling dilemmas faced by Black soldiers fighting in a newly integrated U.S. military. The first Hollywood film based on an actual event, *Pork Chop Hill* depicted the war with almost documentary accuracy. Black soldiers fighting in integrated units is also explored in *All the Young Men* (1960) with Sidney Poitier as a sergeant coping with leadership of white soldiers in a sudden call to command. *New York Times* film critic Bosley Crowther found the film, which costarred Alan Ladd, comedian Mort Sahl, singer James Darren, heavyweight boxing champion Ingemar Johansson, and Blackfeet Indians as Koreans, less than inspiring. "Racial integration in the United States is sluggishly calculated in a variation on a well-used Western plot," he wrote.[42] A sentimental look at the tragic plight of Korean War orphans was presented in *Battle Hymn* (1957), with Rock Hudson hopelessly miscast in the role of the "flying Preacher" Col. Dean Hess, whose memoir recounted airlifting scores of children to a safe haven as Chinese forces advanced on Seoul in December 1950.[43]

In the years immediately after the armistice, both of James A. Michener's two bestsellers led to highly popular movies—*Bridges at Toko Ri* (1955) and *Sayonara* (1957). Realistically depicting the lives and relationships of the U.S. military personnel, Michener's books and the films that resulted tended to ignore the devastation brought to the Korean Peninsula. In the case of *Bridges at Toko Ri*, viewers do not see the devastating result of American bombing of civilian targets. Close cooperation with the U.S. Navy provided viewers with dramatic scenes of aircraft carrier operations off the Korean coast, and Michener's close encounters with U.S. Navy pilots during his work as a wartime journalist gave the story a sense of realism. In *Sayonara* Michener took on racism, prejudice, and interracial marriage in the story of a U.S. Air Force officer, temporarily stationed in Japan during the Korean War, who falls in love with a Japanese woman. An outstanding cast including Marlon Brando, Red Buttons, James Garner, and Miyoshi Umeki, who won the Academy Award for Best Supporting Actress, made *Sayonara* one of the few memorable films depicting the Korean War experience. Both of Michener's works provided a sympathetic and humanizing view of Japanese society, a striking departure from the World War II-era popular images of the Japanese and reflective of the new American-Japanese friendship advanced during the hostilities in Korea.[44]

Almost a decade after the warfare ended, two highly extraordinary and remarkably different films on the Korean War appeared in 1962. Both received excellent critical reviews but earned only mild audience approval and modest box-office success. *War Hunt*, an independently produced film directed by Denis Sanders over a tight two-week schedule and a budget of only $300,000, depicted the nasty realities of modern warfare and the tense relationships of men under the stress of combat with such stark reality that the U.S. Army declined to assist the film's production. Nevertheless, the quality of the film helped launch the careers of Robert Redford, in his first credited movie role, and future Academy Award-winning directors Sidney Pollack and Francis Ford Coppola, the latter who appeared only briefly as an uncredited extra. Praised by the *New York Times* film critic as "one of the most original and haunting war movies in years . . . a singular penetrating study of an American squad in action just before the final cease fire . . . [and] pure unvarnished gold," the National Board of Review selected *War Hunt* as one of the ten best films of the year.[45] Among other films on that year's crowded list were *Lawrence of Arabia*, *Music Man*, and *To Kill a Mockingbird*. Also in the top ten was *The Longest Day*, a big budget film with an all-star international cast that depicted heroic scenes of the D-Day landings on Normandy during World War II, overshadowing *War Hunt* the same way the "Greatest Generation" blocked out the sun on the services of those who fought in Korea.

Unlike *War Hunt* and other Korean War movies, *The Manchurian Candidate* (1962), adopted from a novel by Richard Condon, still holds a special place in public memory. At the time of its release, the film was not a box-office success, finishing only twenty-fifth as a moneymaker in 1963, just ahead of *The Man Who Shot Liberty Valance*. Nevertheless, it received glowing reviews when released, and the movie endures as something of a cult classic, not so much for its superb cast (which included Frank Sinatra, Lawrence Harvey, and Angela Lansbury) and outstanding production value but for its outrageous and paranoid plot. Both the book and movie sensationalized Soviet influence in American politics and the danger of brainwashed American POWs let loose in American society. The film imagined a horrific scheme in which an American POW is returned home to his domineering and politically ambitious mother after being programmed by Communists at the "Pavlov Institute" to murder on command a U.S. presidential candidate. Combining many frightening Korean War themes, *The Manchurian Candidate* left its audience with haunting images of conditions in POW camps, brainwashed and psychologically damaged POWs, momism, and McCarthy-like political demagoguery.[46] Nearly four decades after the film's debut, one movie critic noted that the term "Manchurian candidate even entered everyday speech as a short-hand for a brainwashed sleeper, a subject who has been hypnotized and instructed to act when his controllers pull the psychological trigger."[47] In the twenty-first century, *The Manchurian Candidate* even inspired imitation in which Communist brainwashers are replaced in the era of the "War on Terrorism" with powerful, out-of-control corporate titans in the defense industry. Perhaps more than any other item of popular culture, *The Manchurian Candidate* fixed the notion of brainwashing in the American memory.

While Hollywood produced nearly a hundred movies about the Korean War, most were easily forgettable, and many were farcical depictions of soldiers on leave or otherwise enjoying romps with pretty nurses. Only a few depicted the war realistically, and these too were less than memorable, many accepting popular ideas about brainwashing, momism, the weak and effeminized young American male, and the possible threat of Communist influence embedded in the returning POWs. Some were assisted in this. Yet the movies of the Korean War era, in spite of their short-comings, at least seemed to be profitable.[48] For more serious depictions of the Korean War, audiences had to wait until the dawn of the twenty-first century when the availability of significant new archival material led to the production of documentaries that presented a realistic, often troubling view of the war. Among the more important are *The Korean War: Our Time in Hell* (Discovery Channel, 1997); *Battle for Korea* (PBS, 2001); *Korean War in Color* (Goldhill Home Media International, 2002); *Kill Them All: The American Military in Korea* (BBCTV, 2002); and *The Forgotten War* (ABC, 2003). In addition, *Korea: The Forgotten War* (Mill Creek Entertainment, 2008) offers sixteen hours of gripping footage in both color and black-and-white images.[49]

After a long period of absence from movie theaters, in 2008 *Grand Torino* brought back Korean War memories. Directed by and starring Clint Eastwood as Walt Kowalski, this movie tells another story of a troubled Korean War veteran. Kowalski, a retired autoworker, who stores a 1970s gas guzzler from the good old days in his garage, is upset to see Asians moving into his Detroit neighborhood. While his new neighbors are not Korean, they nevertheless remind him of Korea and his killing of a young enemy soldier attempting to surrender. The 2008 movie shows the dark side of American military actions and depicts Kowalski coming to terms with his demons and acting heroically in the final scene.[50] While the Korean War, seen only in flashbacks of combat, provides the backdrop to the movie's plot, the theme of the troubled veteran remains similar to films made a half century earlier, and the Korean War is presented as a mysterious, daunting, vague, and disturbing memory from the distant past.

It is ironic indeed that the most popular and memorable movie about the Korean War was a comedy. M*A*S*H, a look at the humorous exploits of medical personnel in a mobile army surgical hospital (MASH) unit near the front lines, was released in 1970. Based on Richard Hooker's 1968 novel, Robert Altman directed the creative screenplay by Hooker and Ring Lardner Jr. Hooker was the nom de plume of Dr. Richard Hornberger, who used his experiences with the 8055 MASH unit as the basis for his story. The talented movie cast included Donald Sutherland, Elliot Gould, Sally Kellerman, and Robert Duvall, along with former pro-football star Fred "The Hammer" Williamson. While the setting is Korea, the film is in reality an allegory for the Vietnam War. Filmed near Hollywood in Malibu Canyon State Park, the setting looked nothing like Korea's barren, denuded hillsides. The movie, which won an Academy Award for Best Screenplay, spawned an award-winning television series that ran for eleven seasons on CBS to a wide audience and still reaches millions through unending reruns. The TV series also led to the spin-off *Trapper John M.D.*, which had limited success. In both the movie M*A*S*H and television series, in which Alan Alda played the lead role as Capt. Benjamin "Hawkeye" Pierce, a surgeon assigned to the 4077, the medical staff employ humor and hijinks to relieve tension and escape the horrors of the combat taking place near their chaotic field hospital.[51]

Both the movie and TV series were actually metaphors for Vietnam. Few Koreans were seen either in the movie or the early TV seasons, and Korea's cold winters were filmed in sunny California. Nevertheless, the writers of the television series sought to portray the MASH unit and its characters in a realistic manner. A principal screenwriter, Larry Marks, reached out to doctors who had served in Korea for personal memories to develop original story lines. This was not a small task for a series that included 256 episodes. Marks claimed he made every effort "to make this show a mix of comedy and tragedy [. . . which] occurs daily in a situation like Korea." Indeed, the veteran doctors told him of smoking pot, which grew wild in the Korean countryside, botched abortions on nurses performed in Japan that the MASH doctors tried to correct, and plastic surgeries and "nose jobs" for female medical staff. They had stories of Korean cooks with parasites sneaking out of their noses and "Sears-Roebuck Girls" (local women kept by the GIs and outfitted with mail-order clothing). The doctors related stories of Korean youngsters with limbs blown away by landmines or hand grenades they picked up to use for fishing. They also told of interracial relationships among the American medical personnel and Koreans. The doctors and medical staff Marks spoke to also described piles of boots from amputated legs piled outside a triage room, milk intended for nearby orphanages being sold on the black market, and local prostitutes (called *yobos*, a familiar Korean term for wife) being snuck into camp in U.S. Army ambulances.[52] A quarter century after their service in Korea, the memories appeared sharp and the descriptions were graphic.

Much of the material Marks acquired never found its way into the final scripts; when it did, the material was sanitized, edited out, or significantly altered. Marks's biggest concern, however, was the increasing influence of Alan Alda in the production of the series. The original theme of the movie and series was of people in a dreadful environment making sense of the situation through humor. Alda wanted something more. A pacifist, Alda was involved in antiwar politics in the 1960s and early 1970s, as the American involvement in Vietnam escalated and then lurched violently to a bloody conclusion. In his work as the lead actor, a writer, and often director (and ultimately creative producer), Alda was unapologetic about presenting a strong antiwar message. Alda saw M*A*S*H as more than a TV comedy series and sought to deliver a meaningful point of view to the program's huge audience. "We were nourished and sustained by the feeling that we were doing something of value," Alda wrote. "We could explore compassion and we could rage against death and pain. . . . We threw ourselves into M*A*S*H and we let it soak up our nights and days."[53] Yet at least one doctor who served in Korea during the fighting was troubled by Alda's Hawkeye Pierce character, who expressed remorse at seeing soldiers sent back to the front after medical treatment. This attitude was unfamiliar to the doctor's own experience and unlike the professionalism and dedication he had known among medical staff in Korea. He told Marks that "Alda is moving too fast too far—he's on the Vietnam thing. . . . He's got a seventies head with a fifties situation."[54]

The notion that America's real enemy was the callous, hypocritical, and disingenuous leadership in Washington DC, may have been widespread in the Vietnam War era but not in the early 1950s.

The Korean War never entered American memory theater through the motion picture genre in a significant way. Movie critics identify no great films among the Korean War movies, no classics. The most memorable, and arguably the best, of the Korean War films had little to do with the Korean War itself. *Sayonara* took place in Japan, and in *Bridges at Toko Ri* the jets operated off aircraft carriers and flew high over Korea, descending only to drop bombs on North Korean military sites and infrastructure. *M*A*S*H*, which was really about the Vietnam War, depicted no significant Korean characters and portrayed an unseen version of a fantasized Korean War that was happening somewhere off camera, in the background, from where wounded soldiers arrived by helicopter. Of the better films of the Korean War era, *Steel Helmet*, *The Rack*, *War Hunt*, and *Pork Chop Hill* all depicted harsh realities and concluded with less than heroic and victorious outcomes. Unfortunately perhaps the major contribution of these films to the popular culture in the post–Korean War era was the creation of a national sense that the Korean War was different from previous wars, something far less than a victory, and an event to be put aside and moved on from, if not forgotten altogether.

Popular culture in the United States was quick to adopt erroneous notions that prevailed among political leaders and military officials eager to find something, or someone, to blame for a less than heroic outcome to the war. They were joined and assisted by opportunistic journalists, fraudulent or unqualified social scientists, and outright charlatans. Movies and popular literature focused on the threat of Communists infiltrating American society, the weakness of the American male, momism, and the susceptibility of young soldiers to the techniques of brainwashing. Among the numerous "B" movies that appeared during the Korean War and its aftermath, *The Manchurian Candidate* stands out for its imaginative incorporation of all the misconceptions about both the Korean War and its returning POWs and veterans. The movies and literature of the Korean War also reflected the unsatisfactory conclusion of the conflict. No *Patton*, *The Longest Day*, or *Midway* was produced about the Korean War in Hollywood, and no Korean War general penned anything to match the personal memoirs of Ulysses S. Grant. No novels based on the war approached the lasting greatness of *The Red Badge of Courage*, *From Here to Eternity*, or *The Naked and the Dead*. Meanwhile, political leaders, generals, and journalists proved all too eager to place on the public record their own conflicting views on why the war took place, how it was fought, and what lessons about limited warfare in the nuclear age might have been learned. These first-person narratives tended to shed more heat than light on unresolved issues related to the war.

Soon after the signing of the armistice, the memoirs of prominent participants in the war provided accounts clearly aimed at shaping the public's initial memory of the unpopular conflict that had turned the United States into the world's police chief. The authors presented their readers with contrasting explanations and analyses, although all agreed that the war in Korea had been necessary to check the advance of Communism in East Asia. President Truman's two-volume *Memoirs* were without precedent, as no previous commander-in-chief had written so candidly and extensively about his presidential decisions following his time in office. Truman's memoir went beyond chronicling and justifying his decisions on Korea and East Asian security. He called out major newspapers for dividing the nation during a time of military conflict and weakening the confidence of the American people in their own government through distortion and faulty analysis.[55] The president was soon joined by generals Matthew Ridgway and Mark Clark. While Ridgway viewed Korea as the type of limited and restricted warfare required for the survival of humanity in the nuclear age, the less imaginative Clark saw the failure of the United States to employ full force in Korea, especially after the Chinese intervened, as a mistake.[56] Claiming to understand Eisenhower's decision to reach a negotiated peace and Truman's need to address concerns of American allies, while acknowledging the dangers of igniting a third world war, Clark wrote, "It was beyond my comprehension that we would countenance a situation in which Chinese soldiers killed American youths in organized formal warfare and yet would fail to use all the power at our own command to protect those Americans."[57] A year after his release from three years as a POW, Maj. Gen. William Dean authored a chilling, matter-of-fact memoir telling of his capture and brutal treatment by the North Koreans and Chinese.[58] Admiral C. Turner Joy, who led the UN negotiations with the North Koreans and Chinese for almost the first year, added his account of the frustrating negotiations at Kaesong and Panmunjom. Like Clark, Joy believed U.S. restraint in using its "most effective weapons" severely limited the UNC in the negotiations. He also criticized the removal of General MacArthur, writing that to recall him "when that renowned officer was vigorously advocating a strong and aggressive policy in the Orient, particularly toward Red China, gave further reason for the Communists to believe we had no steel in our own attitude, that we were, in their phrase, 'a paper tiger.'"[59]

War correspondent Marguerite Higgins provided a blunt, candid, and powerful early assessment of the first months of the war, with stark images provided by *Life* magazine photographer Carl Mydans. Higgins warned readers to be prepared for further confrontations with Communist aggression, if not a third world war.[60] Three years later a memoir by journalist Keyes Beech provided an analysis of wartime journalism in Korea. His book included a discussion of issues with military censorship in the introduction provided by James A. Michener. A critic of MacArthur, Beech saw the general as responsible for unnecessary press censorship of great journalists, including war photographer David Douglas Duncan. Beech gleefully observed that, at least by his count, five times as many Japanese turned out to welcome American movie star Marilyn Monroe as lined the streets of Tokyo to bid farewell to General MacArthur following his dismissal by President Truman. Moreover Beech was an early reporter of the "Pavlov technique" used to get American POWs to falsely confess to using "germ warfare."[61] These wartime recollections were followed in a few years with the publication of MacArthur's magisterial and self-serving *Reminiscences*.

MacArthur's autobiography gives his leadership during the Korean War less attention than he provided on the early years of his long career and, as might be expected, glosses over his most notorious failures and miscalculations. In his account of Korea, written a decade after the events, the aged general mentioned that, after his meeting with President Truman on Wake Island and China's unexpected entry into the war, the president lost the courage he had earlier displayed. MacArthur believed he saw a "curious and sinister" change in the administration and worried that the "timidity and cynicism" he saw in Washington DC, might have resulted from Truman coming under the influence of evil forces within the United Nations. He decried the Truman administration's supposed unwillingness to "fight to win" but did not define what he meant by winning. Nor did MacArthur explain his failure to anticipate the Chinese offensive of November 1950, which he had assured President Truman during their Wake Island meeting would never happen. Lawton Collins, U.S. Army chief of staff at the time of the Korean War, wrote in his analysis of the war several years after MacArthur's memoir appeared, "It is different to gauge how much these comments was [sic] actually the feelings of MacArthur at the time of the Wake Island conference and how much was the result of bitterness at being relieved of command."[62]

Early writings on the Korean War by military and political leaders, as well as journalists, clearly influenced both politicians and public opinion. Indeed, during the Vietnam War era, both hawks and doves would look at the Korean conflict and its early literature for lessons. Most would conclude that Korea was difficult, costly, and unpopular. Several argued that the United States should have used all its military might to drive for a complete victory over Communism in East Asia. Nearly all agreed that Korea was a necessary and successful action to halt the advance of Communism without causing a wider war. However, the creative writers with personal experience of the Korean War produced nothing comparable to the literature of earlier twentieth-century wars, or in the volume, quality, and introspectiveness of the Vietnam era.[63]

The early memories of the Korean War forged during the conflict of 1950–53 and in the two decades immediately following the armistice would prove to have lasting impacts on the American political process and public memory. The decisive response of the United States to the outbreak of the war in Korea would have been predictable to anyone familiar with the American political system. Truman, reluctant to take his nation into a foreign war, acted because he had no other option. To protect U.S. interests in East Asia, his administration had to respond with military force to support the fledgling Republic of Korea against a Soviet onslaught, and Truman knew it from the moment North Korean forces crossed the 38th parallel. In addition, Truman was well aware that the credibility of the United Nations was at stake, and it was clear to anyone paying attention that Truman placed great hope in the United Nations. Already damaged politically by his alleged "loss of China" to Communist forces supported by the Soviet Union, Truman could not withstand the political fallout that would be inflicted upon his administration by Republican critics if he failed to make a stand in Korea. Unfortunately, while wanting to keep the war limited in use of military force, he expanded the original objective of the war from saving South Korea to unifying the entire peninsula under the Republic of Korea. This enlarged mission proved impossible to achieve with limited force, leading to a public perception of defeat.

Following the Korean War, American presidents noted and remembered that Truman had failed to seek congressional approval for the "police action" in Korea. As American presidents sent U.S. military forces overseas to Vietnam, the Middle East, and elsewhere, they would not make this mistake again. Pres. Lyndon B. Johnson secured the sweeping Gulf of Tonkin Resolution from Congress in 1964, and Pres. George H. W. Bush sought congressional support for the first Gulf War to drive Saddam Hussein's Iraqi forces from neighboring Kuwait. In 2003 Pres. George W. Bush, eager to gain congressional approval and UN support for another war against Iraq, produced questionable information from intelligence agencies to make his case that the regime in Baghdad had "weapons of mass destruction" to use at any moment against its neighbors, possibly even the United States. Not only had the presidents succeeding Truman learned to seek an authorization of some kind from Congress before taking a major military action abroad, they learned that they could more easily send military forces overseas without seeking a constitutionally mandated but politically more problematic legislative action—a declaration of war.

Although they lacked any coherent plan of their own and vacillated from calling for the reunification of the Korean Peninsula by force to advocating the complete abandonment of South Korea, Republican critics of President Truman learned that charging Democrats with weakness in the face of Communist aggression was a winning strategy. Disregarding the fact that Truman's decisive actions in June 1950 turned back Communist aggression and rescued the Republic of Korea, Republicans claimed fighting a limited war in Korea amounted to a loss, leaving North Korea under Communist control. The charge was employed repeatedly throughout the Korean conflict and in subsequent elections. In 1952 the Republican presidential campaign used the slogan K_1C_2 (Korea, China, and Communism) to defeat Democratic presidential candidate Adlai Stevenson. Four decades later, when campaigning for reelection in 1984, Pres. Ronald Reagan still invoked a central Republican theme of 1952, telling his audience that General MacArthur should have been allowed "to lead us to victory in Korea."[64] The memory of Korea as a loss, or at least something less than a victory, was set in the American memory.

In the first decade following the Korean War, neither the American public nor its political and military leadership could have possibly known what a pivotal moment in U.S. history the Korean War would turn out to be. Most failed to notice just how much the U.S. role in world affairs was changed forever by the Korean War. Likewise, the leaders of the two Koreas, China, the Soviet Union, and Japan could never have imagined that a peaceful and prosperous East Asia would emerge from the rubble and ruins the war had left on the devastated Korean landscape. While public interest in the conflict in the faraway land of Korea diminished quickly once the warfare in Korea ended, lasting impressions remained, and popular mythologies about the war lingered in public memory. The Korean War was never truly forgotten even as other dramatic world events took center stage. The Korean War was a milestone nevertheless. It just was not immediately recognized as such.

3 | Lessons Learned

Throughout the Cold War and beyond, U.S. policy makers drew lessons from the Korean War experience. They remembered the Korean War as a necessary and successful effort to contain Communism and Soviet expansion in Asia. Meanwhile, revisionist historians, led by Bruce Cumings and influenced by the 1960s anti-Vietnam War movement, viewed the U.S. involvement in Korea as an earlier Vietnam, a misguided intrusion into a civil war. While American attention was focused elsewhere, the public's memory of the Korean War remained cloudy, and into the 1980s few public memorials in the United States reminded Americans of the unsettled war in Korea they wished to forget. However, violent incidents on the divided peninsula alerted the world that Korea remained dangerous and volatile.

As a college undergraduate in the 1960s, my U.S. history survey course was taught by a crusty and cynical old professor, who had served as a Navy fighter pilot in World War II. His course syllabus never got as far as that war, and he did not include the Great Depression either. "It is not history if you remember living through it," he often said.

The Korean War brought about both immediate and lasting changes in U.S. foreign and domestic policy. The Korean War experience profoundly influenced the generation of policy makers whose vivid memories of Korea guided the United States through the Cold War decades. The unsettled Korean War left the nation with a new sense of vulnerability to foreign powers and internal threats from elements seeking to destroy the U.S. political system and way of life. The nation proved willing to spend enormous amounts of national treasure on defense. A huge military-industrial complex stood prepared to confront Communism anywhere in the world. Support for any foreign regime, no matter how brutal or corrupt, was considered justified if its leadership espoused an anti-Communist philosophy. As the American determination to halt Communist advances in Southeast Asia led to involvement in a military nightmare in Vietnam, some historians began to reexamine the superpower role of the United States in world affairs. This revisionist school looked at the record of the United States in Korea and believed it to be, like that in Vietnam, fundamentally based on government lies and misinformation. At the same time, as a legacy of the Korean War, the Cold War pasture of the United States hardened as the political dynamics in East Asia underwent a process of transformation. Charles Bohlen, a perceptive U.S. diplomat, observed in the early 1970s, "It was the Korean War, not World War II, that made us a world military-political power."[1]

The Korean War realigned the geopolitical map of East Asia and vastly expanded international security commitments of the United States. In order to coerce South Korea's Syngman Rhee into accepting the terms of the peace agreement negotiated at Panmunjom, the Eisenhower administration concluded a security pact with the Republic of Korea. In addition, with the end of military operations in 1953, the United States had established a virtual protectorate over the Chiang Kai-shek regime by permanently positioning the Seventh Fleet in the Taiwan Strait. The United States also concluded a peace treaty with Japan, placing that nation under U.S. protection as well. At the same time, the United States significantly increased aid to the French in their faltering effort to hold on to their colonial possessions in Indochina. The U.S. defense budget tripled during the Korean War, and the Truman administration accepted the recommendations of NSC-68 to expand the American military in costly new directions. The North Atlantic Treaty Organization (NATO), established under U.S. leadership in 1949, became a genuine military alliance after the Korean War began to address Soviet expansion in Europe, much to the displeasure of the premier Joseph Stalin and the Soviet military. What had been unthinkable prior to the Korean War—the rearmament of West Germany and full partnership for that state in the NATO alliance—became a reality due to the heightened national security concerns in the United States and Europe. A much weaker and less structured alliance system, the Southeast Asia Treaty Organization

(SEATO), was created by Eisenhower's secretary of state John Foster Dulles in 1954 to coordinate the containment of Communism following the French failure to hold Indochina. In effect, by the mid-1950s the United States was committed to a policy of worldwide containment and had made itself the world's policeman in an increasingly bipolar world. Containment had advanced from economic and political policies and actions, such as the International Monetary Fund, the Marshall Plan, and the NATO alliance, into a full-blown military phase. With the signing of the Korean Armistice of 1953, the Cold War became accepted as an international reality.[2]

On the American domestic front, the war in Korea proved to be a godsend to social conservatives. The war had enabled Sen. Joseph McCarthy and his allies to advance their campaign to root out alleged Communists anywhere they might or might not be found, forcing elected government officials, federal bureaucrats, and educators to curb almost any controversial criticism of the established social order. As warfare in Korea stirred emotions and encouraged those who played upon the fears of frightened citizens, even Pres. Dwight Eisenhower was reluctant to criticize or reign in Senator McCarthy's outrageous personal attacks and unsubstantiated charges. Racial integration was slowed down, despite the U.S. Supreme Court's ruling in *Brown v. Board of Education*, and the debt that Americans owed to its returning Black veterans of the Korean War went unpaid. The pent-up frustrations of Black critics in the United States would be delayed until pressure for justice exploded in the 1960s. Issues such as public healthcare, school funding, and gender equality were all placed on hold. While the social advances of the New Deal and Fair Deal remained in place, the 1950s were a time for social conservatives to stifle necessary social reforms and maintain "traditional values." In the post–Korean War United States of the 1950s, dissenters and those seeking to address social ills were forced to the sidelines.[3] And the United States was not alone in viewing the Cold War confrontation with Communism as a threat to the social order. The East-West confrontation with Communism during the Cold War was employed as justification for ruthless supervision of leftist elements and anticolonial leaders in many parts of the world. In Taiwan a reign of "White Terror" against the regime's critics was unleashed; in Japan a "Red Purge" took place; and in Great Britain unions and the Labour Party came under suspicion.[4]

Policy makers in the United States saw lessons from the Korean War as experiences to be followed in addressing Cold War confrontations, most prominently in Vietnam. Here, following the French defeat and withdrawal, the ancient nation was left divided along the 17th parallel, leaving a nationalistic and Communist government in the north and a quasi-democratic government dependent on the United States in the south. A peace conference in Geneva, Switzerland, lasting from April to July 1954, intended to consider elections and reunification in Korea as well as issues concerning Vietnam, ended up leaving both Korea and Vietnam divided.[5] The similarities between the situation in Korea and Vietnam seemed obvious, and American military leaders were quick to look to the recent conflicts in Korea for guidance. Unfortunately, those officers who had fought in Korea disagreed about what lessons had actually been learned. Meanwhile, political leaders understood that any sign of compromise through negotiations with Communist regimes would surely lead to charges of weakness by political opponents. Amid this conflicting process of lessons learned, both military and civilian leaders often misunderstood or overlooked the cultural and geopolitical differences between the situations in Korea and Vietnam. As a result, a series of U.S. presidents received conflicting and misguided advice from their national security officials and top military commanders.

While the American public may have wanted to forget the Korean experience, U.S. foreign policy makers and military leaders made every effort to remember. Ever aware of Korea's significance, they examined the conflict for lessons on how to deal with Communist advances in the former French Indochina. Both the United States and the People's Republic of China directed their attention to these experiences immediately following the armistice in Korea. The defeat of the French and the division of Vietnam following the Geneva Conference of 1954 created a situation seemingly similar to Korea. As the Communist North Vietnamese regime consolidated its hold on power north of the 17th parallel and sought increasing influence in the south, U.S. presidents and their advisors believed that they saw in Korea a successful effort to contain Communist expansion. In particular, military planners assessed Korea as a model for a limited war where the message to the American people for justifying a foreign involvement could be presented in a carefully controlled message.[6] Throughout the 1950s the Eisenhower administration supported the South Vietnamese government in hopes of an outcome similar to Korea—a divided nation with a pro-Western and anti-Communist regime south of a well-guarded demilitarized zone.

Following the establishment of a Communist government in China and a stalemate in Korea, Eisenhower worried about a potential "domino effect," with countries in Southeast Asia falling one after another to internal and external Communist pressures. Eisenhower's concerns for Communist expansion in Southeast Asia were valid; however, he and his successors in office failed to understand important and often unrecognized differences between Korea and Vietnam. In South Vietnam the United States had no political partner with the stubborn determination, local political alliances, and willful ruthlessness of Syngman Rhee. North Vietnam had such a leader in Ho Chi Minh, a nationalist with a long record of fighting French imperial forces. The Vietnamese insurgents in the south were far stronger and had greater popular support than the Communist cadres Kim Il-sung supported and encouraged in South Korea prior to the June 1950 invasion. Moreover, while the South Korean Peninsula had only one border to defend, Vietnam's dense jungles and ill-defined perimeters on two sides made infiltration from the north unstoppable. As Eisenhower and his administration channeled aid to support the anti-Communist regime in South Vietnam, he was both cautious and pragmatic with respect to other areas of U.S. foreign policy. He rejected the isolationists within his own Republican Party as well as those calling for a "roll back" and the liberation of "captive peoples." He believed the national security of the United States could rely on a relatively low-cost military based on nuclear weapons and air power. This "New Look" in American security was to be relied upon to halt Communist advances and realize ambitious national security goals.[7] The Eisenhower strategy seemed to be working in Southeast Asia until the South Vietnamese regime began to implode from internal corruption, poor governance, and increasing Communist pressure. By the time the weakness of the South Vietnamese regime became apparent, it was up to his successors to deal with the new reality in Vietnam and reexamine the lessons of Korea.

Upon taking office in 1961, Pres. John F. Kennedy determined that the "New Look" defense strategy of the Eisenhower administration was ineffective in dealing with Communist insurgencies and "wars of national liberation," where homegrown Communist elements were significantly involved in violent, nationalist movements to free native peoples from their European colonizers. Kennedy's approach to military preparedness, coined the "Flexible Response," relied on more conventional ground forces and highly trained army units prepared for close combat in rough terrain and hostile political environments. As the political situation in South Vietnam deteriorated, a U.S.-backed coup led to the overthrow and murder of the country's ineffective president, Ngo Dinh Diem, and his influential brother. Kennedy himself was assassinated just a few weeks later, and his successor, Lyndon Baines Johnson, inherited the growing crisis in Vietnam. For Johnson, like Kennedy, an overriding concern in setting an anti-Communist strategy in Vietnam was the fear of political attacks from Republicans and conservative Democrats. Johnson understood, based on the Truman administration's experience, that any inaction or appearance of weakness in the face of a Communist challenge would be disastrous.[8] Furthermore, Johnson was acutely aware of the politics surrounding U.S. involvement in Korea and had not forgotten how East Asian policies leading to the "Loss of China" and the war stalemate in Korea doomed Truman's presidency. White House aide Doris Kearns Goodwin later recalled a conversation with the former president. "I knew Harry Truman and Dean Acheson had lost their effectiveness from the day that the Communists took over China," Johnson told Goodwin. And he continued noting that all other problems his own administration faced were "chicken shit compared with what might happen if we lost Vietnam."[9] Yet President Johnson was well aware that Vietnam was a potential military disaster. To his national security advisor McGeorge Bundy, he confided, "It looks to me like we're getting into another Korea. . . . I believe the Chinese Communists are coming into it. I don't think we can fight them ten thousand miles away from home. . . . I don't think it's worth fighting for, and I don't think we can get out."[10]

An experienced politician with a long and unforgiving memory, Johnson inherited a faltering government in Vietnam and an uncertain U.S. policy. Johnson sought in vain to strengthen a succession of weak South Vietnamese leaders with American aid and military advisors, hoping to appear resolute in standing up to Communism, while avoiding a quagmire in Southeast Asia. In the summer of 1964, in the midst of a presidential election campaign against U.S. senator Barry Goldwater, an ultraconservative Republican candidate, the president made a fateful move.

Believing that President Truman had made a political misstep in not seeking congressional support for military actions in Korea, Johnson sought and received congressional approval permitting the president "to take all necessary measures to repel any armed attack against the forces of the United States and to prevent further aggression" in reaction to an alleged North Vietnamese attack on U.S. warships patrolling the waters off the coast of Vietnam. This Gulf of Tonkin Resolution came in response to what would later be proved misleading or erroneous assertions of a second unprovoked North Vietnamese attack on U.S. naval vessels. Nevertheless, the resolutions passed with unanimous support in the U.S. House and only two dissenting votes in the Senate. Just hours prior to the passage of the resolution, Johnson met with congressional leaders from both parties, telling them, "I don't think any resolution is necessary, but I think it is a lot better to have it, in light of what we did in Korea."[11] Escalation of the U.S. role in Vietnam was underway and would continue throughout Johnson's presidency. Henceforth misunderstood lessons of Korea would shape the decision-making.

As the United States became more committed to halting Communist expansion in Vietnam, it became apparent that the lessons of the Korean War were learned in different ways by both the civilians and military leaders charged with advising the president. Memories were in conflict over basic issues. Did the Korean War prove that a "limited war" against Communist aggression could be won? Or did the experience in Korea show that the American public would soon turn against an administration that pursued a costly war where there existed no clearly defined or immediate threat to the United States? Mindful of the unpopularity of the Korean War, President Johnson resisted putting the nation on a wartime footing, imposed no new taxes, avoided calling up the National Guard, and left in place numerous opportunities for many men of draft age with proper social and economic status to secure deferments. For the most part, the war would be fought by the poor, the Black, and the less educated.[12] Meanwhile, Johnson was well aware that opinions among the Joint Chiefs of Staff (JCS) were sharply divided. He knew President Kennedy had been warned in 1963 that any action in Laos (which bordered Vietnam) would require sixty thousand American troops and the possible use of nuclear weapons. When Johnson's secretary of state Dean Rusk asked Gen. Lyman Lemnitzer, the chair of the JCS, about sending the

101st Airborne Infantry Division into Laos, Lemnitzer responded, "We can get in all right. It's getting them out that I'm worried about."[13] Gen. Maxwell Taylor, a former chairman of the JCS who had commanded the Eighth U.S. Army at the end of the Korean War, dismissed public opinion and considered limited military involvement in Southeast Asia a suitable testing ground for the Kennedy administration's "Flexible Response." Gen. David Shoup, commander of the U.S. Marine Corps, challenged Taylor's optimistic assessment. Shoup believed Korea demonstrated exactly the opposite—that the United States was not adept at fighting limited and protracted wars—and expressed the view that the United States should not involve itself in a land war in Asia under any circumstances. Later, when the United States began extensive bombing of targets in North Vietnam, U.S. Army chief of staff Gen. Harold Johnson pointed out that the extensive use of air power in Korea had failed to bring an enemy to its knees.[14]

Another critic of bombing in Vietnam, one with extensive experience in policy making during the Korean War and a sharp memory of that conflict, doubted that the Communists could be pressured into negotiations through bombing or limited military successes. Ambassador Charles Bohlen, a longtime specialist on the Soviet Union, wrote to the Johnson administration's ambassador-at-large Llewellyn Thompson in July 1966 to express his concern that bombing would not lead to a negotiated settlement. He observed that "past history demonstrates this point. For example, in Korea there was no question of an armistice after the Incheon landing when things looked very black for the Communists. I know of no peace feelers from them at that time. The possibility of an armistice suggested by the Russians in June 1951 happened at a time when the military situation was virtually at a stalemate."[15] Presumably Ambassador Thompson passed this memory-based message on to the president's key advisors, if not the president himself.

Among the civilian advisors to President Johnson, undersecretary of state George Ball was the most forceful voice in cautioning the president about military involvement in Vietnam. Like other advisors he used the experience in Korea as the basis for his argument. Ball wrote in an October 1964 memorandum that the Vietnam situation and the U.S. commitment to that country was not at all like Korea in 1950. Ball noted that in Korea there was an unprovoked invasion over a recognized border. Therefore he maintained that the United States had a clear United Nations (UN) mandate, and U.S. action was supported by significant allies. In Korea Ball observed that Rhee had a more stable government and an army prepared to fight. In Vietnam Ball saw a country whose government was in chaos, exhausted by two decades of warfare, and confronted with a popular internal rebellion. Ball foresaw that the entry of U.S. ground forces into Vietnam would lead to bitterness and frustration among the American public that would far surpass the dissatisfaction with Truman's policies in Korea.[16]

Johnson carefully reviewed Ball's memorandum and debated its conclusions with senior advisors. In July 1965 Johnson invited a group of senior government officials and military leaders to the White House to hear their views. The group, known as the "Wise Men," included Truman administration veterans Dean Acheson and Gen. Omar Bradley and largely disagreed with Ball's negative assessment. According to close observers of Johnson's management style, Ball's cautious and reasoned use of historical analogies without offering alternatives caused the president to deal with him as "his official 'devil's advocate,' which granted him a hearing at the cost of weight. Secretary of State Rusk dismissed Ball as merely playing a role 'assigned' to him by the President."[17] In addition to Ball's cautionary memorandum, Johnson had his own sharp memory of the Korean War. "We don't have the allies we had in Korea," Johnson told aides. Furthermore, he recalled ineffective bombings of North Korea, and he reminded his military advisors, who dismissed the possibility of the Chinese entering the conflict in Vietnam, that "MacArthur didn't think they would come in either."[18]

President Johnson's speechwriter Harry Middleton—who in 1965 published his own book on the Korean War—observed that the administration understood the "strong parallels between the Korean experience and escalating war in Vietnam." Based on the Korean experience, Middleton, a veteran of both World War II and Korea, wrote that early on there existed reluctant recognition within Johnson's administration that air power alone would not bring a favorable settlement. Moreover, Middleton saw that it was apparent to the administration that there would be no resolution in Vietnam "until American infantrymen took their places behind their rifles on the ground." In Middleton's view it was clear to all in the administration that Vietnam, like Korea, would be a limited conflict ending with some sort of negotiated settlement, and he concluded that the White House held no illusions about invading and liberating the north in a final battle. He saw in the White House an understanding that "only a hard recognition of what limited and still acceptable ends can be accomplished by force of arms within the new dimensions of war."[19]

Like Korea, the Vietnam War would frustrate the U.S. public because of its government's limitations on use of weaponry and reluctance to attack military targets beyond North Vietnam. While clearly not "limited" for the Koreans or Vietnamese, on whose soil these wars raged, the great powers held much larger geopolitical interests well beyond Korea and Vietnam. In both conflicts the United States, the Soviet Union, and China all placed self-imposed restraints in the conduct of their military operations, accepting limited and controlled warfare in an effort to achieve a limited objective. For the United States, frustration set in when policy makers sought to accomplish with limited military force something beyond a limited goal. In Korea this was the decision in September 1950 to bring about the reunification of the entire Korean Peninsula once the limited goal, repelling the North Korean invasion, was effectively accomplished. In Vietnam the overreach was the attempt, beginning in the 1950s, to create a pro-Western, quasi-democratic state in the southern half of a former French colony already lost to nationalist insurgents led by strong Communist elements. For the United States and its allies, the asymmetrical nature of conflicts since World War II has led inevitably to frustration. Civilian populations of democratic countries are reluctant to endure casualties to establish or preserve repressive regimes in distant lands. The situation tends to be exacerbated when the enemy is perceived to be a weaker military adversary than the United States.[20] Such frustrations lead to reckless calls from pandering politicians for use of ever greater force, including demands for increased superior air power to pound less technically advanced adversaries into submission.

Gen. Matthew Ridgway, whose leadership had saved the Eighth Army from disaster in Korea, was a late addition to the "Wise Men." He noted that politicians and military planners of the Vietnam era seemed to forget that the Korean War demonstrated the limits of air power against a determined foe. "An insistence on going all-out to win a war may have a fine masculine ring, and a call to 'defend freedom' may have a messianic sound that stirs our blood," Ridgway wrote. "But an all-out war in these times is beyond imagining. It may mean the turning back of civilization by several thousand years, with no one left capable of signaling the victory." Ridgway concluded that in the nuclear era wars must be fought with limited means for clearly defined objectives.[21] The very nature of a limited war presents a dilemma, however, as limited use of military force may lead to an unlimited time of conflict before the warring sides achieve a resolution.[22] Certainly this has proved to be the case in the never-ending Korean War, where both sides signaled early on that the warfare would be limited, and the geopolitical situation on the Korean Peninsula remains little changed from what it was in the summer of 1950.

Memory of the Korean War informed the search for answers during the Johnson administration's growing involvement in Vietnam. Unfortunately the misuse of history and memory within the administration led to disaster. Johnson and his principal advisors employed Korean War memories and their understanding of recent history in searching for analogies to shape wartime strategies. No historians served officially or directly in Johnson's administration. However, several prominent historians served as close observers, advisors, and consultants.[23] Among them was Henry Graff, a distinguished professor of history at Columbia University for more than seven decades. Familiar with the workings of government in wartime, Graff had served as a translator and cryptanalyst of Japanese military communications with the Signal Intelligence Service during World War II, built a career studying the presidency, and accepted an appointment by Johnson to the National Historical Public Records Commission. He managed to secure access to the inner workings of the Vietnam policy debates among the senior members of the Johnson administration, which are recorded in his 1970 study, *The Tuesday Cabinet*.[24]

Almost every Tuesday during Johnson's presidency, key presidential advisors gathered for lunch with the president in a private White House dining room to openly discuss foreign policy issues, in particular those related to U.S. involvement in Vietnam. Joining the president were Secretary Rusk, secretary of defense Robert McNamara, JCS chair Gen. Earle Wheeler, aide Bill Moyers, national security advisor McGeorge Bundy, and Walt Rostow, who, along with others like Clark Clifford, replaced departing cabinet members and senior staff. At Johnson's invitation, Graff met periodically for candid, private discussions with the luncheon participants to probe the substance of their meetings and record how decisions on peace and war came to be made. Graff's record of his conversations with the president and his principal advisors on the Vietnam War reveals how history and memory influenced policy makers who had experienced World War II and Korea.[25]

Serving as something of an in-house historian, but with no official duties or responsibilities, Graff enjoyed remarkable and unhindered access to the president throughout the full term in office that followed his 1964 landslide election victory. Graff focused on interviewing the president and the key advisors who met for the Tuesday lunch, naming them the "Tuesday Cabinet." He found Johnson and his advisors well informed and open to sharing their thoughts and arguments. The president, Graff believed, "was interested in history for its own sake, to be sure, but primarily . . . for his own place in it."[26] More helpful to Graff in his analysis of the decision-making process were Secretaries McNamara and Rusk as well as Bundy. These men, Graff wrote, "alluded frequently and spontaneously to the past." He observed that they had all attended "the school of foreign policy of Franklin Roosevelt and Harry S. Truman and it had stamped them indelibly," as they learned that only firmness could counter aggression and actions required the accompaniment of lofty rhetoric. As he proceeded with his post-Tuesday Cabinet meeting interviews with the participants, Graff began to conclude that "the study of history can be misleading as well as instructive. . . . [History] too often simplifies rather than clarifies."[27]

Early in 1965 after the bombing of targets in North Vietnam began and U.S. troop commitments were estimated to top out at sixty thousand, Graff asked the secretary of defense, "Which historical analogy are you finding more instructive and compelling in dealing with Vietnam, the consequences of appeasement at Munich or the consequences of intervention in Korea?" McNamara responded that Korea was "false in logic although significant in psychology." Unlike bombing in Korea, McNamara argued, there would be "no sanctuaries this time," and there would be no major troop buildup for a land war, because "we are not moving in that direction."[28] Three years later, following an extensive bombing campaign and a U.S. ground force buildup of more than a half million, the war remained far from settled, and antiwar opposition at home was destroying Johnson's presidency. Yet members of the Tuesday group still saw analogies to Korea. Rusk considered opposition to war in Vietnam as a new isolationism and believed the American people, especially the younger generation, had either forgotten or never learned about events in Manchuria, the Rhineland, and Austria in the 1930s. He also insisted that "Korea was not a civil war." The only difference between outside Communist aggression in Vietnam and Korea was that the frontier in Korea was more clearly defined.[29] Bundy concurred, noting that "the aggression in Vietnam is less clear than in Korea, so it does not force a moral judgment as it did then."[30] One difference between Korea and Vietnam that seemed to go unnoticed was that Korean combat had ended with an armistice after thirty-six months, while the unpopular war in Vietnam was well into its fourth year when Johnson left office—with no end in sight.

More than a decade after Graff recorded the inner workings of Johnson's Tuesday Cabinet, Harvard professors Richard Neustadt and Ernest May published a study based on their Kennedy School seminar on the use of history and memory in the formation of presidential decisions. They examined Truman's decisions in the Korean conflict and Johnson's actions regarding U.S. involvement in Vietnam. Both Neustadt and May had government experience in times of war, and both were fascinated by the use and misuses of history by policy makers and sought to uncover ways history might be used to make better decisions—or at least avoid catastrophic mistakes. Their groundbreaking study, *Thinking in Time: The Uses of History for Decision Makers*, included analysis of Truman's Korean War decisions and Johnson's policies during the Vietnam War. A decade older than May, Neustadt, a political scientist, served as an Army supply officer in the Pacific during World War II and a White House aide on budget and policy matters at a time when the Korean War dominated the Truman administration's foreign policy agenda. A historian, May saw service in the Navy as a historian for the JCS during the Korean War. Both consulted and held appointments in presidential administrations throughout their long careers.

The two academics observed that memory is subjective and wrote in their assessment of modern presidential decision-making, "Our own histories have influenced [not only] . . . the subject matters of this book but also its conclusions." And in their exploration of the Johnson administration, these two scholars concluded that memories of Korea among principal civilian and military advisors in the Johnson White House usually depended on age and position the individual advisors held during the Korean War. They determined that memory, as a resource for policy making, was influenced by one's personal perspective, or "where they sat depended on where they stood before." The inability to identify essential historical analogies and understand the personal perspective influencing their colleagues hindered the formation of effective decisions.[31] Indeed in spite of detailed knowledge of the war, its historical context, and vivid memories of their personal experiences, Johnson's advisors failed to find consensus and provided the president with conflicting advice. They seemed to universally agree on only one thing: President Truman had demonstrated courage and resolve when confronting a Communist threat in June 1950.[32] Given Johnson's decisions for escalation of the conflict in Vietnam at several critical junctures during his administration, it appears the president concurred with this assessment.

President Johnson and his advisors held powerful memories of World War II and Korea, but there is no evidence they studied the colonial histories of Korea and Vietnam. President Johnson, his cabinet, and his advisors were bright men with excellent memories and a solid understanding of contemporary affairs; but while the historical analogies they looked to made sense to them, they were the wrong analogies and perhaps too recent in the long scope of history to be understood in historical context. Johnson's advisors might have made more informed decisions had they carefully studied the wars for independence fought in the Americas during the eighteenth and nineteenth centuries. The rebellion of the thirteen North American colonies against the rule of Great Britain could have provided an excellent case study for their consideration, as it was in many ways a civil conflict fought far from the capital of the empire, waged often with guerilla tactics against superior military forces, and assisted by significant aid from Britain's rival world powers. Similarly, the independence movements led by Simón Bolívar, José de San Martín, and Toussaint Louverture against European powers would have provided useful studies, as well as the resistance led by Benito Juárez against the French attempt to establish a puppet state in Mexico in the 1860s. In all these instances, local resistance to colonialism, while often internally conflicted, managed to reject attempted takeovers from stronger entities whose attention, interests, and military resources were dispersed elsewhere, and whose essential security was threatened not by colonial rebellions far from home but by competing world powers.

The Korean War changed the international alignments in post–World War II East Asia and served as a major turning point in world affairs; however, it did not provide a valid historical analogy for the events taking place in Vietnam in the 1960s.

As the war in Vietnam staggered on toward a disaster, a generation of Americans emerged with a sense of skepticism and distrust of political leadership. Unlike Korea, where a genuine U.S.-led coalition operating under a UN resolution had halted Communist aggression and reestablished the Republic of Korea as the governing authority over the southern half of the peninsula, nothing but a horrible defeat could be observed in the helicopter evacuation of U.S. troops and terrified South Vietnamese civilians from the rooftop of the U.S. Embassy in Saigon in April 1975. By this time Americans had become exhausted by the war in Vietnam, and opposition to the government's involvement there had nearly torn the nation apart. Meanwhile, on the nation's university campuses amid the often-violent antiwar protests, academics (along with their students) demonstrated a new distrust of the U.S. government.

While Johnson's White House and members of the JCS looked back to Korea for lessons in addressing the contemporary challenges they faced in Vietnam, many historians in the United States looked backward from Vietnam to reassess the early years of the Cold War and the U.S. military involvement in Korea. Disillusioned by the evolving tragedy in Vietnam and the often-disingenuous statements from the U.S. military and the Johnson administration on the war's success, a new generation of scholars began to question the reliability of historical narratives from earlier presidencies—especially that of President Truman. It is not unusual for each generation to reassess the past and challenge existing orthodoxies. *Revisionist historian* is not necessarily a pejorative term, and scholars such as William Appleman Williams, who led the "Wisconsin School" of revisionism with his groundbreaking 1959 study, *The Tragedy of American Diplomacy*, contributed significantly to an understanding of U.S. foreign relations by integrating economic factors and the conflict between idealism and the use of power into the review of diplomatic history. Likewise, historians of the Cold War era, such as Gabriel Kolko and Joyce Kolko, Walter LaFeber, Thomas Paterson, and Barton Bernstein, have added to the historiography of the post–World War II era. Revisionists challenged the prevailing orthodoxy that the Cold War was initiated entirely by the actions of Joseph Stalin. These historians looked elsewhere to assign blame for breaking up the Grand Alliance that had won World War II, and they argued that President Truman failed to understand Stalin's pragmatic quest for security. Revisionists faulted Truman for his failure to adhere to agreements made by his predecessor during World War II and charged that Truman's unnecessarily belligerent actions led to avoidable friction between the Soviet Union and the United States. They saw Truman and his successors as guided by a long-existing U.S. foreign policy in which capitalistic economic factors drove an insatiable need for markets, raw materials, and investment opportunities. Such economic concerns, they argued, caused U.S. policy makers to oppose Socialism and any political forces that might welcome a Soviet-style system—especially in nations recovering from World War II or emerging from colonial rule.[33] These historians saw in Korea an unwise, needless, and tragic American intervention into a civil war in which the United States recklessly allied itself with the most reactionary elements in Korean society to stifle the aspirations of true reformers. As in Vietnam, revisionist historians saw in Korea the United States intervening in a nationalist struggle for independence and self-governance. Forces in Korea's ancient civilization striving for independence, self-determination, and social justice in the modern world were opposed by American policy makers at every turn, according to many revisionists.

Bruce Cumings, the leader among this school of revisionist historians dealing with Korean history, appeared on the scene in the 1970s. His fresh, thorough, and highly controversial studies of the Korean War and its origins challenged the orthodox narrative of the war. A prolific scholar with a lucid and engaging writing style, Cumings had first encountered Korea as a Peace Corps volunteer in the late 1960s, where he sympathized with protesting South Korean students and hard-pressed workers seeking greater academic freedom and a better standard of living. Influenced by the early Korean War narrative of journalist I. F. Stone, *The Hidden History of the Korean War, 1950–1951,* Cumings focused his post–Peace Corps graduate studies at Columbia University on the Korean War, seeking to document misguided policies of the Truman administration, the atrocious behavior by the U.S. military in Korea, and the notion that the Korean War had somehow been initiated in June 1950 by the United States in cooperation with the Rhee regime in South Korea. He also maintained contacts with reform-minded, leftist politicians in South Korea, including peace and reunification advocate Kim Dae-jung. Throughout his long and prolific career, Cumings believed that his hero, Stone, "provided a model of honest inquiry, of which there are all too few examples—particularly in regard to our own recent Asian wars. . . . A truthful book, it remains one of the best accounts of the American role in the war."[34] Cumings's work set a new standard for scholars of U.S. foreign policy in Korea and advanced his professional standing in the academic community, leading to an endowed chair in the history department at the University of Chicago. In addition, his works reached a wide international audience and delighted academics in both the United States and South Korea, who blamed the United States and the Rhee regime for the series of military dictatorships that ruled South Korea until the late 1980s.

In the 1980s Cumings's study of the origins of the Korean War made him an icon of revisionist academics in the United States and leftist intellectuals and activists in South Korea with his argument that the war originated in 1945, not when North Korea invaded in 1950. Amid internal conflicting forces within Korea, Cumings charged that the U.S. military in 1945 favored right-wing political elements and former collaborators with the Japanese, while suppressing groups seeking social and economic reform. His subsequent publications, which made use of Korean language sources, earned him praise from academic admirers as "the acknowledged authority on the Korean War."[35] Although Cumings himself rejected the label "revisionist," scholars in the United States, South Korea, and elsewhere took up Cumings's radical thesis, to the point where he could, with justification, claim, "It is a fact, even if it is immodest to say it, that my own work played a part in this new history."[36]

Cumings's early work deserves considerable credit for examining the internal political struggle among Communist and anti-Communist Korean leaders in the wake of Japan's surrender that ended World War II and thirty-five years of harsh colonial rule in Korea. Largely ignoring the extraordinary influence of the Soviet Union and the Red Army north of the 38th parallel, Cumings faulted the United States for stifling democratic elements in the south, including unions and moderate Socialists, to install a right-wing dictatorship. By 1950 a civil war among Koreans was well underway in Cumings's view, and the eruption of open warfare in June 1950 was only an expansion of ongoing insurrections, rebellions, and pitched battles that had plagued the peninsula for five years. He dismissed the orthodox history that the invasion of June 25, 1950, was a well-planned, all-out military operation authorized, supplied, and carefully coordinated by the Soviet Union with the acknowledgment and support of the PRC. For Cumings, "The Korean War . . . was the handiwork of Dean Acheson and Harry Truman."[37] In his writings on the Korean War, Cumings considered himself to be on a mission "to uncover truths that most Americans do not know and perhaps don't want to know, truths sometimes as shocking as they are unpalatable to American self-esteem."[38]

While criticizing the role of the United States for favoring the rightist Rhee regime, Cumings viewed North Korea's leader Kim Il-sung as a patriotic nationalist, an effective leader, and something much more than a Soviet protégé. He viewed Kim as an authoritarian ruler but one in the ancient Confucian tradition with whom Koreans were comfortable. Cumings further argued that throughout the bitter warfare that raged between 1950 and 1953, the North Korean leadership "conducted itself better than did the American ally in Seoul." As for wartime atrocities, Cumings contended that "Communist atrocities against civilians constituted about one-sixth the total number of cases, and tended to be more discriminating."[39] Even in acknowledging that forces from the DPRK in the north had executed several hundred captured U.S. soldiers in the first months of the conflict, Cumings wrote that these helpless GI captives were shot in a "humane battlefield manner."[40] A July 2010 New York Times review found Cumings's The Korean War "a powerful revisionist history of American intervention in Korea . . . a squirm-inducing assault on America's moral behavior during the Korean War, a conflict that he says is misremembered when it is remembered at all."[41]

Because of the U.S. interference in Korea's civil war, Cumings saw the North Korean regime as reflexively, and understandably, anti-American. In his view the DPRK was warped by profound deformities for which the United States was and remains responsible.[42] Yet North Korea endured and in his view became by the 1980s a highly successful Socialist country, its culture "authentic" and "national." He praised the dictatorial regime of Kim Il-sung for providing "a form of political and social stability known to few nations on earth, with a type of soviet monarchy that ensures continuity." He even credited North Korean leaders with making ingenious and unanticipated advancements while recovering from the effects of U.S.-led bombing campaigns. Collective agriculture, Cumings noted, became "relatively uncontentious, as so many of the boundaries demarcating property (as well as the owners) had been obliterated by American bombing."[43] By any measure the North Korean regime appeared to Cumings as more humane, authentic, and legitimate than the Republic of Korea in the south.

The demise of the Soviet Union led to the opening of Soviet archives in the early 1990s and the discovery of documents that clearly established the extensive role Premier Stalin played in instigating the Korean War. In 1993 historian Kathryn Weathersby published her findings in the Woodrow Wilson Center's Cold War International History Project *Bulletin*, and her work, along with that of other scholars, completely debunked any notion that the Korean War was started by a U.S. attack on North Korea.[44] In fact, materials from the Soviet archives documented the extent to which the North Korean leader Kim Il-sung was dependent on Soviet tutelage, military support, and financial assistance from the day in 1945 when he arrived in Pyongyang accompanied by the Red Army and wearing a Soviet military uniform.

The new evidence failed to convince Cumings. He refused to acknowledge that the war had been ignited by the North Koreans and the Soviet Union. In a heated exchange with historian Kathryn Weathersby, she labeled his work "dishonest" for ignoring the Soviet sources. In response he accused his critics of being guilty of "naivete" and further charged that the U.S. Department of State was actively recruiting "American scholars to refute my work with malice aforethought."[45] He then dismissed the question of who started the international conflict in June 1950 as irrelevant, since the struggle for domination of the Korean War was a domestic, civil conflict that had its origins in 1945 with the end of Japanese rule. "'Who started the Korean War?' is surely the wrong question," he wrote, adding the remarkable assertion that "no Americans care anymore that the south fired first on Ft. Sumter in the [American] Civil War." While still maintaining that there remain basic unresolved questions about the events of June 25, 1950, he believed that some future archival evidence might yet uncover the truth.[46]

Cumings's recent works have become more balanced. Offering his "fresh assessment" of the origins of the Korean War, Cumings claimed "the right to retain interpretations that still seem correct to me and to revise views that may have been found in my work before, on the principle that to change one's mind is a sign of growth."[47] Still, in an updated 2005 edition of his book *Korea's Place in the Sun*, Cumings continues to assert that North Korea was never a Soviet satellite in the 1940s, that Soviet influence in creating the DPRK was minimal, and that Kim built the North Korean army. However, he now assigns to Kim Il-sung's regime "the grave responsibility for raising the civil conflict in Korea to the level of general war, with intended and unintended consequences that no one could have predicted." In addition Cumings wrote in 2011 that "it is now clear from Soviet documents that Pyongyang had made the decision to escalate the civil conflict to the level of conventional warfare many months before June 1950."[48] Of course the decision was never Pyongyang's to make; the final decision was made in Moscow. Documents from Soviet and Chinese archives establish the fact that no invasion would have occurred in 1950 if Stalin had not authorized it and Mao had not agreed to the plan.

Cumings's publications caused celebration among leftist scholars in South Korea. Many academics and students in the ROK believed North Korean propaganda about the DPRK's self-reliance (Juche) and considered their own government illegitimate and dominated by the United States. For those sympathetic to North Korea, Cumings holds the status of a true hero, and his writings remain highly influential.[49] Academics, human rights activists, and labor leaders who chafed under the authoritarianism of the military dictatorships of Rhee, Park Chung-hee, and Chun Doo-hwan were quick to accept this American scholar's conclusions. Those conclusions proclaimed North Korea was not substantially aided by the Soviets and that South Korea had initiated the June 1950 invasion. Korean scholars with leftist sympathies were pleased to find a prominent American academic whose work suggested unification of the peninsula in 1950 would have provided a better life for all Koreans if Americans had just stood aside and let the Koreans settle their internal dispute themselves. Certain South Korean academics and leftist politicians and labor leaders found it impossible to see North Korea as a dictatorship and failed to acknowledge the vast trove of documentary evidence that demonstrates Soviet control in the DPRK. "The Korean War was a civil conflict started by Kim Il-sung for national unity," wrote one Korean scholar. "It would have ended in a month if American forces had not intervened." The scholar continued, "The statue of Gen. MacArthur, the warmonger, should be thrown into the gutter of history. MacArthur is . . . an enemy who scratched away Korean lives. MacArthur was a fanatic. The favorable perception of the war maniac who caused great tragedy to the Korean people should be scrapped. His statue should also be destroyed."[50]

Even as they delighted in the highly critical interpretations of U.S. policy, many of the South Korean scholars who accepted revisionist writings failed to acknowledge that the radical, antiauthoritarian views they cherished and openly expressed could only be held on the Korean Peninsula in the emerging democracy south of the demilitarized zone (DMZ).

As much as the public in the United States may have wanted to put the Korean War behind them, they would find it impossible to forget or ignore. Throughout the decades of uneasy peace that followed the 1953 armistice, violent events on the Korean Peninsula reminded Americans that the limited war of 1950–53 was not yet concluded. The jagged, three-mile-wide DMZ separating the two Koreas remained tense and problematic. Troublesome incidents in and near the DMZ threatened stability and peace almost as soon as signatures were affixed to the armistice documents. Violent acts included commando raids across each other's boundaries by both North and South Korea.

In January 1968 a squad of thirty North Korean infiltrators attempted to assassinate South Korean president Park Chung-hee in a raid on the Blue House, his official residence in Seoul. All the attackers save one were killed by ROK police.[51] Perhaps frustrated and embarrassed by this fiasco, the North Koreans struck again just two days later. This time their target was the USS *Pueblo*, an American intelligence-gathering ship that approached, or maybe crossed into, North Korean waters on January 23, 1968. Supposedly on a "scientific" mission, Capt. Lloyd Bucher and eighty-three crew members were suddenly surrounded by a flotilla of North Korean vessels and captured. President Johnson responded by calling up fifteen thousand Air Force and Navy reservists and ordered the nuclear-powered aircraft carrier *Enterprise* to the waters off the coast of South Korea. But the Tet Offensive in Vietnam, launched on January 31 by the Viet Cong against U.S. forces stationed throughout South Vietnam, demanded the Johnson administration's attention. A long negotiating process led to a settlement with the DPRK. Held for nearly a year, all except one who died of his wounds during the taking of the *Pueblo* were released after signing forced confessions, which the U.S. government disavowed even before the captured seamen were released. While the shock of the Tet Offensive dominated the news, the *Pueblo* incident brought back memories of the prisoners of war (POWs) held by North Koreans during the Korean War. Brainwashing, collaboration with the enemy, and forced confessions once again became topics of concern. Like Korean War POWs in the 1950s, Captain Bucher faced possible career-ending disciplinary action, although no formal charges were ever brought forth.[52]

The peaceful settlement of the *Pueblo* incident did little to ease tension. On August 18, 1976, an incident in the DMZ brought the Korean Peninsula to the edge of open warfare when two American officers were murdered by ax-wielding DPRK soldiers in an incident involving the removal of a large tree. Meanwhile, throughout the 1970s the North Koreans had been secretly digging tunnels under the DMZ to launch an invasion of the south. Then in October 1983 a North Korean terrorist murdered seventeen high-ranking South Korean government officials by detonating a powerful explosive device at a public ceremony in the capital of Burma (now Myanmar).[53] By then it appeared that the two Koreas were about equal in military strength, although still dependent on their much stronger allies, as they competed in their claims to be the legitimate government of the Korean people. As both regimes seemed unable to adequately care for their population without foreign assistance, their ambitions for unification and rivalry for supremacy on the peninsula threatened the stability of the region as well as world peace. Decades after the costly war and compromising armistice agreement, it seemed that nothing positive had resulted from the war's bloodshed, devastation, and expense.

The 1988 Seoul Olympics would provide an unlikely and unanticipated change in the dynamics on the Korean Peninsula. The Olympic movement appeared moribund following the 1980 Moscow Olympics, which the United States and some Western nations boycotted in response to the Soviet Union's invasion of neighboring Afghanistan the previous year. The Soviets and Communist states stayed away from the 1984 Los Angeles Olympics in retaliation. Now the 1988 Olympics were to be hosted in the sprawling city of Seoul, just thirty miles from the DMZ. Seoul was selected following an intensive campaign by officials in the Park Chung-hee government that included lavish spending and the companionship of beautiful, young "hostesses," when the International Olympic Committee (IOC) site-selection committee met in Baden-Baden, West Germany, in the late 1970s. Many around the world found it shocking that the ROK had been selected over Japan and expressed concerns about the safety of Seoul and the ability of a developing country to manage such a complex event. Meanwhile, the North Koreans feared the Seoul Olympics and rightly viewed the games as a political venture by South Korea to enhance its image abroad. As the opening ceremony for the Olympics drew near, the DPRK tried various schemes to disrupt the games and even sought advice from Communist allies, including the East Germans and Cuba's Fidel Castro, who suggested the two Koreas cohost the event and call it the "Chosun" or "Pyongyang-Seoul" games. To keep the DPRK at bay, Seoul and the IOC negotiated with Pyongyang about staging a few of the competitions in North Korea. But the talks went nowhere, as it was always clear that the Kim Il-sung regime would never seriously consider providing a proper welcome to hordes of international athletes, spectators, officials, and journalists.[54]

In a desperate effort to disrupt the preparations, the DPRK turned to terror, placing a bomb on a Korean Air flight from Abu Dhabi to Seoul in November 1987 that killed all 115 people aboard the plane. However, the world's Communist countries were now eager for a true Olympic competition. In May 1987 East German ambassador Hans Maretzki complained, "North Korea is once again putting itself in self-imposed isolation. Through its stubborn behavior, North Korea is granting advantages to South Korea, which will enjoy an improved image."[55] Meanwhile U.S. president Ronald Reagan received assurances from Soviet foreign minister Edvard Shevardnadze that the DPRK would launch no terrorist attacks in attempts to disrupt the Seoul Olympics—a clear indication of the Soviet Union's continuing powerful hold on the DPRK regime as well as concern for the safety of athletes and officials of Soviet and Communist-bloc countries. Frustrated, isolated, and abandoned by its Communist compatriots seeking a place for their athletes on the world stage, the North Korean regime was forced to watch from the sidelines as Seoul hosted 8,454 athletes from 159 countries (the most ever to that point) at the Olympics, including the Soviet Union, PRC, and Soviet satellite countries in Eastern Europe.[56] In the opinion of U.S. ambassador to the ROK James Lilley, "The 1988 Olympics were a crowning achievement."[57]

Around the world, people agreed with the ambassador's assessment. The 1988 Seoul Olympics served as a dramatic watershed in shaping international opinions about the Republic of Korea, and the games facilitated a new paradigm for remembering the Korean War and its consequences. The spectacularly staged Olympic Games showcased the country's amazing economic and social advances and displayed the rising confidence of the South Korean population. The Olympics showcased the ROK's new democratically elected government, installed after relatively free voting in 1987. The event also earned South Korea world recognition as a rising Asian "economic tiger." Within two years both the Soviet Union and China normalized relations with South Korea. The DPRK found itself more isolated than ever, and its economic collapse in the 1990s demonstrated to the world the DPRK's extensive dependence on the financial assistance once provided by the Soviet Union.[58] All these sudden and unexpected developments led to a reassessment of the war's outcome in the United States and other nations involved in supporting the ROK four decades earlier.

With the memory of the Korean War reshaped by the new international realities of the 1980s, the Republic of Korea, the United States, and the nations of the United Nations Command began to reconsider the Korean War. In the following decade, the fall of the Soviet Union and the availability of new documentation from Soviet, Chinese, and declassified American sources set off a firestorm of new Korean War scholarship.

The 1950–53 conflict in Korea came to be seen as a success, in that the Republic of Korea had been saved from Communist aggression. Even into the twenty-first century, American policy makers demonstrated that they remained profoundly influenced by what they understood to be the lessons of the Korean War. The remarkable extent to which U.S. leaders remembered the Korean War, and interpreted its lessons in addressing contemporary conflicts long after the 1953 armistice, was made clear by secretary of state Condoleezza Rice in 2006. Responding to questions about the floundering military intervention in Iraq and its failure to quickly bring about peace and a democratic form of government, Secretary Rice sought to make a historical comparison to South Korea's long, elusive, and ultimately successful struggle to achieve political stability and economic prosperity. "Just because you won't have that democracy that is a beacon for the Middle East in 2007 doesn't mean that you won't have an Iraq that is a beacon of democracy in the Middle East," she stated. "You know, you didn't have that beacon of democracy in South Korea for quite a long time, either, but conditions were there and now you have it."[59]

In the 1980s and 1990s, in an era of positive memory, aging veterans of the war in Korea began to receive long-overdue recognition for their service in a painful war that was no longer remembered as a loss. The time for memorialization of an unfinished war had arrived.

4 | Memorializing across America

An effort to build a Korean War archive in Independence, Missouri, and an ambitious plan for a national Korean War museum in Chicago or New York City both ended in frustration. However, individuals and local communities across the United States found creative ways to memorialize the Korean War while honoring veterans of a war that was overlooked and misunderstood but never completely forgotten. Veterans and their families usually led these endeavors, and often grateful Korean Americans were intimately involved at the local level in the memorialization processes and veteran recognitions.

Eighteen-year-old Paul Edwards found himself in the midst of the Korean War because he smoked a cigarette! Dismissed from college his freshman year for lighting up in his dorm room, he quickly married his teenage sweetheart and volunteered for the U.S. Army. "We thought we'd go fight and come home heroes," Edwards recalled years later. "I was there because I was stupid."[1] Following the trauma of his wartime service, Edwards finished college, earned a doctorate in history, and taught for many years as a popular professor at Graceland University in Lamoni, Iowa. In the late 1970s he began putting together an archive and writing about the war that had altered his life. Starting with the two hundred letters he had written from the front lines in Korea to his young bride, Edwards amassed an archive of nearly thirty-four thousand items related to the experiences of U.S. soldiers and junior officers in Korea by 2010. For a time Graceland University housed Edwards's Center for the Study of the Korean War in a few rooms in the library at its Independence, Missouri, branch campus; however, the university was unable to properly fund the project. Edwards moved his collection off campus and managed to keep it going with the help of dedicated volunteers. "We lived on nickels and dimes for years," Edwards lamented.[2] I became acquainted with Dr. Edwards during my thirteen-year tenure as director of the Harry S. Truman Presidential Library, located just a few blocks down the street from Edwards's center, and began urging my friend to find an appropriate institutional home for his important archive.

While Edwards struggled to maintain his archive in western Missouri, in Chicago another Korean War veteran never let his war experience fade from memory. Denis Healy, cochair of the Turtle Wax corporation, was determined to see his dream of a Korean War museum become a reality, perhaps on Chicago's historic Navy Pier or maybe in New York City. He envisioned a "world-class, dynamic, and instructive museum" and secured thousands of items from fellow veterans. He incorporated the Korean War National Museum and Library in 1997 and stored his collection through the 1990s in an unused U.S. Air Force base in Rantoul, Illinois, surrounded by endless flat fields of corn and soybeans. He later moved his fledgling operation to Springfield, Illinois, hoping that his small storefront museum near the new Abraham Lincoln Presidential Library and related historic sites would increase his project's visibility and aid efforts to raise the tens of millions of dollars his museum would require. Overwhelmed by management problems and financial issues, however, his little museum abruptly closed its doors in July 2017. While their ambitious plans were never realized, the important collections amassed by both Edwards and Healy over many years found a home at the Harry S. Truman Presidential Library.[3]

Meanwhile, in White Rock Lake near Dallas, Texas, two brothers began an online database intended to provide information to veterans, families, students of military history, the Department of Defense, and even the White House. Hal and Ted Barker were sons of a distinguished Korean War veteran. They began collecting personal information from veterans about their Korean War experiences in 1979 as part of a family history project. Hal Barker's enthusiasm had led him to a brief involvement with the initial advocacy efforts that would eventually lead to the building of the Korean War Veterans Memorial in Washington DC. At the same time, the brothers collected an enormous amount of information on individual veterans, battles, skirmishes, and prisoner-of-war (POW) issues. After initiating the Korean War Project in 1991 and then moving it online in 1995, the collection soon held one hundred gigabytes of information on its website (koreanwar.org). Although the Barkers' project initially sought simply to assist Korean War veterans to reconnect, it rapidly expanded into a service for families, scholars, students, and current armed-services personnel.[4] The work Edwards, Healy, and the Barkers put into documenting the Korean War is representative of grassroots efforts by many veterans and families of veterans of the "forgotten war" to somehow preserve or create a remembrance for the sacrifice and service of those who fought in Korea.

In the remembrance of the Korean War, citizens and local groups have led the memorialization drive, with the academic historians as observers and government officials at all levels usually playing a reactive role. American society appeared in the 1980s to be in the era of a memory boom, and the topic of how wars of the twentieth century should be remembered increasingly attracted the attention of the public. Memory, a process distinct from yet related to history, can encompass various theaters: memoirs, films, museums, memorials, and sites of remembrance. The public memory boom in the United States appears to have ignited a deep fascination in the memories and remembrances of war and its victims. In recent decades the need to acknowledge the veterans and victims of war and its ravages has become central to contemporary culture in the United States, and public memory of warfare tends to rise from the bottom up. It is formed and interpreted at the local level in versions of past events interacting among family, friends, and social and fraternal organizations.[5] In such an environment, it is not uncommon for public memory to be in conflict with the historical record, which is based on the analysis of sources such as government documents, manuscripts, audio recordings, and photographs. Ironically, while the study of history at U.S. academic institutions is in decline, the public seems increasingly interested in exploring the past outside the classroom. To an extent history has been replaced by memory. When memory replaces history, myth and legend can become reality.

In the United States the private sector tends to drive commemoration and memorialization of warfare, while a complex process leads to the creation of a society's collective memory. Collective memory is formed through an evolutionary process and is a product of group memories brought to the front by civic clubs, patriotic organizations, unions, and religious communities. Eventually a public (or collective) memory emerges, which homogenizes group memories into a commonly held creed that a central authority can sanction and support. At this point public memory that arose from group memories can become the society's official public memory and a component of the dominant civic culture. In a sense public memory of a war is the result of a merger of the vernacular memory of groups (veterans groups, family, civic organizations) with the officially adopted and approved recollection of cultural leaders and authorities.[6] The memorialization of the Korean War presents an example of the grassroots or public commemoration process.

The study of war memorials and activities of remembrance provides a means for examining the long and complicated developments leading to the establishment of a people's collective memory about a past wartime era. The Korean War is a remarkable example of the evolutionary process by which such a memory is formed by a population over several decades in a complex and ever-changing international environment. Interest in recognizing the service of Korean War veterans came about after celebrating the bicentennial of the American Revolution, which renewed curiosity about the heritage of the United States. A heightened sense of patriotism during the 1980s may have also played a role. Furthermore, a clear connection exists between the 1982 unveiling and 1984 dedication of the Vietnam Veterans Memorial in Washington DC, and the remarkable proliferation of Korean War sites of remembrance that followed. The dedication of the Vietnam Veterans Memorial in Washington DC, sparked a desire for recognition by Korean War veterans and their families. The Korean War Veterans Association (KWVA) organized and began to lobby for recognition.[7] And the change in public opinion toward the Republic of Korea that occurred in the wake of the 1988 Seoul Olympics, along with the dramatic end of the Cold War era, fueled enthusiasm for public remembrances of the Korean War.

The remarkable change in the public's attitude toward POWs (a legacy of the Vietnam War experience) also enhanced the once-tarnished image of the Korean War POWs. Vietnam-era POWs were viewed as heroes to be honored, not weak collaborators or victims of brainwashing as were Korean War POWs (unfairly and inaccurately). Post-Vietnam America paid new attention to military personnel who were missing in action

(MIA) as well. Pres. Richard Nixon declared January 25, 1974, a National Missing in Action Day, and Pres. Jimmy Carter created National POW/MIA Recognition Day in 1979. In 1982 Pres. Ronald Reagan initiated the practice of flying the black MIA flag over the White House and federal buildings on certain commemorative days, and in 1985 Reagan awarded all living American soldiers who had ever spent time as a POW since World War I a U.S. POW Medal. A decade later the U.S. Postal Service produced a stamp displaying the inscription "POW/MIA Never Forgotten" along with an image of a military dog tag. Presidents George H. W. Bush, George W. Bush, and Bill Clinton added days of recognition during their presidencies.[8] All these developments have retroactively benefited Korean War veterans.

In the mid-1980s the United States appeared to be in an era of renewed patriotic fervor. Whatever factors brought about this phenomenon, it is clear that remembrance of war gained a wide public appeal as society attempted to reconstruct a recent past in order to form an understandable and acceptable present. Warfare and its remembrance were always central in defining American memories and patriotic traditions.[9] The public need to commemorate recent wars that emerged in the 1980s boosted interest and support for memorializing the Korean War. Indeed, as the initial planning for the Korean War Veterans Memorial in Washington DC, began slowly to move ahead, states, municipalities, and even universities were already planning and constructing memorials for Korean War veterans and their fallen comrades. The awareness among Korean War veterans generated by the stir surrounding the Vietnam Veterans Memorial on the Mall in Washington DC, along with the nationwide efforts by the local chapters of the newly organized KWVA, led to a new awareness in the American public about the 1950–53 war and greater attention to the ongoing conflict on the Korean Peninsula. Perhaps the renewed concern about threats emanating from North Korea and the remarkable rise of South Korea as a genuine democracy and world economic powerhouse also brought about a greater appreciation for the service of veterans in the Korean conflict. As a result of grassroots efforts in local communities, by 2015 more than thirty states had established Korean War memorials, and others were in the planning stage.[10] The stories behind each of these memorials are as diverse as their architectural designs (almost all of which proved contentious to some degree), but most have certain characteristics in common. The memorials were locally inspired and funded by private sources (although some secured municipal, state, or federal assistance), and in most cases local Korean American communities were significantly involved and highly supportive. Several case studies serve as examples.

HAWAI'I

Well before the Korean War Veterans Memorial was dedicated on the National Mall in Washington DC, some states and communities had already begun the process of memorialization. The territory of Hawai'i was among the first to host a significant site of remembrance. Soon after the 1953 armistice was signed at Panmunjom, the U.S. territory of Hawai'i became the burial site for thousands of military personnel killed in the Korean War. Early in the war, soldiers and marines were buried in a temporary cemetery near Hungnam in South Korea. From July to November 1954, both sides exchanged remains in a process called for in the 1953 armistice agreement. After Congress rejected a suggestion by the American Battle Monuments Commission (ABMC) to place a permanent memorial cemetery in South Korea, the remains of the service personnel killed in Korea were transferred to Hawai'i. Named Operation Glory, more than four thousand U.S. soldiers, sailors, airmen, and marines were returned. The reburial in 1956 placed the remains of those who fell in the Korean War in the National Cemetery of the Pacific (commonly called the "Punchbowl Cemetery"). Located in the vast crater in Honolulu, Hawai'i, where Native Hawaiians practiced ritual human sacrifice in ancient times, the Punchbowl was the site of the battle of Nu'uanu. Here the victorious King Kamehameha the Great unified his control over the islands in 1795 with help from his British and American allies. After the U.S. annexation of Hawai'i in 1898, the Punchbowl served as a navy fortress, training ground, and observation station. Following World War II the Punchbowl was dedicated as a military cemetery in 1949. The earliest of the Korean War dead were interred here beginning in 1956, along with more than thirty thousand soldiers, sailors, and marines killed in the Pacific theater during World War II. In 1964 the ABMC erected a striking memorial depicting a white marble Lady Liberty at the cemetery both to represent grieving mothers and "to honor the sacrifices and achievements of American Armed Forces in the Pacific during World War II and the Korean War." In 1980 the mission of the vast cemetery was expanded to include military of the Vietnam era.[11] The Korean War section of the cemetery served as Hawaiʻiʻs only memorial to that conflict until July 1994.

By waiting until the 1980s to begin a local effort for the memorialization of the Korean War, veterans of that conflict, their families, and Hawaiʻiʻs state officials fit the pattern repeated in almost all the states. Even so, the Honolulu Memorial is unusual, if not unique, in that it serves as a site of remembrance for the fallen in both conflicts. Moreover, Hawaiʻiʻs memorial was initiated by state legislators and largely publicly funded. The construction took place on public land, and state officials guided the process. However, it shares in common with numerous other war memorials, including the Korean War Veterans Memorial on the National Mall in Washington DC, a history of controversy and contention over design issues and cost overruns. The entire planning and construction process frustrated planners for years. Hawaiʻi was still a U.S. territory at the time of the Korean War. Yet 454 uniformed service personnel from the islands died in the Korean War, more per capita than in any state (more than 300 died in Vietnam). In recognition of this exceptional sacrifice, Hawaiʻiʻs legislature authorized a Vietnam War memorial on the state capitol grounds in 1988. The brothers who pushed for the legislation, Hawaiʻi state representative David Hagino and state senator Gerald Hagino, had originally planned for a memorial for their contemporaries who had died in Vietnam. Only as an afterthought did they realize that Hawaiʻi had never recognized the service of the state's Korean War dead, including the uncles of these two prominent state legislators. Once it was decided to include the Korean War in the Vietnam memorial, a legislative committee composed of veterans called for legislation to establish a commission to choose a design. From thirty-five entrants, commissioners selected a grandiose proposal for a tall, abstract structure of three triangular forms, the tallest forty-four feet high, each topped with a prism to disperse light in a rainbow of colors on the capitol.[12]

Although a prominent local architect predicted "it will win national prominence," opposition to the design was immediate and fierce. Local community groups, particularly Honolulu's Downtown Neighborhood Board and the Friends of ʻIolani Palace, were concerned that the height of the structure would overshadow both the nearby capitol and the ʻIolani Palace. Meanwhile, tradition-minded veterans groups seemed to dislike just about everything in the avant-garde design.[13] Nevertheless, the commissioners appointed to select a winning proposal held their ground. They labored stubbornly for four years on the project before the fantastic and futuristic winning design was ultimately abandoned.

In July 1992 the frustrated state legislature enacted a new design competition, specifying that the memorial could not exceed a height of twenty feet, in order to keep any new design in proportion with other structures and statuary in the immediate area. As a result, this new legislation effectively disqualified the original winning design. Furthermore, impatient lawmakers established a new review board of five members "to monitor and review the work of the commission in developing the design and to approve or disapprove the final design of the memorial submitted by the commission or the department of accounting and general services . . . within seven days of a timely submission by the commission."[14] Clearly upset with the original process, the legislature gave the commission, now reduced to advisory status, only ninety days to select a new design or the work would move to state government officials, who would forward their own plan to a review board for final approval.

In protest to this new arrangement, five disgruntled members of the nine original commissioners dropped out of the new selection process. At this low point in the memorialization process, Kenneth Kupchak, a well-regarded local attorney and veteran, stepped forward and coordinated a new competition to select a design that would ultimately satisfy all parties. The second call for proposals generated more than fifty entries, and more than a thousand Hawaiians provided comments on the varied designs. Paul Medley, a young intern with the architectural firm Fritz Johnson Inc., won the 1992 competition with a plan to focus on the names of the fallen soldiers. His design also sought to blend the memorial into the park-like grounds surrounding the capitol and palace. His proposal called for two low serpentine rows of polished granite pedestals that would wind comfortably between native trees and plants on the capitol grounds. On top of each pedestal the name of a fallen soldier would be etched, similar to the Vietnam Memorial on the National Mall in Washington DC, except that Medley's concept required visitors to engage with the monument close up rather than from afar. (To fully appreciate the memorial, visitors must approach it from a vantage point where they can see that the identical-looking pedestals are actually all different when one reads the names.) Although complications with plans

for a parking ramp and underground cable lines, along with a funding shortfall, produced further frustrations, the project was eventually completed and dedicated on July 24, 1994.[15]

Medley's efforts produced a memorial he intended to be "personal and intimate." He had listened attentively to veteran groups and civic organizations, such as the Friends of the ʻIolani Palace. In a modest understatement of his achievement, Medley said, "This memorial is more of an expression of participation than of my own talent." Veterans of Korea and Vietnam immediately found the uncomplicated, quiet, and dignified memorial in a garden-like setting to be a place that encouraged reflection and remembrance, and family and friends of the veterans and fallen found peace and comfort at the site. "The memorial is long overdue," Vietnam veteran William Johnson observed at the memorial's dedication. He spoke for Korean War veterans as well when he observed that "people don't realize Hawaiʻi gave up a lot. A lot of local boys and girls died. . . . [The memorial] gives a brother, a sister, a mother, or a father a place to go and touch."[16]

Nearly a quarter century after the dedication of the memorial to the veterans of the Vietnam and Korean Wars on the capitol grounds in Honolulu, a small ceremony in Hilo on the Big Island dedicated a Korean War memorial specifically for the fifty-two Hawaiians from the Island of Hawaiʻi who died in combat, along with five who died of noncombat causes. This modest memorial had been fifteen years in development and was funded by the sale of "a helluva lot of candy," according to one member of the Big Island Chapter No. 231 of the KWVA. At the dedication ceremony the mayor of Hilo, Harry Kim, the son of Korean immigrants, presided, and the consul general of the Republic of Korea expressed the gratitude of his nation for the sacrifice of U.S. servicemen. A gathering of two hundred, many of whom were Korean Americans who had lost family in the war, watched in silence.[17]

KANSAS

By the time the fiftieth anniversary of the Korean War arrived, family and friends of the fallen, MIAs, and veterans of the 1950–53 conflict on the Korean Peninsula no longer lacked for memorials in most parts of the United States, and in the nation's heartland, the Korean War veterans of Kansas and their comrades who did not return received a long-delayed recognition. The themes of the state and local memorials reflected the growing attitude toward the war as a patriotic, selfless, and ultimately successful endeavor to save South Korea from Communist aggression by the North Koreans and a halt to the spread of Soviet-inspired Communist regimes in East Asia during the early years of the Cold War. Veterans and the public had come to believe that South Korea's freedom further ensured the security of the United States.

Critics see such local memorialization efforts as misguided or overly simplistic, ignoring the cost of war in human carnage and suffering. Suhi Choi, a specialist in mass communication, claims that such memorials, while protecting a society's self-proclaimed ideals and values, actually "promote acts of forgetting as opposed to acts of remembering." Noting that the survivors of the war in Korea often hold memories counter to the officially sanctioned narrative of a war, she believes a "memorial that ceases to question is no longer a mnemonic device in our symbolic world but an ossified relic of our landscape." In her study of the Utah Korean War Memorial in Memory Grove Park in Salt Lake City, she finds the site unsatisfactory as a historical resource. Choi considers Utah's memorial an intentional effort to forget the realities of war while resonating "with three mythical scripts—*resilience, local pride*, and *the good war*."[18]

Perhaps much the same criticism could be directed at the memorial in Overland Park, Kansas, a suburban community located just across the state line from Kansas City, Missouri. Indeed, for many local veterans and citizens involved in the conceptualization, funding, and dedication of this site, including a large and active Korean American community, these characteristics of patriotism, resilience, local pride, and a just war are exactly what the memorial was intended to represent. Clearly the memorial's planners never fixated on the tragic mistakes of American military leadership or complex decisions and compromises made by wartime political leaders. And their narrative of the sacrifice of Kansan soldiers is not necessarily at odds with survivors' personal memories and understanding of the historic events that placed them in a bloody conflict far from home.

The Kansans got off to a relatively late start in their memorialization effort, and the planning, funding, and construction of the Kansas memorial faced the problems, delays, setbacks, and design controversies common to memorialization in a democratic society. Jack Krumme, who launched the campaign to secure funding for the memorial to be located in Overland Park, expressed the project's urgency in 2004 when he said, "We're getting so damn old that we have to hurry." On June 9, 2003, with Democratic U.S. House member Dennis Moore in attendance, the Overland Park City Council approved a site for the memorial. The original design was drawn and redrawn while local funding efforts moved ahead. Pancake breakfasts and garage sales brought in initial funding. A Korean American resident of nearby Leawood, Kansas, Therese Park, who as a young girl fled with her family to Pusan when the North Koreans invaded, served as a key figure in the project. Her childhood memoir of wartime Korea, *When a Rooster Crows at Night: A Child's Experience in the Korean War*, provided publicity for the project in local papers, and she assisted the Korean American Society of Greater Kansas City, led by Youngsik Dokko, in fundraising efforts.[19]

Local funding proved insufficient, however. Corporate support was modest, and a request to the giant Kauffman Foundation for $500,000 resulted in a token contribution of $50,000. So to complete the Overland Park project, planners sought federal assistance. Representative Moore and his Kansas colleagues in the U.S. Senate, Republicans Pat Robertson and Sam Brownback, got busy securing a congressional appropriation (or earmark) for the project. Their efforts paid off when a $388-billion federal omnibus spending bill passed in late 2004, which included a line appropriating funds for a number of worthy projects for Kansas residents living in Johnson County (Moore's district). These included a transit system, local road projects, and new equipment for the sheriff's department. In addition, there was $364,000 for the Korean War memorial in Overland Park. Despite Krumme's frustrations with the federal paperwork, which came along with the funding through the Department of Housing and Urban Development, the monument became a reality.[20]

Depicting heroic statues of unidentified soldiers, the final piece in the memorial paid a special tribute to Fr. Emil Kapaun, a Roman Catholic priest from a small Kansas community and U.S. Army chaplain, who served his fellow captives in a North Korean POW camp until his death. Featuring a curved and polished wall of remembrance with the names of the Kansans lost in the war, the memorial was dedicated on September 30, 2006. The Kansas City Korean Choir performed at the dedication, and ROK consul general Wook Kim arrived from Chicago to speak at the event.[21] Visitors find the Overland Park memorial a beautiful and quiet place for reflection. Those seeking a "counternarrative" of the Korean War's excesses, mistakes, and atrocities will not find it here.

Kansas is home to at least three additional memorials. A most imaginative sculpture exists among memorials to other wars of the twentieth century on the University of Kansas campus in Lawrence. Entitled *Korean Cranes Rising*, a work by Jon Havener, a professor of design at the University of Kansas, was unveiled and dedicated on April 15, 2005. In Korean culture cranes symbolize spirituality, peace, and happiness, and the four rising birds represent the war's major combatants: the United States, China, and North and South Korea. It is perhaps unique that North Korea and China are represented. This memorial honors the forty-four members of the university "family" who died in the Korean conflict. The $100,000 raised to fund the memorial came entirely from former University of Kansas students living in the United States and South Korea.[22] An additional memorial for Kansan Korean War vets is in Topeka. This city's memorial to Kansans was dedicated on July 27, 2003, three years prior to the Overland Park site. Earlier, in May 2001, a memorial was erected in the state's largest city, Wichita, "to pay tribute to acts and sacrifices Kansas made in the war effort." In addition, just across the Kansas-Missouri state line in downtown Kansas City's Pershing Park, the Missouri Korean War Veterans Memorial was dedicated on September 29, 2011, on land provided by the city and built with $270,000 in donations—many from Korean Americans.[23]

OLYMPIA, WASHINGTON

The memorial on the grounds of the state of Washington's capitol fits a pattern seen throughout the United States. At the urging of various veteran groups and prominent business and civic leaders, the Washington State Legislature authorized a state-sponsored Korean War Memorial in 1989. More than 500 of the 122,000 Washington soldiers who fought in the Korean War never returned, and the memorial was to serve as a reminder of their sacrifice and a sign of gratitude to all who served during the Korean conflict. As was often the case with Korean War memorials, the state legislature's authorization and designation of a location was not accompanied by a sufficient allocation of funding. Thus a four-year fundraising effort was soon underway to secure the $400,000 needed for the project. Veterans groups led by the "Chosin Few" raised $320,000 from private sources; the state eventually contributed $70,000 in "matching funds." A three-month design competition resulted in the selection of Deborah Copenhaver Fellows's proposal from neighboring Montana. Known for her western-themed works, Fellows was raised on a ranch in Idaho by her father, Deb Copenhaver, a Korean War veteran, rodeo enthusiast, and a 1991 inductee of the Rodeo Hall of Fame. Her works were of the traditional genre that veteran groups appreciated.[24]

Seeking to create a realistic sculpture that would provide a venue "for people to reflect on war and the price it extracts from those who participate," Fellows's bronze statues depict three weary soldiers of diverse nationalities huddled to warm themselves in the cold around a pile of sticks. One of the soldiers tries to light a fire. Twenty-two flags fly in the background, representing nations contributing to the United Nations Command (UNC). On either end of the statues are plaques designed to provide a brief overview of the war; in front of the memorial, the names of soldiers killed in the war are carved in stone tablets. The memorial was dedicated on July 24, 1993, on the Washington State Capitol campus in Olympia. Following the dedication, names were added to the memorial in 1994, 1998, and 1999 in a process not unfamiliar to other memorials to the Korean and Vietnam Wars. A sentimental poem, "I Am Not Forgotten," by Lt. Col. Richard Kirk on another marker completes the site surrounding the huddled, multiracial trio of soldiers.[25]

The Washington State memorial says much about the culture in which it was created. The memorial is entitled *The Forgotten War*, and both English and Korean text is used several times in the memorial. Seeking inclusiveness, one of the explanatory plaques briefly recognizes the role of women in all American wars, adding that in Korea, women serving as nurses and medical assistants "distinguished themselves by their devotion to duty, utter disregard for working hours and willingness to do anything that needed to be done with courage, stamina, and determination." Other bronze plaques present a map of Korea and a brief summary of Korea's four-thousand-year history, concluding that "South Korea and its allies won the war, forcing the North Koreans back, creating a democratic stronghold in South Korea and enabling over 100,000 North Koreans to emigrate to the South during the evacuation at Hungnam."

Although easily overlooked by visitors to the state's capitol complex, the memorial is among the more impressive of its genre. The effort to provide something of a narrative regarding the origins and conduct of the undeclared war is, while simplistic, useful to the unschooled visitor who might, when first encountering the memorial, easily mistake it for an edifice dedicated to World War II or Vietnam.

While more modest in scale, these local memorials share the themes and focus of the National Mall in Washington DC. All seek to honor service and sacrifice, while providing a quiet and comfortable place for reflection on the cost of the war. None examine the war's causes or consequences, nor do they address diplomatic failures, Cold War crises, wartime atrocities, military misdeeds, political leadership, false confessions of POWs, or instances of failures and cowardice. Graduate seminars, college classes, library shelves, archival collections, and documentary films serve as the proper places to explore those complex aspects of the war's history.

AN INFINITE VARIETY

Although there were a few early Korean War monuments and memorials, sites of remembrance for the Korean War were not in fashion until after the Vietnam Veterans Memorial graced the National Mall in the early 1980s. In fact, with the exception of the Punchbowl Cemetery in Hawai'i and a plaque at the United Nations headquarters in New York City dedicated on June 21, 1956, to the war dead who served in the UNC, the American landscape was devoid of sites commemorating the Korean War. Perhaps this was due to the unhappy and unresolved nature of the Korean conflict (not yet named a war), or maybe the nation was in no mood for war memorials following World War II. Returning veterans of that horrendous warfare, which left more than fifty-five million dead across the globe, seemed content with cemeteries for their comrades in arms and "living memorials," such as highways, bridges, playgrounds, auditoriums, and stadiums. It seemed as though in its time of victory, prosperity, and power, Americans had no need for monuments of stone and metal.[26] Only after the tragedy of Vietnam, when the nation felt vulnerable and weakened, were memorials seen as necessary for the veterans of that war as well as the overlooked Korean War veterans.

Korean War memorials and monuments have dotted the nation in recent decades, along with imaginative, creative, and at times, misinformed projects and programs to honor veterans, remember their service and sacrifice, and commemorate the fallen. Vermilion County in central

Illinois dedicated an early memorial to the soldiers of the Vietnam and Korean Wars in May 1986 on Hazel Street in Danville.[27] Korean American architect Choe Yong-wan (Bryan Choe) donated his talents to a Korean War memorial in Dayton, Ohio. Adding to confusion about the war, a well-intentioned memorial just outside Fort Wayne, Indiana, presents erroneous statistics about the war, as does a monument at Williams College. A diorama at the National Guard Memorial Museum in Washington DC, honors a Medal of Honor recipient who led a heroic attack on a Chinese position in February 1951.[28] And memorials continue to proliferate. After an advocacy campaign of twenty-four years, a Korean War memorial was unveiled in Boulder City at the Southern Nevada Veterans Memorial Cemetery in 2018. Spokane, Washington, dedicated a modest memorial for local veterans of the Korean War on July 27, 2021, the sixty-eighth anniversary of the armistice. On a hot Sunday afternoon, in a ceremony moved indoors, Spokane's mayor told of the memorial's long planning process that began as an afterthought six years earlier. During a discussion of the need to refurbish the city's Vietnam War memorial, a city council member noted there was no Korean War memorial for the veterans of that conflict.[29]

A surprising Korean War Children's Memorial can be found in Bellingham, Washington. This site, dedicated on October 23, 2006, consists of a graceful hilltop pagoda with a bronze plaque honoring the U.S. servicemen and women who saved one hundred thousand Korean children and supported fifty thousand others in four hundred orphanages. The script on the plaque also maintains that U.S. military personnel donated more than $2 million with help from family and friends back home. The website associated with this memorial also takes issue with the legend of Dean Hess, the courageous pilot depicted by the movie star Rock Hudson in the 1950s film *Battle Hymn*, based on Hess's memoir of the same title. The memorial's website claims Hess to be "one of the most shameless frauds of the Korean War," arguing that the true hero in rescuing scores of abandoned children from the region around Seoul in December 1950 was chaplain Col. Russell L. Blaisdell. The memorial's website includes links to Korean adoption information sites.[30]

Americans have found an amazing variety of activities to honor the long-neglected service of Korean War veterans. In one imaginative endeavor, Honor Flight Network has transported groups of aging veterans of the Korean War (as well as World War II and Vietnam) to Washington DC, to view war memorials, remember friends and lost comrades, and share their experiences with other veterans. Honor Flight Network coordinates flights, ground transportation, food, and lodging at no cost to the veterans. Volunteer escorts meet the veterans upon their arrival in Washington DC, and provide assistance, including wheelchairs. The network was cofounded in 2005 by Earl Morse, a physician assistant and retired U.S. Air Force captain, and Jeff Miller, a small-business owner. Both were sons of veterans who realized that many veterans of World War II would never be able to visit the newly completed memorial to their wartime service. The small volunteer organization quickly grew, funding was secured, and 126 World War II veterans were transported in small private planes the first year. Within a year more than three hundred World War II veterans from the founders' hometown Asheville Regional Airport traveled to Washington DC. A decade later the network had expanded to 140 hubs across the United States and escorted more than 200,000 veterans to view the war memorials in the nation's capital.[31]

War is never the heroic and romantic adventure so often depicted in movies and other forms of popular culture. The initial patriotic fervor and martial spirit that can accompany the United States' entry into a war quickly fades, and a profound sense of sorrow and loss soon takes hold. Wars never solve problems—although they may prevent a bad situation from getting worse. Even when ended victoriously on the battlefield, wars often lead to new problems that require pragmatic diplomatic solutions, policy alterations at home or abroad, and sometimes further armed conflict. Memorials and monuments seek to justify the loss and comfort the afflicted once the post-warfare reality sets in. Nations seem to need a common narrative about the war, places where the fallen can be remembered, and activities designed to assist and honor the veteran and his/her family—even if adequate government healthcare, pensions, and other benefits may be lacking or nonexistent.[32]

KOREAN AMERICANS

The Korean American community in the United States has significantly influenced American perceptions of South Korea and the Korean War. They have often played a significant role honoring Korean War veterans and memorializing their service and sacrifice. There are now more than

1.5 million Korean Americans, including those of mixed ethnicity, living throughout the United States, with huge concentrations located in the urban and suburban areas of California, New York, New Jersey, Illinois, and Washington State.

The Korean diaspora began in 1884 with a lone political exile from the corrupt and declining Chosun Dynasty. Seo Jae-pil (Philip Jaisohn), a politically active medical doctor married to a Caucasian woman, became the first Korean naturalized as an American citizen. He returned to Korea to advocate for independence from the Japanese, again faced exile, and finally returned to Korea after independence in 1945 to serve as an advisor to the U.S. Army. In 1904 he was followed to the United States by Syngman Rhee and other exiles, who became advocates for Korean independence and leaders in a growing Korean American community that expanded in Hawai'i and later California. In 1902 the first Korean laborers for Hawai'i's pineapple and sugar cane plantations arrived in Honolulu. This initial wave of immigrants included Christian converts who American missionaries had recruited to work on the Hawaiian plantations. Many of these Koreans relocated in California when their labor contracts with plantation owners in Hawai'i expired. Like other Asian immigrants, Koreans faced discrimination, and Korea was included as a "barred zone" from which immigration was prohibited in the Immigration Act of 1924. However, hundreds of Koreans continued to study at American universities in the 1920s and 1930s with Japanese passports.

The conflict in Korea, and a decade later, the Vietnam War, significantly and permanently altered U.S. immigration policy. Prohibition of Asian immigration ended with the Immigration and Nationality Act of 1952 (known as the McCarran-Walter Act). Although this legislation was less than what President Truman and liberals in Congress wanted, it did end restrictions on Asian immigration. Historian Roger Daniels has noted that, while intended to maintain the status quo, McCarran-Walter became "a vehicle for significant change in both the number of immigrants and the source of immigration."[33]

About this time, war brides and adopted Korean orphans began to enter the families of thousands of Americans. Because some of the Korean war brides had been saloon workers, and many of the orphans were of mixed race, all were subjected to social stigmas widespread in American society. Following the Immigration and Nationality Act of 1965, another and much larger wave of immigrants swelled the populations of Korean American communities, especially in and around Los Angeles, New York City, and Chicago. Whereas only fifteen thousand South Koreans immigrated to the United States prior to 1965, more than four hundred thousand arrived from South Korea in the 1960s and 1970s. (More than one hundred thousand immigrated to Canada, Australia, and Brazil during these two decades as well.) This new Korean American population was diverse economically and socially, with distinct differences in educational levels. This diversity gave these new Korean immigrants greater opportunities for mobility within the first generation, what could be called the "1.5 generation" (those who immigrated as children), and the "2.0 generation" (those of the second generation, born in the United States to immigrant parents). A third generation now appears almost fully integrated into the American mainstream and seems embarrassed, or at least uneasy, when identified as a "model minority."[34]

The adoption of Korean orphans began during the war when more than one hundred thousand children were left abandoned and homeless in South Korea. Some GIS and soldiers of the UNC became particularly fond of certain orphans they encountered near their military bases and informally recruited them to do odd jobs, run errands, or even serve in the Korean Augmentation to the United States Army. A few of these abandoned children were adopted by the foreign soldiers. One such adoptee is Mark Monahan. My family and I shared a house on the Yonsei University campus with him when I was in Seoul as a Fulbright lecturer in 1995. Born Chang Kil-yong in a small village in North Korea, he fled south when Chinese troops crossed the Yalu River the winter of 1950–51. Along with thousands of North Korean landed gentry, shop owners, Christians, and those who were simply fed up with the Soviet-backed government of Kim Il-sung, he left his mother at home, where she hoped to find her imprisoned husband, and he headed south. Upon his arrival on an island south of the 18th parallel, young Chang found himself drafted at age fifteen into the South Korean military where he served as a guerilla fighter along the front lines. He quickly became proficient in English, and a military acquaintance led to his adoption, university studies, and U.S. citizenship. He became Mark Monahan, earned a doctorate, married, and eventually returned to Korea where he taught on the faculty of Yonsei University and the University of Maryland's overseas program.[35] Mark Monahan's story is not unique, and the practice of adopting Korean infants and children soon spread well beyond military personnel and continued for decades after the armistice of 1953.

Since 1950 more than two hundred thousand children have been adopted out of South Korea, mostly to the United States, Canada, Australia, and European countries. As the number of orphans swelled from the war and the slow recovery of South Korea, so too did orphanages and adoptions. Orphanages, a relatively recent institution in the Confucian culture of Korea, saw their populations grow in number from 715 in 1951 to 11,319 in 1964. In 1953 an Evangelical lumberman in Oregon and his wife, Bertha, adopted eight orphan children from Korea and went on to establish Holt International, a Christian-based adoption agency that to this day arranges adoptions from Korea while endeavoring to assist troubled families and single mothers in coping with their issues. The agency has expanded its mission into China and other countries, even while weathering criticism and scandal over the questionable local sources from which some of the more recent adoptees are found. In Korea adoptions peaked in 1985; afterward, the nation's economic situation and social services improved. Also many of the wartime orphans reached adulthood. In 2019 only 259 children were adopted out of Korea, but it is without question that the Korean War served as a template for international adoptions in Vietnam and other countries troubled by revolution, poverty, and war.[36] Furthermore, the presence of the adoptees in the United States and other nations of the UNC reminded the host countries of the war's human cost and suffering, while perpetuating for decades a memory of Korea as a place of tragedy and need.

In recent years a remarkable number of Korean adoptees have gone to great lengths to reconnect with their birth families—often with the full support of their adoptive parents. And many of those who returned to the land of their birth have chosen to relocate and reside permanently in South Korea, even forming their own associations and support groups in Seoul and other cities. The numbers were such that the government in the ROK was forced to alter its residency laws to accommodate the returned adoptees, who arrived in their native land with little or no language skills while holding thoroughly Western views on individualism, women's rights, and social equality that conflicted sharply with traditional Confucian values.[37]

In the United States adoptees tend to be female, as Korea's traditional culture favors males. Although adoption of any children outside the extended family is not looked upon with favor, when adoption does occur, it is usually to fill a family's desperate need for a boy baby to carry on the family name. Thus there seemed to be more female babies available for adoption. Some of these female adoptees and their female contemporaries, born to Korean mothers who came to the United States as war brides, have proven to be bold in telling their stories. Both Grace Cho and Ji-Yeon Yuh write about their own mothers and their sister war brides having sold drinks and sex to U.S. military personnel, coming to terms with a new life in a foreign land, and ultimately reaching an accommodation with their independent, strong-willed, American-born daughters.[38] Other recent memories record first-person experiences of Korean American girls enduring, surviving, and flourishing in a culture that viewed them as foreign.[39] Doubtless these frank, explicit memoirs have assisted the transformation of the recent public memory of the Korean War in the United States and strengthened the prevailing understanding of that conflict as a brutal, costly, and tragic event that has proven over time to be preferable to allowing the fledgling Republic of Korea and its people to fall under domination by the authoritarian regime in the north.

Prior to U.S. immigration reform legislation in the mid-1960s that revised the McCarran-Walter Act, most Americans outside Hawai'i or the West Coast only encountered Koreans who were war brides or orphans who had been adopted by American parents. Many of the war brides were poorly educated and came from impoverished families, whose situations had been made even worse with the outbreak of the Korean War. For young women in unfortunate circumstances, working in bars and night clubs near military bases (and sometimes in prostitution), the opportunity for a move to the United States offered not only a means to survive but also an escape to a better future—or at least a new start in a wealthy, foreign land. The survival rate of these early wartime marriages was not high, as challenging language, custom, and dietary barriers had to be overcome, as well as local prejudices. Beginning in the 1980s marriages of South Korean women with American servicemen no longer occurred as often as they had when young, lonely, and sexually inexperienced draftees were sent abroad to grim military bases. In the 1980s the U.S. military sent older professional soldiers, many of them women, to serve in South Korea. These more mature servicemen and servicewomen were often married and frequently brought their families to bases that hosted schools and family services. Nevertheless, Korean women (and less often men) continued to marry U.S. service personnel and sometimes faced the same problems as the earlier Korean brides. However, by this time the Korean community in the United States had grown following immigration reform and had established support groups and churches to assist these women.[40] The Korean orphan population also benefited from the presence of a larger and more socially and economically diverse Korean American community after the 1960s, as many Korean professionals and their families arrived in the United States seeking refuge from the oppressive military regime in South Korea and better opportunities for their children.[41]

The label "model immigrant" grew out of an appreciation for the low crime rate among Koreans, as well as their work ethic and determined focus on education. The economic success of the Korean American community generated jealousy and outrage at times, notably the 1992 anti-Korean riots that broke out in Los Angeles.[42] Despite some resentment, as Korean immigrants became more numerous and prosperous, they became increasingly engaged in their communities, and through their civic groups and churches supported community projects. Their civic activities included local efforts to memorialize American involvement in the Korean War.

In addition to supporting the local efforts of American Korean War veterans to establish memorials to their fallen comrades and recognize the service of their own relatives, several Korean Americans have taken on their own remarkable projects, expending amazing amounts of time and financial resources. Perhaps no better example of this can be found than the project of Dr. Kim Byong Moon and his family.

THE KIM FAMILY

In the late 1990s Dr. Kim Byong Moon and his wife toured the campus of Massachusetts Institute of Technology (MIT). They were on campus for parents' day because their daughter was a new student at MIT. As they walked through the administration building, they were struck by the plaques honoring the university's students who had been called away for military service during the American wars of the twentieth century.

One of the plaques listed the names of eight MIT students killed in the Korean War. Soon afterward, the Kims visited Harvard University's campus and found a similar memorial plaque with the names of seventeen students lost in the Korean conflict. The Kims realized that their daughter was able to attend MIT only because a half-century earlier students from Boston's great universities had been called to fight and die in a land far from their homes. Dr. Kim was determined to do something to honor American Korean War veterans and the U.S. president whose decision sent soldiers to save South Korea.

Kim was raised in grinding poverty in the small port city of Kunsan, about a hundred miles south of Seoul, Korea. He was six years old in the summer of 1950 when the North Koreans invaded, and he remembered Korean People's Army (KPA) soldiers using the local school building as a headquarters until it was bombed by American airplanes. He remembered the North Korean soldiers were small; many appeared to be only teenagers as they rounded up the town's youngsters and taught them songs in praise of their leader, Kim Il-sung. Then in September the KPA quickly vanished. After they were gone, young Byong Moon heard many stories of executions and murders by the retreating Communists. The North Koreans were soon replaced by tall, often blue-eyed Americans (whom the locals called "utility pole soldiers" because of their height). The town's people were delighted that these American soldiers did not take their rice and kimchee; instead they actually shared their rations and handed out candy. While his crippled and widowed mother eked out a living selling fabric in nearby villages to support her six children, Byong Moon walked several miles to school each day, reciting his English vocabulary along the way. His diligent study paid off. Even after dropping out of school for two years because of the family's poverty, he was able to complete high school and secure a job as a "house boy," shining boots and running errands at a nearby U.S. Air Force base. There his hard work impressed the American officers, who provided forty dollars from a local charity to send him to night school at Myung Ji University in Seoul. His college degree led to an entry-level civil service position with Korea's Ministry of Education. There his exceptional ability in English opened many doors and eventually provided an opportunity to study for a doctorate in educational administration at the University of Minnesota.

During his years of study, Kim married, fathered two daughters, and became a Christian and devout Bible reader. One story in the New Testament held a special meaning for him. In it Jesus cures ten lepers, but only one returned to give thanks. "Were not all ten cleaned? Where are the other nine?" Jesus asks (Luke 17:17–18). Following his experience on the MIT campus, Dr. Kim was determined to be the one who gave thanks.[43]

To demonstrate his gratitude to American servicemen of the Korean War, Dr. Kim and his family organized an annual picnic and concert in Minneapolis for veterans and their families. The first was held in 2004 and funded almost entirely by the Kim family. Volunteers and modest donations helped, along with interest and visits from the Korean consul general in Chicago. Attendees, besides veterans of the war, their families, and descendants, included returned service personnel stationed in Korea to maintain the post-armistice peace. All were treated to a Korean American buffet with rice, kimchee, and fried squid served along with hot dogs and potato chips. Local Korean church choirs and professional Korean and American musicians volunteered their time and talent to entertain. The event expanded over the years, and in 2014 the group began awarding $500 scholarships annually to twelve selected descendants of Korean War veterans. Veterans and family members also have received a souvenir pair of socks, provided with the assistance of one of Dr. Kim's brothers who operated a textile business in Korea. The socks display both the American and Korean flags and the slogan "Appreciation for President Truman and Korean War Vets 1950–1953 The Kims." More than fifteen thousand pairs of socks have been given out to date. The idea for this unique gift came to Dr. Kim while listening to the story of a veteran of the Battle of Chosin Reservoir. He told Dr. Kim there were two enemies in that fierce December 1950 engagement—the Chinese and the cold. Frostbite was a common foe, and Dr. Kim learned that one U.S. Marine recovering at a hospital in Yokosuka, Japan, was admonished by a nurse for walking on his frostbitten feet. The U.S. Marine replied, "I want to walk while I still can. Doctors will amputate parts of both feet today."[44]

The Kims' appreciation for President Truman brought them to his home state of Missouri in October 2010 for a grand concert at the Kansas City Music Hall. The hall is located just a few city blocks from the site Harry Truman and his business partner, Eddie Jacobson, once operated a failed haberdashery and near the historic Muehlebach Hotel where Truman gave his public acceptance address the morning of his surprising victory in the 1948 presidential election. Thousands from Missouri and neighboring states attended the free program, which featured local Korean and American talent and the Korean Choir of Kansas City. The program received support from the Truman Institute for National and International Affairs and the Korean American Society of Greater Kansas City.[45]

Veterans and their families have reciprocated the Kims' generosity and gratitude. They often share personal stories of their service or memories of a loved one who served and then express how they find the programs and events focused on the Korean War to be healing experiences. Many relate the pride they feel when hearing positive news about South Korea and express concern for that country's continued safety. After veterans tell of their delight in seeing Korean teams do well in World Cup soccer, the Olympics, or women's golf tournaments, many say they purchase only Korean-made TVs and automobiles. Once a woman told Dr. Kim of the recent passing of her father, a veteran who was buried proudly wearing his Kim family souvenir socks.[46]

Commemorative programs and events as grand as those of the Kim family are rare but not unique. Documenting each instance of first-generation Korean American gratitude based on personal and highly subjective memories of emotionally charged wartime experiences would be an impossible task. Throughout the United States thousands of Korean Americans who still harbor nightmare memories of the war and near miraculous rescues from the forces of North Korea enthusiastically support efforts to erect local memorials to the service and sacrifice of American servicemen and women of the Korean War. Additionally, they volunteer to participate in all sorts of veteran appreciation events. Just a sampling of the local memorials and activities indicates that gratitude and appreciation within the Korean American population is vastly more common than anti-American protests. Appreciation for U.S. as well as United Nations (UN) assistance during and after the Korean War far outweighs any of the occasionally loud anti-American outbursts, which are easily put forth and require little long-term commitment or the expenditure of long hours and personal financial resources. No other American overseas military engagement has earned the degree of unified gratitude from an immigrant population as the Korean War. The positive memory of the United States in the war for their native land appears likely to be a legacy inherited by the next generation of Korean Americans, and families like the Kims of Minnesota seem determined to make this happen.

DIVERSITY AND SAMENESS

Throughout the United States the ways in which the Korean War has been remembered and memorialized are creative and numerous. Memorials and activities can be found in every corner of the United States, and these differ in many ways. However, elements of memorialization efforts related to the Korean War share common characteristics. These include a sense of confusion about the war's cause, its place in the pantheon of U.S. wars, and its continuing status. Additionally, the varied and creative forms of memorials now found across the U.S. landscape have in common a recent starting date, as most came about only after the outpouring of local and national movements to memorialize the Vietnam War in the 1980s. Their erection also followed the spectacular rise of the Republic of Korea on the world stage due to the success of the 1988 Olympics in Seoul. South Korea's emergence appears to have provided an almost tangible justification for the horrors of 1950–53. Veterans and families of the fallen could now feel a sense of pride and accomplishment. The war in Korea could now be judged as something of a victory. Indeed, the ROK was saved, accomplishing the original UN mandate. And this new awareness of the Korean War's place in the history of the Cold War was almost everywhere enhanced by the outpouring of support from within local Korean American communities now deeply integrated into the fabric of American society.

Memorialization of war in the United States usually involves the resolution of conflicting design ideas and funding challenges, as well as social and political concerns. Reaching consensus involves debate and compromise. The final approval of a project requires agreement among various interest groups in a democratic society, including veterans and their families, local government officials and agencies, funders, and neighborhood residents who might be concerned about such mundane issues as the impact a proposed memorial might have on traffic flow and parking. Participants, victims, and survivors of war retain strong personal emotions about historical events, while political office holders and government officials seek approval and consensus. As a result, any public representation of something as powerful as a war must be addressed with sensitivity and care. Out of necessity a museum exhibit, war memorial, commemorative ceremony, or public program must be kept ambiguous enough to satisfy various factions in competition or disagreement.[47] For the historical community, much can be learned about a society from examining how it commemorates and remembers a war, even though bottom-up, grassroots, or "people" history may be overly simplistic and lacking in nuanced analysis of factual information. We can learn from the scores of Korean War memorials across the varied landscape of the United States that Americans now view the Korean conflict as a real war and a war deserving to be remembered as a victory. It is also possible to trace and document the process through which the first-generation Korean American community integrated itself into the mainstream of American society through their involvement—both individually and through organizations like churches and businesses—in local endeavors to honor the memory and service of Korean War veterans.

Grassroot efforts at memorialization do not necessarily pay much attention to careful historical analysis by academics. Veterans, their families, and survivors of warfare tend to have a selective, narrow, and focused understanding of the war they experienced; their interest in memorialization is largely more emotional and heartfelt than driven by a desire to assess the war's causes, politics, international complexities, and diplomatic wrangling. The losses of the "other side" are not of concern. For the veterans and their families, these memorials serve as a place of remembrance of loss and a site where one can find solace and comfort. Likewise, civilians who experienced the trauma of warfare and found refuge in a foreign land hold memories that are highly personal, emotionally charged, and seldom objective. For critical historical narrative and academic analysis, those interested in such things should look elsewhere.

INDEPENDENCE, MISSOURI

The most telling and memorable artifact in the Harry S. Truman Presidential Library's Korean War exhibit remains a Purple Heart medal, displayed along with a hand-printed letter to former President Truman from a grieving father. Private first class George C. Banning was a young soldier killed in combat just weeks before the signing of the armistice at Panmunjom in July, 1953. Following his son's death, Private Banning's father wrote:

Nursery Rd
New Canaan
Conn.

Mr. Truman,

As you have been directly responsible for the loss of our son's life in Korea, you might as well keep this emblem on display in your trophy room, as a memory of one of your historic deeds.

Our major regret at this time is that your daughter was not there to receive the same treatment as our son received in Korea.

Signed,
William Banning

Curators at his presidential library discovered the medal and letter while processing the former president's papers following his death on December 26, 1972. Both items were found in the letter drawer of the desk in his "working office" centered in the library where the former president spent most weekdays throughout his retirement. For nearly twenty years Truman kept the medal and letter close.[48] As he reflected on what he considered the most difficult decision of his presidency, there is no way of knowing just how frequently Truman looked at the medal and Mr. Banning's letter.

Presidential libraries in the United States serve as centers for serious research and scholarship as well as memorials and sites of remembrance. The thirteen institutions within the system of the National Archives and Records Administration (NARA) hold the official records of each president's administration; private papers; personal artifacts of the president, his family, and associates; and collections of materials related to his life and times. The Harry S. Truman Library in Independence, Missouri, is located just a few blocks from Truman's boyhood homes, the neighborhood drugstore where he got his first job, the church where he attended Sunday school and met a little blonde girl who would become his wife a quarter century later, and the home on Delaware Street where he lived for more than fifty years. President Truman and his wife and daughter are buried in the library's courtyard, and, like other presidential libraries, the building and grounds serve as a monument to the president. The library is both a site for events and public programs and a place for public education with interpretive exhibits, supported by texts and videos, displaying artifacts related to the president's career and achievements. The exhibits, official ceremonies, and public programs are designed to be commemorative, thoughtful, and celebratory. In addition, at the Truman library there is an effort to be accurate and balanced in presenting the president's story, while providing the public with sound history and analysis of President Truman's most controversial decisions.

A personal disappointment of my thirteen-year tenure as director of the Harry S. Truman Presidential Library was a failure to significantly enhance the exhibits on the Korean War in the section of the library dedicated to Truman's presidential years. I arrived at the library in September 2001 just as a $12-million "Classroom for Democracy" capital campaign was nearing completion and a major renovation of the entire facility was entering its final months. Tractors were moving mounds of dirt in the building's courtyard, many of the interior spaces were completely gutted, and installations of planned exhibits on the Truman presidency with high-tech, state-of-the-art exhibits were just beginning. Because the NARA selection process for a new director had taken a full nine months longer than expected (a common problem in NARA personnel issues, I would soon discover), I came on the job with the urgent need to get the new construction completed, exhibits installed, and innovative educational programming up and running. A rededication ceremony was set for just three months after I took office, and expectations among the major donors and the public were high.

There was no time to rewrite a more comprehensive exhibition script on the Korean War—or Truman's civil rights agenda and his role in the establishment of the United Nations, which were also skimpy, in my judgment. The reopening of the library in December 2001 was hailed as a great success, and the educational programs planned and designed under the creative and energetic leadership of my predecessor, Larry Hackman, became models for other presidential libraries. However for a variety of reasons there was little I could achieve in reworking the Korean War section of our exhibits on Truman's presidency. In fact, it took several years following the rededication event just to complete the building renovations and initiate all the ambitious educational programs called for in the Classroom for Democracy campaign I had inherited. In addition, with the board of the Truman Library Institute, we launched a mini campaign to raise even more funding to complete a new gallery to allow public access to and interpretation of President Truman's "working office"—a project on the original renovation wish list but one neither funded nor set in motion with an agreed-upon design.[49]

In 2008 in the midst of the economic meltdown of the "Great Recession," we opened a new "working office" addition with visitor viewing space and interactive exhibits featuring the president's final two decades as "Mr. Citizen." During my tenure as director, I did what was possible to begin the process of advancing the Truman library as a principal location for the study of the Korean War and for greater public understanding of that conflict. Through conferences, programs on C-SPAN, publications, and special events (often supported by the local Korean American community), as well as partnerships with universities in the United States and the ROK, I believe there was as much programming on the Korean War sponsored by the Truman library in the first decade of the twenty-first century as anywhere else in the world. Every Korean consul general from the Chicago region visited at least once during his posting in the Windy City, and ambassadors from the ROK to the United States also visited for special programs. But a major new exhibit on the Korean War at the facility in Independence, Missouri, had to wait for my successor, who successfully completed a major, $22-million update of the library's exhibits with significant private sector support from the Truman Library Institute. Likewise, in spite of my best efforts, the library's acquisitions of the major collections of the Center for the Study of the Korean War (CSKW) and the Korean War National Museum were finalized only after my retirement.

I would like to think that my work at President Truman's library established an environment for current and future advances. Under the leadership of my able successor, Dr. Kurt Graham, the collections of the CSKW and the Korean War National Museum are now safely housed at the library, and there is more out there to be acquired on the war, its aftermath, and the continuing strife on the Korean Peninsula. Already the materials from recent acquisitions have enhanced the new Korean War exhibits at the library following a major renovation of the building and its exhibition galleries. Artifacts from the defunct Korean War National Museum and letters, postcards, photos, and drawings from soldiers once held in the CSKW collection now add to the visitor experience.[50]

President Truman's library still enjoys an uncommon status among NARA facilities with potential for continuing financial support from a 501(c)(3) foundation dedicated solely to assisting the library (Truman Institute for National and International Affairs).[51] If continued, this administrative relationship should enable the library to hold the status as a special, premier place for subsequent acquisitions, research, and public programming in the decades ahead, as the unended war in Korea continues, and new history of the war is constantly generated.

A POSTSCRIPT

Many years of experience on the practical side in the field of public history leaves me concerned about the long-term maintenance and conservation of the plethora of well-intentioned Korean War monuments that have arisen in communities across the United States. During the planning and construction of a memorial, negotiations involving advocacy groups, financial sponsors, patriotic organizations, academic historians, university administrators, government regulators, and various ethnic and religious societies all share an enthusiasm and common goal. Despite differences, they agree on a need to do something for an event or cause that requires remembrance, and a satisfactory solution is usually achieved through compromise, pressure, and eventually a realistic coming to terms with financial restraints and other matters. However, for completed monuments and memorials, along with rescued historic sites, enthusiasm tends to diminish as time moves along and those responsible for the project pass from the scene.

Succeeding generations may question the value of or have no interest in the event being commemorated and remembered, while new and more urgent issues demand their attention. Many long and contentious hours in the legislative hearing rooms of state capitols, county courthouses, and city halls can be spent wrestling with matters of jurisdiction and responsibility for ongoing (necessary but unglamorous) maintenance and repairs. (I know because I've spent many hours on such matters.) Usually these come to the attention of public agencies only after periods of neglect have left the item in question in dire need of extensive and costly renovations and at times when financially strapped public agencies are already underfunded with a huge backlog of delayed maintenance projects. In some cases—for example the CSKW and Korean War National

Museum collections, for which a safe haven has been found at the Truman library—one can reasonably assume that proper care will be permanently provided. However, important collections on the Korean War still need a secure home, and many recently dedicated sites of remembrance may face abandonment within a few decades. Will there be support for these worthy sites of remembrance as those veterans and their families who caused the numerous monuments and memorials to come into existence pass from the scene? Or will the 1950–53 conflict in Korea become a truly forgotten war?

In the American remembrance of the Korean War, it may well be that the process of memorialization has proven to be more important than the scores of edifices produced and left standing in public spaces. Throughout the United States, Korean War memorials tend to be, for the most part, unimaginative, bland, and obviously designed to avoid controversy. Paying respect to current notions of diversity and inclusiveness, Korean War memorials do not honor individual leaders. No generals or presidents can be found standing anywhere other than their own libraries. Instead, Korean War memorials follow recent trends and consist of realistic art depicting common soldiers engaged in routine tasks associated with military services. Soldiers of clearly differing races, ethnicities, and genders are depicted huddled around campfires, on patrol, or tending to wounded comrades. Scenes of violent action are never rendered—nor is death. Even abstract themes, such as peace and humanity, are presented with realistic images: an angelic young woman symbolizes peace (Vancouver, British Columbia) or four cranes represent the common humanity shared by the principal combatant nations on the Korean Peninsula (University of Kansas at Lawrence). And frequently included is some form of wall of remembrance, a variation of the Vietnam Veterans Memorial in Washington DC, with the names of the fallen and MIAs carved in stone or listed on a bronze plaque. With few exceptions these sites of remembrance reflect planning and execution to satisfy the aspirations, concerns, artistic tastes, and budget limitations of veterans and their families, community leaders, elected officials, and a plethora of governing boards and commissions. The memorials present "Middle America" in a sort of regression to the mean. At the same time it is apparent to anyone who looks for the names of planners, donors, and funders for their recent landmarks that the local Korean American community played a prominent role. While these memorials fulfill the worthy purpose of providing comfort and solace to those most impacted by the war and serve to offer a measure of awareness and public education about the war, few if any are likely to be considered by future generations as inspirational or exceptionally noteworthy for their artistic value. Yet the memorials to the veterans of the Korean War do fulfill their mission, and the collaborative effort, even when contentious, to envision, plan, fund, erect, and dedicate these mnemonic sites have had a healing and unifying effect throughout the country on those involved in the process.

Nowhere is the complex nature of the American memorialization process more evident than in the creation of the Vietnam Veterans Memorial on the National Mall in Washington DC.

Fig. 1. Gen. Douglas MacArthur's statue overlooks Incheon Harbor where the landing of United Nations Command (UNC) forces on September 15, 1950, changed the course of the war. Republic of Korea veteran and survivor of the Incheon Landing, Rhee Sun-bak, pays his respects. (Author's photo)

Fig. 2. (*opposite top*) Originally planned as a Vietnam veterans memorial, the elegant, serpentine memorial on the grounds of the Hawaiʻi state capitol in Honolulu was expanded, as an afterthought, to honor veterans of both Vietnam and Korea. (Author's photo)

Fig. 3. (*opposite bottom*) The Korean War Veterans Memorial (KWVM) on the National Mall in Washington DC, was dedicated in 1995, following a contentious ten-year process. Both veterans and planners were determined to have a traditional yet inclusive memorial that would avoid the public criticism that surrounded the abstract design of Maya Lin's Vietnam Veterans Memorial. (Author's photo)

Fig. 4. The lonely kiosk adjacent to the KWVM on the National Mall provided names and information about U.S. service personnel lost in the Korean War, but the kiosk did not offer the emotional appeal of the Vietnam memorial's stark wall of names. (Author's photo)

Outstanding Leadership and Brilliant Victory

KOREA PICTORIAL, Pyongyang, DPRK
1993

Fig. 5. In the English-language guide to the Victorious Fatherland Liberation War Museum in Pyongyang, the Democratic People's Republic of Korea claims the war was a "brilliant victory" that followed "a surprise armed invasion" by the United States and the South Korean puppet state. Kim Il-sung is credited with leading a patriotic defense of the nation with little outside support. (Author's photo)

Fig. 6. The USS *Pueblo*, captured by the North Koreans in 1968, is on display in Pyongyang as a trophy of the continuing conflict on the Korean Peninsula. (Wikimedia Commons, Laika ac from the United States)

Fig. 7. The War Memorial of Korea in Seoul stresses the international support and United Nations (UN) recognition provided to the ROK during the Korean War. Note the flags of the UN member states that assisted South Korea during the 1950–53 conflict on prominent display. (Author's photo)

Fig. 8. The statue of two brothers at the entrance to the grounds of the War Memorial of Korea depicts the southern brother as larger, stronger, and better armed than his sibling from the north. (Author's photo)

Fig. 9. (*opposite top*) Plaques along the entrance to the War Memorial of Korea display the names of the thousands of UNC soldiers killed in the defense of the ROK. (Author's photo)

Fig. 10. (*opposite bottom*) The author meets with Gen. Paik Sun-yup in his office on June 8, 2011, at the War Memorial of Korea to discuss the planning of the museum and its message of peace and reconciliation. (Author's photo)

Fig. 11. The United Nations Cemetery in Pusan, South Korea, is a beautifully maintained thirty-five-acre site. Graves in twenty-two sections designated by nationalities are a clear reminder of the international nature of the Korean War. (Author's photo)

Fig. 12. (*opposite top*) A quiet 2017 anti-American protest in Seoul, South Korea, in the months prior to President Trump's visits with the North Korean leader. (Author's photo)

Fig. 13. (*opposite bottom*)An aging U.S. veteran of the Korean War on a 2016 revisit to South Korea is escorted on the campus of the ROK Military Academy by young army officers. The generous ROK government program for U.S. and UNC soldiers ended in 2020 because of the COVID-19 pandemic and the frail health of most surviving veterans. (Author's photo)

NURSERY RD
NEW CANAAN
CONN.

MR. TRUMAN

AS YOU HAVE BEEN DIRECTLY RESPONSIBLE FOR THE LOSS OF OUR SON'S LIFE IN KOREA, YOU MIGHT JUST AS WELL KEEP THIS EMBLEM ON DISPLAY IN YOUR TROPHY ROOM, AS A MEMORY OF ONE OF YOUR HISTORIC DEEDS.

OUR MAJOR REGRET AT THIS TIME IS THAT YOUR DAUGHTER WAS NOT THERE TO RECEIVE THE SAME TREATMENT AS OUR SON RECEIVED IN KOREA.

SINGED

William Banning

Fig. 14. This Purple Heart medal and the letter from a grieving father were discovered by curators at the Truman Presidential Library in the former president's desk following his death in 1972. (Photo by Phil Licata, courtesy of Harry S. Truman Library)

5 | The Korean War Veterans Memorial

The Korean War Veterans Memorial on the National Mall in Washington DC, came about as the American popular memory of the Korean War was undergoing rapid change. In the 1980s as South Korea suddenly emerged from a long period of military dictatorship into a thriving democracy, people in the United States began to feel a new sense of pride and accomplishment about the long-misunderstood war in Korea. Nevertheless the memorialization project faced serious challenges. A fractious process finally led to the dedication of a striking and popular monument in July 1995. However, critics, including the Korean War Veterans Association (KWVA), remained unsatisfied.

On a hot and muggy July afternoon in 1995, an aging Korean War veteran stood patiently among the huge crowd gathered on the National Mall in Washington DC. He quietly observed the dedication of the long-delayed Korean War Veterans Memorial located near the Lincoln Memorial. A veteran of World War II as well as Korea, Gen. William C. Westmoreland was best known to the American public as the commander of more than a half million soldiers in the Vietnam War from 1964 to 1968. Among the youngest U.S. Army generals in the post–World War II era (he achieved the rank of brigadier general at age thirty-eight), during the Korean War "Westy" (as his West Point classmates called him) commanded the acclaimed 101st Airborne Division before returning home to serve as commandant of the U.S. Military Academy. Following the dedication ceremony, the old general, then in his eighties, was overheard sharing his assessment of the new memorial with a U.S. Marine Corps veteran. "This is beautiful," he said, just before a torrential downpour scattered the crowd. But the heavy rainfall and oppressive heat deterred neither General Westmoreland nor the other elderly veterans, who lingered long after the day's formalities had ended.[1]

In the United States, commemoration of wars and the service of those who fought is often instigated and funded by the veterans of conflicts, and not until the 1980s did Korean War veterans begin to influence public opinion about the conflict that had halted with an uncertain armistice thirty years earlier. They were inspired by the amazing success of the younger generation of Vietnam War veterans in securing a remarkable memorial on the National Mall in Washington DC, which for two hundred years displayed no monument to warfare or veterans. Once the precedent had been set, Korean War veterans quickly saw their opportunity to achieve a measure of national public recognition in Washington DC, for their service and sacrifice in a conflict they felt was overlooked and misunderstood by the American public. The veterans' timing would prove propitious, as the Republic of Korea was about to emerge on the world stage as a vibrant, stable democracy with a powerful and dynamic economy. South Korea's success stood in stark contrast to its misgoverned, isolated, impoverished, and troublesome counterpart to its north, the Democratic People's Republic of Korea. The rise of the ROK was becoming obvious to all, giving U.S. Korean War veterans a sense of pride previously unknown to them. In addition, the democratically elected leadership of the Republic of Korea, major South Korean corporations, and thousands of grateful Korean Americans were now positioned to assist in efforts to remember and memorialize the service of U.S. military personnel.

Whatever the causes or outcome of a war, the American people have come to feel compelled to commemorate it with monuments in the nation's capital. Nonetheless Korea presented unique challenges to those seeking to memorialize a conflict (not yet officially declared a war) that was unpopular at the time it was fought and remained misunderstood by the American public. Moreover, the war had never officially ended, and it remained an ongoing and unsettled struggle for supremacy on the Korean Peninsula with an ultimate outcome far from certain. Even wars with generally agreed upon histories are not readily memorialized in ways that always satisfy the public or achieve a broad popular acceptance. As the Korean War was not even over, planners of the Korean War Veterans Memorial in Washington DC, were forced to confront the task of memorializing an overlooked, inconclusive, and unsettled war put to rest after only an armistice quieted major military operations on the faraway land.

In the pluralistic society and federated system of the United States, many political and societal interests must be taken into account in planning and creating memorials depicting war and sacrifices of veterans. As a result, memorializing warfare in the United States has a long and contentious history. Following the Civil War, the federal government engaged in actively creating monuments, preserving battlefields, and establishing cemeteries for veterans while assigning national holidays to be observed by the public. Washington's federal efforts sought to shape a public memory of the Civil War as well as earlier conflicts, fully aware that, at the same time, local and state traditions and sensitivities had to be considered. For example, the system of Civil War cemeteries allowed for the burial of both Union and Confederate soldiers and the erection of monuments to the deeds of rebellious Confederate military units along with those fighting to preserve the Union.[2] Nevertheless, this policy of inclusion and generosity failed to settle matters. Monuments to Confederate leaders erected in the post-Reconstruction era helped legitimize Jim Crow laws and perpetuate the myth that the Civil War was a heroic "lost cause" to defend states' rights rather than an effort to preserve the institution of slavery. These sites of memorialization tell us more about the South in the decades following the Civil War than they do about the war itself, and to this day the Civil War stirs passions beyond any other conflict in American history.

Beginning in the mid-twentieth century, Americans learned to commemorate wars with ever greater diversity. Artistic renderings and ceremonial events reflected changes in the U.S. understanding of wars, their focus on soldiers and veterans, and an ever-increasing awareness of the diverse ethnicity of U.S. society and its armed forces. With little public opposition, even the meanings of certain national holidays were altered to become more inclusive. For example Armistice Day was changed to Veterans Day following World War I, becoming a day of remembrance to recognize the service of all veterans rather than just those who died in World War I. Not all memorial efforts lent themselves to easy resolution, however. Often public memory and efforts at commemoration of past wars remain contested, and political compromise has proven elusive. Observers of military memorials note that how Americans come to understand the history of a particular war in their national consciousness and culture is as important as the experience of fighting the war itself.[3]

There exists no better example of this than the Vietnam Veterans Memorial on the National Mall in Washington DC. Five years after the last American soldiers evacuated Saigon in April 1975, Vietnam War veterans began to seek a memorial on the National Mall. Led by Vietnam veteran Jan Scruggs and due to the tireless efforts of many vets, a successful campaign raised money from private sources to fund a memorial. Maya Lin's stunning abstract design led to the creation of one of the most beloved shrines in the nation's capital. But the path from design to completion was not without considerable public controversy. The huge, black, polished granite, V-shaped wall displaying the names of the nearly sixty thousand service members who died or were unaccounted for in the conflict between 1959 and 1975 was termed "Orwellian glop" in the pages of the conservative *National Review*. Billionaire businessman and future presidential candidate H. Ross Perot called it a "wailing wall," and another conservative critic considered it a "black gash of shame and sorrow." Pres. Ronald Reagan's secretary of the interior James Watt even refused to allow construction of the wall until a traditional, heroic statuary depicting three soldiers (two men and a woman) was planned to satisfy military "hawks" and political conservatives. Yet in the words of one expert observer, the completed memorial wall "remains remarkable for the degree to which it has bridged the differences and divisions within the nation." Indeed, decades after its opening on November 13, 1982, at a "National Salute to Vietnam Veterans" (two years later the *Three Soldiers* addition was formally dedicated), the stark, powerful wall continues to inspire deep emotions from millions of visitors along with veterans, their families, and friends. In many instances they return year after year.[4]

While the official unveiling of the Vietnam Veterans Memorial helped heal the nation's wounds from that tragic and divisive conflict, the event also provided inspiration to Korean War veterans for the placement of a memorial to their service on the National Mall. The very year the Vietnam Veterans Memorial was dedicated, Korean War veterans saw a bill for a Korean War memorial introduced in Congress only to die in committee. However, a renewed effort in 1985 gained traction. Months earlier the KWVA had come into existence, and this group would prove essential in rallying support for the memorial and assisting in the fundraising efforts.[5]

When Rep. James Florio (D-NJ) introduced legislation to authorize a Korean War veterans memorial, his effort had the support of 143 cosponsors. In the Senate, Sen. William Lester Armstrong (R-CO) introduced a bill to authorize the memorial to Korean veterans with the enthusiastic backing of four Korean War veterans then serving in the U.S. Senate: John Chafee (R-RI), John Glenn (D-OH), Warren Rudman (R-NH), and John Warner (R-VA). After the legislation passed both houses of Congress with overwhelming support, President Reagan signed it into law on October 28, 1986.[6] The first step on the long road to creating a national memorial on the Mall had been taken. Now would come the hard part—the struggle to agree on a design and complete construction of the monument. The process would last three times longer than the 1950–53 conflict on the Korean Peninsula. The new legislation authorized the American Battle and Monuments Commission (ABMC) to build a memorial on U.S. government land in or near Washington DC, and called for the president to appoint a Korean War Veterans Advisory Board to recommend the site and design of the memorial and to encourage private donations to fund the project. It became clear from the beginning that, following the Vietnam memorial model, no government funding would be provided for design and construction of the memorial for Korean War veterans.

Even before the enactment of legislation authorizing a veterans memorial, Hal Barker, son of a Korean War veteran, played a key role in the launch of the Korean War Memorial Trust Fund. This followed Barker's brief and unfortunate relationship in the early 1980s with a shady operation headed by Korean American woman Chayon Kim and involving several ultraconservative political operatives who advocated a memorial featuring Gen. Douglas MacArthur. After a series of exposés in the *Baltimore Sun*, Barker disassociated himself from that group, but his passion for a Korean War memorial remained. Proud of his father's heroic service as a helicopter pilot during the Korean War—for which he was awarded a Silver Star for gallantry in an unsuccessful attempt to rescue a downed fighter pilot—Hal and his brother Ted started raising money. Barker also had a hand in securing passage of the legislation authorizing the Korean monument. His letter to Hollywood actor and film director Clint Eastwood questioning the historical accuracy of the script for the 1986 movie *Heartbreak Ridge* led to a fortuitous relationship. Eastwood, a Korean War-era veteran who had been stateside during his army service, was impressed by Barker's enthusiasm. Eastwood sent a letter to Sen. Malcom Wallop (R-WY) and made a phone call to President Reagan to move ahead legislative action at a critical time in the summer of 1986. Earlier Barker's own modest check for ten dollars (in honor of Art DeLacy, the pilot his father could not save from capture by the North Koreans) served as the initial gift.[7]

The establishment of the Korean War Memorial Trust Fund eventually led to the raising of more than $17 million. For the most part funding came from small donations. American Legion posts and their members were particularly helpful. Corporate donations were also important. Chrysler Corporation, Ford Motor Company, and DuPont contributed $25,000 each for the memorial. However, American companies were far less generous than their South Korean counterparts, who were especially supportive. Altogether Korean corporations contributed about $2.5 million, with Hyundai of Korea providing $500,000 early on. Individual Koreans also contributed large sums, with Sung Hak Baik and Yong Kim each contributing $250,000 and Kyupin Philip Hwang sending in $50,000.[8] The memorial for Korean War veterans would not have been possible without the support of corporate donors from the Republic of Korea.

The KWVA worked in coordination with the Korean War Veterans Advisory Board, employing a variety of activities to raise money. The budget for the project estimated design and construction costs at $17,298,737, with $250,000 set aside for groundbreaking and dedication ceremonies. The board projected that funding would consist of a $1,000,000 federal appropriation for administrative costs, $17,818,000 in contributions, and $6,000,000 in commemorative coin sales. The U.S. Treasury Department issued a commemorative silver dollar (which sold for thirty dollars) and secured several million dollars for the cause. By early 1992 more than $18,000,000 was on hand, enough for the construction of the project to move forward.[9] Even though the board had anticipated a significant surplus to create an endowment for maintenance, cost overruns eliminated any leftover funding.

As the funding effort gained momentum, the advisory board held its first meeting on September 23, 1987. In response to an initial call from the board, more than five hundred artists submitted designs. As usual in such endeavors, differing opinions among those involved in selecting the design led to controversy. Several of the early plans could be easily dismissed for financial or conceptual reasons. But even before the board called for submissions, ideas had begun pouring in. Among the earliest was an extraordinarily ambitious plan put forth in September 1987 by the Mosquitoes, a well-organized veterans group of the 6147th Tactical Control Group. Drawings by James Martin and Lt. Col. Sidney Johnson (USAF Ret.) provided fantastic renderings for a Korean War veterans memorial library at a cost of $63,423,000. The planners of this grand version of a memorial suggested donations of $1,000 for each of the servicemen and servicewomen killed or listed as missing in action (MIA). The group noted that "those who served in the Korean War have been waiting thirty-five years for the nation's tribute to their sacrifice and service to the cause of freedom." The huge complex the Mosquitoes proposed would have included an amphitheater, conference rooms, and offices, as well as a library and archive. The completed project would have books, films, and military records (somehow acquired from both government and private sources) for research purposes and to educate younger generations. Names of the fallen were to be "perpetually enshrined" on the exterior walls of the massive structure, which would have as its centerpiece a forty-two-feet-wide dome. Early on, board member Col. Conrad Hausman (Ret.) echoed the call for all veterans to support plans for a memorial that "would radiate a message that is at once inspirational in context and timeless in meaning . . . and present renewable living aspects of hope, honor, and service."[10] The Mosquitoes' grandiose plan failed to advance, however, and more modest and realistic concepts were considered.

The advisory board would prove to be a relentless force in seeing the memorial through to completion. The members soldiered on through missteps, delays, and disagreements over design issues and legal challenges. All of the board members were Korean War veterans, and its first chair was Gen. Richard Stilwell (Ret.), who had served in the 1970s as commander in chief of the United Nations Command (UNC) in Korea and as commanding general of the U.S. Eighth Army. In addition, Stilwell had previously commanded an infantry regiment during the Korean War. Retired U.S. Marine Corps general and Congressional Medal of Honor recipient Raymond Davis served as deputy chairman. Among the board's members, Col. Rosemary McCarthy, a nurse who had seen duty as a young lieutenant in Korea in a surgical hospital, and Col. William Weber, who as a captain in the 187th Airborne Regiment Combat Team had lost both an arm and a leg, exemplified the varied Korean War experiences of the original advisory board membership. Robert Hansen was named the board's director.[11]

Where to place the memorial presented the advisory board with an early challenge. Board members wanted a highly visible location, and the National Mall, already becoming overcrowded with new monuments and memorials, was a primary objective. The Commemorative Works Act adopted by Congress in 1986 with the intention of halting the placement of additional monuments on the National Mall could neither deter nor withstand pressure from veterans, ethnic minorities, and women's groups; proliferation on the Mall ensued. The advisory board identified a remaining location at the western end of the Mall known as Ash Woods. The site occupied an area in the shadow of the Lincoln Memorial, just across the reflecting pool from the Vietnam Veterans Memorial. Ash Woods was also adjacent to the location where the memorial to Franklin D. Roosevelt was planned. (The FDR memorial was dedicated in 1997 after forty years in development.) However, this site was reclaimed land resulting from the U.S. Army Corps of Engineers dredging and landfill efforts in the late nineteenth century. Any memorial on this site's unstable soil would require steel-reinforced concrete piers. (The nearby Lincoln Memorial sits on 122 such piers driven as much as sixty feet into bedrock.) The necessary underpinning for any sizable structure at Ash Woods would add significantly to its cost. Undeterred, the advisory board agreed with Colonel Weber's statement: "We didn't want an unseen memorial for a forgotten war."[12] Putting aside the problems associated with the Ash Woods site, the board was determined to secure this location—the design and cost would have to conform.

Once Ash Woods was identified as the memorial's place on the Mall, the board focused on the design competition, clearly stating to competitors that honoring the men and women who fought in Korea would be the main theme of the memorial. The hundreds of responses to the design competition provided the board with enough entries to occupy months of review and consultation with architects and artists specializing in memorials. Early in the process, board members' ideas for the memorial included depictions of patriotism and sacrifice, a traditional representational monument, a tribute to General MacArthur, and an emphasis on the international character of the UNC. At some point the recognition of General MacArthur's leadership was quietly discarded. Eventually the advisory board selected a design submitted by an architectural team from Pennsylvania State University. Calling itself BL3, the team consisted of Veronica Burns Lucas, John Paul Lucas, Don Leon, and Eliza Penny-packer Oberholtzer. Their entry called for thirty-eight U.S. soldiers (the number reflected the 38th parallel) advancing in a V formation toward an American flag. The figures, dressed in combat gear and carrying various weapons of the Korean War era, were to be formed from gray Vermont granite. To the side of the advancing soldiers would be a long, black wall with relief sculptures depicting scenes of servicemen and servicewomen from all branches of the armed forces, representing diverse ethnicities and engaged in various wartime activities. Pres. George H. W. Bush hosted an unveiling ceremony in the White House Rose Garden to present the winning design to the public on Flag Day, June 14, 1989. Surrounded by Korean War veterans and their families, the president proclaimed the Korean War to be "an American victory that remains too little appreciated and understood."[13]

The White House event and the publicity surrounding the planned memorial opened the winning design to the usual controversies that accompany new monuments and memorials in the nation's capital—especially those high-profile monuments seeking prominent locations on the Mall. About this same time, the Dwight D. Eisenhower Memorial, Vietnam Veterans Memorial, and World War II Memorial all endured similar criticism. The advisory board insisted on more realism in the figures of the soldiers and at least the indication of combat action—although the members made it clear that they did not want to glorify war. Rather than abstract figures of granite, the advisory board called for the figures to be made of stainless steel to provide more realistic detail. The U.S. Commission of Fine Arts (CFA) and the National Capital Planning Commission (NCPC) both expressed serious concerns, and the board had to consider the power these organizations held over new developments. J. Carter Brown, director of the National Gallery of Art and CFA chair, would prove to be a particularly strong voice on overall design issues. In general CFA members considered the original design to be lacking "concentration, condensation, containment, and focus."[14]

In the board's review process, one member expressed concern over the height and length of the proposed wall, while another considered the depiction of the soldiers being hit by enemy fire as too dramatic and gruesome. Various critics viewed the memorial's design as too militaristic. In their effort to gain final approval of the memorial's design, the advisory board hired Cooper-Lecky Architects, the Washington DC, firm that had constructed the Vietnam memorial, to oversee the building of the memorial and create a landscape design for the 2.2-acre Ash Woods site. All the criticism led to numerous compromises and significant changes in the original design. Excluded from the redesign process, the competition winners expressed frustration and anger. The Penn State team had based their design on an iconic David Douglas Duncan photograph and felt the new architects, Cooper-Lecky, had overly romanticized the original concept, turning it into "a GI Joe battle scene" with soldiers in action, shooting and being shot. Cooper-Lecky viewed the Penn State architects as "unreasonable" and "stubborn." But the board agreed to the proposed changes, as did the ABMC. However, the alterations were so extensive that the BL3 team withdrew from the project altogether and later filed a lawsuit. The board and its director, however, held little sympathy for the BL3 group and their creative concerns. Expressing his displeasure with the prizewinning BL3 team and what he considered their uncompromising attitude, Robert Hansen stated, "They got their $20,000. Now it's property of the United States government."[15]

From their viewpoint and experience with the Vietnam Veterans Memorial, the Cooper-Lecky team understood that the presidentially appointed board was determined to avoid the controversy that had surrounded the Vietnam memorial selection process. They knew this client had conservative tastes and tended to appreciate conventional and realistic designs. "Abstraction was not on their agenda," they noted, viewing the original design concept as flawed as it grew more abstract and allegorical.[16] Serving five years as both architects and coordinators on the project, the Cooper-Lecky group accepted that the congressional mandate stipulated a design to recognize diversity in the U.S. armed services, prisoners of war (POWs) and MIAs, and the addition of women and support personnel. The challenge for Cooper-Lecky was clear if complex: to incorporate a realistic theme into a column of troops advancing toward the U.S. flag while projecting a willingness to serve without glorifying warfare.[17] In the end Cooper-Lecky would succeed in the art of political compromise where the original designers of the memorial had failed.

Finally in 1992 the CFA and NCPC joined the board and the AMBC in approving the revised design. Although the memorial was to commemorate a horrific war in which millions, mostly civilians, had perished, the new design depicted none of the violence and suffering. The final plan reduced the number of combat figures from thirty-eight to nineteen in order to "subdue their impact and better integrate them within the pastoral setting." Furthermore, no figures would be seen engaging in actual fighting, which represented quite a change from many nineteenth-century Civil War memorials. The long granite wall was shortened by fifty-five feet. Other alterations concerned landscaping. Much of the criticism of the early Cooper-Lecky design centered on its size and complexity. At least one board member felt that the memorial was turning into an outdoor museum, and J. Carter Brown called it "overstatement to the point of bombast."[18] But with further revisions there would at last be a Korean War Veterans Memorial, and following three years and heated public controversy after the "winning" design had been unveiled, military and government officials finally gathered in Ash Woods for a groundbreaking ceremony presided over by Pres. George H. W. Bush. "It took longer to get the design approved than it did to fight the war," remarked Hansen, the frustrated executive director of the Korean War Veterans Memorial Advisory Board.[19] "Let's get on with it," exclaimed General Stilwell.[20]

Nearly a decade had now elapsed from the enactment of legislation to the completion of the memorial, which, along with the Lincoln Memorial and Vietnam Veterans Memorial, would form a triad at the western end of the Mall. The completed memorial consists of a circle intersected by a triangular "Fields of Service" displaying nineteen larger-than-life soldiers (about seven feet tall and each weighing a thousand pounds) rendered by sculptor Frank Gaylord in unpolished gray stainless steel. They are placed on granite slabs surrounded by juniper bushes, intended to represent the rugged Korean terrain. The troops, all wearing ponchos over their combat gear, are arranged to be seen as advancing cautiously and anxiously toward an American flag. The nineteen patrolling, racially diverse male soldiers—twelve white, three Black, two Latin, one Asian, and one Native American—represent all branches of the armed service. Behind the flag is a reflecting "Pool of Remembrance." To the north of the Fields of Service, a large, granite block lists the countries that comprised the United Nations Command. All diplomatically receive equal recognition, ignoring the fact that some provided only token support. The final element, on the southern border of the site, consists of a long wall of highly polished black granite, etched with more than 2,400 computer-generated images of infantry men, nurses, sailors, pilots, and even a dog. These figures are engaged in all manner of warfare and combat support activities; however none are actually fighting, nor is there any depiction of the war's devastation. The images are rendered from photographs taken by servicemen and servicewomen themselves and housed in the National Archives and the Smithsonian Institution's Air and Space Museum. The servicemen and servicewomen are unidentified—dog tags and all unit insignia have been removed. Unlike the Vietnam Veterans Memorial, the names of fallen soldiers are not displayed. However, a kiosk at the site operated by the National Park Service (NPS) holds a bank of computers listing the names of all who died in the war, were held as POWs, or are still listed as MIA. In addition to the names, the serviceman or service-woman is further identified by military branch, rank, and hometown. Across from a large stone displaying the toll of those killed, wounded, and missing in action from the nations comprising the UNC, another granite wall bears the message, "Freedom Is Not Free." Below the American flag, another plaque states:

OUR NATION HONORS
HER SONS AND DAUGHTERS
WHO ANSWERED THE CALL
TO DEFEND A COUNTRY
THEY NEVER KNEW
AND A PEOPLE
THEY NEVER MET

South of the memorial, Korean rose bushes (also known as the rose of Sharon), South Korea's national flower, help frame the site.[21]

Now all that remained for the advisory board was the dedication, and this too would prove problematic. By this time there were already more than sixty memorials for Korean War veterans in communities throughout the United States, and given the wide involvement of veteran organizations in planning and funding the memorial, expectations for the program in the nation's capital were high. Perhaps up to a half million would attend the dedication ceremony. Meanwhile, lawsuits continued to be heard in courts from the original Penn State design team over both the design as well as sculptor Frank Gaylord's use of an image of his statues on a commemorative postage stamp. Although legal issues were not yet resolved, Executive Director Hansen was determined to proceed with invitations to Pres. William Jefferson Clinton, all living former U.S. presidents, and the democratically elected president of the Republic of Korea, Kim Young-sam. Writing to Mike Garza of Fox Associates in early June 1994, Hansen stated, "One of my many goals is to provide a series of events that will awaken the world to the true historical significance of the Korean War." For Hansen the Korean War was "no longer a forgotten war but a forgotten victory."[22] This theme would be repeated at the dedication ceremony by President Clinton and his presidential successors as a central part of the new American remembrance of the Korean conflict.

The Korean War Veterans Memorial was finally dedicated on July 27, 1995, forty-two years to the date of the armistice signing. As with all sites administered by the NPS, the memorial was immediately listed in the National Register of Historic Places. President Kim of the Republic of Korea joined President Clinton for the ceremony. The brutally hot and steaming summer day tested the endurance of the aging American and Korean veterans of the unended war in Korea, who heard President Clinton state that their service in the early Cold War era had "put the free world on the road to victory."[23] Many proud Korean Americans attended the ceremony as well.

Not all were satisfied with the completed Korean War Veterans Memorial. Critics found it too compromised by the various interest groups and committees to effectively educate the public. Indeed, the memorial does attempt to provide ethnic representation, recognize all branches of the U.S. Armed Forces, honor the contributions of those nations supporting the UNC, and satisfy the concerns of veterans and their families, all while meeting the aesthetic standards demanded by various parties. In arguing that a memorial should educate visitors to the war's purpose, outcome, and historical significance, as well as provide a site for remembrance, one student of architecture and memorialization saw the Korean War Veterans Memorial as a failure. She found it a poor design that falls short of both communicating an educational message while serving as a place of remembrance and comfort. She attributed these shortcomings to "the democratic nature of the design process and the excessive compromises that were made to resolve conflicting traditional ideas and modernist aesthetics in a national commemoration."[24] Other critics have faulted the memorial for failing to provide "public education about the past."[25] Yet the memorial does acknowledge the erosion of social, gender, ethnic, and racial boundaries that took place during the Korean War.[26]

As can be expected in such a complex artistic and architectural project, criticism came forth from those familiar with the war's specifics. Korean War historian Allan Millett has called the memorial "a monument to American confusion" about the war, noting that the "oversized military statues walk through a 'paddy' of arbor vitae and black marble, which by no stretch of the imagination represents any field I have ever seen in Korea."[27] Questioning the accuracy of the depiction, Stanley Weintraub, a veteran of the conflict and a distinguished historian, wrote that "those who were in Korea in 1950–53 often gaze with chagrin at the bronze GIs wearing ponchos used mostly to shroud the dead and bearing walkie-talkie field radios, which most never saw." He was nevertheless moved by the overall experience. He approved of the inclusion of all the nations that contributed soldiers and support to the UNC and found that "somehow the space evokes their sacrifice."[28] Another veteran saw an "inclusive monument" that "symbolizes the erosion of social boundaries that had previously deprived ethnic, racial, gender, and service groupings of official regard." One former Marine platoon leader in the Korean conflict was simply pleased that at long last, the service of his fellow veterans had achieved appropriate recognition, stating, "Our only anger really, was that so much bravery, so much uncomplaining devotion to duty, went unrecognized for so long. Now that lingering bitterness has been laid to rest at last."[29]

The dedication ceremony and the completion of the Korean War Veterans Memorial Advisory Board's operations on September 30, 1995, did not end the story or the controversy surrounding the memorial. Poor construction and several years of harsh weather conditions, not unusual for the District of Columbia, have caused the reflecting pool to leak, newly planted trees to die, and walkways to crumble.[30] At considerable cost the entire site had to be refurbished in time for a rededication in 1999, at which it was announced that the U.S. Senate would consider legislation to call the military action in Korea "a war" rather than "a conflict."[31]

Meanwhile, Korean War veterans expressed unhappiness with the lack of a wall of remembrance similar to that which comprises the Vietnam memorial. For veterans and their families, the kiosk near the Korean War Veterans Memorial simply did not hold the emotional appeal of the great, imposing black wall displaying the names of the tens of thousands of soldiers lost in the Vietnam conflict. Such a wall had been considered at length but rejected for practical reasons in the advisory board's early deliberations. Given the unresolved nature of the Korean War and the fact that large numbers of service people are still MIA, the task seemed overwhelmingly complex. There also existed confusion about the exact number of those killed in action and their proper names. It was estimated the identification process would take several years and cost $2 million. Hansen felt that the memorial's "current design could not accommodate another wall . . . why open Pandora's box?"[32] But in their demand for a wall of remembrance the veterans proved persistent.

In 2016 Congress enacted the Wall of Remembrance Act (HR1475) to allow certain private contributions "to fund a wall" and authorize the ABMC to request and consider design recommendations from the Korean War Veterans Memorial Foundation (KWVMF). Once again federal funding would not be provided. The legislation was sponsored by Rep. Sam Johnson (R-TX), who, along with House members Charles Rangel (D-NY) and John Conyers (D-MI), was a Korean War veteran. The wall would list the names of members of the U.S. Armed Forces who died in the Korean War theater as well as a summarized number of those wounded in action, held as POWs, or listed as MIA. In addition, a number of names would be displayed for Korean Augmentation to the United States Army (KATUSA) members, ROK Armed Forces, and those of other UNC nations who were killed in action, wounded in action, listed as missing, or held as prisoners of war.

One of the design concerns in the early review of plans for the Korean War Veterans Memorial was that any aboveground obstructions, such as a solid wall, would hinder Mall visitors' views of the Potomac River. Likewise, memorial visitors' view of the Mall from the Ash Grove site would be blocked by a wall. Therefore the act specifically called for an unbroken semicircle of glass panels seven feet high to allow full views of the Mall and the Potomac River from all directions. The NPS expressed opposition to the addition. Although it was to be paid for with private funds, the NPS noted that the memorial already honored veterans of the United States, ROK, and twenty-two UN countries and that original planners had rejected the idea of a wall of remembrance. Officials from the NPS noted the Vietnam Veterans Memorial experience of "determining the list of names to include on the memorial cause[d] a tremendous amount of heartache and grief." Arguing that no action should be taken that would compromise the integrity of "a complete work of civic art," the NPS expressed the view that open space and the original vision of the L'Enfant/McMillan plans for the nation's capital city should be preserved.[33] The veterans' wishes were not to be denied, however, and the legislation became law.[34]

Once Congress had authorized the glass wall, the Korean War Memorial Foundation was tasked with raising funds for the project, including the extensive and costly research required to determine the names to be etched on the panels. The private funding would enable the Department of Defense to provide the list of names. The foundation was also required to establish a maintenance fund to assist in upkeep for the 2.2-acre memorial. The NPS, facing an $11.5-billion backlog of maintenance projects, was in a hopeless situation. Not to anyone's surprise, the foundation struggled, but financial backing slowly emerged, largely from grateful Koreans. Samsung donated $1 million for the fund, and Hyundai provided $20,000 for a ceremony to mark the memorial's twentieth anniversary. "The only backing is coming from overseas," remarked Col. William Weber (Ret.), the foundation's chair. In a 2015 interview, Colonel Weber noted, "Our great support comes from corporate Korea. . . . American corporations— forget it."[35] The Wall of Remembrance remained a dream. Given the costs involved and the complexities of the project, it seemed unlikely that the hopes of the veterans would be fulfilled any time soon.[36]

Modest gifts continued to arrive from veterans groups, civic organizations, and sympathetic citizens. However, the situation changed suddenly and dramatically in the spring of 2021 when the Republic of Korea appropriated $20,000,000 in government funding for the KWVMF to complete the Wall of Remembrance and help endow the memorial's maintenance. The state of Maryland's Gov. Larry Hogan, whose Korean American wife served on the board of the KWVMF, announced a $250,000 contribution to the project. But it was clearly the huge funding from the ROK that changed everything. In announcing the financial assistance, Pres. Moon

Jae-in of South Korea stated that his country had initiated the contribution to the foundation as a demonstration of the ROK's gratitude to the United States.[37] He traveled to Washington DC, for a groundbreaking ceremony on May 21, 2021, at the site of the memorial. The Korean president also had a White House meeting with Pres. Joseph Biden where both leaders pledged continued and close cooperation in matters of mutual security, combating the COVID-19 pandemic, and the eventual denuclearization of the Korean Peninsula. President Moon spoke (in Korean) at the groundbreaking, proudly noting that the U.S. Congress had called for the names of 7,200 KATUSA soldiers to be added to the list of 37,000 Americans who lost their lives in Korea's defense. Gen. John Tilelli Jr. then addressed the assembled crowd, noting that the names of the U.S. service personnel would be provided and verified by the Department of Defense as the project moved toward completion in May of 2022.[38] At last it appeared certain that more than thirty-five years since the process began, the Korean War would be memorialized on the National Mall with a unique international message reflecting the support and appreciation of both the Republic of Korea and the Korean American community in the United States.

There exist unmistakable diplomatic implications to the Koreans' generosity. The awarding of $20,000,000 by the government of the ROK to assist the struggling KWVMF, while clearly motivated by a sense of gratitude for saving the fledgling South Korean state in its hour of desperate need, came at a time of shifting dynamics in internal ROK politics and in the complex relationships among the countries of East Asia. Pres. Moon Jae-in had personal reasons for thankfulness. The child of a refugee family that barely escaped from the North Korean regime on the dangerously overloaded USS *Meredith Victory* as Chinese "volunteers" overran U.S. Marines in their retreat from the Chosin Reservoir in December 1950, Moon was an ardent disciple of former president Kim Dae-jung. A firm believer in Kim's "sunshine" policy of engagement with the North Korean regime, Moon holds a prominent position in a political faction that is frequently at odds with hard-line U.S. policy toward the DPRK. In 2017 he had stated the ROK needed "to learn to say no to the Americans." Moon's leftist political associations and eagerness to engage with the North Koreans had long troubled conservatives in South Korea, and his role in arranging meetings between U.S. president Donald Trump and

North Korean leader Kim Jong-un only enhanced his image as a weak leader—especially when the talks between Trump and Kim led to nothing of substance. Constitutionally prohibited from seeking another term as president, Moon and his liberal Democratic Party of Korea faced a strong challenge in 2021 from the conservative People Power Party, whose leading candidate favored closer ties to the United States in reaction to China's more assertive foreign policies in the region and on the world stage. The issue of direction in South Korea-U.S. relations arose anew in Seoul as Washington promoted the idea of a "Quad," consisting of Japan, India, and Australia in a strategic alliance with the U.S. to counter the People's Republic of China's aggressive and expansionist behavior. Along with the Quad, the U.S. began exploring ROK membership in a "Quad Plus" alliance with New Zealand and Vietnam. Forced into a dilemma, South Korea will have to choose whether to pursue ever closer ties with its longtime ally, or decline membership in the Quad Plus because of the possibility of offending China, its powerful neighbor and largest trading partner.[39] President Moon no doubt viewed the support of the KWVMF as a relatively inexpensive way to shore up good will with Washington and refocus diplomatic efforts on the shared memory of the military action seventy years ago that formed the current order in East Asia and brought to the region many decades of peace and stability.

Meanwhile, an entirely unintended result of the construction of the Korean War Veterans Memorial proved to be the advancement of proliferation of war memorials on the National Mall and other locations in Washington DC. The hyper-memorialization began with the creation of the Vietnam Veterans Memorial; and, like the Korean War, the wars commemorated in the new wave of remembrance all took place before Vietnam. Besides the Korean War, these include the World War II Memorial (2004), the Japanese American Memorial to Patriotism during World War II (completed in 2000 and located between the U.S. Capitol and Union Station), the Women in Military Service for America Memorial (dedicated in 1997 at the entrance of the Arlington National Cemetery), and a proposed yet unfunded Black Revolutionary War Patriots Memorial. Plans are also nearing completion for retroactively memorializing American soldiers who fought more than a century ago in World War I.[40] As with the Vietnam and Korean War memorials, this recent building boom to recognize patriotism and service in times of war was put in motion by various veteran groups and advocates for greater inclusion of minorities and women in the remembrance of the nation's wars. Critics note that these memorials all tend to portray a highly positive, if not heroic, vision of military service and are clearly intended to inspire patriotic emotions. At the same time, these memorials tend to ignore the violence and destruction of warfare.[41] Whether or not this proliferation of war memorials will lead the American people to more readily accept warfare and the suffering and loss that come with it, as some critics have suggested, the future of the National Mall as an open gathering place appears at risk. Further placement of war memorials on the National Mall and in every corner of the nation's capital city may present to future generations an overemphasis on warfare as a component of American history.

Unlike the war on the Korean Peninsula, the long process to complete the Korean War Veterans Memorial has finally ended. In this era the U.S. government seems unwilling to adequately fund new memorials to recent military conflicts and undeclared and limited wars. It is left to the veterans of these violent engagements to advocate for themselves for recognition and to secure funding for their own sites of remembrance. In overcoming numerous challenges, the Korean War veterans have achieved significant success. The memorial has provided the American public with a measure of appreciation for the service and sacrifice of Korean War veterans and the significance of the conflict in which they fought. Their association has brought veterans together for comfort, camaraderie, and a sense of pride in their service to the nation. Many veterans have enjoyed sponsored visits to Washington DC, and received warm and heartfelt gratitude from fellow citizens, many of whom are Korean Americans.[42] The memorial in the nation's capital has also enhanced the image of Korean Americans living throughout the United States and helped solidify the long alliance between the United States and the Republic of Korea.

The Korean War Veterans Memorial offers visitors an image of the Korean War based on memory. It is not a textbook or historical monograph on the subject it memorializes, and the monument's factual information only provides a somewhat sanitized overview of the cruel warfare that ravaged Korea for thirty-seven months in the early years of the Cold War. Like all memorials it is intended to stir emotions, offer comfort and solace, and speak more of the present than of the past. From this memorial visitors learn that soldiers of the United States fought with many allies in a brutal war in Korea, and that these veterans, their families, and survivors of the conflict wanted their service recognized and remembered. And visitors to the memorial will clearly recognize the appreciation of the Korean people for the aid of the United States in saving their country from tyranny—an aspect of the Korean memorial that will always differentiate it from the Vietnam Veterans Memorial and possible sites of remembrance to the United States' lengthy involvements in Iraq and Afghanistan.

An impressive and moving monument now exists on a prime location in the nation's capital. The public may achieve a better understanding of the Korean War through the efforts of the Korean War Veterans Association. Their stated goal, to encourage memorialization of the service of Korean War veterans, has succeeded.[43] Korean War monuments and memorials continue to spread in states, municipalities, and public places across the nation.

6 | Conflicted Memories of Allies and Foes

Adhering to profoundly differing memories of the war, two regimes emerged on the Korean Peninsula: in the south a dictatorship with limited democratic features and a capitalist economy; in the north a harsh, rigid Soviet-style political system under the rule of a single family. Both sides sought legitimacy from the international community, harbored dreams of reunification of the divided nation on their own terms, and told themselves their own version of the war. Meanwhile, in China Mao Zedong proclaimed victory over the Americans, while advancing his stature as a world leader. The Soviet Union remained silent about the tragic conflict it had instigated.

Rhee Soon-bak admired Gen. Douglas MacArthur with an adoration held only for gods. As a seventeen-year-old ROK Navy seaman and radio specialist, Soon-bak had served proudly in the Korean War. Several nights prior to the MacArthur-led amphibious landing of United Nations Command (UNC) forces at the port city of Incheon in September 1950, Soon-bak accompanied a patrol of marines to set up communications on a small island in the harbor. Their goal was to prepare for the decisive counterattack against the North Koreans. After the ROK marines secured the rocky outpost from its Communist defenders, Soon-bak was called back to his ship to take his usual midnight shift in the radio room. The next morning he learned that the North Koreans had retaken the island, killing every one of the ROK marines. The memory of this event seared Soon-bak's soul. Not even MacArthur's dramatic victory at Incheon could ease the pain. And when the great general was removed from his command before unifying all of Korea, the young Korean sailor was heartbroken.

There could be no doubt, Soon-bak believed, if MacArthur had been allowed to continue in his command, he would have reunified Korea.[1]

Soon-bak was not alone among South Koreans in this admiration and reverence for MacArthur. Indeed, his memories were shared by millions of his countrymen, foremost among them the South's Korean War veterans and the nation's dictatorial and messianic president, Syngman Rhee. In 1957 Rhee had a huge, heroic statue of MacArthur placed on a cliff overlooking the site of the Incheon landing. The script at the base of the statue reflects the shared, lasting memory of most South Koreans to this day, stating, "Until the last battle against the malignant infection of Communism has been won, may we never forget it was he who said, 'In war there is no substitute for victory.'" Soon-bak, like many fellow veterans, visited the statue often, placed flowers, fruit, and bottles of rice wine before it, and prayed that their beloved general's spirit would somehow continue to protect South Korea. When loud and violent leftist protestors threatened to remove the general's statue during a fit of anti-American fervor in 2005, the elderly Rhee Soon-bak joined hundreds of his aging fellow veterans to provide protection. As they had on earlier occasions, the veterans held vigils throughout the night to supplement the police guards and keep radical protestors away. Meanwhile, public opinion polls indicated that only 10 percent of the South Korean population wanted the statue removed.[2]

General MacArthur serves as a powerful symbol for those in South Korea, the United States, and elsewhere who remember the United States as South Korea's savior from a hostile Communist takeover. At the port city of Incheon, his monument stands ten feet tall on an eighteen-feet pedestal in Jayu (Freedom) Park. From this lofty lookout, since 1957 he has witnessed the development of the growing, bustling port city, the expansion of the vast harbor, and the construction of a modern international airport while basking in the admiration of millions of Koreans. One Korean American survivor of the war recalled, "My parents never stopped talking about MacArthur. It was as though they had just found a new deity."[3] The foreign general's impressive statue at Incheon remained for decades the Republic of Korea's most prominent memorial as South Koreans sought to get past the bitter memories of a war that had caused such grief and left their people divided. Conservative South Korean leaders felt betrayed that U.S. presidents Harry S. Truman and Dwight

D. Eisenhower failed to demonstrate the will and provide the resources to defeat the North Koreans and drive the Chinese Communists completely off the Korean Peninsula, even at the risk of a third world war. For many South Koreans, MacArthur remains the single most heroic figure of the war. To this day no comparable monument exists in the ROK for Syngman Rhee or any of the ROK's wartime leaders. North of the demilitarized zone (DMZ), the Communist leadership took a different approach to maintaining the war's memory.

In his description of an imagined dystopian society, George Orwell once wrote that "it will be seen that control of the past depends above all in the training of memory."[4] Nowhere on earth has this observation been taken more seriously than in the DPRK, where the regime of three generations of the family of Kim Il-sung have tightly controlled their peculiar version of the public memory of the Korean War. And they have produced a state-sanctioned history to support the officially approved memory. Under the absolute domination of the Kims, the North Korean state has created a mythic past that clearly aims at legitimizing the ruling family's firm grip on power and its claim for recognition as the rightful government of the entire Korean Peninsula. In the self-isolated dictatorship of North Korea, all monuments, memorials, museums, cultural programming, and educational endeavors are aimed at perpetuating a story of heroic resistance to an invasion in the fall of 1950 by the United States and its corrupt, weak, and illegitimate puppet state in the south. The north's gallant resistance against great odds and amid great suffering was led by the northern state's brilliant and courageous founder, Kim Il-sung, who stood alone at the head of his loyal subjects and rallied them to victory. The north's symbols of the mythical wartime legend is intended to form an indisputable reality in the public memory of the entire population, and it is granted a fallacious credibility by the massive size of the country's stone and steel monuments and the all-pervasive nature of the officially sanctioned cultural and educational propaganda. The false legend, perpetuated and advanced by three generations of the Kim family, has not changed for nearly seven decades, and it says much about the determination of the ruling Kim family to maintain their authoritative dictatorship at the expense of the twenty million souls living north of the DMZ.

In the DPRK only one public memory of the Korean War exists. The dictatorial regime has never allowed any deviation from the official

Communist party narrative of the war and the cult of personality surrounding Kim Il-sung. Soon after the armistice ended the fighting along the DMZ, Kim set about consolidating and tightening his hold on power using strong personal alliances with those Korean Communists who had accompanied him along with the Soviet army into North Korea from Manchuria in late 1945. Espousing Marxist zeal and demonstrating suspicion of all Western influences except Communist ideology, Kim and his loyalists would soon prove to be more nationalists than true Communists as they oversaw the creation of a hybrid Soviet-feudalism under a family dynasty. In the 1950s Kim brutally purged the Korean Communist cadres who had returned after 1945 to the north from their exile in China or the Soviet Union. He also eliminated those South Korean Communists who had come to Pyongyang before, during, or after the Korean War. Meanwhile, Kim built a cult of personality around himself that was unmatched anywhere in the world by its pomposity and ostentatiousness. By the late 1980s, nearly thirty-four thousand monuments, including benches where Kim once sat, honored Kim for his enlightened and fearless leadership in war and peace. Pyongyang's main square was named for Kim, as was the state university. A sixty-six-feet statue of Kim, known in North Korea as the "Great Leader," soon overlooked North Korea's capital city on a site once used for worshiping the emperor of Japan. In order to hold the population under strict observation, a system of *inminban* (people's groups), a remnant of and variation on the Japanese colonial practice of civilian control, organized families under a government-appointed neighborhood leader, who reported daily on production goals, social gatherings, suspicious activities, and overnight visits, even by family members. The neighborhood leaders were then themselves carefully monitored by another layer of government overseers. At the same time, Kim kept his state and its subjugated people isolated from the outside world, wasted scarce resources, and made poor planning decisions that kept his country dependent on aid from the Soviet Union. While he cleverly played his Chinese and Soviet allies for vital economic and military support to sustain his flawed regime, he failed to develop a modern economy within the DPRK.[5]

The pervasive nature of Kim's cult of personality even shocked visiting Communist leaders. Reports from officials of Eastern European Communist countries in Pyongyang complained that Kim's cult of personality was ruining the country. A Hungarian diplomat noted in 1955 that in the DPRK, "Mistakes are not revealed openly, only in private and belatedly. . . . *The personality culture has not changed at all, and it is a primary and decisive factor in every mistake.*"[6] Soviet support for Kim's regime persisted nevertheless. Kim was an embarrassment who could not be allowed to fail, and massive assistance was essential for the DPRK's survival. In 1973 the deputy head of the International Department of the Central Committee of the Soviet Union's Communist Party explained the situation to an East German official: "In the interests of our common tasks, we must sometimes overlook their stupidities. None of us agree with the idolatry of Kim Il-sung."[7] Another Soviet Central Committee member reported in 1991 that Mao himself considered Kim "mediocre" and responsible for starting an "idiotic war."[8] Criticism from friends or foes never seemed to trouble Kim, however, as his officially sanctioned narrative of the Korean War underpinned the legitimacy of his regime.

For Kim and his family, the memory of the Korean War would prove to be an effective tool for maintaining the absolute control over his state. Kim required an enemy to justify the many decades of hardships his people were forced to endure; fanning anti-American sentiments and exaggerating fears of a U.S. attack suited his purposes. One careful observer of North Korea has noted that memory of the war "is critical for the state's raison d'être, the suffering that it caused remains a critical part of the society's collective historical memory—and colors how North Koreans and their leaders see almost every issue."[9] To his isolated population, he presented himself as his people's lone champion.

As soon as the 1953 armistice ended the bombing of his capital, Kim began construction of North Korea's national war museum. North Korea makes the claim to be the legitimate Korean state in its national museum by insisting that its leaders never needed or sought foreign assistance. The DPRK's Victorious War Museum (also referred to as the Victorious Fatherland Liberation War Museum), built in Pyongyang's central district, presents a vision of people independent and largely alone in their selfless and heroic effort to unite their homeland. Rising from the ashes of his demolished capital city just months after the end of warfare, the country is depicted in the museum as a nation united under a bold, visionary leader who defeated powerful foreign imperialists and their southern "puppet clique." There is no room for discussion of internal conflict, much less a civil war. The Korean people were all united, except for the lackies of the imperialists. Leading his people singlehandedly, Kim Il-sung's heroic and dominating image appears everywhere throughout the vast facility. An English-language guidebook, *Outstanding Leadership and Brilliant Victory*, claims that as a guerrilla leader in World War II, Kim "led the Korean people to victory in the anti-Japanese revolutionary war by employing Protean tactics of guerilla warfare, and liberated the country on August 15, 1945." Then a few years later he led the Korean People's Army in "shattering the myth of the U.S. imperialists' 'might.'" Readers and visitors to the museum are informed that "the historic victory of the Korean people in the war was only possible thanks to the outstanding guidance of President Kim Il-sung, the great military strategist and ever-victorious iron-willed brilliant commander." In an easily overlooked reference to outside assistance, the text states "units of the (North Korean) People's Army, together with the Chinese People's Volunteers, carried out strong counteractions to check the enemy's attack at the end of October [1950]."

Beyond this slight to the critical regime-saving role of their Chinese allies, throughout the museum it is emphasized that North Korea's victory was "a shining result of his [Kim's] Juche military thoughts and distinguished military art."[10] Kim Il-sung's philosophy of Juche means self-reliance and independence from foreign assistance. This philosophy was never put into practice, certainly not during the Korean War, when the Soviet premier Joseph Stalin's approval, authorization, and military assistance allowed Kim to instigate the June 25, 1950, attack on South Korea. Moreover, there appears only the slightest reference to the quarter million Chinese "volunteers" who saved the North Korean regime in the autumn of 1950 from complete annihilation by UNC and South Korean forces and carried on most of the fighting for the next two years. Juche does not allow for the acknowledgment of decisive outside assistance.

Renovated in 2013 the DPRK's Victorious War Museum displays numerous images, artifacts, and weapons, including some from conflicts and incidents after 1953. The Pyongyang facility consists of eighty rooms displaying dioramas of the highest quality through which only carefully monitored, guided tours (conducted by guides in military uniforms) are allowed. The modest sections addressing Chinese and Soviet involvement are separate and appear to exist only to appease Russian and Chinese visitors. Everywhere the central focus is on Kim Il-sung and his brilliant heroism. The exhibition narrative tells of a surprise attack on the north from the south and the north's successful counterattacks and brave defense of the homeland from invasion by the United States and the hopeless puppet regime in the south. The USS *Pueblo*, seized by the North Koreans in 1968, is an added attraction and exemplifies the ongoing nature of the Korean conflict.[11] The Pyongyang museum offers no message of reconciliation or peace, and a fierce anti-American message permeates the facility's narrative. Visitors from the United States report friendly treatment, while the polite, uniformed North Korean guides emphasize that the DPRK hostility is directed at the U.S. government, not the American people. Every aspect of the exhibit text centers on "U.S. imperial aggressors," the "most brutal slaughter of people ever known in history," and the "barbarous atrocities of using chemical and germ weapons." Renovated recently at obviously great expense, the museum still largely dismisses the decisive participation of the Chinese in the Korean War and ignores the Soviet role altogether.[12]

In the North Korean town of Sinchon, another newly renovated war museum depicts in graphic and gruesome exhibits the story of a massacre attributed to American soldiers in the early months of the war. That a horrific slaughter of civilians took place in Sinchon is certain; however, the facts are contested. It seems most likely that South Koreans, not Americans, committed the murders, and the numbers killed are open to question. The South Korean troops and irregulars moving north with ROK and UNC forces in the autumn of 1950 clearly took revenge on DPRK officials and civilians who were seen as loyal Communists in retaliation for their earlier murders of Christians, landowners, and professionals in both the north and south. To what extent U.S. military commanders were aware of or assisted in the massacres in any way remains unknown. Whatever the facts of the horrific incident, the Sinchon museum places all the blame on U.S. soldiers. Jean Lee, director of the Hyundai Motor-Korea Foundation Center for Korean History at the Wilson Center, viewed the museum's exhibits. He saw these as "a veritable house of horrors, with room after room graphically bringing to life the gruesome atrocities attributed to the Americans. . . . Rabid glee distorts their faces." In 2014 North Korean media touring the facility reported Kim Jong-un as expressing his approval of the exhibits and denouncing the U.S. soldiers as "cannibals seeking pleasure in slaughter."[13] From one room to the next, the horror continues, with displays of hideous massacres of civilians and scenes of atrocities attributed to the vicious U.S. invaders.[14]

The indoctrination continues beyond museum visits and into classroom curricula. Recently at a scheduled meeting at Panmunjom, a North Korean officer posted to the DMZ told an American counterpart that his grandchildren learned to count in school "by saying: One American bastard. Two American bastards. Three American bastards."[15] Given the intensely conflicting memories put forth in both Pyongyang's and Seoul's war museums, it is difficult to imagine anything close to a shared history of the Korean War ever emerging as long as the Kim family regime rules the north.

One questions the extent to which the DPRK can have any genuine popular culture, since an overbearing and tyrannical dictatorship not only spoon-feeds North Koreans a skewed version of "history" but also tightly controls all aspects of their everyday lives and their national culture. Nevertheless, literature and film deserve some analysis as they provide "theaters of memory" for use by the state to generate a common national remembrance of the war as a way that helps underpin the ideology of the governing regime. Even before initiating the Korean War, Kim Il-sung was insisting Korean writers use their words to support his agenda. The DPRK established a cultural life based on the model provided by the Soviet Union, where writers and artists were to serve as soldiers on the front lines of culture. Purges eliminated popular writers unable or unwilling to conform. Before long even Soviet sponsors viewed Kim Il-sung's measures as extreme and suggested that he allow writers to "humanize" their efforts and address themes that did not require enhancing his nascent cult of personality. The Soviet advice was ignored, and to this day the Kim regime carefully scrutinizes every word, even in works of fiction. One current popular writer has stated that obstacles to writing fiction are like "having to swallow the salty water."[16] North Korean film production is also supervised by the state, or the Workers' Party of Korea, and is considered vital for advancing government propaganda. Two themes tend to dominate: the glory of suffering and martyrdom for the state while fighting Japanese colonizers or American invaders, and the joyfulness of living in North Korean society. In the 1970s the production of films became a special interest of the Great Leader's son, Kim Jong-il, who attempted to enhance the poor quality of the regime's cinematic offerings by kidnapping prominent South Korean director, Shin Sang-ok, and his then former wife, Choi Eun-hi, to employ their talents and expertise. After making a few movies, however, his two captives slipped away from their guards and escaped while attending a film festival in Europe.[17] The North Korean film industry has since remained moribund.

The North Korean leadership continues to need the memory of a vicious and threatening enemy to remain in control. Through its museums, memorials, sites of remembrance, and media productions, the Kim family has created a myth of the Korean War and its aftermath to secure and hold power while also creating a sense of community bound together in a state of perpetual crisis. The North Korean population receives life-long indoctrination in the official narrative of the Korean War and Kim Il-sung's courageous and brilliant leadership in defending the homeland from a merciless, flesh-eating invader. Barred from outside sources of information and restricted in their movement, North Koreans are constantly told that their economic hardships are the result of American imperialism and that the danger of another unprovoked attack requires sacrifices. Of course they are also told that only the descendants of the Great Leader, Kim Il-sung, can continue to protect the North Korean populace from devastation. The Korean War, an event fading in the memory of other nations who fought in the conflict, remains a central element of everyday life in the DPRK. The Kim family's mythology strains any significant opening to the outside world. Even relations with its only ally, the People's Republic of China, are strained while North Korea perpetuates its bogus historical narrative.

An entirely different take on the official memory of the war exists across the Yalu River. Like their North Korean neighbors, leaders of the Chinese Communist Party (CCP) take to heart the Orwellian dictum, "Who controls the past controls the future [and] who controls the present controls the past."[18] However, for China's authoritarian regime, the Korean War serves to remind the Chinese people of the heroic sacrifice endured by China's generation of the revolution. Furthermore, the Chinese official memory emphasizes how the war in Korea advanced China's world status. China's entry into the Korean War ended what Chinese leaders consider a "Century of Humiliation" at the hands of Western and Japanese imperialists. The leadership of the PRC has employed history education to glorify the Communist Party, create a national identity in a multiethnic society, and justify an authoritarian political system. This effort has been especially pronounced in the post–Tiananmen Square (1989) era. The large-scale military operation across its own border did indeed immediately establish Mao Zedong's new PRC as a major player in Asian politics and a significant force in world affairs. Chinese history books and museums cite the confrontation with the United States in Korea as the birth of a "New China."[19] In Chinese museums the public is presented with a grand narrative in which the new Chinese Communist regime under Chairman Mao saved a weak Communist neighbor from the aggression of an imperialistic United States; the 1953 armistice that ended the warfare in Korea is identified as ending the unequal treaties that were in place at that time with Western powers.

China's Memorial of the War to Resist U.S. Aggression and Aid Korea (Korean War Museum), located in the town of Dandong, overlooks the Yalu River into North Korea. The museum has a long and complicated institutional history, not at all uncommon among the world's military museums, which must conform to changing international relationships with former allies and one-time adversaries. The museum serves as China's official site for commemoration of the war and was dedicated on July 25, 1993 (because July 27, the fiftieth anniversary of the armistice, was already booked for ceremonies in Pyongyang). Interestingly, the dedication was actually a reopening, as earlier and more modest versions of the museum had existed at the same location. The new museum features weapons, military uniforms, memorabilia, and a 360-degree diorama of an intense battle scene. The current museum came into existence just as the PRC was establishing formal diplomatic relations with the ROK —much to the displeasure of the North Koreans. Other road bumps in the planning of the expanded museum's themes included dealing with the shameful neglect of China's veterans and the brutal and politically awkward purge of legendary Korean War military leader Gen. Peng Dehuai during the Cultural Revolution. Most Chinese soldiers returning home from Korea were treated badly; not until after the Cultural Revolution did the regime recognize their service. By then General Peng had been imprisoned and tortured for pointing out problems with Mao's economic policies. He died imprisoned and in disgrace. Nevertheless, a bronze statue at the museum's entrance depicts a smiling Chairman Mao warmly shaking the hand of General Peng as his steadfast comrade in arms and commander of China's forces in Korea.

China's earlier anti-American displays were also toned down following Pres. Richard Nixon's historic visit to China and meeting with Chairman Mao in 1972. Remodeled in 2014 the current exhibits feature Kim Il-sung's October 1, 1950, letter to Chairman Mao urgently requesting Chinese aid; a hall of fallen heroes (in which Mao's son Mao Anying, who was killed in a U.S. air raid, holds a prominent place); and a revised Chinese death toll. In 2000 the Chinese Military Museum in Beijing opened a Korean War section, and a memorial to the Korean War was dedicated in Shanghai in 2018.[20] In its public history sites, China sees itself as North Korea's protector, and the Korean War helps justify China's current assertiveness and calls for patriotism. It seems China's role in the war on the Korean Peninsula will be held in the forefront of the official national memory for many years to come, especially as tension grows with the United States and neighboring countries over trade and a new, more aggressive Chinese military posture.[21]

Much more than in the West, the memory of the Korean War is a compelling and significant force in forming China's official historical narrative and its citizens' perception of the outside world. Memory of the war aids the shaping of both foreign and domestic policy. Although memory of the war was set aside to some extent for several decades following Nixon's 1972 visit to Peking, the Chinese have never forgotten the war or allowed it to be overshadowed by other foreign military involvements. Especially for younger Chinese, perpetuation of the war's memory has served to justify a lingering mistrust of the United States, supported the regime's claim that only the CCP could protect the population from alien powers, and helped explain the delayed reunification of Taiwan with the rest of China. While the regime's memory is selective, the recent campaigns have generated exceptional patriotism, support for an authoritarian regime, and a determination to never repeat the century of "national humiliation" that existed before the Communist Party achieved power.[22] So sensitive have the Chinese recently become of the memory of the Korean War that the seemingly innocuous remarks from BTS, a South Korean K-pop band, set off a social media outrage in the PRC. The popular and spontaneous reaction to the remarks about the sacrifices of countless men and women in the defense of the Republic of Korea caused a widespread boycott of the band's albums in China and threatened sales of products produced by Hyundai and Samsung. Meanwhile, a number of new films produced in the PRC to commemorate the seventieth anniversary of China's entry into the Korean War present strong patriotic themes that have been absent from Chinese theaters and TV screens for more than thirty years.[23]

In spite of a sometimes-rocky relationship between the PRC and DPRK over the past several decades, the two nations share a common sense of victory in their public remembrances of the outcome of the Korean War. Both understand the 1953 armistice as a turning point in East Asian relations with Western nations, and both view the Korean War as a key element in establishing the legitimacy of their governments—and in the case of the PRC, entry into the major leagues in world diplomatic affairs. Both also harbor resentment that two bystanders to the war, the Nationalist regime of Taiwan and the nation of Japan, emerged from the Korean War secured and strengthened.[24]

South of the DMZ, throughout the Rhee regime and the decades of military dictatorships that followed, the history of the Korean War and its aftermath were largely ignored in public memory. In the ROK the focus, until democracy arrived in the late 1980s, was on the military threat from North Korea and its powerful Communist allies and the need to keep the population prepared for a resumption of all-out warfare. In the 1990s, with a new sense of national pride and confidence, the ROK began to address its contemporary history in museums, memorials, literature, and the arts. The great success of the 1988 Seoul Olympics placed the resurgent ROK in the international spotlight, and both the PRC and the Soviet Union, South Korea's wartime enemies, recognized the ROK. As the North Korean regime found itself further isolated, its economic weaknesses were exposed to the world. Meanwhile, South Korea emerged as one of Asia's "economic tigers," and the first genuinely free elections brought an end to decades of military rule. As its economic status rose to spectacular heights and democracy prevailed, the ROK set about addressing the neglected history of its recent past with themes that focused on national reunification and the brotherhood of all Koreans.[25] In addition, South Korean memorialization efforts emphasized the international nature of the Korean War and the overwhelming support the United Nations provided during a time of crisis for the young republic. With the emergence of democracy, however, came a new openness and freedom to express bitter, antigovernment memories of the war long suppressed under the era of the dictators.

The concept for a Korean War museum arose in the late 1980s during the final years of the popularly elected but less authoritarian regime of the former general Roh Tae-woo. President Roh assigned renowned Korean War hero Gen. Paik Sun-yup the task of securing public and private support for the project through the establishment of a Korean War Memorial Foundation. During the Korean War, Paik was named the ROK's first four-star general at age thirty-three, represented South Korea at the peace negotiations at Panmunjom, and gained the respect of all the top UNC commanders. Following the war he served his country as ambassador to Taiwan, France, and Canada. Later he supervised the initial phases of the construction of Seoul's Metropolitan Subway system. His distinguished career was not without controversy however. Like many ROK military officers of his generation, he had trained in the Japanese Army during World War II; and prior to the Korean War, Paik had saved the career, and possibly the life, of Park Chung-hee, when the young officer was accused of North Korean sympathies. Nevertheless, Paik proved well suited to the task of leading the memorial/museum effort. He commanded respect from the military, the business community, mainstream democratic leaders, and the international community.[26] Most important of all, he had enthusiasm for the project.

Like President Roh, General Paik viewed the proposed museum as both a place to honor those who had died in the Korean War and a site to provide lessons in history and civics to younger generations. Paik served as president of this organization and managed to enlist agreement for the museum from two leading opposition politicians, Kim Yong-sam and Kim Dae-jung, who would serve as democratically elected presidents of Korea in the 1990s. This political support ensured backing for the project over the coming decade. Paik's prestige and leadership would maintain momentum for what would eventually become the War Memorial of Korea.

I met General Paik at his spacious office in the War Memorial of Korea on June 8, 2011. Colleagues at Korea University arranged my visit, and the general could not have been more generous with his time or willing to talk at length about the need to tell the story of the war to new generations of Koreans as well as foreign visitors. I found the aged general energetic and committed to advancing the memorial's mission as he entered his ninth decade. General Paik also saw the memorial as a place where the service and sacrifice of Korean and UNC soldiers could be remembered or honored, and he expressed a special fondness for Pres. Harry S. Truman for his decision to assist South Korea. To my surprise he considered me (then director of the Truman library) as President Truman's personal representative; as we departed his office, he took me by the hand and walked me down the museum's long hallways to my awaiting car and driver.[27]

The massive museum project was initiated and constructed at a time when peaceful reunification of the two Koreas suddenly seemed possible because of the rise of South Korea's economic status, the collapse of the Soviet Union, and the furthered isolation of North Korea. As these factors led to economic disaster in North Korea, there even seemed some hope that the northern regime might implode with the transition to new leadership following the death of Kim Il-sung in 1994. In addition, the DPRK appeared near its end because of a disastrous famine brought on by floods and a poorly planned and managed agricultural policy. Meanwhile, South Korea's rising status as a world economic power continued after a pause during the 1997 East Asian financial crisis. Museum construction continued during the "Sunshine Policy" of South Korean president Kim Dae-jung, as he sought dialogue and cooperation with North Korea. As a result of these political factors, the museum's exhibits ignore or downplay the horrors and atrocities committed by both sides during the Korean conflict. In fact the museum depicts very few examples of combat or aerial bombing or their consequences. Rather, events of the war are presented in dispassionate chronological order. An impressive array of military hardware is displayed both inside and outside the museum. However, peaceful reconciliation remains a persistent theme throughout the museum and its grounds. This theme is reinforced by the giant statue at the entrance to the museum grounds of two brothers in the military uniforms of the two Koreas embracing each other. The larger, more heavily armed brother is from the south; the smaller, weaker sibling from the north appears thankful to be rescued and reunited with his kin. That the memorial seems to promote a tacit forgetfulness of the harsh and brutal realities of the war has not gone unnoticed by thoughtful observers.[28]

South Korea's confident status is on clear display in the War Memorial of Korea, located in the heart of Seoul on a site that once housed a Japanese military compound and later the U.S. Eighth Army. The giant museum complex stresses the legitimacy of the Republic of Korea by emphasizing the country's international support from the United Nations and aid from abroad during the Korean War and its aftermath. Although the conflict of 1950–53 is at the center of its vast indoor and outdoor interpretive spaces, the museum exhibits artifacts related to Korea's struggles to defend itself against foreign forces from China, Mongolia, and Japan over several millennia. Items in state-of-the-art displays include a huge and colorful painting depicting a great Korean victory over a "100,000 strong Khitan army at Kwiju in 1019," an ancient mobile missile launcher from 1451 capable of firing a hundred deadly rocket-propelled arrows, and a small cannon manufactured in 1587. Occupying a prime location among the extensive exhibitions is a large model of an ironclad warship designed by Korea's greatest military hero, Adm. Yi Sun-sin, to fend off repeated Japanese invasions led by Hideyoshi in the 1590s.

A surprising feature to find within an institution dedicated to warfare is the Children's Museum, whose displays present stories of Korea's great military heroes who fought off foreign invaders throughout several millennia and include an elaborate "training grounds . . . where young visitors can experience guerilla training . . . with rock climbing, slides, and rope ladders." No specific foe is identified, and the theme for the youngsters is a patriotic defense of the homeland. The vast Korean War museum complex also offers two exceptional visitor services—an elegant, two-story café offering a wide selection of international cuisine and a "traditional European style wedding hall . . . surrounded by pine forest and fountains amid the perfect feng shui of the Yangsan area."[29] (The huge reception hall can seat two thousand guests, and there exists parking space for two thousand cars.) These popular amenities offer neither support for nor detraction from the museum's central message that the war of 1950–53 was the nation's most recent effort to survive yet another invasion from a hostile foreign intruder. Stalin, Mao, and their handpicked northern enforcer, Kim Il-sung, are depicted as the enemies, not the unfortunate people of the northern half of the Korean Peninsula, who were themselves invaded and overwhelmed by the Chinese and Soviet military during the Korean War.

The War Memorial of Korea also seeks to avoid any sense of triumphalism, although the case is clearly made that the south prevailed with the assistance of allies and survived the unprovoked attack by powerful invading forces. The narrative is that of an emerging republic attacked from the outside and caught off guard. It also highlights the desperate, suicidal tactics the south used to delay the invasion until help could arrive in the person of General MacArthur leading the multinational UNC. The suffering of civilians at the hands of the invaders is depicted in photos of long lines of refugees fleeing south to escape their Communist pursuers. While these photos are disturbing, they hardly tell the complete story of the horrendous toll on the civilian populations, both north and south, because of UNC bombings, the use of napalm, and mass executions by ROK partisans.[30] Throughout the museum complex there is prominent recognition of the crucial participation of forces under the U.S.-led UNC at a time of great crisis for the young Republic of Korea. The UN banner and the flags of the close to sixty countries that provided military and humanitarian aid fill the plaza in front of the main exhibit hall. The names of UNC soldiers from a dozen nations killed in the war are etched on huge granite columns along corridors leading into the main museum building. Those who might question the UNC commitment to saving South Korea and the continuing U.S. alliance with the Republic of Korea cannot help but be deeply moved by walking down the long colonnade of the War Memorial of Korea in Seoul and reading the thousands of names on the plaques.[31] By demonstrating its UN recognition and the support from fifty-eight member states, the ROK is making its case for legitimacy as the true government of all the Korean people. This site also clearly makes the case for continuing the U.S.-ROK alliance that has endured for decades, providing peace and stability for Korea and the region.

In addition to its national war memorial, the ROK built a National Museum of Korean Contemporary History. Housed at central Seoul's most prominent intersection in a building that once served as a U.S. Embassy Annex, this museum tells foreign and domestic visitors the story of Korea's twentieth century, a period glossed over until recently because of national angst over the Japanese colonial period (1910–45) and the horrific trauma of the Korean War. The tragic suffering and conflicted political loyalties during the Japanese occupation and the Korean War and its aftermath still divide communities, families, and civic discourse. Nevertheless, the National Museum of Korean Contemporary History, opened in 2012, boldly strives to address the long and complex Korean struggle for independence, the brutal political strife among rival Korean factions following the end of Japanese rule, the North Korean invasion of 1950, the Korean War's devastation and horrors, and the challenging process of rebuilding under military rule. Emphasis is also placed on South Korea's place in the world of diplomacy, trade, and scientific advancement; and once again foreign assistance to South Korea is acknowledged. For example, a 2017 exhibition tells of the role of Peace Corps Volunteers in Korea from the mid-1960s to the early 1980s. Nonmilitary aid from abroad is presented as a further demonstration of South Korea's international friendships and respected place in the world community.[32]

Among South Korea's new institutions of public history are presidential libraries, including a strikingly modern edifice in Seoul dedicated to the memory of Park Chung-hee, Korea's dictatorial president from 1963 through 1979. Park came to power following a military coup on May 16, 1961, which ousted a democratic but ineffective civilian government that briefly succeeded Syngman Rhee after the elderly leader's forced resignation and exile to Hawai'i. A tough, pragmatic career military officer, Park ruled with an iron fist, but his head was open to enlightened ideas and his motivations were patriotic. The Park Chung Hee Presidential Museum is clearly modeled on the thirteen presidential libraries in the United States managed by the National Archives and Records Administration (NARA) and several others operated by private foundations. However, the Park presidential library is unlike the federal libraries in the United States within the NARA system. It contains no official archival records of his presidency, and the private papers it does contain are sparse and far from comprehensive. In the ROK most official presidential records are held at the National Archives in Daejon; in Park's case, his private materials are still carefully guarded by his family. Nevertheless, the exhibitions give a sense of Park's tough but effective leadership, dedication to economic advancement, and overriding concerns for an orderly society and national security. While unpleasant aspects of his life and career are ignored or glossed over, the Park presidential library's interpretive exhibits are no more protective and misleading than the federally administered libraries of presidents John F. Kennedy, Ronald Reagan, or George W. Bush. One critic of such presidential libraries suggests that such edifices follow more of a heritage tourism model and present only what is attractive, heroic, and favorable, while ignoring the rest, thereby creating a McDonald's "Happy Meal version of presidential history."[33]

During my visit to the Park library in the spring of 2018, I found the exhibitions lacking in presentation and discussion of Park's early life, his World War II and Korean War military career, and suspicion of his youthful Communist sympathies by officials of the Syngman Rhee regime. The stern, forceful approach President Park took toward student demonstrators and opposition to political leaders was also overlooked. Park's governing philosophy was made clear in his poetic messages, several displayed in large scripts presented on the exhibition walls in both Korean and English. Among the more interesting:

> Human rights, democracy . . . these are nice words. But true human rights and democracy become possible only when we have freedom from hunger. We must not play with words in front of people starving to death.
> (no date)

> When future generations ask
> What our nation did for them
> What kind of work we did for the nation
> Let us be able to say proudly
> Without hesitation
> That we worked, worked, and worked
> With faith in our nation's modernization
> —January 17, 1967, President's New Year's Message

And this one is my personal favorite:

> Students are the leaders of our nation
> Tomorrow, not today
> —January 1976, President's New Year's Message[34]

Clearly the planners of the Park presidential library envisioned in the 1990s, as they initiated the project, a type of political reconciliation and nonpartisanship demonstrated in most U.S. presidential libraries, where traditionally former presidents all appear at the opening of a new presidential library and often visit each other's institutions as guest speakers.

Although an ardent political foe of President Park, Pres. Kim Dae-jung, who at one time was imprisoned by Park, supported the development of the Park presidential library, while his future successor Pres. Moon Jae-in, still a civil rights lawyer, ignored an invitation to the library's opening in February 2012.[35] Meanwhile, several of Korea's former democratically elected presidents have established libraries or centers, while Yonsei University in Seoul has systematically endeavored to collect the private papers of Korea's presidents.[36]

In the midst of the recovery of its contentious, contemporary history, the Korean government has sought ways to publicly recognize the important role of the United States and UNC during the Korean War. Foreign veterans receive special gestures of gratitude never, to my knowledge, surpassed by any country to its wartime allies. The ROK has demonstrated its debt to the soldiers of the UNC by sponsoring visits to South Korea for hundreds of veteran groups. These tours began in 1975 and are administered by the Korean Ministry of Patriots and Veterans Affairs. Upon their arrival in Korea, the aging UNC veterans are provided VIP treatment, including complimentary lodging, ground transportation, meals, and tours.[37] Further evidence of South Korea's openness to recognizing the role of international aid during its wartime crisis and struggle for survival can be experienced at the numerous memorials in Seoul and along the southern side of the DMZ, where the military units of the United States and other UNC nations are recognized.[38]

The ROK has now come to acknowledge its recent past and the central role of the devastating 1950–53 conflict in shaping today's South Korean society. Nevertheless, disagreement over the war's history and legacy persists. In the Republic of Korea, where freedom of expression expanded significantly after the free elections of 1987, public outbursts of anti-Americanism have not been uncommon. In South Korean academic circles, where the views of revisionist scholars remain in fashion, some South Korean academics are still convinced the United States is responsible for turning a domestic civil conflict into a horrendous international confrontation. Americans, including diplomats, express surprise at these anti-American sentiments, and former U.S. ambassador Donald Gregg noted that many Korean artists and intellectuals "were not particularly grateful to us for our efforts to keep them free."[39] Of course this view ignores the wartime atrocities committed by UNC and South Korean troops as well as the bombings that killed millions in the north and in the south. Many Koreans who suffered hold justifiable resentment for the U.S. support of dictatorial regimes. In South Korea's open society, even the most outrageous academic hypotheses are tolerated.[40]

In some quarters General MacArthur is vilified as a special symbol of American violence in Korea. Protestors periodically attack MacArthur's heroic statue in Incheon. Leftist sociology professor Kang Jeong-koo of Seoul's Dongguk University claims, "The Korean War was a civil conflict started by Kim Il-sung for national unification. It would have ended in a month if American forces had not intervened. The statue of General MacArthur, the warmonger, should be thrown into the gutter of history. MacArthur was not a person who saved Korean lives, but an enemy who snatched away Korean lives. MacArthur was a war fanatic. . . . His statue should be destroyed."[41] An official with the Incheon Society for Peace and Participation maintains that MacArthur "was a contributor to so many civilians' deaths and must be answerable for his conduct. His statue is a symbol of war, it must be torn down."[42] Efforts to destroy or remove the statue of MacArthur have been unsuccessful because there remains genuine and widespread admiration for the general in most sectors of Korean society. Korean veterans are particularly fond of MacArthur, and hundreds rally to protect the statue when radical students try to deface it during demonstrations.

The arrival of democracy in the ROK changed international realities, and a prosperous economy altered memories of war among a new South Korean generation. The admiration for the DPRK and the Kim regime once held by many Korean leftists began to dissipate in the 1990s, as the economic weakness of the north became apparent to the entire world. The once-feared Soviet Union vanished. Russia could no longer serve as the guarantor of North Korea's struggling economy. In fact Russia became a debtor to the emergent Republic of Korea as the "Nordpolitik," an opening of relations by the south initiated a decade earlier under the administration of Gen. Roh Tae-woo, paid off handsomely. The appeal of North Korea was gone for all but a small group of diehard leftists, labor-union leaders, Christian pacifists, and academics who refused to recognize changing international realities. Moreover, the south's so-called Generation 386 (those in their thirties, educated in the 1980s, and born in the 1960s) came of age in the 1990s with no firsthand memories of the Korean War. This generation held little concern for the DPRK as a security threat and knew only about the unpleasant issues of the continuing U.S. military presence and the persistent social problems of South Korean society. Unlike their parents and grandparents, Generation 386 had little enthusiasm for a contentious and costly reunification with the north. The succeeding generation seems even less interested in reunification. A 2018 poll conducted by Seoul National University found that while 67 percent of South Koreans over the age of sixty want reunification, the percentage drops to 41 percent of those in their twenties.[43]

Memory of the U.S. role in the Korean War, while acknowledged, is fuzzy concerning the specifics. Surprisingly many South Koreans still have little awareness or appreciation for the role of President Truman, who as MacArthur's commander in chief ordered the general to defend South Korea in June 1950. For most South Koreans, Truman is remembered, if at all, as the world leader who caused Korea to be divided. After all, it was Truman who agreed to the division along the 38th parallel following the Potsdam Conference in 1945, and many Koreans hold Truman responsible for the dismissal of MacArthur, whom they are taught would have reunited all of Korea if allowed to expand the war. And of course there exists a vocal leftist minority in South Korea who accept the notion that Korea would be better off today if the Truman administration had not intruded into a domestic quarrel on the Korean Peninsula. Truman's place in Korean history is publicly memorialized only in a small sculpture park at Imjingak along the DMZ. There a diminutive, gnome-like Truman statue stands as a lonely sentry near a UNC monument surrounded by an amusement park and a visitor center where souvenirs, snacks (including Popeyes chicken), and bottles of North Korean liquor are sold to tourists.

Truman's sense of modesty may in part be responsible for his lack of recognition and the general indifference in the Republic of Korea. In 1967 Fr. Paul White, a Catholic missionary in the South Korean city of Inju-myeon, asked permission from the former U.S. president to name a new hospital there under construction in his honor. Truman declined and responded by writing, "It has been my personal preference not to encourage any monuments or memorial to me. I consider whatever useful acts may have been performed during my administration were in fact acts of the American people."[44]

Over the past two decades, South Korean literature and film have earned international recognition. Among the most notable works are realistic and nuanced depictions of the Korean War and its aftermath. With the openness that arrived with democracy in 1988, South Korean writers and film producers often focus on divided Korean families and losses suffered during the war. These art forms have provided numerous compelling visions of tragedy.[45] However, as the older generations pass from the scene, memories of the war fade among a population that grew up knowing their poor, isolated northern cousin only as economically backward, cut off from its regional neighbors, and pariahs among the world's advanced nations. Even the north's nuclear weapons and threats to use them are not viewed as issues requiring serious concern. Among the south's younger generation, close family ties to the north no longer exist, making reunification with an impoverished, badly governed, and xenophobic nation seem undesirable.

Meanwhile, North Korean refugees numbering in the tens of thousands now live in the ROK. These people have arrived, often after frightening experiences, several failed escape attempts, and years wandering through China and Southeast Asian countries, only to face an uncertain life in Seoul. Most fear for the family members they left behind in the DPRK, while trying to establish a new identity for themselves in a culture that is both familiar and strange. They know their friends and relatives will be forever lost to them, while their lives in the fast-paced South Korean society will always remain somewhat foreign. A new genre in South Korean literature (and film) tells of the firsthand experiences of these people. The escape narrative books written by North Korean refugees are similar in their descriptions of a harsh regime that provided no hope and no end to physical abuse and psychological torture. Almost always written with a coauthor, these accounts of a brutal and dehumanizing life in the north have become something of a cottage industry in the publishing world.[46]

The continuing struggle over the telling of South Korea's recent past in an era of openness and freedom of expression has recently played out in the secondary-school classrooms of teachers (many of whom are enrolled in left-leaning unions), who often express harsh criticism of their country's conduct during the Korean War. Leftist teachers dislike the alliance with the United States and object to everything that happened during the four decades of dictatorial rule under presidents Rhee, Park, Chun Doo-hwan, and the less authoritarian Roh Tae-woo. Ignored in South Korean classrooms are North Korean wartime atrocities, the harsh and brutal rule of Kim Il-sung and his family, and the economic failures of the North Korean regime. A 2018 survey reported by one of the ROK's leading newspapers found that 69 percent of the teenagers in South Korea believed that the south invaded the north in June 1950. During the presidency of Park Geun-hye, the daughter of Park Chung-hee sought to produce what conservative leaders considered a more balanced and fact-based textbook in the schools. This action led to controversy and protests in the streets of Seoul by a half million marchers. Teachers, university professors, and politicians opposed to Park's ruling party saw the state-produced *Correct Textbook of History* as an effort to dismiss the dictator's faults, while emphasizing economic progress brought about during Park Chung-hee's regime. The more balanced historical treatment of Japan's colonial rule was an additional issue at a time when Park Geun-hye was seeking to improve relations with Korea's longtime rival, foe, colonial master, and essential partner for trade and economic development. Faced with strong opposition and beset with charges of corruption in her administration, the government backed down. Confronted with increasing calls for her resignation following a range of charges, President Park was eventually removed from office following massive street demonstrations by hundreds of thousands of marchers carrying lighted candles.[47] She was replaced following a national election in 2018 by left-leaning opposition political leader Moon Jae-in. The textbook controversy demonstrated that deeply conflicted memories about the Korean War and its aftermath remain lasting and fundamental obstacles to reconciliation efforts that might allow for a common understanding of the country's recent past.

Principal allies in the UNC seemed to share with the United States a type of forgetfulness about the Korean War following the 1953 armistice. While the United Nations remembered those who died in the international organization's first peacekeeping operation with a plaque at its New York headquarters, dedicated on June 21, 1956, similar markers of remembrance were slow to be established in the principal countries that formed the United Nations Command.[48] Memory of the war never held a strong place and quickly faded for the British and the French, as their involvement in the Korean War was diminished by the powerful remembrance of the two world wars. These were both fought on or near their own homelands and took a staggering toll on their military and civilian populations. Furthermore, both nations were preoccupied at the time of the Korean conflict with recovery from World War II and costly colonial wars in Malaysia, Indochina, and Algeria. In addition they came to see their roles in decision-making as marginalized by U.S. policy makers in Washington. Confronted with threatening economic challenges at home, bogged down in failing efforts to hold on to the remnants of their colonial empires, and left on the sidelines by Washington in strategic planning, European allies grew disillusioned and frustrated.[49] Moreover, as in the United States, returning prisoners of war (POWs) were seen as problematic and possibly a threat to national security.

The conservative government of Winston Churchill considered "reeducation" for all returning POWs. In these circumstances veterans of the Korean conflict were overlooked and their service forgotten. In Britain calls from Korean War veterans for the government to erect a memorial for their service and sacrifice went unanswered. Eventually several South Korean firms came forward with financial support.[50] Fear that returning POWs might present a threat to the general population influenced early memories of the Korean War in Britain just as it had in the United States. Concerned that some POWs had collaborated with their captors, many British citizens suspected there might be hardened Communists among those returned from the prison camps. Thus the British Chiefs of Staff decided all returning indoctrinated POWs needed to be thoroughly interrogated to obtain intelligence information. In addition, those determined to be "brainwashed" were considered in need of thorough vetting and continuing supervision—especially if they remained in the military.[51]

The declining role of France as a world power had become apparent in the Korean War. The French contributed one of the smaller military forces in the Korean War, the fourteenth largest behind much weaker nations such as the Philippines, Thailand, the Netherlands, Colombia, Greece, and Ethiopia. Nevertheless the French fought with valor, and forty-four French soldiers are buried in the UN memorial cemetery in Pusan. Furthermore, French president Charles de Gaulle drew lessons from the conflict in Korea. He believed, as he stated to New York Times's Cyrus Sulzberger, the war demonstrated the United States' willingness to use its military power to resist aggression and established a beginning of détente with the Communist world, "a modus vivendi . . . an armed peace."[52]

Other UNC nations experience the same postwar disinterest, malaise, and disappointment as the United States, Britain, and France. In Canada the war was never popular, and an overwhelming majority of French Canadians opposed conscription during the Korean War.[53] Disillusioned and forgotten veterans of the Korean War did not organize an association until 1983. Australia and New Zealand found themselves threatened at the end of the Korean War by the United States' "soft" peace treaty with an emerging Japan and, as in the United States, questioned the effects of the Korean War on the mental fitness of returning veterans.[54]

In recent decades UNC veterans have received overdue appreciation. Memorials to soldiers from the nations supporting the UNC are now located in every corner of the world as well as across South Korea. These have become too numerous to list and range from small, rectangular plaques and diminutive monuments, to special exhibits in large war museums, to huge memorials commanding the surrounding landscape. In South Korea's Paju City along the DMZ, the visitor center at Imjingak, which attracts more than three quarters of a million visitors each year, displays modest memorials to soldiers of several UNC nations, and on a large plaza, the flags of all UNC participants fly every day of the year. Among the memorials a monument to Filipino soldiers is particularly attractive. Curiously, most of the foreign visitors to Imjingak's international memorials are Chinese. A few miles away, a vast memorial to the Gloucester regiment that held off a Chinese onslaught resembles the American memorial to its veterans on the National Mall in Washington DC. South of Seoul in Anseong, a South African memorial, while not prominently located, presents its message in English and Afrikaans while honoring the South African Air Force squadron known as the "Flying Cheetahs." In 1968 Ethiopia placed a monument in the city of Chuncheon, presenting text in English, Korean, and Amharic. A memorial dedicated in 1976 in a crowded development in Seoul, now almost completely obscured by new construction, recognizes the participants of Colombian soldiers, while a tasteful monument in Osan tells the story of French fighters who fought with Task Force Smith in the first weeks of the Korean War. Turkish soldiers are recognized in a memorial built in Gyeonggi-do in 1974. Perhaps the most moving and beautiful of all the memorials to the multinational UNC is the vast cemetery in Pusan.[55] Although the size, attractiveness, and quality of the UNC memorials of the various nations that sent soldiers to Korea may vary greatly, it is clear that the service of those who fought the Korean War, while perhaps overshadowed by other events of the twentieth century, has not been forgotten.

Ironically, as the nations of East Asia have become increasingly inter-connected, the memories of the Korean War remain as contested as ever and contribute to political tensions. Furthermore, in East Asia, as else-where, the memory of the war remains frequently clouded by misinfor-mation, myths, hyper-nationalism, political ideologies, and long-outdated Cold War images and narratives. Recent initiatives by East Asian nations to remember the war in museums and monuments have only furthered the gap in historical understanding. In particular the conflicting public histories of the Korean War found in the ROK and DPRK only serve to perpetuate instability on the Korean Peninsula. Here two regimes present widely differing national memories in an ongoing contest for legitimacy in a divided land.

Meanwhile, in East Asia and beyond, an unlikely agreement seems to have emerged on one critical question of the war's legacy. By the beginning of the twenty-first century, all parties came to see themselves as victors. Each participant, in their museums and sites of remembrance, point to their own successful accomplishments. For South Korea it is the survival of the nation (albeit just the southern half) from a foreign invasion by Soviet-sponsored elements to North Korea and a massive wave of Chinese soldiers. The North Koreans tell themselves, and any foreign visitors who will listen, that the war was a great and glorious patriotic effort to unify the nation and a heroic victory over the Americans who invaded the fatherland by crossing the 38th parallel in autumn 1950. The Chinese see their role in Korea as a heroic and selfless campaign to assist a struggling Communist neighbor, which propelled the People's Republic and Mao Zedong into a position of world leadership. And in the United States, as well as among the nations in the UNC, the war in Korea is remembered as a critical turning point in the Cold War, where Soviet aggression was halted, a third world war was avoided, and a fledgling democracy was set on a course toward freedom and prosperity.

The claims of victory cannot ignore the fact that the war remains unre-solved. Wounds, both physical and psychological, are yet to be healed, and Korea remains divided. In spite of the peace and prosperity known in that part of the world over the past decades, the potential for violence along Korea's DMZ is ever present, and North Korea's possession of nuclear weapons adds to the regional tensions. True peace and reconciliation seem distant dreams.

7 | Memory, Truth, and Reconciliation

With democratization in South Korea came a new openness and a questioning of the official memory of the Korean War maintained throughout the era of dictatorship. Inquiries into wartime and postwar massacres and atrocities began, and politics became a factor in the work of the Truth and Reconciliation Commission for Korea (TRCK). Revelations of wartime U.S. military actions, particularly the 1950 murder of hundreds of civilians under a bridge at No Gun Ri, caused a resurgence of anti-American outbursts. Meanwhile, in North Korea and China the official historical narrative of the Korean War has never been questioned. Differing public memories of the Korean War continue to hinder multinational negotiations to address threats to peace and stability on the divided Korean Peninsula.

East Asia was profoundly and permanently changed because of the tragic conflict that raged across the Korean Peninsula from 1950–53. To this day the contentious and conflicted memories of that war continue to fuel tensions in the region and throughout the world, and these memories complicate efforts to achieve a peaceful settlement to the continuing struggle for supremacy between the two Koreas, which remain physically divided by the heavily armed demilitarized zone (DMZ). Unfortunately memory is often substituted for historical analysis in efforts to uncover the truth about the origins, conduct, and consequences of the war. Ignoring history in favor of memory can only exacerbate unresolved issues resulting from warfare; in seeking resolution to the unended war in Korea, diplomats and national leaders are stymied by the persistence of conflicted memories, as well as ignorance of how important these memories are.

Memory is not history, although the two overlap and can share common spaces. Moreover, memory can never serve as a substitute for history; memory is more subjective and selective. Over time memory can fade or become increasingly vivid, all-consuming, and emotionally charged. Memory can be a nightmare that leaves no opening for peace, or memory can be therapeutic, bringing about a kind of willful amnesia that allows living to go on and make reconciliation possible. Unlike history, memory is not based on the study of evidence or the thoughtful examination of documents. Popular culture and physical symbols of the past, such as monuments and memorials, are based not on history but on memory. When memory threatens to replace history, there is a need for dialogue between the scholars and the public. History and public memory can complement each other but neither can substitute for the other. One keen observer of this phenomena has written that archives exist for history, while the process of erecting monuments is for forgetting. Nevertheless, public memory, no matter how it comes about, is essential for holding together nation-states as well as civilization itself. Furthermore, in spite of the intense interest in the study of public memory, real and imagined, in recent years there still exists no method of measuring memory's impact on society or the relationship between collective memory and national policymaking and actions by government officials.[1] Public memory is clearly at work in forming national identity in the countries of East Asia.

In the Republic of Korea, as in other emerging nations throughout the world, historic sites dedicated to the memory and commemoration of tragic events, sometimes referred to as "sites of conscience," have come into existence since the 1990s following the establishment of democratic governments.[2] At times newly democratic governments incorporate long-suppressed memories of minorities and marginalized groups into a more comprehensive historical narrative. While the aim of their activity is reconciliation, this process can become divisive and political. In efforts to display sensitivity to those who suffered from past abuses, old wounds are reopened. Demands come forth for assignment of responsibility, apologies, compensation, and even revenge. But sites that commemorate horrific and tragic events need not be places where people go only to express their grief, remorse, and anger. These places have the potential for healing, and visitors to these locations might resolve to work toward a more peaceful, just, and humane society.[3] Occurring in a highly charged political atmosphere, endeavors to achieve justice and recognition through exposing the truth in South Korea have led to a more comprehensive and balanced understanding of the war. Meanwhile, the deliberate disregard of the factual historical record in the Democratic People's Republic of Korea and the People's Republic of China has perpetuated officially sanctioned public memories and myths.

Remembrance of the Korean War is plagued and haunted by memories of the war crimes and atrocities both sides committed against civilian populations and captured soldiers. Exposing these horrific acts and assigning guilt can both impede the finding of a peaceful resolution to the war and stoke tension on the Korean Peninsula. In many instances aggressors on both sides deliberately executed soldiers and civilians and participated in outright acts of terror designed to intimidate or force submission. In the frantic and confusing vortex of chaotic warfare in Korea, civilians as well as soldiers found themselves caught up in horrific violence, and often there was no escape. Cruel decisions by combatants were at times morally ambiguous, yet there can be no doubt that the Korean War involved thousands of deliberate attacks on civilian targets and the execution of partisan fighters, prisoners of war (POWs), and government officials in both North and South Korea, as well as innocent civilians seeking to escape the warfare that surrounded them.[4] Atrocities took place on both sides of the 38th parallel, and both North Koreans and South Koreans perpetuated horrific acts before and after the invasion of June 25, 1950, often with their principal allies' assistance or acquiescence.

While the Communist regime in North Korea refuses to acknowledge any role whatsoever in atrocities or war crimes, since democratization in 1987, the ROK has made initial efforts to determine the truth and seek reconciliation. In 2005 the South Korean government established the TRCK to examine instances of wartime atrocities and abuses of power during the era of Syngman Rhee and the military dictators who succeeded him. Memories long suppressed or ignored came before the public. Victims' families and sympathetic human rights organizations demanded justice, as memorial services were conducted at sites of atrocities. Meanwhile, TRCK also sought to explore and expose misdeeds of the Japanese colonial period (1905–45). Created during the administration of Pres. Roh Moohyun, TRCK was modeled after the truth and reconciliation commission set up in South Africa a decade earlier. The newly formed organization employed twenty staff members and had a budget of nearly $20 million. During its existence the TRCK examined and confirmed more than two hundred cases of alleged war crimes and atrocities and explored the issue of possible compensation to families of the victims. Markers or monuments were placed at various locations following historical research and archaeological examinations of sites where massacres were identified. Of special attention was Cheju Island. There, in the years prior to the Korean War, distrust of the government in Seoul, partisan strife, and agitation often enhanced by a large number of North Korean infiltrators led to a violent government crackdown and the deaths of thousands. In Koch'ang the discovery of yet another mass burial site confirmed the ROK forces' use of executions. In both instances the work of the TRCK led to attempts to honor victims. While the memorials told of the victims, their brief narrative failed to place the incident in the broader historical context of the war and its aftermath. The memorials appeared to leave all sides unsatisfied, and assessing blame became a contentious and partisan exercise. After Pres. Lee Myung-bak came into power in 2008, and his conservative government disbanded the TRCK in 2009, the work of identifying and interpreting the murderous sites was left unfinished.[5]

Among the memories of tragic events, one stands out for special consideration. Because of the clear documentation proving that the event occurred, no wartime atrocity generated more international attention or controversy than the massacre of hundreds of Korean civilians (and possibly a few intermingled North Korean military personnel) who sought refuge under a bridge that spanned the small river known as No Gun Ri. This undisputed killing of civilians took place about a hundred miles southeast of Seoul between July 26 and 29, 1950, in the first panic-filled weeks of the war as South Korean and United Nations Command (UNC) forces were retreating from the Soviet-supported North Korean onslaught. The estimated numbers of those killed range from fewer than two hundred to more than four hundred—some sources claim as many as five hundred civilians died in this four-day period.[6] It is also unclear as to who ordered the cold-blooded killing. And soon after the publication of a Pulitzer Prize-winning report on the incident, questions surfaced regarding the reliability of some of those who claimed to be eyewitnesses. Nevertheless, U.S. secretary of defense William Cohen ordered a review by the military, insisting that the examination process "devote whatever resources are appropriate to accomplish this review as thoroughly and as quickly as possible."[7]

Following weeks of friction between American and South Korean investigations, the U.S. Defense Department and the South Korean Ministry of National Defense simultaneously released reports on the massacre at No Gun Ri in July 1950. Both reports became public on January 11, 2001. The evidence does indicate that senior U.S. military officers were aware of what happened at No Gun Ri and had issued vague and hastily written general orders that allowed for shooting fleeing refugees, as DPRK soldiers might be embedded with them. The South Korean report stated that U.S. pilots had been ordered to strike at South Korean refugees, as it seemed to American commanders that North Korean infiltrators likely were mixed in with refugees fleeing south to escape the conflict and being captured by the Korean People's Army. The South Korean report also suggested that U.S. ground troops might have had orders to open fire on refugees. In issuing its three-hundred-page report on the four days of indiscriminate slaughter at No Gun Ri, the Pentagon acknowledged that the U.S. military had killed or wounded an "unknown number" of South Korean refugees, and that the victims had been killed with small arms, artillery, and mortar fire, in addition to aerial strafing. However, the report of the inquiry headed by the U.S. Army inspector general maintained that U.S. pilots were not instructed to strafe civilians at No Gun Ri, and no army officers had issued orders to shoot the fleeing refugees. The clear implication in the report was that enlisted men acting on their own committed the massacre. The killings were described as an unfortunate tragedy inherent in war but not a deliberate premeditated killing.[8] The U.S. report identified no official wrongdoing and assigned no blame.

It soon became clear that the U.S. Army's inspector general had omitted or misrepresented important information and documentary evidence and had not shared key materials with South Korean counterparts. Former U.S. representative and Korean War veteran Paul "Pete" McCloskey Jr. (R-CA), who served as one of eight "outside" members of an advisory panel overseeing the U.S. Army inquiry, was so upset with the Pentagon report that he called it a failure to report the truth. Another advisory committee member, retired Marine Lt. Gen. Bernard Trainor, stated in a letter to Sec. Cohen, "My conclusion is that the American command were responsible for the loss of innocent life in or around No Gun Ri.

At the very least, it failed to control the fire of its subordinate units and personnel. At worst, it ordered the firing."[9]

A spokesman for the No Gun Ri petitioners in South Korea decried the failure of the report to assess responsibility for the killings and called it a Pentagon attempt to whitewash the massacre. But an official South Korean government commission led by Gen. Paik Sun-yup, one of the ROK's most distinguished wartime commanders, was more understanding of the chaos of the early combat in the Korean War. Meanwhile, Pres. Bill Clinton, with fewer than two weeks left in his presidency, issued a statement expressing deep regret for the No Gun Ri incident. He established a scholarship fund to honor all Korean civilians in the 1950–53 conflict and promised to have a memorial constructed in remembrance of the No Gun Ri victims. Although President Clinton called South Korean president Kim Dae-jung to express regrets, the U.S. government made no formal apology and offered no compensation to survivors of the No Gun Ri massacre.[10]

The focus on No Gun Ri renewed attention to memories of atrocities and savagery during the Korean War and its aftermath and rekindled the embers of anti-American sentiment that had been smoldering in South Korean society since the war. Memories of old grievances and outrage over postwar incidents sparked mass protests during the decades of dictatorship that followed the 1953 armistice. During the years of postwar dictatorship, the United States was often seen as a hindrance to efforts by South Koreans to achieve democracy, a friend to military dictators, and an untrustworthy partner.[11] No postwar incident seared itself more deeply into the South Korean public memory of U.S. betrayal than the brutal suppression by the South Korean military regime of the pro-democracy uprising that erupted in the southern city of Kwangju in the spring of 1980. In reaction to huge, frenzied, and disruptive street protests led by student radicals, labor leaders, and Christian activists against the dictatorship of Gen. Chun Doo-hwan, Korean military units were removed from the DMZ and ordered to Kwangju by the regime in Seoul to quell the protests. Using force that many viewed as excessive, the military put down the rebellion that local authorities had been unable or unwilling to control. Hundreds (some in Kwangju claimed thousands) died in the chaotic melee. Photographs and videos depicted bloody street fights and graphic images of the dead, which circulated around the world. At the time of the military actions against the protestors, many Koreans believed Pres. Jimmy Carter, a self-proclaimed champion of human rights and frequent critic of Pres. Park Chung-hee and his successor, could have done more to support the people of Kwangju. However, as the military crackdown became increasingly violent, the U.S. ambassador to Korea observed that the ruling generals under President Chun felt threatened as the situation raged out of control. Meanwhile in Washington, diplomats urged President Carter to follow a "carefully calibrated posture of disapproval, public and private, of the military crackdown in Korea, while avoiding statements which imply that we are encouraging the opposition to the government at a time of disorder." The goal, they argued, should seek to halt violence while preventing "erosion of the ROK defense posture, which could invite North Korean efforts to exploit the situation." The diplomats believed that such a stance would allow "the Korean military to discover for themselves the consequences of their recent actions."[12] Throughout the rioting the U.S. government stood aside as a brutal military crackdown and the killing of civilians went on for days.[13] Kwangju served as the nadir for the unpopular military regime and led to the emergence of democracy in South Korea less than a decade later.

A decade and a half later, in 1997, a financial crisis in East Asia hit the newly democratized and prosperous South Korean economy. Millions suffered, and hundreds of suicides were attributed to job losses and business failures. As with the Kwangju incident, some South Koreans believed the United States had somehow manipulated the situation to its own advantage.[14] Then a few years later, another incident leading to a diplomatic crisis and anti-American mass demonstrations occurred in June 2002 when a U.S. military vehicle accidentally struck and killed two young schoolgirls walking along the side of a road near a military base. An American diplomat in Seoul at the time witnessed U.S. embassy staff dealing with another media snowball effect in which one story fed into the next about new and different instances of alleged American disrespect for Koreans. Immediately upon receiving news of the accident, he predicted trouble. "This is going to be bad, very bad," he told a colleague. Indeed, following several huge anti-American demonstrations, numerous harsh editorials, and four investigations into the accident by various Korean civic organizations, most Koreans still demanded greater sincerity in U.S. apologies for the incident.[15] While the anti-American protests during this period were loud and fierce, they did not lead to a breakdown in U.S.-ROK relations, a weakening of the military alliance, or a disruption of mutually beneficially economic and cultural exchange. Indeed, in my experience it was not at all uncommon to see a young participant in an anti-American demonstration return home and stay up late studying for the Graduate Record Exam in hopes of earning a master's degree in business administration from Harvard, Stanford, or the Massachusetts Institute of Technology.

Nonetheless, the protests against the U.S. presence in South Korea illuminated the genuine anti-American feelings that have existed in South Korean society since liberation from Japanese colonialism as both North and South Korea continue to struggle for identity and legitimacy. The continued American military presence in the ROK is resented, while at the same time it is recognized by South Korea (and North Korea) as necessary for peace and stability in the region where the Korean Peninsula is flanked by an emerging PRC and an economically powerful Japan.[16] Donald Clark, the son and grandson of missionaries and a long observer of Korea, has noted the fierce nationalism of all Koreans. While fighting to advance under different political and economic systems, Koreans tend to feel embarrassed that their nation ever needed the assistance of missionaries, aid workers, Peace Corps Volunteers, assorted modernizers, and do-gooders. Koreans often see Western intervention and influence in Korea, even when well-intended, as a kind of imperialism no better than Japanese colonial rule. Clark explained that South Koreans also consider the Allied occupation after 1945 "an especially violent disruption of their natural life by foreigners and blame Americans for decades of military dictatorship in the South." In this environment a longtime observer notes Koreans often view "evildoers more evil, the innocents more innocent, and the people from the colonial and postcolonial powers more selfish and cynical than they actually were."[17]

While memories of the war on both sides of the DMZ remained sharp and bitter through the end of the twentieth century, the dawn of a new century appeared, at least briefly, to signal a more optimistic time on the Korean Peninsula. Even as anxiety persisted between the competing regimes on the Korean Peninsula over security, it seemed the moment might have arrived for the possible achievement of a peaceful reconciliation between North and South Korea in spite of anti-American episodes in South Korea and the DPRK's continued policy of stoking wartime memories and hatred for the United States in North Korea. As the Cold War ended, the 1990s seemed to offer the real prospect of agreements between Washington, Seoul, Moscow, Beijing, and Pyongyang. At least diplomats were talking to each other; early in the 1990s, the South Korean minister for the Ministry of Unification predicted, "We can look forward with great expectations."[18] Even though the 1990s was a crisis-filled decade, signs of genuine progress steadily grew.

Progress did not come easily, however. In 1995 a DPRK mini-submarine washed up on the eastern coast of South Korea with eleven dead crew members, all executed by the thirteen North Korean commandoes on board, who were themselves tracked down and killed by the ROK military and police.[19] This outrageous behavior came at a time of crisis initiated just one year earlier, when the DPRK began testing missiles that could hit Japan and announced plans to develop nuclear weapons. Although the DPRK had signed the Treaty on the Non-Proliferation of Nuclear Weapons (often referred to as the Non-Proliferation Treaty, or NPT) and Safeguard Agreement with the International Atomic Energy Agency (IAEA) in 1985, the aging Kim Il-sung withdrew from the NPT in 1994 following the earlier DPRK withdrawal from the IAEA. Former president Jimmy Carter soon arrived in Pyongyang as the unofficial representative of the United States and secured an agreement to halt North Korea's nuclear development in return for concessions from the United States. Negotiations led to what was referred to as the "Agreed Framework," signed October 21, 1994, in Geneva. This deal between the United States and the DPRK froze the North Korean illicit plutonium program for eight years, although the nuclear facility at Yongban remained. In return the United States pledged aid, sanctions relief, 500,000 tons of oil per year, and the construction, at a cost of $4 billion, of two light-water nuclear reactors (LWRs) to generate electricity in North Korea.[20] A conflict over nuclear weapons was averted, but tension and uncertainty remained along the DMZ. Additionally, even as its economy worsened, the DPRK continued to develop long-range missiles.

Despite provocative incidents from North Korea and uncertain diplomatic fits and starts, the situation on the Korean Peninsula in 2000 seemed relatively stable, and there existed hope for improvement. South Korea was now a democracy, recognized by both Moscow and Beijing, and the ROK economy was thriving (except for the 1997 financial hiccup). North Korea as yet possessed no nuclear weapons and was severely weakened by the loss of the Soviet Union as its financial backer. In addition, four years of floods and famine (known as the Arduous March) resulted in more than three million deaths and further ravaged the north's economy, and the sudden death of Kim Il-sung in 1994 had left governance in the hands of his son Kim Jong-il, a young, untested, and seemingly inexperienced new leader. In mid-June 2000 South Korea's president and longtime advocate for democracy and human rights, Kim Dae-jung, visited Pyongyang in an unprecedented effort to open relations with North Korea. Elected in 1997, Kim Dae-jung had dealt successfully with the fallout of the financial crisis that year and now sought to improve relations with North Korea through more open communication. A longtime peace and pro-democracy advocate, his new effort, labeled the "Sunshine Policy," was criticized by his conservative political opponents as giving the DPRK too much for too little in return.[21] Nevertheless, meeting in Pyongyang, the leaders of the two Koreas agreed to improve dialogue, initiate social and economic exchanges, and ease tensions in the DMZ. The North Korean leader even agreed to a reciprocal visit to Seoul. Although marked by scandal when it was revealed that Hyundai Corporation had transferred $500,000 to the DPRK just prior to the visit by the South Korean president, the Pyongyang encounter led to Kim Dae-jung receiving the Nobel Peace Prize and a public gesture of goodwill when the two Korean teams marched behind a "Korean Unification Flag" as they entered the opening ceremony at the 2000 Sydney Olympics.[22] Hope that the new leader of the DPRK might be more flexible that his father filled the hearts of Western and South Korean diplomats alike. All appeared moving toward a peaceful resolution of a decades-old conflict.

In 2000 the prospects for real reconciliation, if not reunification, seemed brighter than they had been at any time since the end of World War II. As Clinton's presidency neared its end, his administration was determined to proceed with a peace initiative. In June 1999 William Perry, the secretary of defense, visited Pyongyang. The following year Secretary of State Madeleine Albright arrived in North Korea's capital for cordial meetings with the "Dear Leader," as Kim Jong-il had insisted on being called by his subjects. All this was preparation for a planned summit with President Clinton during the waning months of his presidency. In the wake of several years of difficult negotiations, President Clinton now offered a gradual normalization of relations and a lifting of sanctions in return for a moratorium on the North Korean missile programs.[23] However, the disputed U.S. presidential election of November 2000 and the U.S. Supreme Court's selection of George W. Bush as president brought an abrupt end to the pathway toward détente between the United States and North Korea. President Bush and his powerful vice president, Richard Cheney, seemed determined to set a new and more assertive U.S. foreign policy in the Far East and elsewhere.

President Bush's policies quickly soured U.S. relations with the ROK and set back any chance for reconciliation with the DPRK. Bush came into office at a time when the United States enjoyed good relations with the South Korean leadership and saw real possibilities for progress toward a settlement with North Korea. When Clinton left office, the United States had no human rights issues with the ROK, the status of U.S. forces in South Korea was stabilized, North Korea's Yongbyon nuclear plant was frozen and under inspection by the IAEA, and negotiations were underway to limit the DPRK's missile program. Nevertheless, Bush decided on taking a new direction. Serious problems already existed with the Agreed Framework. The U.S. Congress had refused to eliminate trade restrictions with the north, promised oil shipments were slow to arrive, and the eight water nuclear reactors were on hold. Once in office, the new, inexperienced U.S. president called for a policy review concerning U.S. relations with the two Koreas and rejected his secretary of state Colin Powell's expressed interest in following the course set by the previous administration. President Bush accepted the hard-line policy advocated by Vice President Cheney, his national security advisor, Condoleezza Rice, and other hard-liners in the new administration. In keeping with his "hawk" approach, the new U.S. president told Republic of Korea Pres. Kim Dae-jung that the United States rejected his "Sunshine Policy" of openness toward the North Korean regime. Kim's visit to Washington early in 2001 resulted in a stunning humiliation for the South Korean leader as the American president publicly chided the South Korean leader for his efforts to reach out to North Korea. Relations with both Koreas were now rapidly sliding downhill, and the Agreed Framework of multinational talks seemed about to be scrapped.[24] In his January 2002 State of the Union Address, President Bush included North Korea as a charter member of what he labeled the world's Axis of Evil (the other nations being Iraq and Iran) and announced that he wanted "regime change" to eliminate the North Korean leader, calling him a "pygmy," "tyrant," and someone to be "loathed." John Bolton, undersecretary of state for Arms Control, summed up the administration's new direction when he stated that "rogue states such as Iran, North Korea, Syria, Libya, and Cuba, whose pursuit of weapons of mass destruction makes them hostile to U.S. interests, will learn that their covert programs will not escape either detection or consequences." What the consequences might be was never articulated. With no clear plan to replace the strategy of his predecessor, one critic saw the Bush policy as "no talks, no carrots, no sticks."[25]

The North Koreans reacted to President Bush and his new aggressiveness by pointing out that the Agreed Framework of 1994 stood "at the crossroads" because the United States had pledged to provide the DPRK with two LWRs, which were now eight years overdue. The DPRK also noted that the June 13–15, 2000, talks during the Clinton administration had been a turning point for the DPRK, and further negotiations had led to restored diplomatic relations with sixteen countries, including four of the (then) G-7 nations and all the European Union members except France and Ireland. Clearly upset with the U.S. government's abrupt change in direction, DPRK officials complained in 2002 that the United States had stockpiled nuclear weapons for decades on or near the Korean Peninsula and threatened North Korea with nuclear destruction as a component of an overall strategy of world domination.[26] The North Koreans were clearly upset with the American government's abrupt change in direction, and they were prepared to act.

South Korean diplomats were as shocked as their North Korean counterparts by the Bush administration's policy change and harsh attitude. South Korean ambassador to the United States, Yang Sung-chul, immediately noted that "the policy of the United States shifted from one of collaboration during the Clinton presidency to dismantling during the Bush presidency." The ambassador viewed President Bush as creating "irreparable damage in mutual trust, particularly between North Korea and the United States." He also feared the possibility of a new arms race in what he came to view as "the flawed approach of President George W. Bush's security team as manifested in its unilateral abandonment of the [1972] Anti-Ballistic Missile Treaty and indiscriminate missile defense push."[27] The rapid downhill trajectory in U.S.-ROK relations had early on become public during President Kim's 2001 White House visit when Bush referred to the South Korean leader as "this man." The remark appeared disrespectful, especially to the South Korean news media.[28] As the Bush administration pursued its hard-line policies, and the North Koreans reacted by successfully developing nuclear weapons, as an ROK ambassador to Washington observed, "The United States did not want to admit that its hard-line policy had failed to prevent North Korea from becoming a bona fide weapons-possessing nuclear state." The ambassador saw the United States as unable to destroy the DPRK's growing nuclear arsenal or do anything to prevent its proliferation. At the same time, as relations between Washington and Seoul continued to decline, he viewed his own role as striving to avert a "diplomatic train wreck."[29]

South Koreans with long experience and sharp memories of sudden fluctuations in U.S. policy have grown accustomed to policy shifts as administrations in Washington display little appreciation for history while attempting to make their own mark on the diplomatic record. They know as well that the U.S. Congress also ignores history and often undercuts policies of the presidential administrations of the opposing party for short-term political gain. Aware of these factors in creating uncertainty, South Koreans reacted with cynicism, observing with frustration that there is only one major difference between their U.S. ally and the DPRK: one can always count on the North Koreans.

The North Koreans reacted to the Bush administration's hard-line policy by arming itself with nuclear weapons. The process had already begun when the United States seemed unwilling to fulfill the terms of the Agreed Framework. With assistance from Pakistan's Abdul Qadeer Khan, a nuclear physicist and leader of Pakistan's nuclear enrichment program, the DPRK had secretly restarted its nuclear program. With the collapse of the Agreed Framework and North Korea's announcement in 2003 of its withdrawal from the NPT, Pyongyang openly restarted its nuclear facilities. In response the Bush administration initiated the Six-Party Talks, involving both Koreas, China, Japan, and Russia, along with the United States. The first of the Six-Party Talks were held in Beijing in August, and several sessions followed. Once again there appeared to be a breakthrough in 2005 when the North Koreans promised to do away with all nuclear weapons and existing nuclear programs and rejoin the NPT.

Later all parties agreed on steps to implement the terms of the agreement, only to have things fall apart in 2009 over verification procedures. Meanwhile, on October 9, 2006, the DPRK announced that it had detonated its first nuclear device, and more tests of nuclear weapons followed. North Korean tests of missiles capable of reaching targets well beyond South Korea and Japan also continued, in spite of UN resolutions, economic sanctions, and the annoyance of neighboring China. Beyond its harsh words and warnings, the Bush administration, preoccupied with new wars in the Middle East, did nothing to ease tensions with North Korea.[30] The United States never appeared committed to a military action to take out North Korea's new nuclear arsenal during the Bush years, nor could the Bush administration admit that its hard-line policy and tough rhetoric had failed to prevent North Korea from becoming a nuclear armed state.

Amid further nuclear testing in North Korea, Barack Obama became president in January 2009, and he and his administration announced that they intended to pursue something other than the failed no-carrot-and-no-stick policies of the previous administration. However, just a year after Obama's inauguration, the Council on Foreign Relations released its *Report of Task Force 64*, an early critique of Obama's policy. The task force document concluded that the DPRK presented the "gravest threat" to U.S. security and noted that efforts to negotiate with the DPRK had been unsuccessful. President Obama's measures appeared "reactive" and "halfhearted," and the task force argued that the new administration's "current approach does not go far enough."[31] The task force also recommended plans to resume Six-Party Talks (involving the United States, the two Koreas, China, Russia, and Japan), engagement in limited bilateral talks with the DPRK, and renewed pressure on the North Korean regime with enhanced continuation of economic sanctions. The report listed as priorities preventing horizontal proliferation of nuclear weapons with other countries (for example North Korea assisting nations like Syria to acquire nuclear weapons), halting vertical proliferation of nuclear weapons within the DPRK, the eventual denuclearization of the DPRK, and ongoing engagement to support efforts aimed at improving human rights and the lives of the North Korean people. The report's authors also called for plans to implement punishments if the DPRK broke any agreements and took note of the Obama administration's lack of a stern response to the DPRK's attack on a South Korean naval vessel in 2010 that killed forty-six sailors.[32] Almost the same time, meeting with ROK president Lee Myung-bak in Toronto on June 26, President Obama praised the South Korean leader's "judgment and restraint" and stated, "We stand foursquare behind him." Referring to the North Koreans, the U.S. president also said, "There have to be consequences for such irresponsible behavior on the international stage." He then sent the matter to the United Nations Security Council.[33] President Obama called for no direct action against the DPRK, however, and beyond the rhetoric, nothing happened.

President Obama's approach of "strategic patience" did nothing to halt the North Korean nuclear program and long-range missile testing. Then in 2011 Kim Jong-il died, leaving DPRK leadership in the hands of his thirty-something-year-old son, Kim Jong-un. During the transition in the DPRK, the Obama policy employed neither more carrots nor a stronger stick, seeming to indicate that Obama hoped existing sanctions would, over a period of years, make North Korea's young leader break with the past and find reasons to negotiate. The North Koreans were not about to change course, however, and continued their dangerous weapons programs while engaging in a new form of mischief, launching cyberattacks on Sony Pictures and other corporations. Meanwhile Kim Jong-un consolidated his power, eliminated rivals (including family members), and advanced the development of nuclear weapons and the missiles to deliver them.[34] Obama, like his immediate predecessor, left his successors in the new Donald J. Trump administration to face the challenges of dealing with a nuclear armed North Korea.

Not surprisingly given the new American president's outrageous personal style, inexperience in world affairs, hostile rhetoric, and threats of military action ("fire and fury"), problems with North Korea arose early and often in the Trump White House. President Trump, in his customary campaign style, resorted to name calling, labeling Kim Jong-un as "Little Rocket Man." The North Korean leader responded by calling the septuagenarian American leader a "dotard." Suddenly the tone changed dramatically when President Trump saw an opportunity, provided by South Korea's new left-leaning president Moon Jae-in (who in 2017 replaced conservative president Park Geun-hye). President Trump jumped at the opportunity to meet with the North Korean leader for a high-profile, unprecedented media event. They met first in Singapore in June 2018. The two leaders agreed only to a generally worded statement of principles and a pledge that the DPRK would facilitate the return of the remains of UNC missing in action (MIA) soldiers. Nevertheless, returning from his first encounter with North Korea's young leader, President Trump declared North Korea no longer posed a nuclear threat.[35] They met a second time over two days in February 2019 in Hanoi. However, American aspirations for a comprehensive deal in Hanoi led to frustration, as the North Koreans were unwilling to accept U.S. demands for total denuclearization (CVID— complete, verifiable, irreversible denuclearization) of its weaponry in return for vague promises similar to those the United States had offered before about lifting economic sanctions and formally ending the Korean War. Even modest progress to ease tensions in the DMZ by removing all weapons from the Joint Security Area and the return of the remains of U.S. MIAs began to disintegrate.[36] Talk of a Nobel Peace Prize for any of those involved in these summits quickly melted away.

A third meeting in January 2019 between Trump and Kim at Panmunjom in the DMZ led to nothing more than a pleasant photograph opportunity for both leaders. It was now clear there was no deal to be struck. The United States would not budge from an insistence on CVID. On the other side, the North Koreans, as careful observers of the world scene, were well aware of the recent fate of leaders in Libya and Iraq who lacked the leverage of nuclear weapons when dealing with the United States.[37] Zero nuclear warheads was not an option for the DPRK, and it never would be. Furthermore, the North Korean regime saw the promise of integration into the world economy and open relationships with the world's democracies as more of a threat from the Americans than a bargaining chip.[38] In negotiations with the United States, the North Koreans have long, fixed memories of the Korean War, as well as every incident since the war that posed any threat to their regime's survival.

Ongoing strife on the Korean Peninsula demonstrates that conflicting public memories matter in current East Asian international relations. How contested memories of past issues form national identities requires the thoughtful attention of policy makers on all sides. Along with the conflicting narratives of the Korean War, grievances related to Japanese colonial exploitations and American support for past dictatorial regimes in South Korea hinder any diplomatic efforts to advance peace and reconciliation in the region. The Korean War created lasting consequences and bitter memories for all parties involved in the conflict. More importantly the war's memory continues to provide the foundational experience for both North and South Korea. Deep ideological conflicts based on concepts of national identity, public memory, and interpretations of history will not be easily forgotten or resolved. Ignoring both memory and history will only lead to continued stalemate.[39]

East Asia has remained a relatively peaceful and stable region since the Korean War, yet much has changed.[40] Koreans are no longer passive actors in regional and world affairs. South Korea is one of the globe's economic powerhouses and an exporter of popular culture throughout the world. North Korea is now a member of the exclusive nuclear weapons club, fully capable of threatening and intimidating its larger neighbors and the United States. Furthermore, both the ROK and DPRK occupy a strategically located small peninsula in the middle of one of the most dynamic regions of the earth.[41] Each claims legitimacy and strives for control over the other, while holding profoundly conflicting memories and historical narratives to justify their claim.

In seeking reconciliation on the Korean Peninsula, the contested memory of a troubled past cannot be ignored. While the heavily fortified DMZ presents a formidable physical barrier to a unified Korea, sharply contested and conflicting memories of the war of 1950–53 and its aftermath continue to obstruct efforts toward reconciliation. The north and south do not even agree about basic facts on when and how the war began. Moreover, the role of the United States in Korean affairs remains a contentious point of disagreement. To many Koreans, more so in the north than in the south, the United States is seen as a power that interfered with Korean efforts at unification in 1950 and caused a disastrous war that took the lives of nearly five million of their countrymen, the vast majority being civilians. The United States is also viewed as the force behind a series of authoritative dictatorships in South Korea that suppressed civil rights, denied individual freedoms, and perpetrated horrible atrocities on opponents of their regimes. Even those in the ROK who are grateful for U.S. support during the Korean War and afterward find the United States a much-needed but frequently frustrating ally. In North Korea, where only one memory and official historical narrative of the Korean War is permitted, the war is remembered as a heroic defense of the fatherland against a savage American-led invasion and a nuclear military threat that has continued for seven decades. The divergent memories and conflicting

understandings of history continue to hinder the effort the Koreans themselves must initiate to achieve reunification or even peaceful coexistence.

The People's Republic of China, meanwhile, continues to insist that
its population must understand the Korean War only as a heroic and
honorable sacrifice to halt U.S. aggression and save a weaker Communist neighbor. This narrative was set aside for decades by the Chinese
government following Richard M. Nixon's visit to the PRC in 1972 that
brought about positive developments in U.S.-China relations.[42] In 2020,
however, as relations with the United States deteriorated amid trade
disputes with the Trump administration and charges that the COVID-19
virus resulted from Chinese carelessness, the government of Xi Jinping
noticeably ramped up its patriotic rhetoric and claims of victory in 1950
over U.S. Armed Forces in Korea. In addition, seventieth-anniversary
commemoration activities related to the PRC's role in standing up to
the United States during the Korean War have accompanied the new and
more assertive foreign policy.[43] In adopting a "Wolf Warrior" approach
to foreign relations, the Chinese leadership appears intent on building
its armed forces, suppressing minorities, and eliminating any criticism of
the ruling elite. At the same time, the Chinese Communist Party (CCP)
is clearly intent on enforcing an orthodox history and public memory of
the recent past from which no counternarrative is allowed.[44]

Actions of the current regime governing China cannot be understood
without careful attention to the importance of historical memory. Using
the public memory of the past, Communist Party officials have largely
succeeded in redirecting a young generation who threatened the party's
rule in the 1980s by advocating for Western-style democracy into supporters of the increasingly authoritarian government's nationalist and
expansionist foreign policies. The party achieved its goal with a restless
campaign beginning in the 1990s to place China's "century of national
humiliation" at the forefront of historical education and crediting the party
with bringing the humiliation to an end. Certainly the period from the
Opium Wars of the 1840s through the end of World War II was a time of
disunity, suffering, and humiliation. The unification of the nation under
Mao Zedong's leadership brought Western and Japanese abuse of China to
an abrupt end. But the Communist Party further claims a great victory in
Korea over U.S. imperialism while glossing over CCP-led disasters, such as
the "Great Leap Forward" and the Cultural Revolution (which combined

may have devastated the Chinese population more in just two decades than foreign imperialists did in an entire century). Whatever its merits in the realm of truth and accuracy, the party's campaign has succeeded in developing a new and virulent nationalism that supports the government's assertive policies in the South China Sea, the expansionist "Belt and Road" international trade initiative, and the suppression of dissent in Hong Kong and in the northwestern regions populated by Uyghurs.[45] It appears that the official public rhetoric of the "Never Forget the Century of National Humiliation" campaign has produced a strident and well-entrenched national memory that allows for the public approval of the government's efforts to make China a dominant force in world affairs and reformulate the order that has existed in East Asia since the Korean War.

For seventy years the trilateral relationship between the United States, South Korea, and Japan has been close and highly cooperative—in spite of occasional disagreements, misunderstandings, and painful, conflicted memories of World War II and the Korean War. President Trump disrupted this relationship in his effort to set his own distinctive mark on U.S. foreign policy by questioning and destabilizing traditional alliances worldwide. As this book goes to press, it remains to be seen if the administration of Pres. Joe Biden will be able to restore the trust and confidence of both Japan and the Republic of Korea in the reliability of the United States as a partner in maintaining peace and stability in East Asia. Clearly President Biden understands the importance of the trilateral relationship and in the early weeks of his administration sent a high-powered delegation, headed by the secretary of state, Anthony Blinken, to meet with Japanese and South Korean leaders. In addition, Japanese prime minister Yoshihide Suga and ROK president Moon Jae-in were the first foreign leaders to be invited to the White House following Biden's inauguration. Meanwhile, Japan and the Republic of Korea must overcome festering problems in their relationship with each other before there can be progress in trilateral diplomacy.

As President Biden strives to reassure the two important allies, serious long-standing issues of trust sour the relationship between the Republic of Korea and Japan. Koreans remain bitter about Japan's economic recovery following World War II, which is viewed by many in Korea as Japan's profiteering during the devastation of the Korean War. The economic advancements at the expense of Koreans during the harsh decades of

Japanese imperialism (1910–45) is still an unpleasant memory, and the inability to satisfactorily resolve the World War II "comfort women" apology and compensation issue stirs contentious memories in both nations about the sexual exploitation of thousands of Korean women.[46] While the United States would like to move ahead on the resolution of pressing current issues (the security of Taiwan, open waters in the South China Sea, and climate change), its two key East Asian allies appear stuck in the mire of memory. North Korea and China, meanwhile, appear eager to create new challenges to the long-standing trilateral relationship.

Is reconciliation among the United States, North Korea, South Korea, and other nations that supported the UNC possible? Although there exists a myriad of differences between the Korean War and the long U.S. military involvement in Vietnam, the U.S. reconciliation with Vietnam may offer something of a model for what an eventual peace with North Korea may look like. The reconciliation process will likely take decades (the United States did not establish full diplomatic ties with Vietnam until 1995, twenty years after the last U.S. military helicopter took off from the roof of the U.S. Embassy in Saigon), and any genuine reconciliation will require a long, complex, and incremental process to build trust. And close cooperation with the government of South Korea will be necessary, making reconciliation a three-way process. Initial steps will include finding and identifying remains of MIAs (a collaborative effort already underway), dealing with unexploded land mines and bombs along the DMZ, creating business partnerships and organizing trade, exchanging scholars and students, and establishing a Fulbright office and possibly a Peace Corps program. Above all, if U.S.-Vietnam ties are to be looked upon for guidance, honesty about the past will be required by all sides. The process will be emotional and gradual.[47] Furthermore, as with Vietnam, North Korea will need to realize that a solid relationship with the United States, as well as South Korea and Japan, is beneficial for geopolitical and security issues related to the more assertive and expansionist military and foreign policies of the PRC. As with the United States and Vietnam, reconciliation with North Korea will most likely come about, in large measure, because of concerns over national security.[48] Adjustments to national memories will be required on all sides, but particularly in North Korea, where selective public memories of the Korean War and the restless telling of a mythological national history have underpinned a regime's claim to power and legitimacy. The process will be risky and may take an entire generation and some major transformation or replacement of the Kim regime.

In finding a peaceful resolution to the continuing division of the Korean Peninsula, the bitter and contrasting memories of the Korean War and its aftermath will prove more difficult to remove than the tens of thousands of land mines and hundreds of miles of barbed wire placed along both sides of the DMZ.

Conclusion

On my return visits to South Korea, I am often asked what is the single greatest difference I notice from the memory of my first arrival in the country more than fifty years ago? I always say it's the trees. I well remember landing at Seoul's Kimpo Airport in the frigid winter of 1970 and seeing barren hills and rugged, treeless mountainsides. Even before napalm bombs, flamethrowers, and artillery blasts of the Korean War denuded the mountains and hills, the Korean landscape was largely deforested by people using the trees for fuel and the Japanese colonial rulers' exploitation of Korea's timber resources for their own benefit. On Arbor Day I saw school children planting thin, little sprouts, expecting them to survive and grow amid narrow, jagged cracks in the mountainside rocks. To me, their effort seemed hopeless. Now, thanks to the children and a determined government policy of reforestation, the beautiful, tree-covered landscape of South Korea appears as a vivid symbol of stability and prosperity in the land south of the demilitarized zone (DMZ). Since the 1953 armistice agreement, the Republic of Korea has enjoyed an era of economic and social advancement unknown in its thousands of years of recorded history, and the trees present an undeniable sign of this remarkable development.

The 1950–53 war in Korea stands as a major turning point in the history of East Asia as well as the Cold War. Korea experienced direct military involvement of the United States and its allies, set against the Soviet Union and China as adversaries in a massive and costly foreign war. Yet the conflict in Korea suffered from a lack of deserved recognition because of the enormous shadow cast on it by the conclusion of the greatest of

207

all wars just a few years earlier, and also because the war's violence was contained on the Korean Peninsula. In addition, the Korean War failed to fulfill the expectations for the kind of decisive victory World War II had provided its victors—especially the United States. It appeared that the United States had lost a war for the first time in its history—and to a much weaker foe, no less. Americans were unprepared for a "limited war" and appeared to believe that their nation always fought for unconditional surrender, followed by a capitulation ceremony, victory parades, and trials of enemy war criminals. A war that ended in something less than a complete victory seemed at odds with the very character of the American people. Yet most wars are limited in their objectives, and those of the United States are no exception. World War II was an outlier. Wars rarely conclude with total conquest and occupation of an enemy. Almost always wars end with treaties or agreements, the exchange of hostages and prisoners, the ceding or taking of real estate, and the transfer of treasure.

Korea set a new pattern for post–World War II U.S. military actions. Not only was the Korean conflict of 1950–53 similar to earlier and forgotten U.S. military engagements with foreign adversaries, but it was also quite different in nature and outcome from World War II.[1] Henceforth for Korea the United States would enter overseas conflicts seeking a limited objective and without a declaration of war by Congress, although there would be vaguely written resolutions authorizing the president to use necessary force. After Korea, Americans would grow accustomed to fighting far from American shores for reasons other than an immediate response to a foreign military attack or direct threats to the survival of the homeland. Wars would be fought for certain limited objectives, employing professional soldiers along with highly paid mercenaries and contractors. U.S. presidents would scrupulously avoid mobilization of the home front and employ far less than the full array of available lethal weaponry. In the wars following Korea, professional soldiers and their career-focused commanders would rotate in, out, and back again into combat zones as conflicts continued over long periods. In these seemingly interminable conflicts, the American public would grow numb to the death tolls and the gruesome reports of ebbs and flows of fierce combat in far-off places. Negotiating for months or years while fighting continued, or even accelerated, would characterize post-Korea warfare in Vietnam and the Middle East, where settlements of conflicts would be reached only after the attention of the American public had moved elsewhere. In these wars, as with the Korean War, American veterans returned alone to a society not fully aware of where and for what they had been fighting, and the nation would find it difficult to remember or memorialize these wars in which no vital interest of the United States ever seemed truly threatened.

Practical lessons from the experiences of the Korean War remain difficult to discern, because the Korean War had its own defining national and international factors and unique geopolitical context. The conflict grew out of decades of civil strife that involved two Western philosophies competing for dominance in an ancient, stultified society that had lost faith in its ineffective and corrupt dynastic rulers, outdated Confucian codes of conduct, and rigid isolationist tradition. Both Communism and free-market capitalism (which included powerful elements of Western democracy and Christianity) vied for dominance among reform-minded Korean leaders in the waning days of the five-hundred-year-old Chosun dynasty. That competition continued within the exiled Korean independence movement throughout the thirty-five years of Japanese colonial rule (1910–45). Following the independence from Japanese colonial rule granted to Koreans after World War II, the ideological conflict continued. When the Japanese surrendered, allied forces, the Soviet Union, and the United States immediately occupied a divided Korean Peninsula. In the north the Soviet Union installed a useful Korean national loyal to Moscow in the same manner it used to set up Communist regimes in Eastern Europe following the demise of Nazi Germany. In the south the American military presided over a messy and contentious process that eventually allowed a highly imperfect democratic form of government to emerge following United Nations (UN) supervised elections in 1948. Leading Korean factions of various political philosophies continued to struggle violently for political advantage, from the Yalu River to Cheju Island, even after two competing regimes were established on either side of the 38th parallel.

Both the ROK and the DPRK had considerable local support but were dependent on outside forces to hold power and challenge their rival for supremacy on the peninsula. A standoff ensued until the Communist regime in North Korea secured the authorization and weaponry from the Soviet Union to launch an attack on an overmatched but more populous

South Korea. In June 1950 the civil strife that had destabilized Korea since the end of World War II erupted into a full-blown war. As with most modern civil wars, foreign interests and influences were present before, throughout, and following the conflict. In Korea circumstances in 1950 soon led to a worldwide confrontation involving an international array of nations focused on combat in a small but strategically located peninsula. Massive Soviet aid and more than a quarter million Chinese soldiers confronted a United Nations Command (UNC) led by a determined United States and UN allies, who were committed to halting the advance of Communism, preserving stability in East Asia, and establishing the credibility of the United Nations.

Wars frequently result from misunderstandings, and Korea was no exception. The war in Korea came about and continued for thirty-seven months because both sides made judgments that proved to be erroneous. While Pres. Harry S. Truman may have overlooked or underestimated the threat to South Korea posed by the Soviet-backed regime in North Korea, Joseph Stalin clearly failed to appreciate that he had pushed the Truman administration to the point where the only possible response to an attack on South Korea would have to be military action. By this time Soviet-sponsored Communist governments had taken hold in Eastern Europe, and Mao Zedong had assumed power in China. Truman could see no credible alternative but to respond with force to the Soviet-sponsored North Korean invasion of June 25, 1950. Faced with Republican charges that his administration was responsible for the "loss of China," and needing to shore up the Western European nations within the new North Atlantic Treaty Organization (NATO) alliance, Truman had to demonstrate strength and resolve. Stalin not only miscalculated the American response in Korea but also failed to see that the Korean conflict would lead immediately to developments he did not want: a major American rearmament, a rapid strengthening of NATO's defenses in Europe, and a new security partnership between the United States and Japan. Also the war led to the surprising rise of Mao's China to the status of the Soviet Union's coequal among Communist states.

All sides made critical miscalculations leading to prolonged warfare in Korea. Perhaps Kim Il-sung, Stalin, and Mao all miscalculated the internal strength of Communist cadres operating in South Korea in the years leading up to the invasion of June 1950, although it is likely Kim knew his operations in South Korea were in decline following the brutal, relentless, and effective anti-Communist campaigns of the Syngman Rhee government. There never was overwhelming support in South Korea for Soviet-style Communism or for the northern invaders. In fact, by 1950 Communism was not all that popular in North Korea, as more than a million refugees fleeing to South Korea would attest. Meanwhile Rhee, realizing his dependence on the United States, needlessly hindered his own cause in the years before the war by unnecessarily violating the rights of legitimate democratic opposition, ignoring economic development, and employing reckless militaristic rhetoric about his military invading North Korea. Rhee's actions and words worried the Truman administration, which withheld military equipment for fear he might use it to attack the north. In China, Mao soon realized that his trust in Stalin was misplaced, as the Soviet leader failed to provide the military assistance promised when China sent hundreds of thousands of soldiers across the Yalu River. And in the United States, the Truman administration failed to anticipate the North Korean attacks of June 25, 1950, and then ignored the warnings that China would enter the conflict to rescue the defeated regime of Kim Il-sung.

When war came the United States and the countries contributing to the UNC found it increasingly difficult to explain and justify their military efforts in Korea to their own populations who saw no immediate threat to their security. Censored and often erroneous reports of civilian and prisoner of war (POW) treatment by the combatants, charges that the United States deployed chemical weapons, and false legends surrounding Chinese brainwashing techniques all contributed to the notion that perhaps the war was a misguided effort. With no direct threat to U.S. security, or the survival of the People's Republic of China and the Soviet Union, the purpose of the fighting seemed only an expensive effort to achieve some vague and undefined outcome. Support for the war in the United States and the nations of the UNC was initially strong, but it soon waned. Political opposition in the United States was divided and unable to articulate a coherent strategy other than relentless criticism of the unpopular but seemingly necessary course the Truman administration was pursuing. Unlike World War II, the American people were never fully engaged in the war effort, and most continued their lives with little or no disruption. Men of draft age could secure deferments with some ease, and most of those drafted into the military never saw Korea. Major U.S. allies in the UNC, the British and French in particular, were preoccupied during the Korean War with desperate efforts to hold on to the remnants of their colonial empires as they tried to rebuild war-torn economies. The war in Korea never excited the popular imagination in Western nations, and the popular culture of the 1950s largely ignored the conflict limited to a distant, small, and unknown land. Popular protests were few and without influence on policy. Furthermore, in the decade following the 1953 armistice, the threats presented by Soviet nuclear weapons and its advances in missile and satellite technology, as well as the frightening Cuban Missile Crisis of 1962, all dominated American and NATO security concerns. In this atmosphere, memories of the inconclusive war in Korea were easily pushed aside.

With certain aspects of the Korean War—such as concerns over brainwashing of POWs and notions about a perceived weakness in the American male—becoming ingrained in the nation's culture, the remembrance of the war in monuments and memorials was slow to come about. Perhaps too, the unsatisfactory, negotiated outcome of the war, or the fact that there was no result of the unended conflict other than a return to the status quo ante, left the public, including veterans, in no mood for commemoration. All this changed in the 1980s, three decades after the fighting ended. Both the success of the Vietnam War veterans in securing a memorial on the National Mall for their service and the sudden, unexpected, and spectacular rise of the ROK as a vibrant democratic state fueled the efforts by veterans and their families to place the Korean War Veterans Memorial on the National Mall and simultaneously erect scores of monuments in communities throughout the country. Because a democracy had been saved from Communist aggression, Korea could now be understood as a success worthy of memorialization. In these endeavors, grateful Korean Americans played prominent roles as planners, advocates, fundraisers, and celebrants at dedication ceremonies. South Korean corporations provided assistance, and the government of the ROK has also participated in the memorialization efforts, most notably in providing $20 million for the Korean War Veterans Memorial to fund a Wall of Remembrance and an endowment for maintenance. While monuments, memorials, sites of remembrance, and ongoing commemorative activities appeared throughout the landscape, these failed to generate the emotional appeal of World War II or the American Civil War. In spite of its significance in altering the United States' role in East Asian and world affairs, while permanently changing the nation's society and political culture, the Korean War is still recalled, in contrast to World War II and the Civil War, with a certain ambivalence and lack of passion.

In contrast, memories of the Korean War in the two Koreas remain central to the psyche of each regime. However, each holds to radically differing official narratives of the war and its origins. In North Korea, Kim Il-sung rapidly created a history of the war that placed himself at the center of a heroic effort to lead the Korean people in a patriotic fight to unify their nation and stand boldly against an American-led military invasion of the homeland. In creating a cult of personality, while purging all Communist elements in the north not absolutely loyal to him, Kim's memory of the war left no place to include any mention of Soviet or Chinese guidance, authorization, and assistance. Instead he adopted the notion of Juche—self-reliance and independence from all outside influences. Construction of a huge war museum with himself at the center of a victorious defense of the fatherland began as the ashes of his ruined capital city cooled in the months following the 1953 armistice. Gigantic statues and portraits of Kim began to appear everywhere. Even his Communist allies in China, the Soviet Union, and Eastern Europe were shocked by his audacious cult of personality. Meanwhile, in South Korea, the government, as well as most of the population, remained bitter over the armistice agreement that took effect without President Rhee's signature, and memory of the unresolved war was too distasteful to commemorate publicly. Only in 1957, when a monumental statue of Gen. Douglas MacArthur was positioned overlooking the harbor at Incheon, along with a text lamenting that victory and reunification had not been allowed, did the official (and popularly held) memory of the war have any memorial in South Korea. This situation continued until the 1990s, when democracy and prosperity brought about a reevaluation of the war in that country's popular memory.

In the decades following the armistice, an uneasy peace took hold on the Korean Peninsula. At the same time, there were expressions of concern in the government of the ROK over the reliability of the United States as an ally, as well as popular resentment over U.S. support of dictatorial regimes. Amidst government crackdowns on protests, ROK citizens expressed cries of outrage over multiple aspects of the war, including U.S.-condoned or sanctioned atrocities committed by Rhee's cruel, vindictive, and insecure government and the authoritarian military regimes that followed him. The United States sat on the sidelines, hoping for democratic reforms while concerned about the larger issue of stability in East Asia. Outrage by South Koreans was without doubt justified; however, in the years following the armistice, there were real threats from North Korea. Communist sympathizers supported by North Korea, and murderous cadres dispatched to South Korea by ruthless North Korean tyrants, sought to disrupt, destabilize, and undermine the ROK. North Korean commandos and assassins were dispatched to kill South Korean leaders and prominent civilians.[2] Strong South Korean countermeasures were clearly required, and the practice by naïve antigovernment factions in South Korea of ignoring the real misdeeds of the northerners continues to this day to present a false historical narrative.

Standing at an overlook on the southern side of the three-mile-wide DMZ while gazing toward North Korea, one cannot help but be impressed by the calm beauty of the expansive vista. Whatever the season, the DMZ appears as a vast, forested nature preserve. Beyond the lush canopy of the treetops are picture-perfect farms and pristine North Korean villages, perhaps kept tidy because no permanent residents seem to be living in them. In the distance, through the mist and low clouds, stately mountains appear. This picturesque scene offers no suggestion of what lies beyond or of the lethal, well-hidden military force. Only the enormous statues of King Il-sung, the Great Leader, all placed within sight of one another, suggest that matters north of the DMZ are not what they initially seem. At the same time, the viewer is surrounded on the southern side of the DMZ by huge, heavily armed guards. The military presence is intermingled with busloads of tourists from all over the world. There are souvenir shops, various food stands, monuments to U.S. and UNC forces, and carnival rides to keep the children occupied and entertained. All this creates an atmosphere of a weird and bizarre theme park on the edge of a dangerous no-man's-land. But this is a dangerous place. There are more than a million soldiers on high alert along the two sides of the 150-mile-long DMZ, and more than fifty Americans and hundreds of North and South Koreans have died in skirmishes along this dangerous border since the Korean War ended.

Keen observers of East Asian affairs have noted that the Korean War is viewed differently by the populations of these nations that participated in the 1950–53 conflict. For many Americans, Korea remains the "forgotten war," lost and overshadowed in public memory by the unquestioned triumph of the "Greatest Generation" in World War II and the nation's long, agonizing nightmare in Vietnam. The North Koreans have no choice but to remember it as the "Fatherland Liberation War," while South Koreans tend to refer to the horrific conflict more generically as the "six-twenty-five war"—referencing the date of the Soviet-sponsored invasion across the 38th parallel on June 25, 1950. For the Chinese the war was glorified in slogans such as "Resist American Aggressions, Aid Korea War" and serves today as an important early milestone in the history of the People's Republic of China. There can be no doubt that the differing names define the conflicting memories held by the participants of a still unfinished contest for dominance and legitimacy on the Korean Peninsula.

Americans hold only a vague awareness of the Korean War, and the public memory that exists is often clouded by myth and long-outdated images. There appears to be a lack of understanding that many changes in U.S. domestic life and foreign policy owe their origins to the "forgotten war." Public remembrance of the war may be fading even more with the loss of the Korean War generation. Yet scholars and policy makers are well aware of the war's significance as a turning point in the history of the Cold War, the shaping of "limited" wars in Vietnam and the Middle East, and in the nation's complex international relations with the nations of East Asia. In the United States, the memory of the Korean War continues to evolve as hopes for peace rise and fall amid diplomatic realignments, while for the two Koreas, the war remains at the center of their national identities and their quests for legitimacy.

While the domestic and international consequences of the war's outcome are facts of everyday life in the United States and among the nations who participated in the UNC, these changes are seldom attributed to the Korean War of 1950–53. For the American public, the "police action" in Korea did not seem like a real war. Nevertheless, Korea brought about profound and lasting changes in U.S. society. No future presidential administration (especially not a Democratic one) would risk appearing weak by not sending troops abroad to address a perceived threat, and policy makers came to see Korea as a model for future limited wars in far-off countries such as Vietnam, Afghanistan, Iraq, and Libya. After Korea the U.S. military concentrated on air power and the ability to quickly move huge conventional forces of professional soldiers and private contractors to distant battlefields. Korea has served as the prototype of the warfare in which the United States engaged from after the Korean armistice through the present.

In spite of some hopeful signs for peace and denuclearization of the DPRK, issues on the Korean Peninsula remain far from resolved at the time of this writing. There are few signs that a genuine reunification will come at any time in the near future, and the contested historical narratives of the conflicting sides will certainly hinder meaningful reconciliation. The only point of agreement on the horrific conflict started on June 25, 1950, seems to be who won—remarkably, all parties now consider themselves victors. Perhaps the conflicting historical narratives that have left all parties claiming victory in the Korean War will help to eventually lead to a settlement that will actually allow all parties to be true victors.

For decades the United States and the major powers surrounding the Korean Peninsula have appeared satisfied with the status quo. The People's Republic of China seems content to have a Communist ally (albeit a difficult one) located between itself and a dynamic South Korea with its worrisome U.S. military bases. While the United States would like to see the two Koreas united under a free and democratic ROK, it is unwilling to risk a nuclear war to achieve such a goal. Having centuries of troubled relationships with its neighbor, Japan appears unconcerned with a divided Korea. And Russia, unlike the late Soviet Union, seems uninterested in any major involvements with the geopolitical affairs on the Korean Peninsula. Expressing displeasure and dissatisfaction with aspects of the 1953 armistice, the PRC, Japan, Russia, and the United States all understand that the agreement reached at Panmunjom has held for nearly seven decades and are aware that disrupting the current international alignment in East Asia could be problematic. Furthermore, since 1953, with the notable exception of North Korea, the nations of East Asia have experienced a seventy-year period of peace and economic prosperity unknown at any time during their four millennia of recorded history.

Except for the Communist Party elite, the population of the DPRK has been denied the prosperity enjoyed by their neighbors. Nevertheless, the state's governing regime has proved remarkably resilient, even advancing the isolated and impoverished country to the status of a nuclear power. The DPRK has never ceased to be troublesome and threatening to those across its borders, and its nuclear arsenal adds considerable tension to the divided Korean Peninsula. Bad behavior and nuclear weapons aside, it seems unlikely that the leadership of North Korea is prepared to initiate a war that would upset the existing order in East Asia and lead to its own annihilation. After all, the North Koreans would not have invaded South Korea in 1950 without the explicit approval and massive military assistance of Joseph Stalin's Soviet Union.

Memories of the Korean War held by the nations who fought it have remained contested and conflicted into the first two decades of the twenty-first century. In spite of once-warring East Asian nations increasing their commercial, educational, and cultural interaction with each other and the outside world, radically differing narratives about the Korean conflict of 1950–53 continue to hinder efforts to resolve tensions in the region. In international relations the DPRK holds out as an exception. Yet even with its self-imposed isolation and adherence to the mythical notion of Juche, it appears to be gradually giving way to new international realities, in particular the rise of China as a global power.[3] The Kim family regime seems to be struggling to keep absolute control of all aspects of life in North Korea, while holding its more powerful neighbors at bay with threats of nuclear holocaust.

On the other side of the DMZ, South Korea, with its dynamic economy and free, democratic society, finds within itself sharp divisions in the collective memory of the war, its causes, and its consequences. Rival political parties in the ROK seek to open old wounds, assess guilt for past wrongs, and blame each other for dealings with North Korea and failed reunification efforts. While China's emergence as a world power in the past two decades has forever altered the relationships of East Asian nations, across the Pacific the United States remains deeply and inescapably entangled in East Asian affairs but seemingly incapable of navigating a consistent and reliable course. While U.S. presence in the Asia-Pacific region is unavoidable and necessary, internal political divisions hinder Washington's unsteady diplomatic efforts. A sudden and significant change in the status quo could lead to dangerous instability. While all parties would welcome a resolution of the ongoing conflict on the Korean

Peninsula, none are in a position to force an outcome that would completely satisfy memories of the war or fulfill the unique historical vision each has of a true victory.

For the United States and its UNC allies, the Korean War is remembered, if at all, as a justified and necessary stand against the aggression of the Soviet Union and the People's Republic of China. Indeed, the Republic of Korea was saved and eventually became a prosperous democracy. The "containment policy" initiated by President Truman was followed by all his successors in the White House until the Soviet Union eventually imploded. Yet the current situation in East Asia is far from ideal. The Korean Peninsula remains divided, with the isolated and nuclear-armed north now dependent on China. Meanwhile, the south is allied with the United States and maintains close economic and cultural ties to the nations of the Pacific Rim. Amidst the tension, the armistice of 1953, while unsatisfactory to all parties, has led to a stable era in East Asia that twenty-first-century peace negotiators will be challenged to improve upon—or even match. Whatever the outcome of efforts to resolve the continuing Korean hostilities may be, the conflicted memories of this unfinished conflict will continue to evolve, as the final chapter of the unended Korean War has yet to be written.

Notes

PREFACE

1. My thoughts on the challenges and rewards of a career in public history institutions are expressed in M. J. Devine, "The Education of a Public Historian"; and M. J. Devine, "Administrators."
2. Devine, *The Voices of Heaven*; Devine, "What Was Said in the Bamboo Grove"; and Devine, "Crane's Grace." Additional information at www.maijarheedevine .com.
3. M. J. Devine, *Korea in War, Revolution, and Peace*.

INTRODUCTION

1. Winter, *Remembering War*, 1, 281. See also Kammen, *Mystic Chords of Memory*, 13; Ballal and Joshi, "Forgetting and Remembering in Bhopal," 325; and Kelland, *Clio's Foot Soldiers*, 2. The standard study of collective or public memory remains Halbwachs, *On Collective Memory*.
2. Winter, *Remembering War*, 283–89.
3. Van Wagenen, *Remembering the Forgotten War*, 5. On public memory see Bodnar, *Remaking America*, 13–20. How those who died in U.S. wars are remembered is examined in Bontrager, *Death at the Edges of Empire*, 2–3, 4, 26–27.
4. In all, sixty-three nations contributed to the Republic of Korea's defense, including sixteen that provided military units. Others sent medical and humanitarian aid, including the nonmember United Nations countries of West Germany and occupied Japan. Kim Jiyul and Sheila Miyoshi Jager, "The 'Greater' UN Coalition during the Korean War," *Sources and Methods* (blog), Wilson Center, History and Public Policy Program, May 26, 2020, wilsoncenter.org/blog-post/greater -un-coalition-during-korean-war.
5. President Truman clearly explained his rationale in the second volume of his memoirs, *Years of Trial and Hope*. For analysis of the decision-making process

during the first weeks of the war in Washington DC, and Seoul, see Millett, *The War for Korea*; and Beschloss, *Presidents of War*, 435–73.

6. Casey, *Selling the Korean War*, 325–41, 367.

7. Casey, "The United States," 51.

8. Edwards, *The Korean War* (2006), 169. Also see Carlson, *Remembered Prisoners of a Forgotten War*, 1–21; and Lech, *Broken Soldiers*, 2–5.

9. Wells, *Fearing the Worst*, 472–89.

10. Stueck, *Rethinking the Korean War*, 236–37; Halberstam, *The Coldest Winter*, 647–56; and Yuen, *Analogies at War*, chapter 5.

11. Jinwung Kim, *A History of Korea*, 468–518; and Jager, *Brothers at War*, 416–24, 566, n 6.

12. Kathryn Weathersby, "The Amazing Aftermath of the 1988 Seoul Olympics," *Korea Times*, April 18, 2018; and Oberdorfer and Carlin, *The Two Koreas*, 180–86.

13. West and Suh, *Remembering the Forgotten War*, ii.

14. A summation of polls since 1948 and a current evaluation of the methodologies employed in the rating of U.S. presidents is presented in Watson, "Their Place in History," 1–22, especially 8–9. Truman ranked as the nation's sixth-best president in 2017 and 2018 in a C-SPAN poll and American Political Science poll, respectively. Dwight Eisenhower, Truman's successor at the time of the 1953 Korean War Armistice agreement, was ranked fifth and seventh, respectively, in the same polls. In 1962 Eisenhower ranked twenty-first in historian Arthur M. Schlesinger's survey.

15. Among the revisionist school of Korean War historians, Bruce Cumings is the acknowledged leader. For examples of his writings, see his introduction to *Child of Conflict*; Cumings, *Korea's Place in the Sun* (1997); and Halliday and Cumings, *Korea*. On the "revisionists" and what he considers the "unhappiness school of Korean War history," see Millett, *The War for Korea*, 596–97.

16. Regarding North Korean efforts to court leftist groups in South Korea, undermine the south's democratic institutions, and influence sympathetic Western journalists and academics, see Jager, *Brothers at War*, 351, 355, 424, 556–57, n 61, n 62; Jinwung Kim, *A History of Korea*, 464–65, 532–33; Seongho Jhe, "Recent Aspects and Future Prospects of North Korea's South Korean Operation," (unpublished paper, Chung-Ang University, in emails to author, August 18 and 20, 2021). Copies in Michael J. Devine Papers, Harry S. Truman Library (HSTL). Also see Stella Young Yee Shin, "North Korean-South Korean Relations Since the Korean War. Ethics of Development in a Global Environment," December 1, 2001, https://web.stanford.edu/class/e297a/North%20Kores-%20South%20Kores %20Relations%20Since%20the%20Korean%20War.

17. Suhi Choi, *Embattled Memories*, 7–52, 95–114; and Choe Sang-hun, "Tens of Thousands March in Seoul, Calling for Ouster of President," *New York*

Times, November 14, 2015, https://www.nytimes.com/2015/11/15/world/asia
/antigovernment-protest-seoul-south-korea.html?partner=bloomberg.

18. Hakjoon Kim, "A Review of Korean War Studies Since 1992–1994," 215–346;
and William Stueck, "Korean War in International History since 1995," *Sources
and Methods* (blog), Wilson Center, History and Public Policy Program, June
22, 2020, https://www.wilsoncenter.org/blog-post/korean-war-international
-history-1995.

19. Stueck, *The Korean War in World History*, 179–80.

20. Edwards, *Korean War* (1999), xii, 165, 173; and Pash, *In the Shadow of the Greatest
Generation*, 183–226.

21. Halberstam, *The Coldest Winter*, 645. The sense of loss kept Korean War veterans
from forming an association for more than four decades after the end of the
conflict. See Edwards, *To Acknowledge a War*, 145.

22. Quoted in the English-language guide to the Democratic People's Republic of
Korea's museum entitled *Outstanding Leadership and Brilliant Victory* (Pyongyang, DPRK: Korean Pictorial, 1993). Also see the positive review of the museum
in Cumings, *War and Television*, 223–27.

1. THE "POLICE ACTION"

1. Philip D. Lagerquist recorded this observation on numerous occasions. He is
quoted in Ferrell, *Harry S. Truman*, 321, 440, n 15.

2. An excellent, recent synthesis of the events leading to war in Korea is presented
in Wells, *Fearing the Worst*, 7–60, 507–13. A detailed contemporary account of
President Truman's reaction to the North Korean invasion is provided in Beverly Smith, "Why We Went to War in Korea," *Saturday Evening Post*, November
10, 1951.

3. On the international and domestic challenge Truman faced upon taking office
in April 1945, see Hamby, *Man of the People*, 338–86; and Ferrell, *Off the Record*,
80–81.

4. Elsey, *An Unplanned Life*, 80–89. Elsey had served as a young naval officer
assigned to the secret White House "Map Room" during World War II and then
stayed on as a staff member in the Truman administration. Elsey's memoirs and
papers at the Harry S. Truman Library provide a fascinating insider's view of the
Truman White House. See also Miscamble, *From Roosevelt to Truman*, 34–86.

5. Ferrell, *Off the Record*, 53.

6. Harry S. Truman to Bess Truman, July 18, 1945, in Ferrell, *Dear Bess*, 519.

7. Miscamble, *From Roosevelt to Truman*, 26–27; and Matray, *Reluctant Crusade*,
254.

8. Truman, *Memoirs*, Vol. 1, *Years of Decisions*, 440, 445. Also see Truman, *Memoirs*, Vol. 2, *Years of Trial and Hope*, 265–317; Matray, "Captive of the Cold War,"

145–68; and Charles Kraus, "Failed Diplomacy: Soviet-American Relations and the Division of Korea, History and Public Policy Program," *Sources and Methods* (blog), Wilson Center, May 8, 2020, https://www.wilsoncenter.org. Matray notes that the decision to divide the Korean Peninsula at the 38th parallel was made in August 1945—after the Potsdam Conference. "Potsdam Revisited," 259–280.

9. Henry L. Stimson to President Truman, "Trusteeship for Korea," July 16, 1945, https://history.state.gov/historicaldocuments/frus1945Berlinv02/d732. See also Truman, *Memoirs*, 1:317; and Blaine, *The Accidental President*, 287. The Truman administration was also concerned about the credibility of various Korean political leaders. To Gen. William Donovan, head of the Office of Strategic Services, who was working with associates of Korean political strongman Kim Ku, chair of the Korean Provisional Government, "as intelligence agents in Korea," the White House advised that the administration would not receive communication from "officials of self-styled governments that are not recognized by the Government of the United States." See "Confidential" memorandum, August 22, 1945, prepared by Admiral Leahy, White House Central file 1, HSTL, Independence MO.

10. Truman, *Memoirs*, 1:310–11.

11. Truman to Bess, July 31, 1945, in Ferrell, *Dear Bess*, 522. On Stalin's concerns for the postwar security of the Soviet Union, see Mastný, *The Cold War and Soviet Insecurity*.

12. Truman, *Memoirs*, 1:308.

13. Edwin Pauley to Truman, June 22, 1946, Pauley Papers 17, HSTL. During its nearly four decades of colonial rule, the Japanese had developed the rich mineral resources in the northern regions of Korea, leaving it the most industrialized area in Asia—except for Japan. Lankov, *The Real North Korea*, 69.

14. Press Release, July 23, 1946, Pauley Papers 17, HSTL.

15. Truman to Pauley, July 16, 1946, Pauley Papers 17, HSTL. Pauley would later claim that he recommended more decisive action, even the possibility of war. Prepared Remarks by Edwin Pauley before the U.S. Senate Armed Services Committee, August 3, 1950, Pauley Papers 17, HSTL.

16. Chong-sik Lee, *Materials on Korean Communism*, 174.

17. For a concise overview of the development of competing regimes on the Korean Peninsula from 1945 to 1950, see Jinwung Kim, *A History of Korea*, 367–403. For developments in Soviet-controlled North Korea, see Lankov, *From Stalin to Kim Il Sung*, 16–19, 49–76; and Suzy Kim, *Everyday Life in the North Korean Revolution*. Cumings, *The Origins of the Korean War, Vol. 1, Liberation* presents a thorough and highly critical analysis of the U.S. role in South Korea during the period.

18. Truman, *Memoirs*, 1:329. Also see General Hodge Report to War Department and Secretary of State, January 17, 1947, B file, "Prelude to Korean War," HSTL;

and the Diary Entries of Owen T. Jones, Associate Chief of Korean Economic Mission, July 20 and 22, 1947, Jones Diaries 4, HSTL.

19. An excellent account of the Truman administration's trials and missteps in the occupation of a democratizing South Korea is presented in Kornel Chang, "Independence without Liberation," 77–106.

20. Lankov, *Real North Korea*, 4; see also 6–9 for further assessments of Kim's relations with the Soviets.

21. Jeon and Kahng, "The Shtykov Diaries," 69, 92–93. For an assessment of Kim Il-sung's rise to power, see Martin, *Under the Loving Care of the Fatherly Leader*, 47–62, 735–49. On Rhee's American education and long career in exile as an advocate for Korean independence from Japanese rule, see Fields, *Foreign Friends*, 15–174.

22. Jager, *Brothers at War*, 45. Jager's study offers a concise, balanced, and scholarly analysis of the Korean conflict from 1945 through the first decade of the twenty-first century. Her work is particularly valuable in assessing the international setting in which war has continued over nearly seven decades.

23. Weathersby, "To Attack or Not Attack," 1–9. Weathersby's work ended any question about Stalin's role in initiating the attack of June 25, 1950. Her research in the Soviet archives, opened after the demise of the Soviet Union, was accompanied by other studies and disclosures about Soviet control of the DPRK. These confirmed Kim to be a Soviet vassal (albeit a troublesome one), who took direction from Col. Gen. Terentii F. Shtykov and others sent to Pyongyang by Moscow. On the opening of the Soviet sources, see Hakjoon Kim, "A Review of Korean War Studies since 1992–94"; and Wada, *The Korean War*, xxii. There no longer exists any doubt among scholars of the Cold War that North Korea attacked the south and there would have been no North Korean invasion in June 1950 without Stalin's assistance, approval, and authorization. See Westad, *The Cold War*, 169.

24. Subject: Vulnerabilities of Communists in the Far East, September 20, 1949, CIA, NSC file, HSTL. A year earlier Kim Ku, a Rhee rival for political leadership in southern Korea, had noted the potential for a Soviet-led attack on South Korea. Record of a conversation between Kim Ku and Republic of China minister Liu Yuwen, July 11, 1948, Rhee Papers, Woodrow Wilson Digital Archive, https://digitalarchive.wilsoncenter.org/document/119630.

25. CIA Report: Consequences of U.S. Troop Withdrawal in Spring, 1949, February 28, 1949, B file, "Prelude to Korean War," HSTL. Recent historical analysis of the CIA's work prior to the outbreak of the Korean War gives the agency fairly high marks. See Laurie, "Describing the Elephant," 259–79; and Shtykov, Notes on Conversation, March 5, 1949, Sino-Soviet Relations, Wilson Center Digital Archive, https://digitalarchive.wilsoncenter.org/document/112127.

26. Conversation with the President, April 19, 1949, Dean G. Acheson Papers, B file, "Prelude to Korean War," HSTL.

27. Memorandum of Conversation, July 11, 1949, Acheson Papers, copy in B file, "Prelude to Korean War," HSTL.

28. Memorandum of Conversation, February 1950 and March 22, 1950, B file, "Prelude to Korean War," HSTL. For an examination of Gen. Douglas MacArthur's lack of attention to events in Korea prior to June 25, 1950, see Halberstam, *The Coldest Winter*, 60–62.

29. Truman, *Memoirs*, 2:331. Clay Blair notes that Truman "pursued curious and dichotomous foreign and military policies. On the one hand he was tough and bellicose, urging containment of communism. On the other hand, he savaged the American armed forces which were required to give his containment policy strength and credibility." Clay Blair, Remarks at Carnegie Symposium, Washington DC, June 22, 1988, Clay Blair Papers, box 357, folder 3, American Heritage Center (AHC), University of Wyoming.

30. The Blair House incident is based on several conversations between the author and former White House aide George Elsey over the years 2003 to 2013. Also see Elsey, *An Unplanned Life*, 194–95.

31. June 30, 1950, in Ferrell, *Off the Record*, 185. On the immediate reaction of the Truman administration to the North Korean attack, see Beisner, *Dean Acheson*, 339–47.

32. Anthony Leviero, "U.S. 'Not at War,' President Asserts," *New York Times*, June 30, 1950. White House aide Ken Hechler, a future member of the U.S. House of Representatives, commented on Truman's terminology fifty years later, saying, "I think Truman made a mistake in insisting that this was a police action. When the body bags started to come back, Americans began to realize that this was more than a police action." Brian Burns, "For Truman, 'Whole House of Cards Fell in,'" *Kansas City Star*, June 25, 2000.

33. Stueck, *Rethinking the Korean War*, 220–21. Cold War historian Melvyn Leffler contended that the Truman administration was already committed to the strengthening of U.S. military might before the North Korean invasion. See Leffler, *A Preponderance of Power*, 361–97. Derek Leebaert argues that NSC-68 was, upon its completion in April 1950, "essentially a fantasy: there was no way the Congress would agree to triple defense spending" before the attack in Korea. Leebaert, *Magic and Mayhem*, 27. Also see Leebaert, *Grand Improvisation*, 226–27.

34. George C. Marshall to Gen. Douglas MacArthur, September 29, 1950, in U.S. Department of State, *Foreign Relations of the United States, 1950, Vol. 7, Korea* (Washington DC: GPO, 1976), 826.

35. On the early months of combat in Korea, see Millett, *The War for Korea, 1950–1951*, 107–290. On the extensive record of the Wake Island meeting of October 15, 1950, see 282–83 and 537.

36. Qing, "The U.S.-China Confrontation in Korea," 93–118. See also Jian, "In the Name of Revolution"; and Shen, "The Discrepancy," 237, 242. For a recent assessment, see Donggil Kim, "China's Intervention," 1002–26.

37. Millett, *War for Korea, 1950–1951*, 291–416. Initially U.S. military leaders believed air power could turn the tide in the Korean conflict, but they had abandoned this notion by 1951. See Crane, "To Avert Impending Disaster," 72–88.

38. Tomedi, *No Bugles, No Drums*, 104. Also see Jae Soon Choe, "Korean War's Lost Chapter Has Reports of Attacks on Civilians," *Taipei Times*, August 6, 2008; and Choe Sang-hun, "South Korea Says U.S. Killed Hundreds of Civilians," *New York Times*, August 3, 2008, https://www.nytimes.com/2008/08/03/world/asia/03korea.html. The plight of foreigners caught up in the war is chronicled in D. Clark, *Living Dangerously in Korea*, 359–96.

39. Jager, *Brothers at War*, 96, and also see 85–96 for an account of DPRK, ROK, and U.S. atrocities. On North Korean atrocities, including murders of United Nations Command (UNC) and ROK prisoners of war (POWs), see Chinnery, *Korean Atrocity!*

40. Crane, *American Airpower Strategy in Korea*, 9, 183; West and Suh, *Remembering the Forgotten War*, 87.

41. Maxwell, *Brotherhood in Combat*; Gropman, "The Korean War and Armed Forces Integration," 83–107; James J. Fisher, "War's Effort Yields Rapid Rise to Integration," 50th Anniversary Special Edition *Kansas City Star*, June 24, 2000. Nearly four decades after the signing of an armistice that ended combat in Korea, the Korean War Veterans Memorial on the National Mall in Washington DC, would attempt to depict the racial diversity of the U.S. military operation in Korea.

42. Efforts to reverse Appleman's negative assessment of the Black 24th Regiment at the fighting around Yechon in July 1950 can be found in Clay Blair Papers, 8295, box 356, AHC, University of Wyoming. The collection includes correspondence between Blair and Carlisle, as well as Carlisle's correspondence with Sec. of the Army John O. Marsh and Sec. of Defense Frank Carlucci. Also see Col. Harry G. Summers Jr., "Korean War Vet Aims to Correct a Biased History," *Congressional Record*, March 29, 1988; Bowers, Hammond, and MacGarrigle, *Black Soldier White Army*; and Phillips, *War! What's It Good For?*

43. On the possible use of nuclear weapons in early 1951, see Crane, "To Avert Impending Disaster," 72–88; and Matray, *Historical Dictionary of the Korean War*, 350–51.

44. News Conference, November 30, 1950, *Public Papers of the Presidents: Harry S. Truman*, 6:724–28; Jager, *Brothers at War*, 143–44; and Millett, *War for Korea, 1950–1951*, 357–58. For a recent assessment, see Beschloss, *Presidents of War*, 470–71; and Leebaert, *Grand Improvisation*, 272–77. Leebaert sees Atlee as a

calm and decisive statesman, who supported U.S. policies but viewed Acheson with concern.

45. Brands, "The Redacted Testimony." For an exhaustive review of events surrounding the dismissal of General MacArthur, see H. W. Brands, *The General vs. the President.*

46. On reaction to the dismissal of General MacArthur, see Hamby, *Man of the People*, 557–69.

47. White House aide George Elsey was instructed by assistant to the president John Steelman to share the transcript of the Wake Island meeting with *New York Times* correspondent Anthony Leviero, with whom Elsey was on friendly terms. The Republicans were outraged that in this leaked document their hero was shown to be wrong in assessing the Chinese threat. Meanwhile, the White House press security, State Department, and Defense Department all honestly claimed no knowledge of the leak's origin. Leviero's reporting on the Wake Island meeting won a Pulitzer Prize. See Elsey, *An Unplanned Life*, 206–8.

48. Firsthand accounts of the peace negotiations are found in M. J. Devine, *Korea in War*, 158–89; Joy, *How Communists Negotiate*; Paik, *From Pusan to Panmunjom*, 164–79; and Goldhamer, *The 1951 Korean Armistice Conference.* For analysis of the negotiations, see Vatcher, *Panmunjom*; Foot, *A Substitute for Victory*; and Bernstein, "The Struggles over the Korean Armistice," 261–307.

49. Weathersby, "Stalin, Mao, and the End of the Korean War," 90–116.

50. Vetter, *Mutiny on Koje Island.* Charles Young argues that the issue of repatriation was complex as both Communists and anti-Communists competed, often violently, for POW converts to their side. Young, "Voluntary Repatriation and Involuntary Tattooing of Korean War POWs," 145–67. For an eyewitness account, see Weintraub, *War in the Wards.* Also see M. Kim, "Empire's Babel," 1–28; and M. Kim, *The Interrogation Rooms of the Korean War.* On the fate of Chinese POWs, see D. Chang, *The Hijacked War.*

51. Paik, *From Pusan to Panmunjom*, 215–16; M. Clark, *From the Danube to the Yalu*, 237–39; and Garfield, *I Remember Korea*, xvi.

52. MacArthur's "Memorandum for Ending the Korean War," dated December 14, 1952, is printed in MacArthur, *Reminiscences*, 410–12.

53. Rhee expected the armistice to fail, as North Korea would not abide by its terms. Memorandum of President Rhee to All Diplomatic Officials, August 14, 1953, Rhee Papers, Woodrow Wilson Center, Digital Archive. See also Jager, *Brothers at War*, 272–77; and Thomas, *Ike's Bluff*, 81.

54. On Soviet and Chinese positions at the Geneva Conference, see Jian and Zhihua, "Introduction: The Geneva Conference of 1954," 7–84; and Wingrove, "Introduction: Russian Documents on the 1954 Geneva Conference," 85–104.

55. Matray, *Historical Dictionary of the Korean War*, 349–50.

56. Wada, *Korean War*, 300.

57. Weintraub, *MacArthur's War*, 353. See also Dingman, "Truman's Gift," 46–72.

58. For the impact of the Korean War on the U.S. military, world affairs, and the course of the Cold War, see Leffler, *Preponderance of Power*, 447–93; Herring, *From Colony to Superpower*, 646–50; Wells, *Fearing the Worst*, 472–89; and Leebaert, *Magic and Mayhem*, 27–31.

59. Stueck, *Korean War*, 3.

60. Wells, *Fearing the Worst*, 237–489; Gaddis, *The Cold War*, 129–31.

61. Mark Perry, *The Most Dangerous Man in America*, 81–85, 353–55; Halberstram, *The Coldest Winter*, 621–37; "Behind the Myth: General Douglas MacArthur," *Gwangju News*, November 13, 2013; and Tom Moran, "The Tale of President Harry S. Truman and General Douglas MacArthur," *Chicago Tribune*, October 5, 2016. For a harsh critique of MacArthur's World War I service, see Ferrell, *The Question of MacArthur's Reputation*. Seymour Morris Jr. notes that MacArthur's military record overshadows his most spectacular and longest-lasting success—the building of a democratic, peaceful, and prosperous Japan in the years immediately following World War II. Morris, *Supreme Commander*, xvii.

62. Halberstram, *The Coldest Winter*, 622.

63. David McCullough assesses Miller's work in *Truman*, 801, 901, 977–80; *Plain Speaking* is reviewed by Robert Sherrill, "Cursing and Yarning and Bragging," *New York Times*, February 10, 1974; and Roger Ebert, *Give 'em Hell, Harry!*, review, January 1, 1975, https://www.rogerebert.com/reviews/give-em-hell-harry -1975.

64. McCullough, *Truman*; Hamby, *Man of the People*; and Ferrell, *Harry S. Truman*.

2. FORGING MEMORIES

1. The GI's story is found in A-0955, box 11, Center for the Study of the Korean War, Harry S. Truman Library (CSKW-HSTL). The story is told by Dr. Paul Edwards. Since the extensive collections of the CSKW were placed at the HSTL, staff have begun reprocessing the papers, and a comprehensive new finding aid was not yet available at the time of writing.

2. Journalist Clay Blair seems to have popularized the term in his widely read study, *The Forgotten War*. Also see Edwards, *To Acknowledge a War*, 92–102.

3. *U.S. Commission on Veterans: Pensions, Records, 1954–1958*, Bradley Commission Records 1954–58, box 6, Dwight D. Eisenhower Presidential Library and Museum, Abilene KS. For a discussion on this report and veterans' views, see Pash, *In the Shadow*, 219–26. Also see Wiltz, "Korean War and American Society," 127–34, especially 134; and Zachary Matusheski, "Forgotten Veterans of a Forgotten War: Remembering Those Who Served in the Korean War," *Sources and Methods* (blog), Wilson Center, History and Public Policy Program, June 17, 2020, https://www.wilsoncenter.org/blog-post/forgotten-veterans-forgotten -war-remembering-those-who-served-korean-war.

4. For information on additional prominent Korean War veterans, see www
.koreanwar-educator.org. Military historian Gen. S. L. A. Marshall interviewed
seventy-three enlisted U.S. soldiers who survived combat and were recommended
for decorations. He found that "not one came from a family that could have
afforded to send them to college." Most were from families of three or more
children. See Marshall, *Pork Chop Hill*, 15.

5. Gen. S. L. A. Marshall (*Pork Chop Hill*, 14) believed "the policy of individual
rotation . . . was ruinous to good morale and good administrative order within
an armed force . . . it sacrificed most of the traditional values, such as earned
promotion and citation, pride in unit and close comradeship." See also Tomedi,
No Bugles, No Drums, 292; Clay Blair, Papers Presented at the Carnegie Council
on Ethics in International Affairs, June 22, 1998, box 357, Clay Blair Papers, AHC,
University of Wyoming; Keene, "Lost to Public Commemoration," 1095–113;
and Matray, "Revisiting Korea." On the uneven treatment of U.S. veterans in
the twentieth century, see Kinder, *Paying with Their Bodies*.

6. Doenecke, *Not to the Swift*, 189–209; and Wiltz, "Korean War and American
Society," 32.

7. Steve Crabtree, "The Gallup Brain: Americans and the Korean War," *Gallup*,
February 3, 2003, https://news.gallup.com/poll/7741/gallup-brain-americans
-korean-war.aspx.

8. Edwards, *Korean War*, 45. See also Wiltz, "Korean War and American Society,"
131–32.

9. Quotations from Suchman, Goldsen, and Williams, "Attitudes Towards the
Korean War," 171, 184.

10. For an exhaustive study of Korean War-era public opinion and politics, see
Casey, *Selling the Korean War*, 325–41, 367.

11. Casey, *When Soldiers Fall*, 245; Pierpaoli, "Beyond Collective Amnesia," 92–102;
and "United States" in Casey, *The Ashgate Research Companion to the Korean
War*, 51.

12. Millett, *The Korean War*, 129–30. For a highly favorable view of Stone's journalism and theories, see Cumings, "Introduction: Korea Is Near."

13. Wittner, *Rebels against War*, 202. The radical opposition to the Korean War by W.
E. B. DuBois is examined by Honda, "W. E. B. DuBois and the Paradox of American Democracy," 93–104; and Wiltz, "Korean War and American Society," 131.

14. Johnson and Bentsen quoted in Beschloss, *Presidents of War*, 463. Steven Casey
notes that the Korean War caused Republicans to politicize President Truman's
actions in Korea. Casey, "Harry Truman, the Korean War and the Transformation of U.S. Policy in East Asia," 192–93. Also see Casey, "The United States," 50.
On isolationist opposition, see Doenecke, *Not to the Swift*, 189–209.

15. Sen. Lyndon Johnson's role as a critic is explored in McMaster, *Dereliction of
Duty*, 52. On the McCarthy era, see Oshinsky, *A Conspiracy So Immense*.

16. In his study of the 1952 presidential election, John Robert Greene argues that no Democrat could have defeated Eisenhower in 1952 (*I Like Ike*, 174). See also Casey, "United States," 49; and Beschloss, *Presidents of War*, 490–91. As a U.S. representative, Kennedy had criticized Truman and Acheson for their lack of aggression in Korea. Kennedy had also supported the anti-Communist efforts of Sen. Joseph McCarthy, stating, "He may have something" (quoted in Dallek, *An Unfinished Life*, 162).

17. Heller, *The Korean War*, 1970. Also see Hamby, "Public Opinion," 137–41; and Beschloss, *Presidents of War*, 489.

18. Edwards, *Korean War*, 170. On the notion of the Korean War as a U.S. military defeat, see Alexander, *Korea*.

19. Colonel Schwable faced a possible court-martial upon his release from the North Korean POW camp in 1953 but remained in the Marine Corps and retired following thirty years of service. On Colonel Schwable's career and his ordeal as a POW, see Millett, "The Marine Colonel Becomes a War Criminal," 249–55. On additional allegations of U.S. war crimes, see "Statement of Two Captured U.S Air Force Officers on Their Participation in Germ Warfare in North Korea," with supporting materials published by the World Council of Peace, May 6, 1952, box 9, A-0861, CSKW-HSTL.

20. Edwards, *Korean War*, 170. Clay Blair maintained that the twenty-one POWs who defected did not shake the U.S. public or U.S. military leadership as much as the U.S. Air Force pilots who made false confessions of germ warfare (Blair Papers, 357, AHC). See also Carruthers, *Cold War Captive*, 76; and Wiltz, "Korean War and American Society," 143. By 1966 all but two of the POWs who remained behind in 1953 had returned to the United States. Rather than being "brainwashed," these soldiers had accepted Communist propaganda promising a classless paradise. In addition, several had been awarded material and sexual compensation by their captors. Of special interest is the story of Clarence Adams, a Black soldier who grew up in Memphis, Tennessee, and suffered discrimination in his hometown and in the military. Hoping for a better life, he defected to China where he received an education, married a Chinese student at Wuhan University, and fathered several children. His happy life as a teacher was disrupted by the Chinese government's brutal campaign against intellectuals during the Cultural Revolution. In 1965 Adams returned to the States with his family and opened several Chinese restaurants in Memphis. His daughter, Della, edited his memoir with Lewis Carlson. See Adams and Carlson, *An American Dream*. Stuart Heaver, "POW Chose Mao's China over Home," MCLC Resource Center, The Ohio State University, May 27, 2016, https://u.osu.edu/mclc/2016/05/28/pow-chose-maos-china-over-home/.

21. For examples of recent scholarship, see Dunne, *A Cold War State of Mind*, 223. Several important recent studies have focused on Korean War POWs and their

treatment. See Young, *Name, Rank and Serial Number*; McKnight, *"We Fight for Peace"*; Carlson, *Remembered Prisoners of a Forgotten War*; and Lech, *Broken Soldiers*.

22. On the treatment of POWs by the North Korean and Chinese, see Chinnery, *Korean Atrocity!* See also Carlson, *Remembered Prisoners*, 270n9. The CSKW-HSTL holds a wealth of firsthand accounts of POW mistreatment. Precise numbers on this issue remain elusive. The numerical information provided here was compiled by Sheila Miyoshi Jager with Allan R. Millet and presented in Jager, *Brothers at War*, 535. For additional details see Lech, *Broken Soldiers*, 212–13, 264–76.

23. Johnson shared his documentation and list of POWs who died in captivity with U.S. Army officials at the end of the war, but it remained overlooked and ignored until the 1990s when the Department of Defense (DOD) began to use his notes to cross-check the names of missing POWs. See press clippings, "Soldier Secretly Chronicles Death in North Korean POW Camps," *Rocky Mountain News*, September 2, 1996, and related materials in box 100, A-6327, CSKW-HSTL. Johnson's story is told in McConnell, "Jonnie's List," 49–55. Additional items related to POWs and their treatment and exploitation for propaganda by the North Koreans and Chinese are located in box 9, CSKW-HSTL. Firsthand accounts of life in Communist POW camps include Dean, *General Dean's Story*; and the account of South Korean escapee Lee Young Ido, in Peters and Li, *Voices from the Korean War*, xx.

24. "Subject: Interrogation of Returned Prisoners of War, Headquarters, Korean Communications Zone, Staff Judge Advocate, War Crimes Division, October 21, 1953." A copy of this document was provided to the author by Doctor Boysen's daughter, Catherine Madison, who wrote of her father's Korean War ordeal and the psychological scars the war left him with in *The War Came Home with Him*.

25. Anderson et al., "Medical Experiences in Communist POW Camps in Korea," 120–22, quotation on 120.

26. Anderson et al., "Medical Experiences," 122. In January 1955 Boysen also provided testimony and a sixty-nine-page document in the court-martial of Maj. Ambrose Nugent, who was held at a POW camp with the doctors. Nugent was acquitted on all thirteen charges of collaborating with his captors. See Madison, *War Came Home*, 211–18. Catherine Madison, in discussion with the author, July 25, 2020.

27. RECAP-K Program Case files of Returnees on Exchanged Captured American Personnel, 1953–1958, Record Group (RG) 153 O/JAG (Army), National Archives and Records Administration, College Park MD (NARA II), is a voluminous record of interrogations. See Interrogations Guide, RG153 O/JAG Army, Miscellaneous Paley Documents box 4, NARA-II. See also Keene, "Lost to Public Commemoration," 1089, 1100–106, 1112.

28. Mayer, "Why Did Many Captives Cave In?" 56–72; and Mayer, "Communist Indoctrination," 3–47.

29. Spock, "Are We Bringing Up Our Children Too 'Soft,'" 20. Ironically in the 1960s and 1970s, as a critic of the Vietnam War, Spock was accused of helping create a generation of wimps because he advocated permissive behavior.

30. Wylie, *A Generation of Vipers*, 198–99.

31. Friedan, *The Feminine Mystique*, 285–86. For an analysis of this post–Korean War literature, see Young, *Name, Rank and Serial Number*, 109–26, in his chapter entitled "Target Mom: Disciplining a Misplaced Sympathy."

32. Edward Hunter, "Testimony before the U.S. House Un-American Activities Committee," U.S. House of Representatives, 85th Congress, 2nd Sess. (March 13, 1958), 3ff. Also see Hunter, *Brainwashing: From Pavlov to Powers*, which is the enlarged edition of Hunter, *Brainwashing: The Story of Men Who Defied It*; and Hunter, *Brainwashing in Red China*. For the origins of brainwashing as a national phenomenon, see Seed, *Brainwashing*. On POW escapes and attempted escapes from North Korean and Chinese captors, which almost always took place within the first day or so of captivity, see Pash, *In the Shadow*, 139–40.

33. Dulles, "Brain Warfare," 56. Also see Mayo, "Destroying American Minds," 97–101.

34. Kinkead, "The Study of Something New," 114. Kinkead expands on his theories in *In Every War but One* and *Why They Collaborated*.

35. Dunne, *A Cold War State of Mind*, 3, 4, 8, 235. See also Lorraine Boissoneault, "The True Story of Brainwashing," *Smithsonian*, May 27, 2017, https://www .smithsonianmag.com/history/true-story-brainwashing-and-how-it-shaped -america-180963400/; and Blanco-Saurez, "The Art of Brainwashing," *Psychology Today*, March 21, 2018, https://www.psychologytoday.com/intl/blog/brain -chemistry/201803/the-art-brainwashing.

36. Biderman, "Communist Attempts," 616–25, especially 619; and Biderman, *March to Calumny*.

37. Biderman, *March to Calumny*, 1–2, 271.

38. Following the terrorist attacks in the U.S. on 9/11, 2001, the George W. Bush administration authorized interrogation methods similar to those used by Communists in POW camps holding U.S. POWs, based on the mistaken belief that these tactics had been successful. Leebaert, *Magic and Mayhem*, 130–36. On the notion of brainwashing in today's American culture and society, see M. J. Devine, "The Korean War, American POWs and the Legacy of Brainwashing," 163–73.

39. Rubin, *Combat Films*, 72. Dozens of low-quality and easily forgotten Korean War movies were also produced. See Jeansonne and Luhrssen, *War on the Silver Screen*, 100–104; and May, "Reluctant Crusaders," 110–36. Also see Lentz, *Korean War Filmography*; Young, *Name, Rank and Serial Number*, 162–97; and Edwards, *A Guide to Films on the Korean War*. For an overview of U.S. war movies, see Suid, *Guts and Glory*.

40. The authenticity of the story is a topic of dispute. See Carlson, *Remembered Prisoners*, introduction.

41. Rubin, *Combat Films*, 73–77; and Latham, *Cold Days in Hell*, 240.

42. "Screen: Bias under Fire Seen in *All the Young Men*," *New York Times*, August 27, 1960.

43. The story of Dean Hess is told in "By Faith I Fly" in Millett, *Their War for Korea*, 179–85.

44. *Bridges at Toko-Ri* was well received and won an Academy Award for special effects. "The Bridges at Toko-Ri: The Real Story of Capt. Paul N. Gray, U.S.N," *USS* Bennington, accessed February 18, 2021, http://www.uss-bennington.org /non-benn-bridges_at_toko_ri.html, tells of a December 1951 attack upon which Michener based his story. See Bosley Crowther, "The Screen in Review: *Bridges at Toko-Ri*," *New York Times*, January 12, 1955. *Sayonara* was nominated for five Academy Awards and received box-office success. A more realistic view of the air war in Korea is provided in the less known *One Minute at Zero* (1952) in which Col. Steve Janowski (played by Robert Mitchum) orders an attack on a refugee column because North Korean soldiers have infiltrated the group. A solid overview of Korean War films is in Eperjesi, "The Unending War in Korean Film," 787–809.

45. Bosley Crowther, "Screen: 'Wonder World of the Brothers Grimm': George Pal Production at Lowe's Cinerama Lawrence Harvey Heads Cast of Stars," *New York Times*, August 8, 1962; and Suid, *Guts and Glory*, 202.

46. Carruthers, "*The Manchurian Candidate* (1962) and the Korean War Brainwashing Scare," 75–94.

47. Roger Ebert, "*The Manchurian Candidate*," review, December 7, 2003, https:// www.rogerebert.com/reviews/great-movie-the-manchurian-candidate-1962; Leebaert, *Magic and Mayhem*, 136. According to Ebert, at the time of Pres. John F. Kennedy's assassination, speculation arose that his assassin, Lee Harvey Oswald, was a Manchurian candidate. There were also rumors that Frank Sinatra, who starred in the film, pulled it from theaters because of the Kennedy assassination. In fact Sinatra, who had a financial interest in the production, withdrew the film because of a dispute with United Artists over what he considered their "funny bookkeeping."

48. Ken Hatfield, "Helping Us Remember the 'B' Movie War," *Lee's Summit (MO) Journal*, June 23, 2000, and related material in box 9, A-0906, CSKW-HSTL; and Shaw, *Hollywood's Cold War*, 111, 301. One list of memorable Korean War films includes *MacArthur* (1976), a box office bomb starring Gregory Peck as the general. Other long-forgotten films include *Men in War* (1957), *The Hook* (1963) with Kirk Douglas, and *Incheon* (1981) with Sir Lawrence Olivier as General MacArthur in "one of the worst war movies ever made." James Baker, "8 Must-See Korean War Movies," July 27, 2021, https://www.military.com/off-duty /movies/2021/07/27/8-must-see-korean-war-movies.html.

49. Suhi Choi, *Embattled Memories*, 56; and Morris-Suzuki et al., *East Asia beyond History Wars*, 129. On issues related to the media and the Korean War, see Morris-Suzuki, *The Past within Us*. The historian's role in the production of a documentary on the American wars of the post–World War II era is explored in Cumings, *War and Television*.

50. Morris-Suzuki, "Remembering the Unfinished Conflict," 2.

51. Reiss, *M*A*S*H*. See Howard Fishman's analysis of the movie and TV series in "What *M*A*S*H* Taught Us"; and Strausbaugh, "Meatball Surgery."

52. "Interview with Doctors Saxon and Dishell," July 26, 1973, Lawrence Marks Papers, box 67, AHC. Born in 1915 Marks was an award-winning writer of comedy and humor for Fred Allen, Groucho Marx, and Bob Hope. Marks often collaborated with Larry Gilbert and Gene Reynolds and had several hit television series, including *Bachelor Father* and *Hogan's Heroes*. See finding aid to Marks Papers, AHC. Also see extensive research notes on Stanley Weintraub's *War in the Wards*; undated document "Black Doctor White Nurse"; Stacel interview, March 15, 1974; "notes dictated by Gene Reynolds," May 24, 1974; and Dr. Nathan, July 10, 1973, transcript entitled "DRAPKIN," all in box 67, Lawrence Marks Papers.

53. Alda's foreword in Reiss, *M*A*S*H*.

54. Saxon Interviews, August 27, 1973, Marks Papers, box 67, AHC.

55. Truman, *Memoirs*, Vol. 2, *Years of Trial and Hope*, 433–34. For an analysis of Truman's *Memoirs* in addressing Korean issues, see Casey, "United States," 50.

56. Ridgway, *Soldier*. Ridgway believed that the United States was placing too much reliance on nuclear weapons in the post–Korean War years. In 1955 he wrote to the Secretary of Defense, "No nation could regard nuclear capabilities alone as sufficient, either to prevent, or to win a war" (325).

57. M. Clark, *From the Danube to the Yalu*, 315.

58. Dean, *General Dean's Story*.

59. Joy, *How Communists Negotiate*, xx.

60. Higgins, *War in Korea*, 52.

61. Beech, *Tokyo and Points East*, 13, 230–50.

62. Collins, *War in Peacetime*, 227. See also MacArthur, *Reminiscences*.

63. Herring, "Vietnam Remembered," 152–64, esp. 152.

64. Halliday and Cumings, *Korea*, 202.

3. LESSONS LEARNED

1. Bohlen, *Witness to History*, 303.

2. Stueck, *Rethinking the Korean War*, 213–39; Wada, *The Korean War*, 295–303; Pierpaoli, "Beyond Collective Amnesia," 96–97; and Kaplan, *NATO Divided, NATO United*, 10, 21–22.

3. Masuda, *Cold War Crucible*, 1–2, 86–113, 200–221. For the impact of McCarthyism on U.S. society, see Oshinsky, *A Conspiracy So Immense*; and Schrecker, *Many Are the Crimes*.

4. Masuda, *Cold War Crucible*, 222–79.

5. The Geneva Conference included the United States, China, the Soviet Union, both North and South Korea, and the sixteen United Nations (UN) member nations (except for South Africa) that sent troops to fight in Korea. The move away from negotiations to settle issues in Korea and a focus on Indochina is documented in Jian and Zhihua, "Introduction: The Geneva Conference of 1954," 7–9, 12–84; Wingrove, "Introduction: Russian Documents on the 1954 Geneva Conference," 85–104; and Jinwung Kim, *A History of Korea*, 465.

6. Gibbons, *The U.S. Government and the Vietnam War*, 65, 73–77, 188; Casey, *Selling the Korean War*, 366; Bacevich, *America's War for the Greater Middle East*, 274, 305–6, 318, and 360; Yuen, *Analogies at War*, chapter 5. An opposing view is presented by historian Marilyn Young, who found U.S. leaders' inattention to the Korean War experience as partly to blame for allowing the United States to slip into a deepening military involvement in Vietnam. Young, "Hard Sell: The Korean War," 10.

7. Anderson, *Trapped by Success*, 4–5, 15–18, 21, 207–9.

8. Stueck, *Rethinking the Korean War*, 336. In his exhaustive study of U.S. involvement in Vietnam, Brian VanDeMark (*Road to Disaster*, 9) sees President Kennedy as not viewing Vietnam as a pressing issue upon taking office in 1961. For a detailed study of President Kennedy's policies in which the author argues that Kennedy had become prepared to end U.S. involvement in Vietnam despite his public rhetoric to the contrary, see Newman, *JFK and Vietnam*.

9. Goodwin, *Lyndon Baines Johnson and the American Dream*, 252–53.

10. Updegrove, *Indomitable Will*, 186. Sheila Miyoshi Jager has noted that "of the many analogies evoked to justify America's involvement in Vietnam, it was 'Lessons' of Korea that played the most influential role in the U.S. decision of the summer of 1965" (*Brothers at War*, 541n11).

11. Beschloss, *Presidents of War*, 509–22. See also Gulf of Tonkin Resolution, Public Law 88–408, 88th Congress, August 7, 1964, https://www.govinfo.gov/content/pkg/STATUTE-78/pdf/STATUTE-78-Pg384.pdf#page=1; and Moise, *Tonkin Gulf and the Escalation of the Vietnam War*. Historian Fredrik Logevall's intensive study of Johnson's road to an expanded war in Vietnam has little to say about the Korean War analogy and argues that Johnson rejected the possibility of a negotiated settlement between 1963 and 1965. Francis Bator sees LBJ expanding the war in Vietnam to secure congressional support for his domestic agenda, the Great Society. See Logevall, *Choosing War*. Francis Bator's ("No Good Choices," 309–40) essay on LBJ's choice of war in Vietnam, followed by commentary by

six leading historians of his administration's foreign policies, is an exhaustive and detailed analysis of the subject.

12. Beschloss, *Presidents of War*, 578.

13. McMaster, *Dereliction of Duty*, 7. McMaster faulted the Joint Chiefs of Staff for not adequately warning Johnson of the dangers of military involvement in Vietnam. However, much of McMasters's scholarship shows that Johnson was well aware of the risk but concluded that the political danger of appearing soft on Communism was a greater threat to his presidency than entering a quagmire in Vietnam.

14. McMaster, *Dereliction of Duty*, 43–44, 214, 244.

15. Bohlen to Thompson, January 31, 1996, in Bohlen, *Witness to History*, 254.

16. George W. Ball to LBJ, October 5, 1964, reprinted as "Top Secret: The Prophecy the President Rejected," memorandum published in *Atlantic* 230, no. 1 (July 1972): 35–49. Johnson respected Ball's opinion, but the undersecretary of state never provided the president with a politically acceptable alternative strategy. See Updegrove, *Indomitable Will*, 191–92.

17. Graff, *The Tuesday Cabinet*, 136. See also Neustadt and May, *Thinking in Time*, 161. On the "Wise Men," see VanDeMark, *Road to Disaster*, 289–90, 420–21, and 471–75; and Jonathan Kirshner, "When the 'Wise Men' Failed," *New York Times*, October 31, 2017, https://www.nytimes.com/2017/10/31/opinion/lyndon -johnson-vietnam-war.html. The optimism for the war faded; and when an enlarged "Wise Men" committee, including Gen. Matthew Ridgway, Arthur Goldberg, and Henry Cabot Lodge, met in March 1968 following the Vietcong's Tet Offensive, the consensus was to halt bombing and begin negotiations. See "Editorial Note," *Foreign Relations of the United States 1964–1968*, Vol. 6, *Vietnam*, doc. 155 (March 25 meeting), www.history.state.gov.

18. VanDeMark, *Into the Quagmire*, 195 and 197, respectively. VanDeMark makes extensive use of the *Pentagon Papers* in citing examples where President Johnson looked to the Korean War in assessing the Vietnam solution (29, 77, 88–89, 260). To access the *Pentagon Papers*, see https://www.archives.gov/research/pentagon -papers.

19. Middleton, *The Compact History of the Korean War*, 232. Middleton served as director of the LBJ Presidential Library in Austin, Texas, for thirty years until he retired at age eighty in 2002.

20. Stoker, *Why America Loses Wars*, 106–20. Also see the preface in the reissue of Fehrenbach, *This Kind of War*, x–xi (the original was published as T. R. Fehrenbach, *This Kind of War: Korea—A Study in Unpreparedness* [New York: Macmillan, 1963]); and Millett, *The War for Korea, 1950–1951*, 6.

21. Ridgway, *The War in Korea*, 245.

22. Stoker (*Why America Loses Wars*, 81) sees limited conflicts like Korea as "forever wars." He considers U.S. military interventions in the Middle East as forever wars where the definition of success or victory is not sufficiently limited.

23. The extent to which academic historians should seek to influence public policy is an unresolved question upon which professional historians have failed to reach a consensus. For discussion of this issue, see Graham, "Uses and Misuses of History in Policymaking"; Jones, "The Promise of Policy History in the Public History Curriculum," 28–42; and Alix Green, "Public History and Public Policy: A View from Across the Pond," *History@Work* (blog), NCPH, July 16, 2012, https://ncph.org/history-at-work/public-history-and-public-policy-a-view-from-across-the-pond/.

24. Graff, *The Tuesday Cabinet*.

25. Graff, *The Tuesday Cabinet*; Sam Roberts, "Henry F. Graff, Columbia Historian of Presidents, Dies at 98," *New York Times*, April 15, 2020, https://www.nytimes.com/2020/04/15/books/henry-f-graff-columbia-historian-of-presidents-dies-at-98.html; and Kenneth T. Jackson, "In Memoriam: Henry F. Graff (1921–2020)," *Perspectives on History*, September 30, 2020, https://www.historians.org/publications-and-directories/perspectives-on-history/october-2020/henry-f-graff-(1921%E2%80%932020). President Johnson appointed Graff to the National Historical Publications and Records Commission, and President Clinton appointed him to the President John F. Kennedy Assassination Records Review Board.

26. Graff, *The Tuesday Cabinet*, 4.

27. Graff, *The Tuesday Cabinet*, 180–81. In early 1965 Rusk told Graff that "dictatorships . . . underestimate democracy's willingness to do what it has to do," and noted that since World War II, the United States had suffered 160,000 casualties and spent a trillion dollars on the saving of Iran, Greece, Berlin, Korea, the Philippines, and Malaysia from Communism (42).

28. Graff, *The Tuesday Cabinet*, 37. On the political ramifications of a buildup of U.S. forces in Korea, Bundy stated that memory of Korea "causes pain" in Congress, especially among Democrats, but added that "Johnson is not terrified by Korea, though knowing that it shakes the party" (46).

29. Graff, *The Tuesday Cabinet*, 136.

30. Graff, *The Tuesday Cabinet*, 94.

31. Neustadt and May, *Thinking in Time*, 161, also see xi–xii.

32. Neustadt and May, *Thinking in Time*, 34–48, 160–70.

33. On the revisionists of U.S. diplomatic history, see Gaddis, "The Soviet Side of the Cold War," 523–26; and Gaddis, "The Tragedy of Cold War History," 1–16. For recent assessments of orthodox, revisionist, and postrevisionist Cold War historiography, see Iber, "Cold War World"; Targ, "Cold War Revisionism Revisited"; and Charles Edel and Hal Brands, "The Real Origins of the U.S.-China Cold War," *Foreign Policy*, June 2, 2019, https://foreignpolicy.com/2019/06/02

/the-real-origins-of-the-u-s-china-cold-war-big-think-communism/. On the nature of revisionism in historical studies, see Banner, *The Ever-Changing Past*.

34. Cumings, "Introduction," xiii. On Cumings's career, see http://history.uchicago.edu/faculty.cumings; commentary by Clark Sorensen in Kim and Robinson, *Peace Corps Volunteers*, 43, 210.

35. Hak-joon Kim, "International Trends in Korean War Studies," 326–70, quotation on 331. See also McCormick, *America's Half Century*, 268; and William Stueck, "Bruce Cumings's *The Korean War*, reviewed by William Stueck," *Washington Post*, September 12, 2010, http://www.washingtonpost.com/wp-dyn/content/article/2010/09/10/AR2010091002925.html. Stueck acknowledges Cumings's position as a leading scholar on the Korean War but faults his "limited grasp of sources that have emerged [in recent years]."

36. Jager and Mitter, *Ruptured Histories*, 282.

37. Cumings, *War and Television*, 146.

38. Cumings, *Korean War*, xv.

39. Cumings, *Korean War*, 190, 202.

40. Cumings, *Korea's Place in the Sun* (2005), 272.

41. Dwight Garner, "Carpet-Bombing Falsehoods about a War that Is Little Understood," *New York Times*, July 21, 2010, https://www.nytimes.com/2010/07/22/books/22book.html.

42. Cumings, "The Korean War," 281.

43. Halliday and Cumings, *Korea*, 215.

44. Kathryn Weathersby, "Soviet Aims in Korea and the Origins of the Korean War, 1945–1950: New Evidence from the Russian Archives," (working paper 8, Cold War International History Project, Woodrow Wilson International Center, November 1993); and Weathersby, "The Soviet Role in the Early Phase of the Korean War," 425–58. On the opening of Soviet archives and other documentary evidence from Communist sources, see Wada, *Korean War*, xxii–xxiv; and Stueck, "Revisionism and the Korean War," 17–27.

45. Cumings quoted in Jager and Mitter, *Ruptured Histories*, 292, 365, n 12. Weathersby, "An Exchange in Korean War Origins," 120–22; and Martin, *Under the Loving Care of the Fatherly Leader*, 364–65, 735–36, 748–51, and 824–25.

46. Halliday and Cumings, *Korea: The Unknown War*, 33. Actually naming aggressors in wars is important. Who fired the first shots at Fort Sumter in 1861 was of great importance to Pres. Abraham Lincoln. The Confederate aggression in Charleston Harbor sparked a wave of support for the Union cause, as Lincoln anticipated, and the issue remains relevant to any serious student of the Civil War. See McPherson, *Battle Cry of Freedom*, 264–74. Even Adolf Hitler recognized the value of assigning blame for starting World War II. Thus in August 1939 he set in motion a plot to stage a fake Polish provocation for his invasion of that nation. See Kennedy, *World War II Companion*, 72.

47. Cumings, *Korea's Place in the Sun* (2005), 14. In a review of *Korea's Place in the Sun*, Nicholas Kristof takes issue with Cumings's assessment of the DPRK as the more "genuine" state of the Korean Peninsula and calls Cumings "nuts" for blaming the United States for the division of Korea ("What to Read If You Want to Know More about North Korea," *New York Times*, January 1, 2018, https://www.nytimes.com/2018/01/01/books/review/nicholas-kristof-north-korea.html).

48. Cumings, *Korea's Place in the Sun* (2005), 225–27, 263; and Cumings, *Korean War*, 9.

49. Hak-joon Kim, "A Review of Korean Studies Since 1992–94," 317–19. Revisionist British scholarship influenced by Cumings includes Callum MacDonald, *The War before Vietnam*; Hastings, *The Korean War*; and Foot, *The Wrong War*. On South Korean sympathies toward North Korea, see Lankov, *The Real North Korea*, 9, 156.

50. Choi, *Embattled Memories*, 106. See also Jager, *Brothers at War*, 419–22.

51. For an account of tensions between the north and south during the 1960s and 1970s, see Jinwung Kim, *History of Korea*, 449–67.

52. Graff, *The Tuesday Cabinet*, 153. For detailed examinations of the *Pueblo* incident, see Cheevers, *Act of War*; Lerner, *The Pueblo Incident*; Lerner, "A Dangerous Miscalculation," 3–21; Morrow, "Bridges at Panmunjom," 16; and James Brooke, "Camp Bonifas Journal; It's Korea, and GI's Sleep with Their Boots On," *New York Times*, March 18, 2003, https://www.nytimes.com/2003/03/18/world/camp-bonifas-journal-it-s-korea-and-gi-s-sleep-with-their-boots-on.html.

53. Jinwung Kim, *History of Korea*, 468–518.

54. Ambassador James Lilly, *Ambassadors' Memoir*, 17–21; Oberdorfer and Carlin, *Two Koreas*, 181–83; Pound, *Five Rings over Korea*; Radchenko, "Sport and Politics on the Korean Peninsula."

55. Oberdorfer and Carlin, *Two Koreas*, 183.

56. Aloysius M. O'Neill III, "The 1988 Olympics in Seoul: A Triumph of Sport and Diplomacy," *38 North*, February 8, 2018, https://www.38north.org/2018/02/aoneill020818/.

57. Lilly, *Ambassadors' Memoir*, 21.

58. Kathryn Weathersby, "Amazing Aftermath of the 1988 Seoul Olympics," *Korea Times*, April 18, 2018, https://www.koreatimes.co.kr/www/nation/2020/11/177_247388.html; and Oberdorfer and Carlin, *Two Koreas*, 180–86. For a largely negative critique of the Seoul Olympics, see Burma, "The Jingo Olympics," 44–50.

59. "Transcript of Interview with Condoleezza Rice," *Washington Post*, December 15, 2006, http://www.washingtonpost.com/wp-dyn/content/article/2006/12/15/AR2006121500529.html.

4. MEMORIALIZING ACROSS AMERICA

1. Ken Hatfield, "Helping Us Remember the 'B' Movie War," *Lee's Summit Journal*, June 23, 2000. Also see Cara Skodack Day, "Worth Remembering: He Fought the

Good Fight. Now He's Fighting to Save the Memory of It," vfw *Auxiliary* (April–May 2001), 9; and Janell Coppage, "Four Men: Stories of the War They Can Not Forget," typed manuscript, a-0955, box 11, cskw-hstl. Also based on numerous discussions between the author and Paul Edwards between 2001 and 2017.

2. Frank Haight, "Korean War Center Short on Funding, Long on Dedication," *Examiner*, April 8, 2016.

3. Denis Healy Sr., "U.S. Had a Huge Role in Amazing Story of South Korea," *State Journal-Register*, November 11, 2010, https://www.sj-r.com/story/opinion/columns /2010/11/11/denis-j-healy-sr-u/43166082007/; Tim Landis, "The Korean War Museum in Financial Trouble Long before Shutdown," *State Journal-Register*, August 4, 2017, sj-r.com/news/20170804/korean-war-museum-in-financial -trouble-long-before-shutdown; and Jeff Fox, "Korea, at the Front Lines," *Examiner*, June 26, 2018, https://www.thedailyreporter.com/story/news/local/2018/06 /26/veterans-artifacts-help-tell-story/11885777007/. Also see the notice and funding request for the proposed Korean War National Museum and Library (then located in Tuscola il) in *Graybeards* 16, no. 6 (November–December 2002): 67. For more information see Truman library director D. Kurt Graham to Paul and Greg Edwards, January 26, 2016; library archivist Sam Rushay to Lacey Helmig, March 15, 2018, with supplemental materials; and Stephanie Rohr and Natalie Walker, comp., "National Korean War Museum Collections Report," n.d., all in working files of hstl.

4. The organization can be found at www.koreanwar.org. Hal and Ted Barker to Michael J. Devin (*sic*), February 12, 2021 (in author's papers at hstl); "Brothers behind 'Korean War Project' Keep Watchful Eye on History, Veterans," *Dallas Morning News*, November 8, 2013, https://www.dallasnews.com/news/2013/11/08 /brothers-behind-korean-war-project-keep-a-watchful-eye-on-history-veterans/; and Bruce Langer, "The Forgotten Veterans," *Sunday Camera Magazine*, March 11, 1984, https://www.koreanwar2.org/memorial/kwvm_news_boulder_daily _camera_mar_11_1984.pdf. At this time I am aware of efforts by the Barkers to locate an institution to permanently house their collection; the Truman library seems a logical choice.

5. Winter, *Remembering War*, 1, 281. Winter's clear analysis of the "boom" in memory of remembrance sets a high standard. Particularly useful are his introduction and chapter 12, "Controversies and Conclusions." On public history, see Glassberg, *Sense of History*, 13.

6. Bodnar, *Remaking America*, 13–14; Kammen, *Mystic Chords*, 3–13; and Van Wagenen, *Remembering the Forgotten War*, 4–5. On grassroots efforts to add forgotten or overlooked groups to the historical narrative, see Kelland, *Clio's Foot Soldiers*.

7. Organized in 1985 the Korean War Veterans Association (kwva) grew to 330 chapters by 2020 and publishes a magazine, *Graybeards*, six times a year.

8. Keene, "Lost to Public Commemoration," 1106–7; and Pash, *In the Shadow*, 219.

9. For a discussion of warfare and its memory in defining American culture, see Kammen, *Mystic Chords*, 3–13, 588, 657–88.

10. For an up-to-date listing of Korean War memorials in the United States, see "Korean War Memorials . . . Around the Country & the World," KWVA, accessed February 21, 2021, kwva.org/memorials/index.htm.

11. Government Records Inventory, vol. 24, com. 30, box 6, Hawai'i State Archives; www.ambc.gov. *National Memorial Cemetery of the Pacific*, pamphlet NMCP, Department of Veterans Affairs (December 2011); and Pacific War Memorial Commission, 1949–81.

12. A Bill for an Act Relating to the Vietnam War Memorial, H. B. 3658, approved July 6, 1992. Press clippings and design plans are located in the working files of the Hawai'i Department of Accounting and General Services, Honolulu, Hawai'i.

13. A. A. Smyser, "The Battle over the Korean-Vietnam Memorials," *Honolulu Star Bulletin*, September 2, 1993. Also see Peter Rosegg, "We Will Not Forget Our Fallen Warriors," *Honolulu Advertiser*, July 24, 1994.

14. Smyser, "The Battle," *Honolulu Star Bulletin*, September 2, 1993.

15. Sandi Magooay, "Impact Led to Project's Visitor Friendly Design," *Honolulu Star Bulletin*, July 24, 1994; and Jon Yoshishige, "Memorial to Veterans to be Dedicated Today," *Honolulu Star Bulletin*, July 24, 1994.

16. Medley and Johnson quote in Magooay, "Impact." See also Sandi Magooay, "Markers to be a Healing Place," *Honolulu Star Bulletin*, July 24, 1994; Peter Rosegg, "Speeches, Tears at Veterans Memorial," *Honolulu Advertiser*, July 25, 1994; and Jon Yoshishige, "Schofield Soldiers Remember Sister," *Honolulu Star Bulletin*, July 24, 1994.

17. John Burnett, "Korean War Memorial Dedicated in Hilo," *Hawaii Tribune-Herald*, June 23, 2019.

18. Choi, *Embattled Memories*, 73. See also Choi, "Mythologizing Memories," 61–82.

19. Therese Park, *When a Rooster Crows at Night*; and "Press Release," n.d., KWVA, chapters 1–181, personal archive of Tom Stevens, Overland Park KS. Park wrote an informative blurb on the planned memorial in the Johnson County, Kansas, magazine *Best of Times* (February 2004), 31. Stevens shared many archival materials during my May 5, 2017, interview with him.

20. Finn Bullers, "Past, Future Await U.S. Funding," *Kansas City Star*, December 2, 2004; U.S. Department of Housing and Urban Development to Jack Krumme, April 25, 2005; and press clipping, *Overland Park Sun*, September 30, 2006, Stevens Archive. Even after the official dedication, the Overland Park project was $15,000 short of the funding needed. A mini-campaign to sell 8"x4" paving bricks for $125 each and bench for $7,500 was quickly launched.

21. Therese Park, "Veterans Day Ceremony at Korean War Veterans Memorial on November 11, 2011," *Kansas City Star*, November 11, 2011. See also Travis Heying,

"Kapaun Sainthood Could Be One Step Closer," *Wichita Eagle*, February 18, 2020.

22. Terry Rombeck, "ku Pursues Memorial to 'Forgotten War,'" *Lawrence Journal-World*, June 18, 2003; and Terry Rombeck, "Korean War Memorial Finally Complete," *Lawrence Journal-World*, April 2, 2005.

23. www.accesskansas.org; and *Associated Press*, September 29, 2011, www.cjonline .com.

24. www.leg.wa.gov (memorials) and records of the Washington State Department of Enterprise Services. www.des.wa.gov. Also see "Korean American Day," *Puget Sound* (blog), January 13, 2015, www.pugetsound.blogspot.com.

25. For more on Washington's Korean War Memorial, see Washington State Department of Veterans Affairs, "Memorials," https://dva.wa.gov/about-wdva/memorials.

26. Hass, *Sacrificing Soldiers on the National Mall*, 155; and Pash, *In the Shadow*, 219.

27. A-0932, box 10, cskw-hstl.

28. For a detailed description of the Williams College monument, see Millett, *The War for Korea, 1950–51*, 1–2. Also see Tomedi, *No Bugles, No Drums*, 109–16.

29. Kyndell Nunley, "Korean War Memorial Unveiled in Southern Nevada Veterans Cemetery," *3 News Las Vegas*, March 4, 2018, https://news3lv.com/news/local /korean-war-memorial-southern-nevada. The author attended the program in Spokane, Washington.

30. George F. Drake, "Final Editorial–Closing Down the Project," Korean War Children's Memorial, Bellingham wa, September 20, 2006, http://koreanchildren .org/docs/Closing%20Down.htm. For a favorable depiction of Dean Hess, see Millett, *Their War for Korea*, 179–85.

31. Honor Flight Network, https://www.honorflight.org/.

32. David S. Heidler and Jeanne T. Heidler, "Series Foreword," in Edwards, *Korean War*, ix–x.

33. Daniels, *Guarding the Golden Door*, 124; and Hong, *Opening the Gates of Asia*, 12.

34. Yoo, *The Koreas*, 88–90; S. Chung, "History of Immigration to America"; John Kim, "In Observance of Centennial of Korean Immigration to the U.S."; and National Association of Korean Americans, http://naka.org/. A comprehensive study of Korean orphans, adoptees, and women in the aftermath of the war is presented in Woo, *Framed by War*. Also of interest is chapter 9 in the 2005 updated edition of Bruce Cumings's *Korea's Place in the Sun*, which presents an anecdotal account of Koreans Americans facing discrimination and uncertainty in their American environment.

35. Mark Monahan, based on many discussions with the author, September–December, 1995. The story of Chang/Monahan is recorded in the chapter, "The Teenage Guerrilla," from Millett, *Their War for Korea*, 51–56.

36. E. T. Kim, "Return Flights," 19–20; John Leland, "For Adoptive Parents, Questions Without Answers," *New York Times*, September 16, 2011, https://www.nytimes.com

/2011/09/18/nyregion/chinas-adoption-scandal-sends-chills-through-families-in
-united-states.html. Children born to Korean women and Black fathers created
special needs and efforts to place these children with African American parents,
altering adoption patterns in the United States. See Graves, *A War Born Family*.

37. E. T. Kim, "Return Flights," 21–23; E. Kim, *Adoptive Territory*; and Wool-Rim
Sjöblom, *Palimpsest*.

38. G. Cho, *Tastes Like War*; Yuh, *Beyond the Shadow of Camptown*.

39. For examples of this genre, see *Voices from Another Place*; N. Chung, *All You
Can Ever Know*; and Wills, *Older Sister, Not Necessarily Related*.

40. For an overview of Korean War brides, see Yuh, *Beyond the Shadow of Camptown*. Also see Ryan Schuessler, "Korean-American Military Brides Find Refuge
in a Tiny Missouri Church," *Al Jazeera*, March 21, 2015, http://america.aljazeera
.com/articles/2015/3/21/missouri-community-korean-american-military-brides
.html, for an account of distraught Korean women whose marriages to GIs did
not turn out well. Daniels, *Coming to America*, 364–68.

41. Yoo, *The Koreas*, 201–5; and A. Oh, *To Save the Children of Korea*. The stories
of Korean adoptees who returned to Korea to search for their birth parents are
presented in Jones, "Why a Generation of Adoptees." Jones's conclusions were
challenged by Jane Aronson in "A Saga Comes to an End: From the Horse's
Mouth on Korean Adoption," *Huffington Post*, April 7, 2015. Aronson wrote
that from her experiences, only a tiny fraction of Korean adoptees felt a need
to reconnect with Korea, and the majority have adjusted to their adopted status
the same as adoptees throughout America and other Western societies. Also see
Erin Raftery, "Korean War Babies Still Searching for GI Fathers," *USA Today*,
July 26, 2015.

42. Alderman and Lie, *Blue Dreams*.

43. Dr. Kim Byong Moon, to Michael Devine and Maija Devine, February 28, 2020;
and notes of phone call, June 22, 2020, Michael J. Devine Papers, HSTL.

44. Kim Byong Moon, "Thank You, Vets, for a Free South Korea," *Star Tribune*,
May 26, 2003; K. B. Moon, "A Perspective," 8–12; Kim Byong Moon, "A Show of
Appreciation for Korean War Vets," *Star Tribune*, September 1, 2014; and Valle,
"Kim Family's 12-Year Devotion," 26–27.

45. "Appreciation Concert Honoring President Harry S. Truman and Korean War
Veterans," press release, September 17, 2010; and Appreciation Concert, pro-
gram, dedicated to Pres. Harry S. Truman and Korean War Veterans, Saturday,
October 30, 2010, both in Michael J. Devine Papers, HSTL.

46. Dr. Kim, author's notes from a phone call, June 22, 2020.

47. Glassberg, *Sense of History*, 13.

48. www.trumanlibrary.gov/museum/ordinary-man/trumans-second-term.

49. The presidential years section of the exhibitions opened in December 2001 and
required significant piecemeal upgrading throughout my tenure as technological

advances made audiovisual components obsolete every few years. For documentation, consult the director's files at HSTL.

50. Clay Bauske to the author, February 24, 2022, with three attachments; and Samuel Rushay to the author, February 23, 2022, in the author's papers at HSTL. Bauske and Rushay are chief curator and supervisory archivist, respectively, at the Truman library.

51. The future of the presidential library system and the role of the private foundations in supporting the libraries have become uncertain during the tenure of David Ferriero, Archivist of the United States, whose reorganization of the agency in 2009 made presidential libraries a low priority. Meanwhile, over the past ten years, foundations have become increasingly independent in pursuing their own agendas. The Barack Obama Presidential Library will not be included in the NARA system, and it is uncertain at the time of this writing what kind of presidential library there will be for Pres. Donald Trump. On the future of presidential libraries and their collections, see B. Clark, "In Defense of Presidential Libraries," 96–103; and M. J. Devine, "Presidential Libraries and Their Foundations," 111–15. A still-useful assessment of presidential libraries is Hufbauer, *Presidential Temples*, 1–9, 139–99, 226–34.

5. THE KOREAN WAR VETERANS MEMORIAL

1. Westmoreland quoted in Stein, *Korean War Veterans Memorial*, 9.

2. Piehler, *Remembering War*, 1–9.

3. Hagopian, "Korean War Veterans Memorial," 215–53, especially 217.

4. Piehler, *Remembering War*, 3. For an example of Vietnam veterans' continuing emotional attachment to their memorial, see *Rolling Thunder XXX*, Palm Coast FL, 2017, Michael J. Devine Papers, HSTL. This program accompanied the reunion of thousands of Vietnam War veterans who arrive at the nation's capital each year by motorcycle from throughout the country. For more on Rolling Thunder, visit https://www.rollingthunder1.com/?fbclid=IwAR0TrK8x1y56b8xAg-evvyKjbQqkIYIgEkRwrrahJHhE_B1AMQFvDe03mp0.

5. The KWVA was formed in the summer of 1985 when more than fifty veterans met at a hotel in Arlington VA, following a ceremony held in Washington DC, to unveil a first-day issue of U.S. Postal Service stamps recognizing the Korean War. The organization was incorporated on June 14, 1985, in New York and later granted a charter by Congress on June 30, 2008. The KWVA now lists 330 chapters and publishes a magazine, *Graybeards*, six times a year. See www.kwva.us.

6. Public Law 99–572, April 20, 1986. Korean War Veterans Memorial Advisory Committee. The American Battle Monuments Commission was created in 1923 to commemorate the service of U.S. Armed Forces wherever they served in overseas conflicts. It later was charged with custodianship of military memorials in the United States. See Hagopian, "Korean War Veterans Memorial," 244;

and Albert J. Parisi, "In Pursuit of a Korean War Memorial," *New York Times*, July 10, 1988, https://www.nytimes.com/1988/07/10/nyregion/in-pursuit-of-a -korean-war-memorial.html.

7. For reasons still unclear to this author, the Barkers had a falling out with the advisory board, the foundation, and the KWVA. Ted Barker, in discussion with the author, April 24, 2020. See also Judie (Mr. Eastwood's secretary) to Hal Barker, August 7, 1986, and Clint Eastwood to Sen. Malcolm Wallop, TELEX message, August 7, 1986, https://www.koreanwar2.org/memorial/hb_clint_eastwood _august_1986.pdf; and Hal Barker, "Korean War Veterans Memorial Story: From Disaster to Dedication," April 27, 2018, https://www.koreanwar.org/html /korean-war-veterans-memorial-story.html. Hal and Ted Barker also established a Korean War database that, by 2013, had a hundred gigabytes of data on battles and servicemen and servicewomen. See Scott Baltic, "Rescue Mission," *Chicago Tribune*, July 23, 1995; and "Brothers behind the Korean War Project Keep a Watchful Eye on History, Veterans," *Dallas Morning News*, November 8, 2013.

8. Budget document, June 23, 1994, National Archives, Temporary Committees, Commissions and Boards, RG 220 (series 32940), Korean War Veterans Memorial Board (KWVMAB), correspondence of executive director, box 1, NARA II. The board's records include correspondence (series 32940) and minutes (series 40335). A fifty-eight-page computer printout of donors to the memorial from 1984–88 can be found on the website of the Korean War Project, https://www .koreanwar2.org/memorial/kwvm_memorial_donation_list_full.pdf.

9. Budget document, June 23, 1994. See also Hagopian, "Korean War Veterans Memorial," 220, 246.

10. Proposal by 1647 Tactical Control Group, "The Mosquitoes," September 23, 1987, A0370, box 5, CSKW-HSTL.

11. Two of the original board members, Gen. Richard Stilwell (U.S. Army Ret.; chair) and Col. Conrad Hausman (USAF Ret.), died before the project was completed. See RG 220 (32940), box 1, correspondence, NARA-II.

12. Ashabranner, *Remembering Korea*; and Hass, *Sacrificing Soldiers on the National Mall*, 196. Also see National Archives, KWVMB, RG 0220, minutes 40335.

13. Ashabranner, *Remembering Korea*, 37. For a detailed review of the board's design selection process, see Hagopian, "Korean War Veterans Memorial," 222–44.

14. Benjamin Forgey, "Memorial Design Rejected; Commission Wants Korean Monument Scaled Down," *Washington Post*, January 18, 1991.

15. Barbara Gamarekian, "Architects Clash over Korean War Memorial," *New York Times*, December 15, 1990. Also see Benjamin Forgey, "More Salvos in Memorial Fight; Commission Delays Decision on Korean War Memorial," *Washington Post*, December 14, 1990; and Roger Lewis, "War Memorial Design Symbol of Controversy," *Washington Post*, November 17, 1990.

16. Cooper and Lecky, "Korean War Veterans Memorial," 248.

17. Cooper and Lecky, "Korean War Veterans Memorial," 248–51.

18. Benjamin Forgey, "Memorial Design Rejected; Commission Wants Korean Monument Scaled Down," *Washington Post*, January 18, 1991.

19. *Houston Chronicle*, August 1, 1953. See press clippings in Vertical file, CSKW-HSTL.

20. Sarah Booth Conroy, "Korean Memorial Design Rejected: Arts Panel Decides Plan was 'Overloaded,'" *Washington Post*, June 29, 1991.

21. *Korean War Veterans Memorial*, National Park Services Brochure, 383-644-30300 (Washington DC: GPO, [2009]). Also see Stein, *Korean War Veterans Memorial*; Ashabranner, *Remembering Korea*; and an excellent critique of the memorial in Darda, *Empire of Defense*, 54–59.

22. Gen. Joseph S. Laposata, Memorandum of Board, June 28, 1994; and Robert Hansen to Mike Garza, June 2, 1994, both in RG 220, KWVMB, box 1, NARA-II.

23. President Clinton quoted in Stein, *Korean War Veterans Memorial*, 6; and Todd S. Purdum, "War in Korea, Fast Receding, Gets Memorial," *New York Times*, July 28, 1995, https://www.nytimes.com/1995/07/28/us/war-in-korea-fast-receding -gets-memorial.html. On Korea's participation in the ceremony, see Amb. Park Kun-woo, in *Ambassadors' Memoir*, 87–88.

24. Banta, "Memorializing the 'Forgotten War,'" abstract.

25. Schwartz and Schwartz Bayma, "Commemoration and the Politics of Recognition," 9xx.

26. Also see Hagopian, "Korean War Veterans Memorial," 244.

27. Millett, *Their War for Korea*, xvii.

28. Weintraub, *MacArthur's War*, x–xi.

29. Stein, *Korean War Veterans Memorial*, 39.

30. Millet, *Their War*, xiii; and *Kansas City Star*, May 11, 1997, CSKW-HSTL. Press clipping in vertical file.

31. The official name change from "Korean Conflict" to "Korean War" was included in the National Defense's Defense Authorization Act for Fiscal Year 1999 (Section 1067). See Edwards, *Korean War*, 173.

32. Robert Hansen to Col. William F. Ryan, minutes, March 4, 1988, RG 220 (40335), KWVMAB, no. 2, 52–57, NARA-II. The Korean War Project of Hal and Ted Barker is a website with extensive information on Korean War personnel killed in action and missing in action (MIA) and POWs, along with information on veterans and their survivors. The Barker brothers were among the skeptics. See www .koreanwarproject.org; and David Winkie, "Thousands of Massive Errors Possible in New Korean War Remembrance Wall, Advocates Fear," *Military Times*, April 6, 2021. Korean War veteran Stanley Weintraub noted that while MIAS following the Vietnam War became a huge political issue, the more than six thousand missing from the Korean War were soon forgotten by the American public. Weintraub, *MacArthur's War*, x.

33. Statement of Peggy O'Dell, NPS testimony to accompany H. R. 1475, is included in the files related to the Korean War Veterans Memorial Wall of Remembrance Act of 2016, 114th Congress, 2nd session 5–8, February 24, 2016, Amends PL 99–572, approved November 14, 1986.

34. The Korean War Veterans Memorial Wall of Remembrance Act (Public Law 114–230), enacted October 7, 2016, authorized the Korean War Veterans Memorial Foundation to construct a wall listing the 36,574 members of the U.S. Armed Forces and 8,000 members of KATUSA (Korean Augmentation to the U.S. Army) who died in the Korean War "as determined by the Secretary of Defense." This wall may include information about UNC personnel and is to be "low angled," so as not to obstruct the view across the Mall. Work was to begin in January 2021. See Executive Director's Recommendations, National Capitol Planning Commission, Commission Meeting, October 3, 2019, file 8107, https://www .ncpc.gov/docs/actions/2020October/8107_Korean_War_Veterans_Memorial _Wall_of_Remembrance_Graphics_Package_Staff_Report_Oct2020.pdf. On the twentieth-century trend to place the names of ordinary soldiers on war memorials, see Winter, *Remembering War*, 281.

35. Jada Smith, "Korean War Memorial Group Finds More Aid in Korea than in U.S.," *New York Times*, November 11, 2015, https://www.nytimes.com/2015/11/11 /us/politics/korean-war-memorial-foundation-wonders-where-the-us-corporate -aid-is.html; and Leo Shane, "Korean War Veterans Memorial gets $1M donation from Samsung," *Military Times*, October 12, 2015.

36. Col. James Fisher (U.S. Army Ret.), telephone call with the author, March 4, 2019. The Korean government appears especially interested in the Wall of Remembrance because it will list the names of eight thousand Koreans who served as KATUSA. Hal and Ted Barker remained convinced that the DOD's list of U.S. service personnel is highly incomplete and doubted that the necessary funding would ever be secured. Ted Barker, in discussion with the author, April 24, 2020.

37. Col. James Fisher (U.S. Army Ret.), in discussion with the author, April 2, 2021; Michel Au Buchon (KWVMF Secretary-Treasurer), in discussion with the author, May 17, 2021; and Michel Au Buchon, in email discussion with the author, May 18 and June 10, 2021, Michael J. Devine Papers, HSTL. Michael Ruane, "Korean War Veterans Memorial to Add List of Those Who Died in Combat," *Washington Post*, March 15, 2021, https://www.washingtonpost.com/history/2021/03/15 /korean-war-memorial-wall/; and "Maryland Governor Pledges $250,000 for Wall of Remembrance," *Dong-A-Ilbo*, May 24, 2021.

38. Video of the groundbreaking ceremony can be found on KWVMF's website, facebook.com/KWVMFUSA.videos/272194194268791.

39. For a discussion of foreign policy issues in Korean politics as of the summer of 2021, see Jason Li, "South Korea's Formal Membership in the Quad Plus: A

Bridge Too Far?" *38 North*, September 30, 2021, https://www.38north.org/2021/09/south-koreas-formal-membership-in-the-quad-plus-a-bridge-too-far/.

40. James Reston, "Monument Glut," *New York Times*, September 10, 1995, https://www.nytimes.com/1995/09/10/magazine/the-monument-glut.html; and David Montgomery, "A Wave of War Memorials Is Coming to DC. Are We at Peace with That?" *Washington Post*, July 31, 2018. On the evolution of the Mall since the founding of the District of Columbia, see Savage, *Monument Wars*, 1–22.

41. Hass, *Sacrificing Soldiers*, 196–98.

42. Hundreds of aging veterans of World War II and Korea arrive in Washington DC, each year aboard an Honor Flight, where each veteran is assigned a guide and wheeled around the Mall and other sites by their hosts upon landing at an area airport on all-expense-paid flight: www.honorflight.org.

43. For a frequently updated list of Korean War memorials, see the KWVA website. As with the Korean War Veterans Memorial in Washington DC, local Korean War monuments and activities of remembrance do not tell a "counternarrative" of wartime atrocities, civilian deaths, and lingering anti-Americanism among vocal leftist elements in South Korean society sympathetic to the North Korean regime. Some academic critics see the memorialization of the Korean War as overly simplistic and neglectful of the war's darker side. For example see Suhi Choi, *Embattled Memories*, 115. Choi claims that "the Korean War is exemplary in that its theme is shaped by the act of forgetting. Its official narrative—the American mission of saving South Korea from merciless Communist aggression—has maintained an absolute hegemonic power through forgetting a substantial body of counter memories that historians and journalists have cultivated since the war broke out" (13).

6. CONFLICTED MEMORIES OF ALLIES AND FOES

1. M. R. Devine, "General MacArthur, My Brother and I," 65–75.

2. Jinwung Kim, *A History of Korea*, 596; Jon Rabinoff and Yoo Kyong Chang, "Refurbished MacArthur Statue to be Unveiled at Incheon," *Stars and Stripes*, August 16, 2012; and Suhi Choi, *Embattled Memories*, 95–114, 128–31.

3. Therese Park, *When the Rooster Crows at Night*. A rooster crowing at nighttime is seen as a bad omen in Korean culture. *Kansas City Star*, press clipping, n.d., in KWVA, Tom Stevens Archives, Overland Park KS.

4. Bodnar, *Remaking America*, 10.

5. Lankov, *From Stalin to Kim Il Sung*, x, 11–20, 145, 195; Armstrong, *Tyranny of the Weak*, 241–45; Isozaki, *Understanding the North Korean Regime*, 40–41; Oberdorfer and Carlin, *The Two Koreas*, 18; and Darcie Draudt, "People's Groups and Patterns in Neighborhood Surveillance: Another Tool in State Control over Daily Life," *38 North*, December 10, 2020, https://www.38north.org/2020/12/ddraudt121020/. Also see the overview of North Korean society in Hassig

and Oh, *The Hidden People of North Korea*, 52–60, and their updated version, *North Korea in a Nutshell*.

6. "Report from Embassy of Hungary in North Korea," 107, emphasis in original.

7. Weathersby, "New Evidence," 5.

8. Shimotomai, "Pyongyang, 1956," 460.

9. Brazinsky, "Open Question," 34–37, especially 36. Also see Kristof, "What to Read."

10. *Outstanding Leadership and Brilliant Victory* (Pyongyang, DPRK: Korean Pictorial, 1993), copy in A-6337, box 101, CSKW-HSTL. On the origins of the Juche philosophy, see Jager, *Brothers at War*, 548–49.

11. Morris-Suzuki, "Remembering the Unfinished Conflict," 1–8. On the *Pueblo* display, see Cheevers, *Act of War*, 373–76.

12. For a recent review of the museum and everyday life in Pyongyang, see the commentary of British celebrity and world traveler Michael Palin, "Inside the World's Most Secretive State: Michael Palin Ventures to North Korea . . . and Finds Out What Locals Really Think of Kim Jong-un," *Telegraph*, September 13, 2019, https://www.telegraph.co.uk/books/biography-books/inside-worlds -secretive-state-michael-palin-ventures-north-korea/.

13. Stallard-Blanchette, "Past Present," 30, 31. See also Han, "The Ongoing Korean War," 152–77; and Oh and Hassig, *North Korea in a Nutshell*, 22. Historian Bruce Cumings visited the site in 1987 and concluded "a terrible atrocity had taken place, although the evidence on its authorship is impossible to document" (*The Korean War: A History*, 198).

14. Stallard-Blanchette, "Past Present," 31; and Isozaki, *Understanding the North Korean Regime*, 47–52.

15. Morrow, "Bridges at Panmunjom."

16. Paek Nam-Nyong quoted in Pinkham, "Something Resembling Normal Life," 12. Also see Immanuel Kim's afterword in Paek, *Friend*, 217–24; and Gabroussenko, *Soldiers on the Cultural Front*.

17. Martin, *Under the Loving Care*, 326–35. For an overview and analysis of North Korean films, see Schönherr, *North Korean Cinema*; Fischer, *A Kim Jong-Il Production*; and Simon Fowler, "The Five Best North Korean Films," *Guardian*, August 15, 2014, https://www.theguardian.com/world/2014/aug/15/five-best -north-korean-films.

18. Orwell, *1984*, 34.

19. Wang, *Never Forget National Humiliation*, 99. Also see Jager, *Brothers at War*, 311–21; and Millett, *The War for Korea, 1950–1951*, 590.

20. Jung, "China's Memory and Commemoration of the Korean War." Also see Morris-Suzuki et al., *East Asia beyond the History Wars*, 140–42. On the rise and fall of Gen. Peng Duhuai and the treatment of China's veterans, see D. Chang, *The Hijacked War*, 363–66; and Millett, *Their War for Korea*, 106–11, 132–33, 139.

21. For more on China's more assertive foreign policies, see Sec. of State Michael Pompeo's views in "Confronting Iran," 60–70. On South Korean apprehension over China's more aggressive policies, see Sang-hun Choe, "South Koreans Now Dislike China More Than They Dislike Japan," *New York Times*, August 20, 2021, https://www.nytimes.com/2021/08/20/world/asia/korea-china-election-young -voters.html. China sees the United States as the aggressor. Weihua Chen, "More People Must Oppose the U.S.'s Bid to Trigger a New Cold War," *China Daily, Global Edition*, June 16, 2021.

22. Wang, *Never Forget*, 6; Denmark and Myers, "Eternal Victory," 1–9; Andrew Salmon, "China Honors 'Human Wave' Heroes of Korean War," *Asia Times*, October 24, 2020; Steven Myers and Chris Buckley, "In Xi's Homage to Korean War, a Jab at U.S.," *New York Times*, October 23, 2020; and Delury, "China as Equal," 21–23.

23. "BTS in Trouble in China over Korean War Comments," BBC, October 13, 2020, https://www.bbc.com/news/world-asia-54513408; Oiwan Lam, "K-Pop Band BTS Targeted by Chinese Netizens over Korean War Comments," *Hong Kong Free Press*, October 17, 2020, https://hongkongfp.com/2020/10/17/k-pop-band -bts-targeted-by-chinese-netizens-over-korean-war-comments/; "Animated Korean War Film *Salute to the Heroes* Gets Release Date," *Global Times*, October 18, 2020, https://www.globaltimes.cn/content/1203851.shtml; and Ai Pang, "New Korean War Film Remembers Brave Chinese Soldiers," *Global Times*, October 20, 2020.

24. Wada, *The Korean War*, 299–301; and Morris-Suzuki, "You Don't Want to Know?"

25. Gibney, *Korea's Quiet Revolution*, 50–158; and Oberdorfer and Carlin, *Two Koreas*, 180–86.

26. Sang-hun Choe, "Paik Sun-yup, Lighting Rod General in South Korea, Dies at 99," *New York Times*, July 11, 2020. Korean War historian Millett considers Paik South Korea's equivalent of Gen. Ulysses S. Grant. Millet, *Their War for Korea*, xvi.

27. Gen. Paik Sun-yup, interview and tour of the War Memorial of Korea with M. J. Devine, June 8, 2011; and Paik, *Without My Country I Cannot Exist*, 509–13.

28. See Jager, "Manhood, the State, and the Yongsan War Memorial," 33–39; Jager and Kim, "Korea after the Cold War," 234, 242; and Jager, *Brothers at War*, 446–49.

29. All quotations from the War Memorial of Korea's English-language guide, www .warmemo.or.kr.

30. For an excellent critique of the War Museum of Korea, see Morris-Suzuki, "Remembering the Unfinished Conflict," 6–8.

31. Millett, *Their War for Korea*, xxi.

32. I attended the opening ceremony for this exhibition with more than a dozen former Peace Corps Volunteers. I remember that in 1970, while serving as a Peace Corps Volunteer, no museums, monuments, or images of the Korean War were

available to the public. There was little public mention of the 1950–53 conflict; and beyond the constant preparedness for another attack from North Korea, little information on the DPRK was available. Even magazine photographs of North Koreans and the DPRK flag were censored by ROK officials. This included Western magazines and periodicals. The leadership of the National Museum of Korean Contemporary History appears to have changed following presidential elections, and the left-leaning administration of Moon Jae-in appeared in 2019 to be set for reinterpreting the economic expansion of the Park Chung-hee era among other revisions. See National Museum of Korean Contemporary History website, http://www.much.go.kr.

33. Hufbauer, *Presidential Temples*, 173. Hufbauer saw the Truman Presidential Library as an exception, a credit to President Truman's open-minded family and the good judgment of the director who served as my immediate predecessor, Larry Hackman (172–75).

34. Photographs and notes in author's personal possession.

35. "Park Chung Hee Memorial-Library Opens Today," *Korea JoongAng Daily*, February 20, 2012, https://koreajoongangdaily.joins.com/2012/02/20/socialAffairs/Park -Chung-Hee-MemorialLibrary-opens-today/2948781.html. The Park Chung-hee Presidential Museum is managed by the President Park Chung-hee Memorial Foundation (www.presidentparkchunghee.org). Syngman Rhee's papers are located at the Institute for Modern Korean Studies, Yonsei University (www .gsis.yonsei.ac.kr). Many of Rhee's papers are housed at the Institute for Modern Korean Studies at Yonsei University and can be accessed at www.alarchive .wilsoncenter.org.

36. The Kim Dae-jung Library is located near the Yonsei University campus in Seoul (see www.kdjlibrary.org). It proclaims itself to be "Asia's First Presidential Library." The institution houses President Kim's private papers and artifacts, including his Nobel Prize medallion. His institution also conducts research and oral history projects on Korea's democratic movements. See Rhyu, *Democratic Movements and Korean Society*, 5–6.

37. Tom Clawson, "KWVA Revisit Program—A Twenty Year History," https://kwva.us /uploads/files/revisit_program_history_141028.pdf. Also see Bernard E. Trainor, "A Return to No Man's Land," copy in file ARO186, CSKW-HSTL; and Clyde Farnsworth, "Korea War Veterans Return for Another Look," *New York Times*, October 27, 1985, https://www.nytimes.com/1985/10/27/world/korea-war-veterans -return-for-another-look.html. I have also witnessed and attended dinners and special recognitions provided by Korean Counsels General in the United States for Korean War veterans and groups of former Peace Corps Volunteers.

38. For an overview of the numerous demilitarized zone (DMZ) memorials to American and UNC forces, see Tharp, *The Western DMZ, Paju*.

39. West and Suh, *Remembering the Forgotten War*, ii.

40. On sources of anti-Americanism in South Korea, see Sheila Miyoshi Jager, "Rewriting the Past/Reclaiming the Future: Nationalism and the Politics of Anti-Americanism in South Korea," *Japan Focus*, July 29, 2005, http://www.apjjf.org/Sheila-Miyoshi-Jager/1772/article.html; Straub, *Anti-Americanism in Democratizing South Korea*, 36–49; Hakjoon Kim, "A Brief History of the U.S.-ROK Alliance," 7–45; and Matray, "Irreconcilable Differences?" 1–26.

41. Suhi Choi, *Embattled Memories*, 106.

42. Jon Rabiroff and Yoo Kyong Chang, "MacArthur—Statue at Incheon," *Stars and Stripes*, August 16, 2012.

43. Oh and Hassig, *North Korea in a Nutshell*, 23, 247, n 7. Oberdorfer and Carlin, *Two Koreas*, 197; and Lankov, *Real North Korea*, 158.

44. Rev. Paul White to Harry S. Truman, October 15, 1967, and Truman to White, November 28, 1967, both in Truman Papers, Post Presidential file, box 47, HSTL.

45. Hughes, *Literature and Film in Cold War South Korea*; Keene, "Cinema and Prosthetic Memory"; and Diffrient, "'Military Enlightenment' for the Masses," 22–49.

46. Alice Martin, "6 Powerful Novels that Capture the Impact of the Korean War," OFF *the Shelf*, May 26, 2020, https://offtheshelf.com/2020/05/korean-war-fiction-books/; and W. Kim, "The Korean War, Memory, and Nostalgia," 3–6. Also see Susan Choi's foreword to Richard Kim's novel, *The Martyred*. Among the escape narratives are Tudor, *Ask a North Korean*; Kim and Kim, *Long Road Home*; Lee and McClelland, *Every Falling Star*; and Park and Vollers, *In Order to Live*.

47. For opposition to replacing leftist interpretations in South Korean textbooks, see Jeff Kingston, "South Korea's New State Textbook 'Corrects History,'" *Japan Times*, November 7, 2015; "Clashes in South Korea at Rally for Ouster of President: A State-Issued History Textbook and Labor Change Fuel Outcry," *New York Times*, November 15, 2015; and "South Korea Unveils Controversial State History Textbooks," *Straits Times*, January 31, 2017, https://www.straitstimes.com/asia/east-asia/south-korea-unveils-controversial-state-history-textbooks. On protests against President Park, see M. Park, *South Korea's Candlelight Revolution*.

48. Pash, *In the Shadow*, 215. For a listing of Korean War memorials throughout the world, see Korean War Memorials website, www.koreanwarmemorials.com.

49. Sandler, *The Korean War*, 4, 15.

50. Hennessey, *Britain's Korea War*, 242–43, 259–60. For British and French memories of the Korean War, see comments by Steven Casey, "Truman Legacy Symposium," Key West Florida, 2016, video tape, CSKW-HSTL. Also see Parritt, *Chinese Hordes and Human Waves*, 101–2, 191. According to British journalist and longtime resident of South Korea Andrew Salmon, "Few memorials to the [Korean] War stand in the UK." He also wrote that "the Korean War faded almost totally from the public memory; it was too far from home, and far too opaque a cause to inspire a populace still getting over the struggle against Hitler." Salmon quotes

veterans as stating, "'We were not welcomed back as heroes. . . . Everybody was already fed up with World War II.' . . . 'It was not like the Falklands. . . . Victories get all the publicity. The Korean War is still on'" (*To the Last Round*, 319, 320).

51. Hennessey, *Britain's Korea War*, 242–43, 246–48, 259–60.

52. Weintraub, *MacArthur's War*, 356.

53. John Melady notes that ROK-sponsored visits to Korea for Canadian veterans left them stunned by the progress. Melady, *Korea*, 179. Also see Granatstein, *Canada's Army*, 332–34.

54. On the memories of the ANZUS allies, Vojtěch Mastný comments at the "Legacy of the Korean War," a symposium held at the Harry S. Truman Little White House in Key West FL, 2016, video tapes held at HSTL. Also see Ikin et al., "Comorbidity of PTSD and Depression in Korean War Veterans," 279–86; and Ikin et al., "Life Satisfaction and Quality in Korean War Veterans," 359–65.

55. For reviews, commentary, and listings of international sites of remembrance in South Korea and countries participating in the UNC, see Morris-Suzuki, "Remembering the Unfinished Conflict"; and Tharp, *Western DMZ*, Paju.

7. MEMORY, TRUTH, AND RECONCILIATION

1. Winter, *Remembering War*, 283–89; Kammen, *Mystic Chords*, 13, 713, n 45; and Wang, "The Past's Transformative Power."

2. Ashton and Wilson, "Remembering Dark Pasts," 281, 290.

3. Ashton and Wilson, "Remembering Dark Pasts," 285.

4. Also see Jager, *Brothers at War*, 85–97, 506, n 91–92. Researchers working for Korea's Truth and Reconciliation Commission assisted Jager and provided material for her book (xiii).

5. Suh, *Truth and Reconciliation*. See Suh's introduction to the book for an overview. See also Charles J. Hanley and Jae-Soon Lee, "Truth and Reconciliation Commission, Republic of Korea," https://web.archive.org; Hanley, *Ghost Flames*, 453; Sang-Hum Choe, "Unearthing War's Horrors Years Later in South Korea," *New York Times*, December 3, 2007; and Charles J. Hanley and Jae-soon Chang, "Seoul Probes Civilian Massacres by U.S.," *Associated Press*, August 18, 2007, https://www.statesboroherald.com/local/associated-press/ap-impact-seoul-probes-civilian-massacres-by-us/. Early efforts to seek justice for wartime atrocities are explored in Wright, "Raising the Korean War Dead." Also see Do and Kim, "Crimes, Concealment, and South Korea's Truth."

6. Hanley, Choe, and Mendoza, *The Bridge at No Gun Ri*; Hanley and Mendoza, "The Massacre at No Gun Ri"; Conway-Lanz, "Beyond No Gun Ri," 49–81; and Suhi Choi, *Embattled Memories*, chapter 1. A large file of press clippings on the No Gun Ri incident and its reporting is in box 9, A-0914, CSKW-HSTL.

7. Elizabeth Becker, "U.S. to Revisit Accusations of a Massacre by GIs in '50," *New York Times*, October 1, 1999; Felicity Barringer, "A Press Divided: Disputed

Accounts of a Korean War Massacre," *New York Times*, May 22, 2000, https://www.nytimes.com/2000/05/22/business/a-press-divided-disputed-accounts-of-a-korean-war-massacre.html; and Galloway, "Doubts Raised About a Korean Massacre."

8. *No Gun Ri Review*, Office of the Inspector General, Department of the Army, Washington DC, January 2001.

9. Thomas E. Ricks, "No Gun Ri Massacre Blamed on Panic," *Washington Post*, December 6, 2000, https://www.washingtonpost.com/archive/politics/2000/12/06/no-gun-ri-massacre-blamed-on-panic/ba966bab-4014-4fd8-94bd-2fbb9912d4cc/. Also see Thomas E. Ricks, "No Gun Ri Survivors Denounce Report," CBS News, January 11, 2001.

10. Hanley responded to criticism of his reporting and attacked the official U.S. government's 2001 report on the incident, calling it "whitewashed and distorted at every turn." See Hanley, "In the Face of Amnesia."

11. For an eyewitness to history account of the late 1960s to the arrival of democracy in South Korea, see Baker, "The Rough Road to Democracy," 90–103.

12. For example, Ambassador Gleysteen to Secretary of State, May 21, 1980, and Richard Holbrooke and Anthony Lake to Secretary of State (Secret), May 22, 1980, both in www.digitalarchive.wilsoncenter.org. Also see Jefferson Morley, "The Empty Legacy of Richard Holbrooke," *Asia Times*, June 13, 2019, https://asiatimes.com/2019/06/the-empty-legacy-of-richard-holbrooke/.

13. Benjamin Engel, "5–18 and the Forgotten Lesson on Anti-Americanism in South Korea," *Diplomat*, May 17, 2019, https://thediplomat.com/2019/05/5-18-and-the-forgotten-lesson-on-anti-americanism-in-south-korea/. There exists extensive and highly personal literature on the Kwangju Uprising of 1980. Perhaps the most balanced assessments are found in the essays in D. Clark, *The Kwangju Uprising*. Also see foreword by Kim Dae-jung in Scott-Stokes and Lee, *The Kwangju Uprising*; Drennan, "The Tipping Point"; Byun and Lewis, *The 1980 Kwangju Uprising After 20 Years*; the recent accounts of two Peace Corps Volunteers serving in Kwangju in 1980, Baker, "Kwangju, Trauma and the Problem of Objectivity in History-Writing," 9–29; and Lewis, *Laying Claim to the Memory of May*.

14. The 1997 East Asian financial crisis caused a painful drop in ROK living standards and the loss of jobs, homes, and businesses. Faced with the largest default in history, the ROK agreed to huge loans from the International Monetary Fund (IMF). It was widely reported that the United States pressured the IMF to open Korean markets to foreign investments as a condition for the loans. Whatever the truth of the matter, the IMF bailout led to financial stability and renewed economic growth. See Straub, *Anti-Americanism*, 1–3, 5.

15. Straub, *Anti-Americanism*, 159, and see 160–63.

16. Albright, *Madame Secretary*, 465. Secretary Albright reported that Kim Jong-il felt U.S. troops in Korea were a force for stabilization. See Straub, *Anti-Americanism*, 42; Cumings, *Korea's Place in the Sun* (2005), 502–3.

17. D. Clark, *Living Dangerously in Korea*, xii.

18. "40 Years after Korea: The Forgotten War," *U.S. News & World Report*, June 25, 1990, 31.

19. James T. Laney, *Ambassadors' Memoirs*. Limited relations with the DPRK eventually resumed but remained tense following the submarine incident, after which Ambassador Laney described "unbending determination by the United States and some tough talk between the United States and North Korea in New York," 78.

20. "Statement from Former President Jimmy Carter on Current U.S.-North Korea Relations," Carter Center, August 10, 2017, https://www.cartercenter.org/news /pr/north-korea-081017.html; and Harrison, *Korean Endgame*, 98.

21. The policy's name derived from an ancient Aesop fable about an argument between the wind and the sun over which had more power. Each tried to force a man's coat off his body. The wind blew but only caused the man to tighten his hold. But the warmth of the sun induced the man to gladly remove his coat.

22. Jinwung Kim, *A History of Korea*, 224–29. Kim's presidency was tarnished by financial scandals involving his three sons, and several of his closest aides were arrested and imprisoned for various illegal activities.

23. Sherman, *Not for the Faint of Heart*, 100–105; and Albright, *Madam Secretary*, 455–71. Analyst of East Asian affairs Victor Cha noted that President Bush undercut a "Sunshine Policy" that was already discredited and failing ("America and South Korea," 279–84).

24. Chinoy, *Meltdown*, xx; and Russell Goldman, "How Trump's Predecessors Dealt with the North Korean Threat," *New York Times*, August 17, 2017, https://www .nytimes.com/2017/08/17/world/asia/trump-north-korea-threat.html.

25. Chinoy, *Meltdown*, xxii. An American diplomat's assessment of the Bush administration's policy toward the two Koreas is presented in a chapter entitled "Bush-whacked: North Korea Policy," in Straub, *Anti-Americanism*, 115–31. Also see Eisendrath and Goodman, *Bush League Diplomacy*, 162, 225–28. A detailed assessment of the Bush administration's "Hawk" diplomacy is James I. Matray, "The Failure of the Bush Administration's North Korean Policy," 140–177.

26. Yonhap News Agency, *North Korea Handbook*, xvii–xviii, 511–13.

27. *Ambassadors' Memoirs*, 145, 149–50. In the early weeks of the Bush administration, Sec. of State Colin Powell informed Ambassador Yang that the new administration would "engage with North Korea to pick up where President Clinton and his administration had left off" (150). The policy was quickly reversed by the neocons (hardline conservatives), including Vice Pres. Dick Cheney, Sec. of Defense Donald Rumsfeld, and Undersec. of State for Arms Control John

Bolton. An observer of the White House believed that President Bush struggled between head and heart in forming decisions on Korean affairs. Chinoy,
Meltdown, xxii.

28. Amb. Sung-joo Han, *Ambassadors' Memoirs*, 150.

29. Amb. Sung-joo Han, *Ambassadors' Memoirs*, 192–96.

30. For detailed insiders' accounts of the Bush administration's diplomatic missteps
leading to a nuclear-armed North Korea, see Pritchard, *Failed Diplomacy*; and
Joseph R. DeTrani, "Negotiating with North Korea," *38 North*, September 23,
2019, https://www.38north.org/2019/09/jdetrani092319/.

31. Pritchard, Tilelli Jr., and Snyder, *U.S. Policy toward the Korean Peninsula: Report
of Task Force 64*, 10, 11. See also Goldman, "Trump's Predecessors"; and Rob-
bie Gramer and Emily Tamkin, "Decades of Diplomacy with North Korea: A
Timeline," *Foreign Policy*, March 12, 2018, https://foreignpolicy.com/2018/03/12
/a-timeline-of-u-s-negotiations-talks-with-north-korea-trump-kim-jong-un
-pyongyang-nuclear-weapons-diplomacy-asia-security/.

32. Pritchard, Tilelli Jr., and Snyder, *Report of Task Force 64*, 43–44. On reaction to
the sinking of the *Cheonan*, see Brian Reynolds Myer, "South Korea's Collective
Shrug," *New York Times*, May 27, 2010, https://www.nytimes.com/2010/05/28
/opinion/28myers.html; and Jun-suk Yeo, "Eight Years since *Cheonan* Sinking,
South Korea Still Mired in Controversy," *Korean Herald*, April 5, 2018, https://
www.koreaherald.com/view.php?ud=20180405000692.

33. Obama, "Remarks Following a Meeting with President Lee Myung-bak," 829.

34. Goldman, "Trump's Predecessors."

35. According to Secretary of State Pompeo, a U.S.-led pressure campaign had
driven Kim to the negotiating table in Singapore: "Chairman Kim committed to
final, fully verified denuclearization of North Korea. . . . This was the first time
there was a personal, leader-to-leader commitment on denuclearization." See
Pompeo, "Confronting Iran," 60–70, quotation on 61. President Trump's disregard for history is discussed in MacMillan, "Which Past Is Prologue?" 12–22.
Also see David P. Fields, "The Lessons of the Korean War in the Age of America
First," *Sources and Methods* (blog), Wilson Center, History and Public Policy
Program, July 1, 2020, https://www.wilsoncenter.org/blog-post/lesson-korean
-war-age-america-first.

36. Morrow, "Bridges at Panmunjom," 13–25, especially 20; and Robert Carlin,
"Gentlemen Apparently Do Read Other Gentlemen's Mail: Kim Jong-un's Letters to President Truman," *38 North*, September 11, 2020, https://www.38north
.org/2020/09/rcarlin091120/.

37. Terry, "North Korea's Nuclear Family," 115–27; DeTrani, "Negotiating with North
Korea"; and George F. Will, "South Koreans Worry about the North. But It's
Japan that Inflames Their Emotions," *Washington Post*, October 2, 2019, https://
www.washingtonpost.com/opinions/the-us-has-shouting-matches-over-north

-korea-south-koreans-actually-live-with-the-threat/2019/10/02/03b6eefc-e48a
-11e9-b403-f738899982d2_story.html.

38. The Wilson Center's Robert Litwack suggests that instead of complete "transitional" nuclear disarmament or regime change in the DPRK, the U.S. policy should strive for a limited, incremental, or "transformational" pursuit of objectives. Beginning with a freeze on testing nuclear weapons and ballistic warheads in exchange for lifting economic sanctions, both parties could move ahead on denuclearization. See Litwack, *Preventing North Korea's Nuclear Breakout*, 2–5. Also see Litwack, "Myth/Misconception."

39. Jager, *The Politics of Identity*, v; Keene, "Lost to Public Memory," 1; Myers, *The Cleanest Race*, 166; and Jean Lee, "Guns and Hunger," 13.

40. Koreans count four hundred invasions of their homeland over a four-thousand-year history. This is likely an exaggeration as it would mean warfare once every ten years. However, the seventy years since the Korean War have seen no invasions or major international military confrontations, unlike much of the proceeding millennium.

41. Oberdorfer and Carlin, *The Two Koreas*, 411. In recent years South Koreans have expressed less interest in reunification than they did in past decades. A new generation of Koreans, with no personal memories of the war, appears more interested in maintaining its prosperity and way of life than taking on the economic burden of North Korea, even if reunification somehow came about peacefully. See Timothy S. Rich and Madelynn Einhorn, "South Koreans Rarely Think about North Korea—And Why It Matters," *38 North*, November 13, 2020, https://www.38north.org/2020/11/trichmeinhorn111320/; and S. Park, "Together Apart."

42. Pottinger, "Beijing's American Hustle," 102–3; Delury, "China as Equal," 21–23.

43. Wang, "The Past's Transformative Power in China"; Zhang Han and Xu Liuliu, "'Chinese Cannot Be Trifled with'; Viewers Inspired after Korean War Film Special Screening," *Global Times*, September 25, 2021, https://www.globaltimes.cn/page/202109/1235045.shtml; Salmon, "China Honors 'Human Wave'"; and Pang, "New Korean War Film."

44. Brands and Gaddis, "The New Cold War," 10–20.

45. Wang, "The Past's Transformative Power." U.S.-China watchers and experts on national security issues have assessed China's recent diplomatic and military initiatives, and their work is reviewed by former California governor Jerry Brown in "Washington's Crackpot Realism," 12–14.

46. Discussion of Daniel Sneider and Amb. Kathleen Stephens, Korean Economic Institute Webinar, June 8, 2021, www.events@kei.org; Bong-geun Jun, "Getting Back to Talks: Why the Biden Administration Should Reaffirm the Singapore Joint Statement," *38 North*, March 26, 2021; and H. Lim, "Not 'Final and Irreversible.'"

47. On reconciliation with Vietnam, see the work by former U.S. Ambassador to Vietnam (2014–2017) Osins, *Nothing Is Impossible*, especially chapter 5 on the

issues related to the war's legacy. In a December 9, 2021, Zoom conference sponsored by the Stimson Center in Washington DC, Osins discussed two issues with China during Vietnam's developing relationship with the United States: the control of the Mekong River and navigation of the East Sea (South China Sea).

48. Osins, *Nothing Is Impossible*, 256–70; on the People's Republic of China as a threat to North Korea, see Jager, *Brothers at War*, 464–79.

CONCLUSION

1. For a recent analysis of U.S. involvement in warfare since World War II, including the notion of the Korean War as a defeat for the United States, see Filkins, "War With a Human Face," 68–72.

2. Jinwung Kim, *A History of Korea*, 533.

3. Sheila Miyoshi Jager explores the changing dynamics in the relationships of the East Asian nations in her thoughtful epilogue, "China's Rise, the War's End?" in *Brothers at War*, 464–80. Although written a decade ago, it remains prescient and insightful.

Bibliography

ARCHIVAL SOURCES

American Heritage Center, University of Wyoming

Dwight D. Eisenhower Presidential Library

Harry S. Truman Library / Center for the Study of the Korean War (HSTL-CSKW)

Institute for Korean Studies, Yonsei University

Korean War Legacy Project, Korea University

National Archive and Records Administration, National Archives, College Park MD

State of Hawaiʻi, Hawaiʻi Department of Accounting and General Services, working file, Honolulu, Hawaiʻi

Woodrow Wilson Center, Cold War International History Project, Digital Archive

Government documents, ephemera, newspapers, and blog posts are cited in the notes but not included in the bibliography.

PUBLISHED WORKS

Abrahamian, Andray. *North Korea and Myanmar: Divergent Paths*. Jefferson NC: McFarland, 2018.

Adams, Della, and Lewis H. Carlson, eds. *An American Dream: The Life of an African American Soldier and POW Who Spent Twelve Years in Communist China*. Amherst: University of Massachusetts Press, 2007.

Ahn, Junghyo. "A Double Exposure to War." In *America's Wars in Asia: A Cultural Approach to History and Memory*, edited by Philip West, Steven I. Levine, and Jackie Hiltz, 161–71. Armonk NY: M. E. Sharpe, 1998.

Albright, Madeleine. *Madame Secretary: A Memoir*. New York: Hyperion, 2003.

Alderman, Nancy, and John Lie. *Blue Dreams: Korean Americans and the Los Angeles Riots*. Cambridge: Harvard University Press, 1995.

Alexander, Bevin. *Korea: The First War We Lost*. New York: Hippocrene, 1986.

Ambassadors' Memoir: U.S. Korean Relations through the Eyes of the Ambassadors. Washington DC: Korean Economic Institute, 2009.

Anderson, Clarence L., Alexander M. Boysen, Sidney Esensten, Gene N. Lam, and William R. Shadish. "Medical Experiences in Communist POW Camps in Korea." *Journal of the American Medical Association* 156, no. 2 (September 11, 1954): 39–40.

Anderson, David. *Trapped by Success: The Eisenhower Administration and Vietnam, 1953–1961.* New York: Columbia University Press, 1991.

Appleman, Roy E. *South to the Naktong, North to the Yalu.* Washington DC: Office of the Chief of Military History, Department of the Army, GPO, 1961.

Arkin, William. *The Generals Have No Clothes.* New York: Simon and Schuster, 2021.

Armstrong, Charles K. *Tyranny of the Weak: North Korea and the World, 1950–1992.* Ithaca: Cornell University Press, 2013.

Ashabranner, Brent K. *Remembering Korea: The Korean War Veterans Memorial.* Brookfield CT: Twenty-First Century Books, 2001.

Ashton, Paul, and Jacqueline Z. Wilson. "Remembering Dark Pasts and Horrific Places: Sites of Conscience." In *What Is Public History Globally: Working with the Past in the Present,* edited by Paul Ashton and Alex Trapeznik, 281–94. New York: Bloomsbury, 2019.

Atkins, E. Taylor. "Book Review: *From Cultures of War to Cultures of Peace: War and Peace Museums in Japan, China, and South Korea* and *Embattled Memories: Contested Meanings in Korean War Memorials.*" *Public Historian* 37, no. 2 (May 2015): 152–54.

Bacevich, Andrew J. *America's War for the Greater Middle East: A Military History.* New York: Random House, 2016.

———. *The New American Militarism.* New York: Oxford University Press, 2005.

Baik, Crystal Mun-hye. *Reencounters: On the Korean War and Diasporic Memory Critique.* Philadelphia: Temple University Press, 2019.

Baker, Dan. "Kwangju, Trauma and the Problem of Objectivity in History-Writing." In *Peace Corps Volunteers and Korean Studies in the United States,* edited by Seung-kyung Kim and Michael Robinson, 9–29. Seattle: University of Washington Center for Korean Studies, 2020.

Baker, Edward. "The Rough Road to Democracy in Korea, 1960–1992: The Observations of an American Friend." In *Democratic Movements and Korean Society,* edited by Rhyu Sang-young, 90–103. Seoul: Yonsei University Press, 2007.

Bakich, Spencer D. *Success and Failure in Limited War: Information and Strategy in the Korean, Vietnam, Persian Gulf, and Iraq Wars.* Chicago: University of Chicago Press, 2014.

Baldovi, Louis. *A Foxhole View: Personal Accounts of Hawaii's Korean War Veterans.* Honolulu: University of Hawai'i Press, 2002.

Baldwin, Frank, ed. *Without Parallel: The American-Korean Relationship since 1945.* New York: Pantheon, 1974.

Ballal, Amritha, and Moulshri Joshi. "Forgetting and Remembering in Bhopal: Architects as Agents of Memory." In *What Is Public History Globally? Working with the Past in the Present*, edited by Paul Ashton and Alex Trapeznik, 323–35. London: Bloomsbury Academic, 2019.

Banner, James M., Jr. *The Ever-Changing Past: Why All History Is Revisionist History.* New Haven: Yale University Press, 2021.

Banta, Cora. "Memorializing the 'Forgotten War': The Korean War Veterans Memorial in Context." PhD diss., University of Michigan, 2014.

Baptism by Fire: CIA Analysis of the Korean War: A Collection Previously Released and Recently Declassified Intelligence Documents. Washington DC: Center for the Study of Intelligence, 2010 (documents printed in conjunction with a conference held at the Harry S. Truman Library).

Barnhart, Michael A., ed. "Special Issue: The Impact of the Korean War." *Journal of American-East Asian Relations* 2, no. 1 (Spring 1993): 261–307.

Bateman, Robert L. *No Gun Ri: A Military History of the Korean War Incident.* Mechanicsburg PA: Stackpole, 2002.

Bator, Francis M. "No Good Choices: LBJ and the Vietnam/Great Society Connection." *Diplomatic History* 32, no. 3 (June 2008): 309–40.

Becker, Jasper. "John Everard, Only Beautiful, Please: A British Diplomat in North Korea." *Asian Affairs* 45, no. 2 (May 4, 2014): 385–88.

Beech, Keyes. *Tokyo and Points East.* Garden City NY: Doubleday, 1954.

Beisner, Robert L. *Dean Acheson: A Life in the Cold War.* New York: Oxford University Press, 2006.

Bélanger, Stéphanie A. H., and Renée Dickason, eds. *War Memories: Commemoration, Recollections, and Writings on War.* Montreal: McGill-Queen's University Press, 2017.

Bell, Duncan, ed. *Memory, Trauma, and World Politics: Reflections on the Relationship between Past and Present.* New York: Palgrave Macmillan, 2006.

Berinsky, Alan J. *In Time of War: Understanding American Public Opinion from World War II to Iraq.* Chicago: University of Chicago Press, 2009.

Bernstein, Barton. "The Struggles over the Korean Armistice: Prisoners of Repatriation." In *Child of Conflict: The Korean-American Relationship, 1943–1953*, edited by Bruce Cumings. Seattle: University of Washington Press, 1983.

Berry, Henry. *Hey Mac, Where You Been? Living Memories of the U.S. Marines in the Korean War.* New York: St. Martin's, 1988.

Beschloss, Michael. *Presidents of War: The Epic Story, from 1807 to Modern Times.* New York: Crown, 2018.

Biderman, Albert D. "Communist Attempts to Elicit False Confessions from Air Force Prisoners of War." *Bulletin of the New York Academy of Medicine* 33, no. 9 (1957): 616–25.

———. "The Image of 'Brainwashing.'" *Public Opinion Quarterly* 26, no. 4 (1962): 547–63.

———. *March to Calumny: The Story of the American POWs in the Korean War.* New York: Macmillan, 1963.

Blaine, A. J. *The Accidental President: Harry S. Truman and the Four Months that Changed the World.* Boston and New York: Houghton Mifflin Harcourt, 2017.

Blair, Clay. *The Forgotten War: America in Korea, 1950–1953.* New York: Times Books, 1987.

Bleiker, Roland, and Young-Ju Hoang. "Remembering and Forgetting the Korean War: From Trauma to Recollection." In *Memory, Trauma, and World Politics: Reflections on the Relationship Between Past and Present,* edited by Duncan Bell, 195–212. London: Palgrave Macmillan, 2006.

Bodnar, John. *The "Good War" in American Memory.* Baltimore MD: The Johns Hopkins University Press, 2010.

———. *Remaking America: Public Memory, Commemoration, and Patriotism in the Twentieth Century.* Princeton: Princeton University Press, 1992.

Bohlen, Charles E. *The Transformation of American Foreign Policy.* New York: Norton, 1969.

———. *Witness to History, 1929–1969.* New York: Norton, 1973.

Bontrager, Shannon. *Death at the Edges of Empire: Fallen Soldiers, Cultural Memory, and the Making of an American Nation.* Lincoln: University of Nebraska Press, 2020.

Borden, William S. *Pacific Alliance: U.S. Foreign Economic Policy and Japanese Trade Recovery, 1947–1955.* Madison: University of Wisconsin Press, 1984.

Borthwick, Mark. *Pacific Century: The Emergence of Modern Pacific Asia.* 3rd ed. Boulder CO: Westview, 2007.

Bowers, William, William M. Hammond, and George L. MacGarrigle. *Black Soldier White Army: The 24th Infantry Regiment in Korea.* Washington DC: U.S. Army Center for Military History, 1996.

Bradbury, William C., Samuel M. Meyers, and Albert D. Biderman, eds. *Mass Behavior in Battle and Captivity: The Communist Soldier in the Korean War.* Chicago: University of Chicago Press, 1968.

Brady, James. *The Scariest Place in the World: A Marine Returns to North Korea.* New York: Thomas Dunne, 2005.

Brands, Hal. *The Twilight Struggle: What the Cold War Teaches Us about Great-Power Rivalry Today.* New Haven: Yale University Press, 2021.

Brands, Hal, and John Lewis Gaddis. "The New Cold War: America, China and the New Cold War." *Foreign Affairs* 100 (November–December 2021): 10–20.

Brands, H. W. *The General vs. the President: MacArthur and Truman at the Brink of Nuclear War.* Garden City NY: Doubleday, 2016.

———. "Redacted Testimony that Fully Explains Why General MacArthur Was Fired." *Smithsonian Magazine* (September 28, 2016): https://www.smithsonianmag .com/history/redacted-testimony-fully-explains-why-general-macarthur-was -fired-180960622/.

———. *What America Owes the World: The Struggle for the Soul of Foreign Policy.* Cambridge: Cambridge University Press, 1998.

Brazinsky, Gregg. *Nation Building in South Korea: Koreans, Americans, and the Makings of a Democracy.* Chapel Hill: University of North Carolina Press, 2009.

———. "Open Questions: The Lived Experiences of North Koreans in the War." *Wilson Quarterly* (Summer 2020): https://www.wilsonquarterly.com/quarterly /korea-70-years-on/korean-war-open-questions.

Briley, Ron. "*M*∗*A*∗*S*∗*H* by David Scott Diffrient (review)." *Film & History: An Interdisciplinary Journal* 45, no. 1 (Summer 2015): 94–96.

Britton, Diane. "Public History and Public Memory." *Public Historian* 19, no. 3 (1997): 1–17.

Brooks, Matthew Stephen, and Lawrence Fulton. "Evidence of Poorer Life-Course Mental Health Outcomes among Veterans of the Korean War Cohort." *Aging and Mental Health* 14, no. 2 (2010): 177–83.

Brown, Jerry. "Washington's Crackpot Realism." *New York Review of Books* 69, no. 5 (March 24, 2022): 12–14.

Burma, Ian. "The Jingo Olympics: Playing for Keeps." *New York Review of Books* 35, no. 7 (November 1988): 44–50.

Byun, Juna, and Linda Lewis. *The 1980 Kwangju Uprising After 20 Years: The Unhealed Wounds of the Victims.* Seoul: Dahae, 2000.

Carlson, Lewis H. *Remembered Prisoners of a Forgotten War: An Oral History of Korean War POWs.* New York: St. Martin's, 2002.

Carruthers, Susan L. *Cold War Captive: Imprisonment, Escape, and Brainwashing.* Berkeley: University of California Press, 2009.

———. "*The Manchurian Candidate* (1962) and the Cold War Brainwashing Scare." *Historical Journal of Film, Radio, and Television* 18, no. 1 (March 1988): 75–94.

Casey, Steven. "Harry Truman, the Korean War and the Transformation of U.S. Policy in East Asia, June 1950–June 1951." In *Northeast Asia and the Legacy of Harry S. Truman: Japan, China, and the Two Koreas,* ed. James I. Matray, 185–202. Vol. 8 of *The Truman Legacy Series.* Kirksville MO: Truman State University Press, 2012.

———. *The Korean War at Sixty: New Approaches to the Study of the Korean War.* London: Routledge, 2012.

———. *Selling the Korean War: Propaganda, Politics, and Public Opinion in the United States, 1950–1953.* Oxford: Oxford University Press, 2010.

———. "The United States." In *The Ashgate Research Companion to the Korean War,* edited by James I. Matray and Donald W. Boose Jr., 49–60. Surrey, UK: Ashgate, 2014.

————. *When Soldiers Fall: How Americans Have Confronted Combat Losses from World War I to Afghanistan*. Oxford: Oxford University Press, 2014.

Casey, Steven, and Jonathan Wright, eds. *Mental Maps of the Early Cold War Era, 1945–1968*. Basingstoke, UK: Palgrave Macmillan, 2011.

Cha, Victor D. "America and South Korea: The Ambivalent Alliance?" *Current History* 102, no. 665 (September 2003): 279–84.

————. *The Impossible State: North Korea, Past and Future*. New York: Harper Collins, 2012.

Chang, David Cheng. *The Hijacked War: The Story of Chinese POWs in the Korean War*. Palo Alto: Stanford University Press, 2020.

Chang, Gordon G. *Nuclear Showdown: North Korea Takes on the World*. New York: Random House, 2006.

Chang, Gordon H. "JFK, China, and the Bomb." *Journal of American History* 74 (March 1988): 1287–310.

Chang, Kornel. "Independence without Liberation: Democratization as Decolonization Management in U.S.-Occupied Korea, 1945–1948." *Journal of American History* 107, no. 1 (June 2020): 77–106.

Cheevers, Jack. *Act of War: Lyndon Johnson, North Korea, and the Capture of the Spy Ship* Pueblo. New York: NAL Caliber, 2013.

Chen, Jian. *China's Road to the Korean War: The Making of the Sino-American Confrontation*. New York: Columbia University Press, 1994.

————. "In the Name of Revolution: China's Road to the Korean War Revisited." In *The Korean War in World History*, edited by William Stueck, 93–125. Lexington: University of Kentucky Press, 2004.

————. *Not Yet a Revolution: Reviewing China's "New Cold War Documentation."* College Park MD: Cold War International History Conference, 1998.

————. "Open Question: The 'Long Peace' Between America and China." *Wilson Quarterly* (Summer 2020): https://www.wilsonquarterly.com/quarterly/korea-70-years-on/korean-war-open-questions.

Chen, Jian, and Shen Zhihua. "Introduction: The Geneva Conference of 1954: New Evidence from the Archives of the Ministry of Foreign Affairs of the People's Republic of China." *CWIHP Bulletin* 16 (2007): 7–84.

————. *Mao's China and the Cold War*. Chapel Hill: University of North Carolina Press, 2001.

Cheong, Sung-Hwa. *The Politics of Anti-Japanese Sentiment in Korea: Japanese–South Korean Relations Under American Occupation, 1945–1952*. Westport CT: Greenwood, 1991.

Chinnery, Philip D. *Korean Atrocity! Forgotten War Crimes, 1950–1953*. Annapolis MD: Naval Institute, 2000.

Chinoy, Mike. *Meltdown: The Inside Story of the North Korean Nuclear Crisis*. New York: St. Martin's, 2008.

Cho, Grace. *Haunting the Korean Diaspora: Shame, Secrecy, and the Forgotten War.* Minneapolis: University of Minnesota Press, 2008.

———. *Tastes Like War: A Memoir.* New York: Feminist Press (CUNY), 2021.

Cho, Il Hyun. *Global Rogues and Regional Orders: The Multi-Dimensional Challenge of North Korea and Iran.* New York: Oxford University Press, 2016.

Choi, Deokhyo. "The Empire Strikes Back from Within: Colonial Liberation and the Korean Minority Question at the Birth of Postwar Japan, 1945–1947." *The American Historical Review* 126, no. 2 (June 2021): 555–84.

———. "Fighting the Korean War in Pacifist Japan: Korean and Japanese Leftist Solidarity and American Cold War Containment." *Critical Asian Studies* 49, no. 4 (December 2017): 546–68.

Choi, Suhi. *Embattled Memories: Contested Meanings in Korean War Memorials.* Reno: University of Nevada Press, 2014.

———. "Mythologizing Memories: A Critique of the Utah Korean War Memorial." *Public Historian* 34 (2012): 61–82.

Choi, Susan. "Foreword." In *The Martyred*, by Richard Kim, xiii–xvi. New York: Penguin Books, 2011. First published 1964 by George Braziller (New York).

Chung, Hye Seung, and David Scott Diffrient. *Movie Migrations: Transnational Genre Flows and South Korean Cinema.* New Brunswick: Rutgers University Press, 2015.

Chung, Nicole. *All You Can Ever Know: A Memoir.* New York: Catapult, 2018.

Clark, Bob. "In Defense of Presidential Libraries: Why the Failure to Build an Obama Library Is Bad for Democracy." *Public Historian* 40, no. 2 (May 2018): 96–103.

Clark, Donald N., ed. *The Kwangju Uprising: Shadow over the Regime in South Korea.* Boulder CO: Westview, 1988.

———. *Living Dangerously in Korea: The Western Experience, 1900–1950.* Norwalk CT: EastBridge, 2003.

Clark, Mark W. *From the Danube to the Yalu.* New York: Harper, 1954.

Clifford, Clark, with Richard Holbrooke. *Counsel to the President: A Memoir.* New York: Random House, 1991.

Clifford, Mark. *Troubled Tiger: Businessmen, Bureaucrats, and Generals in South Korea.* Armonk NY: M. E. Sharpe, 1994.

Cohen, Warren, and Akira Iriye. *The Great Powers in East Asia.* New York: Columbia University Press, 1990.

Coldwell, John D. *Anatomy of Victory: Why the United States Triumphed in World War II, Fought to a Stalemate in Korea, Lost in Vietnam, and Failed in Iraq.* Lanham MD: Rowman & Littlefield, 2018.

Collins, J. Lawton. *War in Peacetime: The History and Lessons of Korea.* Boston: Houghton Mifflin, 1969.

Conway-Lanz, Sahr. "Beyond No Gun Ri: Refugees and the United States Military in the Korean War." *Diplomatic History* 29, no. 1 (2005): 49–81.

Cooper, Kent, and William Lecky. "The Korean War Veterans Memorial: Some

Thoughts from the Designers." In *The Korean War Veterans Memorial: A Tribute to Those Who Served*, edited by Robert J. Martin, 248–60. Paducah KY: Turner, 1995.

Core, Dublin. *War's Hidden Chapter: Ex-GIs Tell of Killing Korean Refugees*. No Gun Ri Digital Archive, 1999.

Cotton, James, and Ian Neary, eds. *The Korean War in History*. Atlantic Highlands NJ: Humanities Press International, 1989.

Crane, Conrad. *American Airpower Strategy in Korea, 1950–1953*. Lawrence: University Press of Kansas, 2000.

———. "No Practical Capabilities: American Biological and Chemical Warfare Programs During the Korean War." *Perspectives in Biology and Medicine* 45, no. 2 (2002): 241–49.

———. "To Avert Impending Disaster: American Military Plans to Use Atomic Weapons during the Korean War." *Journal of Strategic Studies* 23, no. 2 (June 2000): 72–88.

Crouse, Eric R. *An American Stand: Senator Margaret Chase Smith and the Communist Menace, 1948–1972*. Lanham MD: Lexington, 2010.

Crowe, David M. *War Crimes, Genocide, and Justice: A Global History*. New York: Palgrave Macmillan, 2014.

Cumings, Bruce. "American Policy and Korean Liberation." In *Without Parallel: The American-Korean Relationship since 1945*, edited by F. Baldwin, 39–108. New York: Pantheon, 1974.

———, ed. *Child of Conflict: The Korean-American Relationship, 1943–1953*. Seattle: University of Washington Press, 1983.

———. "Introduction: Korea Is Near." In *The Hidden History of the Korean War, 1950–1951*, edited by I. F. Stone and Mark Crispin Miller. New York: Open Road Integrated Media, 2014.

———. *Korea's Place in the Sun: A Modern History*. New York: Norton, 1997.

———. *Korea's Place in the Sun: A Modern History*. Rev. ed. New York: Norton, 2005.

———. *The Korean War: A History*. New York: The Modern Library, 2010.

———. "The Korean War: What Is It that We Are Remembering to Forget?" In *Ruptured Histories: War, Memory, and the Post-Cold War in Asia*, edited by Sheila Miyoshi Jager and Rana Mitter, 266–90. Cambridge: Harvard University Press, 2007.

———. "A Murderous History of Korea." *London Review of Books* 39, no. 10 (May 18, 2017): https://www.lrb.co.uk/v39/n10/bruce-cumings/a-murderous-history -of-korea.

———. *The Origins of the Korean War: Liberation and the Emergence of Separate Regimes, 1945–1947*. Princeton: Princeton University Press, 1981.

———. "The South Korean Massacre at Taejon: New Evidence of U.S. Responsibility and Cover Up." *Asia-Pacific Journal: Japan Focus* 6, no. 7 (July 23, 2008): https://apjjf.org/-Bruce-Cumings/2826/article.html.

———. *War and Television*. London: Verso, 1992.

———. "The Wicked Witch of the West Is Dead. Long Live the Wicked Witch of the East." In *The End of the Cold War: Its Meaning and Implications*, edited by Michael J. Hogan, 87–102. New York: Cambridge University Press, 1992.

Cunningham, Cyril. *No Mercy, No Leniency: Communist Mistreatment of British Allied Prisoners of War in Korea*. Barnsley, UK: Pen & Sword, 2000.

Dallek, Robert. *An Unfinished Life: John F. Kennedy, 1917–1963*. New York: Little, Brown, 2003.

Daniels, Roger. *Coming to America: A History of Immigration and Ethnicity in American Life*. New York: Harper Collins, 1990.

———. *Guarding the Golden Door: American Immigration Policy and Immigration Since 1882*. New York: Hill and Wang, 2004.

Darda, Joseph. *Empire of Defense: Race and the Cultural Politics of Permanent War*. Chicago: University of Chicago Press, 2019.

Day, Cara Skodack. "Worth Remembering: He Fought the Good Fight. Now He's Fighting to Save the Memory of It." VFW *Auxiliary* (April–May 2001): 8–10.

Dean, William F. *General Dean's Story as Told to William L. Worden*. New York: Viking, 1954.

Delury, John. "China as Equal: Putting China as Rival into Historical Context." *Perspectives on History* 58, no. 7 (October 2020): 21–23.

Demick, Barbara. *Nothing to Envy: Ordinary Lives in North Korea*. New York: Spiegel & Grau, 2015.

Denmark, Abraham, and Lucas Myers. "Eternal Victory." *Wilson Quarterly* (Summer 2020): https://www.wilsonquarterly.com/quarterly/korea-70-years-on/eternal-victory.

Devine, Maija Rhee. "Crane's Grace." *Kenyon Review* (Summer–Fall 1999): 22–32.

———. "General MacArthur, My Brother and I. South Koreans Remember the Korean War." *Korean War Symposium III* (December 9, 2017): 57–64. Korean War Archive, Korea University, Seoul.

———. *The Voices of Heaven*. Seoul: Seoul Selection, 2013.

———. "What Was Said in the Bamboo Grove." *Boulevard* 18 (Fall 2002): 121–36.

Devine, Michael J. "Administrators." In *Public History: Essays from the Field*, edited by Peter LaPaglia and James Gardner, 45–56. 2nd ed. Malabar FL: Krieger Co., 2004.

———. "The Education of a Public Historian: A Case Study with Reflections on Professional Wrestling." *Public Historian* 22 no. 4 (Fall 2000): 11–18.

———, ed. *Korea in War, Revolution, and Peace: The Recollections of Horace G. Underwood*. Seoul: Yonsei University Press, 2001. Korean language ed., 2002.

———. "The Korean War, American POWs and the Legacy of Brainwashing." *Transactions of the Royal Asiatic Society* 92 (2017): 163–73.

———. "Open Questions: Memorials—Remembering an Unfinished War?" *Wilson*

Quarterly (Summer 2020): https://www.wilsonquarterly.com/quarterly/korea
-70-years-on/korean-war-open-questions.

———. "President Harry S. Truman and the Korean War." *Korean War Symposium III* (December 9, 2017): 57–64. Korean War Archive, Korea University, Seoul.

———. "Presidential Libraries and Their Foundations: Time for Reform." *The Public Historian* 40, no. 4 (May 2018): 111–15.

———. "Professional Issues beyond the Classroom." *Perspectives* 38, no. 5 (May 2000): 48–49.

Diffrient, David Scott. *M*A*S*H.* Detroit: Wayne State University Press, 2008.

———. "'Military Enlightenment' for the Masses: Genre and Cultural Intermixing in South Korea's Golden Age War Films." *Cinema Journal* 45, no. 1 (2005): 22–49.

Dingman, Roger. "Truman's Gift: The Japanese Peace Settlement." In *Northeast Asia and the Legacy of Harry S. Truman: Japan, China, and the Two Koreas*, ed. James I. Matray, 46–72. Vol. 8 of *The Truman Legacy Series*. Kirksville MO: Truman State University Press, 2012.

Do, Kheim, and Kim Sung-Soo. "Crimes, Concealment, and South Korea's Truth and Reconciliation Commission." *Asia-Pacific Journal: Japan Focus* 6, no. 8 (August 1, 2008): https://apjjf.org/-Do-Khiem/2848/article.html.

Doenecke, Justus D. *Not to the Swift: The Old Isolationists in the Cold War Era.* Lewisburg PA: Bucknell University Press, 1979.

Dolski, Michael R. *D-Day Remembered: The Normandy Landings in American Collective Memory.* Knoxville: University of Tennessee Press, 2016.

Doyle, Robert. *Voices from Captivity: Interpreting the American POW Narrative.* Lawrence: University Press of Kansas, 1994.

Drennan, William M. "The Tipping Point: Kwangju, May 1980." In *Korean Attitudes toward the United States: Changing Dynamics*, edited by David I. Steinberg, 280. Armonk NY: M. E. Sharpe, 2005.

Dulles, Allen. "Brain Warfare: Russia's Secret Weapon." *U.S. News & World Report* 34, no. 19 (May 8, 1953): 55–57.

Dunne, Matthew W. *A Cold War State of Mind: Brainwashing and Postwar American Society.* Amherst: University of Massachusetts Press, 2013.

Du Toit, Fanie. "En(Countering) Silence—Some Thoughts on Social Justice after Memoricide." *International Public History* 3, no. 2 (October 2020): https://doi.org/10.1515/iph-2020-2005.html.

Eckert, Carter. *Park Chung Hee and Modern Korea: The Roots of Militarism, 1866–1945.* Cambridge: Harvard University Press, 2016.

Edelman, Robert, and Christopher Young, eds. *The Whole World Was Watching: Sport in the Cold War.* Palo Alto: Stanford University Press, 2020.

Edwards, Paul M. *Combat Operations of the Korean War: Ground, Air, Sea, Special, and Covert.* Jefferson NC: McFarland, 2009.

———. *A Guide to Films on the Korean War*. Westport CT: Greenwood, 1997.

———. *The Hill Wars of the Korean Conflict: Dictionary of Hills, Outposts and Other Sites of Military Action*. Jefferson NC: McFarland, 2006.

———. *Historical Dictionary of the Korean War*. Lanham MD: Scarecrow, 2010.

———. *The Inchon Landing, Korea, 1950*. Westport CT: Greenwood, 1994.

———. *The Korean War*. Malabar FL: Krieger, 1999.

———. *The Korean War*. Westport CT: Greenwood, 2006.

———. *Korean War Almanac*. New York: Facts on file, 2006.

———, comp. *The Korean War: An Annotated Bibliography*. Westport CT: Greenwood, 1998.

———. *The Korean War: A Historical Dictionary*. Lanham MD: Scarecrow, 2003.

———. *The Mistaken History of the Korean War: What We Got Wrong Then and Now*. Jefferson NC: McFarland, 2018.

———. *To Acknowledge a War: The Korean War in American Memory*. Westport CT: Greenwood, 2000.

———. *The United Nations Participants in the Korean War: The Contributions of 45 Member Countries*. Jefferson NC: McFarland, 2013.

———. *Unusual Footnotes to the Korean War*. London: Osprey, 2013.

Eisendrath, Craig R., and Melvin Goodman. *Bush League Diplomacy: How the Neoconservatives Are Putting the World at Risk*. Amherst NY: Prometheus, 2004.

Elsey, George. *An Unplanned Life: A Memoir*. Columbia: University of Missouri Press, 2005.

Eperjesi, John R. "The Unending Korean War in Film: From *The Bridges at Toko-Ri* to *Welcome to Dongmakgol*." *Journal of American Studies* 52, no. 3 (2018): 787–809.

Feffer, John, ed. *The Future of U.S.-Korean Relations: The Imbalance of Power*. New York: Routledge, 2006.

Fehrenbach, T. R. *This Kind of War: The Classic Korean War History*. Dulles VA: Potomac, 2008.

———. *This Kind of War: Korea—A Study in Unpreparedness*. New York: Macmillan, 1963.

Ferrell, Robert H, ed. *Dear Bess: The Letters from Harry to Bess Truman, 1910–1959*. New York: Norton, 1983.

———. *Harry S. Truman: A Life*. Columbia: University of Missouri Press, 1994.

———, ed. *Off the Record: The Private Papers of Harry S. Truman*. New York: Harper & Row, 1980.

———. *The Question of MacArthur's Reputation: Côte De Châtillon, October 14–16, 1918*. Columbia: University of Missouri Press, 2008.

Fields, David P. *Foreign Friends: Syngman Rhee, American Exceptionalism, and the Division of Korea*. Lexington: University Press of Kentucky, 2019.

Filkins, Dexter. "War with a Human Face." *New Yorker* (September 13, 2021): 68–72.

Fine, Sherwood M. "The Impact of the Korean War on the Japanese Economy." In *The Occupation of Japan: The Impact of the Korean War*, edited by Richard B. Rice and William Nimmo, 139. Norfolk VA: MacArthur Memorial, 1990.

Finn, David. "Korean War Veterans Memorial." *Sculpture Review* 46 (1998): 22.

Fischer, Paul. *A Kim Jong-Il Production*. New York: Flatiron, 2015.

Fishman, Howard. "What M*A*S*H Taught Us." *New Yorker* (July 24, 2018): https://www.newyorker.com/culture/culture-desk/what-mash-taught-us.

Foot, Rosemary. "Making Known the Unknown War: Policy Analysis of the Korean Conflict in the Last Decade." *Diplomatic History* 15, no. 3 (Summer 1991): 411–31.

——. *A Substitute for Victory: The Politics of Peacemaking at the Korean Armistice Talks*. Ithaca: Cornell University Press, 1990.

——. *The Wrong War: American Policy and the Dimensions of the Korean Conflict, 1950–1953*. Ithaca: Cornell University Press, 1985.

"Forty Years After Korea: The Forgotten War." *U.S. News & World Report* (June 25, 1990): 31.

Friedan, Betty. *The Feminine Mystique*. New York: Norton, 1963.

Fulton, Bruce, Ju-Chan Fulton, and Bruce Cumings. *The Red Room: Stories of Trauma in Contemporary Korea*. Honolulu: University of Hawai'i Press, 2009.

Gabroussenko, Tatiana. *Soldiers on the Cultural Front: Developments in the Early History of North Korean Literature and Literary Policy*. Honolulu: University of Hawai'i Press, 2010.

Gaddis, John Lewis. *The Cold War: A New History*. New York: Penguin, 2005.

——. "The Soviet Side of the Cold War: A Symposium. Introduction." *Diplomatic History* 15, no. 4 (1991): 523–26.

——. "The Tragedy of Cold War History." *Diplomatic History* 17, no. 1 (1993): 1–16.

Galloway, Joseph L. "Doubts Raised about a Korean 'Massacre.'" *U.S. News & World Report* 128, no. 21 (May 22, 2000).

Garfield, Linda. *I Remember Korea: Veterans Tell Their Stories of the Korean War, 1950–1953*. New York: Clarion, 2003.

Gibbons, William Conrad. *The U.S. Government and the Vietnam War: Executive and Legislative Roles and Relationships, Part I: 1945–1960*. Princeton: Princeton University Press, 1986.

Gibney, Frank. "The First Three Months of the War: A Journalist's Reminiscences of Korea." *Journal of American-East Asian Relations* 2, no. 1 (Spring 1993): 101–10.

——. *Korea's Quiet Revolution: From Garrison State to Democracy*. New York: Walker, 1992.

Gills, B. K. *Korea versus Korea: A Case of Contested Legitimacy*. New York: Routledge, 1996.

Glassberg, David. *Sense of History: The Place of the Past in American Life*. Amherst: University of Massachusetts Press, 2001.

Gleason, Abbott. *Totalitarianism: The Inner History of the Cold War.* New York: Oxford University Press, 1995.

Gleysteen, William H., Jr. *Massive Entanglement, Marginal Influence: Carter and Korea in Crisis.* Washington DC: Brookings Institution, 1999.

Goldhamer, Herbert. *The 1951 Korean Armistice Conference: A Personal Memoir.* Foreword by Andrew Marshall and introduction by Ernest R. May. Santa Monica CA: Rand, 1994.

Goldstein, Gordon. *Lessons in Disaster: McGeorge Bundy and the Path to War in Vietnam.* New York: Times Books, 2008.

Gonchrov, Sergei. *Uncertain Partners: Stalin, Mao, and the Korean War.* Palo Alto: Stanford University Press, 1993.

Gong, Gerrit W., ed. *Remembering and Forgetting: The Legacy of War and Peace in East Asia.* Washington DC: Center for Strategic and International Studies, 1996.

Goodwin, Doris Kearns. *Lyndon Baines Johnson and the American Dream.* New York: St. Martin's, 1991.

Graff, Henry. *The Tuesday Cabinet: Deliberations and Decisions on Peace and War under Lyndon B. Johnson.* Englewood Cliffs NJ: Prentice Hall, 1970.

Graham, Otis L. "Uses and Misuses of History in Policymaking." *Public Historian* 5, no. 2 (Spring 1983): 5–19.

Granatstein, J. L. *Canada's Army: Waging War and Keeping Peace.* 3rd ed. Toronto: University of Toronto Press, 2021.

Graves, Kori. *A War Born Family: African American Adoption in the Wake of the Korean War.* New York: NYU Press, 2020.

Green, Alix R. *History, Policy, and Public Purpose: Historians and Historical Thinking in Government.* London: Palgrave MacMillan, 2016.

Greene, John Robert. *I Like Ike: The Presidential Election of 1952.* Lawrence: University Press of Kansas, 2017.

Gropman, Alan L. "The Korean War and Armed Forces Integration." In *A Revolutionary War: Korea and the Transformation of the Postwar World*, edited by William J. Williams, 83–107. Chicago: Imprint, 1993.

Haass, Richard. "Present at the Disruption—How Trump Unmade U.S. Foreign Policy." *Foreign Affairs* 99, no. 5 (September–October 2020): 24–34.

Hagopian, Patrick. "The Korean War Veterans Memorial and Problems of Representation." *Public Art Dialogue* 2 (September 2012): 215–53.

———. *The Vietnam War in American Memory: Veterans, Memorials, and the Politics of Healing.* Amherst: University of Massachusetts Press, 2009.

Halberstam, David. *The 1950s.* New York: Villard, 1993.

———. *The Best and the Brightest.* New York: Random House, 1972.

———. *The Coldest Winter: America and the Korean War.* New York: Hyperion, 2007.

Halbwachs, Maurice. *On Collective Memory.* Edited and translated by Lewis A. Coser. Chicago: University of Chicago Press, 1992.

Halliday, Jon, and Bruce Cumings. *Korea: The Unknown War*. New York: Pantheon, 1988.

Hamby, Alonzo L. *Man of the People: A Life of Harry S. Truman*. New York: Oxford University Press, 1995.

———. "Public Opinion: Korea and Vietnam." *Wilson Quarterly* 2, no. 3 (Summer 1978): 137–41.

Han, Sung-hoon. "The Ongoing Korean War at the Sinchon Museum in North Korea." *Cross-Currents: East Asian History and Culture Review* 4, no. 1 (March 2015): 152–77.

Hanley, Charles J. *Ghost Flames: Life and Death in a Hidden War, Korea 1950–1953*. New York: Public Affairs, 2020.

———. "In the Face of Amnesia, the Grim Truths of No Gun Ri Find a Home." *Asia-Pacific Journal: Japan Focus* 13 (March 9, 2015): https://apjjf.org/2015/13/9/Charles-J.-Hanley/4294.html.

Hanley, Charles J., and Martha Mendoza. "The Massacre at No Gun Ri: Army Letter Reveals U.S. Intent." *Asia-Pacific Journal: Japan Focus* 5, no. 4 (April 15, 2007): https://apjjf.org/-Charles-J.-Hanley/2408/article.html.

Hanley, Charles J., Sang-hun Choe, and Martha Mendoza. *The Bridge at No Gun Ri: A Hidden Nightmare from the Korean War*. New York: Holt, 2001.

Harden, Blaine. *Escape from Camp 14: One Man's Remarkable Odyssey from North Korea to Freedom in the West*. New York: Viking, 2012.

———. *The Great Leader and the Fighter Pilot: The True Story of the Tyrant Who Created North Korea and the Young Lieutenant Who Stole His Way to Freedom*. New York: Viking, 2015.

———. *King of Spies: The Dark Reign of America's Spymaster in Korea*. New York: Viking, 2017.

Harrison, Selig S. *Korean Endgame: A Strategy for Reunification and U.S. Disengagement*. Princeton: Princeton University Press, 2002.

Hass, Kristin Ann. *Sacrificing Soldiers on the National Mall*. Berkeley: University of California Press, 2013 (e-book).

Hassig, Ralph, and Kongdan Oh. *The Hidden People of North Korea: Everyday Life in the Hermit Kingdom*. Lanham MD: Rowman and Littlefield, 2009.

Hastings, Max. *The Korean War*. New York: Simon & Schuster, 1987.

Hechler, Ken, and Robert P. Watson. "Truman's MacArthur and MacArthur's Truman: The Roots and Ramifications of the General's Removal." In *Northeast Asia and the Legacy of Harry S. Truman, Japan, China, and the Two Koreas*, ed. James I. Matray, 185–223. Vol. 8 of *The Truman Legacy Series*. Kirksville MO: Truman State University Press, 2012.

Heller, Francis, ed. *The Korean War: A 25-Year Perspective*. Lawrence: Regents Press of Kansas, 1977.

Henderson, Gregory. *Korea: The Politics of the Vortex*. Cambridge: Harvard University Press, 1968.

Hennessey, Thomas. *Britain's Korea War: Cold War Diplomacy, Strategy and Security 1950–53*. Manchester: Manchester University Press, 2013.

Herring, George C. *From Colony to Superpower: U.S. Foreign Relations Since 1776*. New York: Oxford University Press, 2008.

———. *LBJ and Vietnam: A Different Kind of War*. Austin: University of Texas Press, 1994.

———. "Vietnam Remembered." *Journal of American History* 73, no. 1 (June 1986): 152–64.

Hess, Dean. *Battle Hymn*. New York: McGraw-Hill, 1956.

Hettiarachchi, Radhika, and Ricardo Santiago. "Identity, Memory, and Transitional Landscape: Public History in the Context of Transitional Justice." *International Public History* 3, no. 2 (October 2020): doi:10.1515/iph-2020-2014.

Higgings, Marguerite. *War in Korea: The Report of a Woman Combat Correspondent*. Garden City NY: Doubleday, 1951.

Highsmith, Carol M., and Ted Landphair. *Forgotten No More: The Korean War Veterans Memorial Story*. Washington DC: Chelsea, 1995.

Hogan, Michael J., ed. *The End of the Cold War: Its Meaning and Implications*. New York: Cambridge University Press, 1992.

Honda, Kazuhisa. "W. E. B. Du Bois and the Paradox of American Democracy: A Battle for World Peace." *Journal of Applied Sociology* 58 (2016): 93–104.

Hong, Jane H. *Opening the Gates of Asia: A Transpacific History of How America Repelled Asian Exclusion*. Chapel Hill: University of North Carolina Press, 2019.

Hopkins, Michael. *Dean Acheson and the Obligations of Power*. New York: Rowman & Littlefield, 2017.

Horowitz, Dorothy G., ed. *We Will Not Be Strangers: Korean War Letters between a MASH Surgeon and His Wife*. Foreword by James I. Matray. Urbana: University of Illinois Press, 1997.

Hudson, Walter M. *Army Diplomacy: American Military Occupation and Foreign Policy after World War II*. Lexington: University Press of Kentucky, 2015.

Hufbauer, Benjamin. *Presidential Temples: How Memorials and Libraries Shape Public Memory*. Lawrence: University Press of Kansas, 2005.

Hughes, Theodore. *Literature and Film in Cold War South Korea: Freedom's Frontier*. New York: Columbia University Press, 2012.

Hunt, Michael H., and Steven I. Levine. *Arch of Empire: American Wars in Asia from the Philippines to Vietnam*. Chapel Hill: University of North Carolina Press, 2012.

Hunter, Edward. *Brainwashing: From Pavlov to Powers*. New York: Bookmailer, 1965.

———. *Brainwashing in Red China: The Calculated Destruction of Men's Minds*. New York: Vanguard, 1951.

———. *Brainwashing: The Story of the Men Who Defied It*. New York: Farrar, Straus, and Cudahy, 1956.

Hwang, Su-Kyoung. *Korea's Grievous War*. Philadelphia: University of Pennsylvania Press, 2016.

———. "Silence in History and Memory: Narrating the Comfort Women." *Trans-Humanities Journal* 2, no. 1 (June 2010): 195–224.

Hwang, Sun-won. *Lost Souls*. Translated by Bruce Fulton and Ju-chan Fulton. New York: Columbia University Press, 2010.

Hynes, Samuel. "Personal Narratives and Commemoration." In *War and Remembrance in the Twentieth Century*, edited by Jay Winter and Emanuel Sivan, 205–20. Cambridge: Cambridge University Press, 1999.

Iber, Patrick. "Cold War World." *New Republic* 48, no. 11 (2017): 60.

Ikin, Jillian F., Mark C. Creamer, Malcolm R. Sima, and Dean P. McKenzie. "Comorbidity of PTSD and Depression in Korean War Veterans: Prevalence, Predictors, and Impairment." *Journal of Affective Disorders* 125 (September 2010): 279–86.

Ikin, Jillian F., M. R. Sim, D. P. McKenzie, K. W. A. Horsley, E. J. Wilson, W. K. Harrex, M. R. Moore, P. L. Jelfs, and S. Henderson. "Life Satisfaction and Quality in Korean War Veterans Five Decades after the War." *Journal of Epidemiology and Community Health* 63, no. 5 (2009): 359–65.

"The Impact of the Korean War." *Journal of American-East Asian Relations* 2, no. 1 (Spring 1993): 1–110.

Iriye, Akira. *The Cold War in Asia: A Historical Introduction*. Englewood Cliffs NJ: Prentice-Hall, 1974.

Isozaki, Atsuhito. *Understanding the North Korean Regime*. Washington DC: Woodrow Wilson Center, 2017.

Jager, Sheila Miyoshi. *Brothers at War: The Unending Conflict in Korea*. New York: Norton, 2013.

———. "Manhood, the State, and the Youngan War Memorial, South Korea." *Museum Anthropology: Journal of the Council of Museum Anthropology* 21, no. 3 (1997): 33–39.

———. *Narratives of Nation-Building in Korea*. Armonk NY: M. E. Sharpe, 2003.

———. *The Politics of Identity: History, Nationalism, and the Prospect for Peace in Post–Cold War East Asia*. Carlisle PA: Strategic Studies Institute, U.S. Army War College, 2007.

———. "Re-Writing the Past/Re-Claiming the Future: Nationalism and the Politics of Anti-Americanism in South Korea." *Asia-Pacific Journal: Japan Focus* 3, no. 7 (July 29, 2005): https://apjjf.org/-Sheila-Miyoshi-Jager/1772/article.html.

———. "Woman, Resistance and the Divided Nation: The Romantic Rhetoric of Korean Reunification." *Journal of Asian Studies* 55, no. 1 (1996): 3–21.

Jager, Sheila Miyoshi, and Jiyul Kim. "The Korean War after the Cold War: Commemorating the Armistice Agreement in South Korea." In *Ruptured Histories:*

War, Memory, and the Post–Cold War in Asia, edited by Shelia Miyoshi Jager and Rama Mitter, 233–65. Cambridge: Harvard University Press, 2007.

———. "Open Questions: The Lasting Legacies of Korean War Special Operations." *Wilson Quarterly* (Summer 2020): https://www.wilsonquarterly.com/quarterly /korea-70-years-on/korean-war-open-questions.

Jager, Sheila Miyoshi, and Rana Mitter, eds. *Ruptured Histories: War, Memory, and the Post–Cold War in Asia.* Cambridge: Harvard University Press, 2007.

Jang, Jin-sung. *Dear Leader: Poet, Spy, Escapee—A Look Inside North Korea.* Translated by Shirley Lee. New York: Simon & Schuster, 2014.

Jeansonne, Glen, and David Luhrssen. *War on the Silver Screen: Shaping American's Perception of History.* Lincoln: University of Nebraska Press, 2014.

Jeon, Hyun-su, and Gyoo Kahng. "The Shtykov Diaries: New Evidence on Soviet Policy in Korea." cwihp *Bulletin* 6/7 (Winter 1995–96): 69, 92–93.

Jeppeson, Travis. *See You Again in Pyongyang: A Journey into Kim Jong Un's North Korea.* New York: Hachette, 2018.

Jones, Arnita A. "The Promise of Policy History in the Public History Curriculum." *Federal History* 4 (April 28, 2012): 28–42.

Jones, Maggie. "Why a Generation of Adoptees Is Returning to South Korea." *New York Times Magazine* (January 14, 2015): https://www.nytimes.com/2015/01/18 /magazine/why-a-generation-of-adoptees-is-returning-to-south-korea.html.

Joy, C. Turner. *How Communists Negotiate.* Foreword by Matthew B. Ridgway. New York: Macmillan, 1955.

Jung, Kuen-Sik. "China's Memory and Commemoration of the Korean War in the Memorial to Resist America and Aid Korea." *Cross-Currents: East Asian History and Culture Review* 14, no. 14 (March 2015): 63–90.

Kammen, Michael. *Mystic Chords of Memory: The Transformation of Tradition in American Culture.* New York: Knopf, 1991.

———. "Public History and the Uses of Memory." *Public Historian* 19, no. 2 (1997): 49–52.

Kang, Chol-hwan, and Pierre Rigoulot. *The Aquariums of Pyongyang.* Translated by Yair Reiner. New York: Basic, 2001.

Kaplan, Lawrence. "NATO: An Atypical Alliance and Its Longevity." In *Legacy of the Cold War: Perspectives on Security, Cooperation, and Conflict*, edited by Vojtech Mastny and Szhu Liqun, 123–45. Lanham MD: Rowman & Littlefield, 2014.

———. *NATO Divided, NATO United: The Evolution of an Alliance.* Westport CT: Praeger, 2004.

Keene, Judith. "Aesthetics versus Ownership: Artists and Soldiers in the Design of the National Korean War Veterans Memorial in Washington DC." In *War Memories: Commemoration, Recollections, and Writings on War*, edited by Stéphanie A. H. Bélanger and Renée Dickason, 33–54. Montreal: McGill-Queens University Press, 2017.

———. "Bodily Matters Above and Below Ground: The Treatment of American Remains from the Korean War." *Public Historian* 32, no. 1 (February 2010): 59–78.

———. "Framing Violence, Framing Victims: Picasso's Forgotten Painting of the Korean War." *Cultural History* 6, no. 1 (2017): 80–101.

———. "Lost to Public Commemoration: American Veterans of the 'Forgotten' Korean War." *Journal of Social History* 44, no. 4 (July 1, 2011): 1095–113.

———. "War, Cinema, Prosthetic Memory and Popular Understanding: A Case Study of the Korean War." PORTAL *Journal of Multidisciplinary International Studies* 7, no. 1 (January 2010): 1–18.

Kelland, Lara Leigh. *Clio's Foot Soldiers: Twentieth Century Social Movements and Collective Memory*. Amherst: University of Massachusetts Press, 2018.

Kennedy, David M., ed. *World War II Companion*. New York: Simon & Schuster, 2007.

Kerin, James R. *The Korean War and American Memory*. Philadelphia: University of Pennsylvania Press, 1994.

———. "Monument as Metaphor: The Korean War Veterans Memorial." *Proceedings of the Centre for the Study of the Korean War* 1 (2001): 107–21.

Kern, Robert. *We Were Soldiers Too: The Second Korean War—The DMZ Conflict*. Scotts Valley CA: CreateSpace, 2017.

Kim, Byong Moon. "A Perspective on Advancing the Legacy of the Chosin Reservoir Campaign." *The Chosin Few* (April–June 2019): 8–12.

Kim, C. I. Eugene, and B. C. Koh, eds. *Journey to North Korea: Personal Perceptions*. Berkeley: Institute for East Asian Studies, 1983.

Kim, Dong-Choon. "Forgotten War, Forgotten Massacres—The Korean War (1950–1953) as Licensed Mass Killings." *Journal of Genocide Research* 6, no. 4 (December 2004): 523–44.

———. *The Unending Korean War: A Social History*. Translated by Kim Sung-ok. Larkspur CA: Tamal Vista, 2000.

Kim, Donggil. "China's Intervention in the Korean War Revisited." *Diplomatic History* 40, no. 5 (2016): 1002–26.

Kim, E. Tammy. "Return Flights." *New York Review of Books* 59, no. 1 (January 13, 2022): 19–20.

Kim, Eleana J. *Adopted Territory: Transnational Korean Adoptees and the Politics of Belonging*. Durham NC: Duke University Press, 2010.

Kim, Hakjoon. "A Brief History of the U.S.-ROK Alliance and Anti-Americanism in South Korea." *Shorenstein Asia-Pacific Research Center Paper Series* 31 (2010): 7–45.

———. "International Trends in Korean War Studies." *Korean War Studies* 14, no. 2 (Summer 1990): 326–70.

———. "A Review of Korean War Studies since 1992–94." In *Northeast Asia and the Legacy of Harry S. Truman: Japan, China, and the Two Koreas*, ed. James

I. Matray, 315–46. Vol. 8 of *The Truman Legacy Series*. Kirksville MO: Truman State University Press, 2012.

———. "Trends in Korean War Studies: A Review of the Literature." In *Korea and the Cold War: Division, Destruction, and Disarmament*, edited by Kim Chull Baum and James I. Matray, 7–34. Claremont CA: Regina, 1993.

Kim, Hong-nack, ed. "The Korean War (1950–1953) and Its Impact." *International Journal of Korean Studies* 5, no. 1 (Spring–Summer 2001): http://icks.org/n/bbs /content.php?co_id=SPRING_SUMMER_2001.

Kim, Hun Joon. *The Massacre of Mt. Halla: Sixty Years of Truth Seeking in South Korea*. Ithaca: Cornell University Press, 2014.

Kim, Il-sung. *Selected Works*. Pyongyang, DPRK: Korea Pictorial, 1975.

Kim, Jinwung. *A History of Korea: From "Land of the Morning Calm" to States in Conflict*. Indianapolis: Indiana University Press, 2012.

Kim, John H., ed. "In Observance of Centennial of Korean Immigration to the U.S." *National Association of Korean Americans* (2003): http://www.naka.org /resources/history.asp.

Kim, Kyung-A, and Clark W. Sorenson, eds. *Reassessing the Park Chung Hee Era, 1961–1979: Development, Political Thought, Democracy, and Cultural Influence*. Seattle: Center for Korean Studies, University of Washington Press, 2011.

Kim, Monica. "Empire's Babel: U.S. Military Interrogation Rooms of the Korean War." *History of the Present* 3, no. 1 (Spring 2013): 1–28.

———. *The Interrogation Rooms of the Korean War: The Untold History*. Princeton: Princeton University Press, 2019.

Kim, Seung-kyung, and Michael Robinson, eds. *Peace Corps Volunteers and the Making of Korean Studies in the United States*. Seattle: University of Washington Center for Korean Studies, 2020.

Kim, Suki. *Without You, There Is No Us: My Times with the Sons of North Korea's Elite, A Memoir*. New York: Crown, 2014.

Kim, Suzy. *Everyday Life in the North Korean Revolution, 1945–1950*. Ithaca: Cornell University Press, 2013.

———. "Introduction." *Cross-Currents: East Asian History and Cultural Review* 4, no. 1 (May 2015): 1–13.

———. "Introduction to '(De)Memorializing the Korean War: A Critical Intervention.'" *Cross-Currents: East Asian History and Cultural Review* no. 14 (March 2015): https://cross-currents.berkeley.edu/sites/default/files/e-journal/articles /s._kim_introduction_0.pdf.

———. "Specters of War in Pyongyang: The Victorious Fatherland Liberation War Museum in North Korea." *Cross-Currents: East Asian History and Culture Review* 4, no. 1 (2015): 71–98.

Kim, Tong-ch'un, and Sŭng-ok Kim. *The Unending Korean War: A Social History.* Larkspur CA: Tamal Vista, 2009.

Kim, Won-Chung. "The Korean War, Memory, and Nostalgia." In CLC *Web Comparative Literature and Culture* 17, no. 3 (2015): http://www.docs.lib.purdue.edu /clcweb/vol17/iss3/7.

Kim, Yong, and Suk-Young Kim. *Long Road Home: Testimony of a North Korean Camp Survivor.* New York: Columbia University Press, 2009.

Kinder, John. *Paying with their Bodies: American War and the Problem of the Disabled Veteran.* Chicago: University of Chicago Press, 2015.

Kinkead, Eugene. *In Every War but One.* New York: Norton, 1959.

———. "The Study of Something New in History." *New Yorker* (October 26, 1957): 114.

———. *Why They Collaborated.* London: Lowe and Brydone, 1959.

Kinzer, Stephen. *The Brothers: John Foster Dulles, Allen Dulles, and Their Secret World War.* New York: Times Books, 2013.

———. *Poisoner in Chief: Sidney Gottlieb and the CIA Search for Mind Control.* New York: Holt, 2019.

Kolenda, Christopher. *Zero Sum Victory: What We're Getting Wrong About War.* Lexington: University Press of Kentucky, 2021.

Kolko, Joyce, and Gabriel Kolko. *The Limits of Power: The World and United States Foreign Policy, 1945–1954.* New York: Harper & Row, 1972.

The Korean War: An Assessment of the Historical Record. Conference Report (July 24–26, 1995). Washington DC: Georgetown University, 1995.

Korean War Veterans Memorial Advisory Board. *Final Report.* American Battle Monuments Commission. Washington DC: National Archives, 1995.

Korean War Veterans Memorial Brochure. Washington DC: National Park Service, 2007.

Lankov, Andrei. *From Stalin to Kim Il Sung: The Formation of North Korea, 1945–1960.* New Brunswick: Rutgers University Press, 2002.

———. *The Real North Korea: Life and Politics in the Failed Stalinist Utopia.* New York: Oxford University Press, 2013.

Lankov, Andrei, and Kwak In-ok. "The Decline of the North Korean Surveillance State." *North Korean Review* 7, no. 2 (Fall 2011): 6–21.

Lansdale, Edward. *In the Midst of Wars: An American's Mission to Southeast Asia.* New York: Harper & Row, 1972.

Lansford, Tom, Douglas M. Brattebo, and Robert P. Watson, eds. *Leadership and Legacy: The Presidency of Barack Obama.* Albany: State University of New York Press, 2021.

Latham, William C. *Cold Days in Hell: American POWs in Korea.* College Station: Texas A&M University Press, 2013.

Laurie, Clayton D. "Describing the Elephant: CIA Reporting in Korea, 1949–50." In

Northeast Asia and the Legacy of Harry S. Truman: Japan, China, and the Two Koreas, ed. James I. Matray, 259–79. Vol. 8 of *The Truman Legacy Series*. Kirksville MO: Truman State University Press, 2012.

Lech, Raymond B. *Broken Soldiers*. Urbana: University of Illinois Press, 2000.

Lee, Chang-rae. *The Surrendered*. New York: Riverhead, 2010.

Lee, Chong-sik, trans. and ed. *Materials on Korean Communism, 1945–1947*. Occasional Papers, no. 7. Honolulu: Center for Korean Studies, 1977.

Lee, Jean H. "For North Koreans, the War Never Ended." *Wilson Quarterly* (Spring 2017): https://www.wilsonquarterly.com/quarterly/trump-and-a-watching-world /for-north-koreans-the-war-never-ended/.

———. "Guns and Hunger." *Wilson Quarterly* (Summer 2020): https:// www .wilsonquarterly.com/quarterly/korea-70-years-on/remembering-conflict-one -familys-story/.

Lee, Jongsoo James. *The Partition of Korea after World War II: A Global History*. New York: Palgrave Macmillan, 2006.

Lee, Karin, and Adam Miles. "North Korea on Capitol Hill." In *The Future of U.S. Korean Relations: The Imbalance of Power*, edited by John Feffer, 160–77. New York: Routledge, 2006.

Lee, Sungju, and Susan McClelland. *Every Falling Star: The True Story of How I Escaped North Korea*. Translated by Shirley Lee. New York: Atria/Simon & Schuster, 2014.

Lee, Wayne E., Anthony E. Carlson, and David Silbey. *The Other Face of Battle*. Oxford: Oxford University Press, 2021.

Leebaert, Derek. *Grand Improvisation: America Confronts the British Superpower, 1945–1957*. New York: Farrar, Straus and Giroux, 2018.

———. *Magic and Mayhem: The Delusions of American Foreign Policy from Korea to Afghanistan*. New York: Simon and Schuster, 2010.

Leffler, Melvyn P., and David S. Painter, eds. *Origins of the Cold War: An International History*. New York: Routledge, 2005.

———. *A Preponderance of Power: National Security, the Truman Administration, and the Cold War*. Palo Alto: Stanford University Press, 1992.

Lemay, Kate C. "In Memory's Eye: The Improbability of War's Remembrance." *Reviews in American History* 45 (2017): 323–29.

Lentz, Robert J. *Korean War Filmography: 91 English Language Features through 2000*. Jefferson NC: McFarland, 2003.

Lerner, Mitchell B. "A Dangerous Miscalculation: New Evidence from the Communist -Bloc Archives about North Korea and the Crisis of 1968." *Journal of Cold War Studies* 6, no. 1 (Winter 2004): 3–21.

———. *The* Pueblo *Incident: A Spy Ship and the Failure of American Foreign Policy*. Lawrence: University Press of Kansas, 2002.

Lew, Young Ik, Byong-kie Song, Ho-min Yang, and Hy-sop Lim. *Korean Perceptions of the United States: A History of Their Origins and Formation.* Translated by Michael Finch. Seoul: Jimoondang, 2006.

———. *The Making of the First Korean President: Syngman Rhee's Quest for Independence, 1875–1948.* Honolulu: University of Hawai'i Press, 2013.

Lewis, Linda. *Laying Claim to the Memory of May: A Look Back at the 1980 Kwangju Uprising.* Honolulu: University of Hawai'i Press, 2002.

Li, Xiaobing. *China's Battle for Korea: The 1951 Spring Offensive.* Bloomington: Indiana University Press, 2014.

Li, Xiaobing, Allan Millett, and Bin Yu. *Mao's Generals Remember Korea.* Lawrence: University Press of Kansas, 2001.

Lim, Dong-won. *Peacemaker: Twenty Years of Inter-Korean Relations and the North Korean Nuclear Issue.* Palo Alto: Shorenstein Asia Pacific Research Center, 2012.

Lim, Hyun-Soo. "Not 'Final and Irreversible': Explaining South Korea's January 2018 Reversal on the 'Comfort Women' Agreement." *Yale Journal of International Law* (February 1, 2018): https://www.yjil.yale.edu/not-final-and-irreversible-explaining-south-koreas-january-2018-reversal-on-the-comfort-women-agreement/.

Lind, Jennifer. *Sorry States: Apologies in International Politics.* Ithaca: Cornell University Press, 2010.

Litwack, Robert S. "Myth/Misconception: North Korea Is a Crazy State (with Nuclear Weapons), Korea: 70 Years On." *Wilson Quarterly* (Summer 2020): https://www.wilsonquarterly.com/quarterly/korea-70-years-on/korean-war-myths-and-misconceptions/.

———. *Nuclear Crises with North Korea and Iran: From Transformational to Transactional Diplomacy.* Washington DC: Woodrow Wilson Center, 2019.

———. *Preventing North Korea's Nuclear Breakout.* Washington DC: Woodrow Wilson Center, 2017.

Logevall, Fredrik. *Choosing War: The Lost Chance for Peace and the Escalation of the War in Vietnam.* Berkeley: University of California Press, 1999.

Macaluso, Laura. *Monument Culture: International Perspectives on the Future of Monuments in a Changing World.* Lanham MD: Rowman and Littlefield, 2019.

MacArthur, Douglas. *Reminiscences.* New York: McGraw-Hill, 1964.

MacDonald, Callum A. *Britain and the Korean War.* Oxford: Basil Blackwell, 1990.

———. *The War before Vietnam.* New York: Free Press, 1986.

Macdonald, Donald Stone. *The Koreas: Contemporary Society and Politics.* 3rd ed. Boulder CO: Westview, 1996.

———. *U.S.-Korean Relations from Liberation to Self-Reliance: The Twenty-Year Record.* Boulder CO: Westview, 1992.

MacIntyre, Donald A. L., Daniel C. Sneider, and Gi-wook Shin. *First Drafts of Korea: The U.S. Media and Perceptions of the Last Cold War Frontier.* Palo Alto: Shorenstein Asia-Pacific Research Center, 2009.

MacMillan, Margaret. "Which Past Is Prologue? Heeding the Right Warnings from History." *Foreign Affairs* 99, no. 5 (September–October 2020): 12–22.

Madison, Catherine. *The War Came Home with Him: A Daughter's Memoir*. Minneapolis: University of Minnesota Press, 2015.

Mansourov, Alexandre Y. "Stalin, Mao, Kim, and China's Decision to Enter the Korean War, September 16–October 15, 1950: New Evidence from the Russian Archives." *Cold War International History Project Bulletin* nos. 6–7 (Winter 1995–96): 94–119.

Marks, John. *The Search for the "Manchurian Candidate": The CIA and Mind Control*. New York: Norton, 1978.

Marshall, S. L. A. "Combat Stress." *Conference on Recent Advances in Medicine and Surgery, Army Medical Services Graduate School*. Washington DC: April 30, 1954.

———. *Pork Chop Hill: The American Fighting Man in Action, Korea, Spring, 1953*. New York: Morrow, 1956.

———. *The River and the Gauntlet: Defeat of the Eighth Army by the Communist Chinese Forces, November 1950, in the Battle of the Chongchon River, Korea*. New York: Times Books, 1962. First published 1953 by William Morrow and Company (New York).

Martin, Bradley K. *Under the Loving Care of the Fatherly Leader: North Korea and the Kim Dynasty*. New York: St. Martin's Press, 2004.

Martin, Daniel. "South Korean Cinema's Postwar Pain: Gender and National Division in Korean War Films from the 1950s to the 2000s." *Journal of Korean Studies* 19, no. 1. (Spring 2014): 93–114.

Mastný, Vojtěch. *The Cold War and Soviet Insecurity: The Stalin Years*. New York: Oxford University Press, 1996.

Mastný, Vojtěch, and Liqun Zhu, eds. *The Legacy of the Cold War: Perspectives on Security, Cooperation and Conflict*. New York: Lexington, 2014.

Mastro, Oriana Skylar. *The Cost of Conversation: Obstacles to Peace Talks in Wartime*. Ithaca: Cornell University Press, 2019.

Masuda, Hajimu. *Cold War Crucible: The Korean Conflict and the Post War World*. Cambridge: Harvard University Press, 2015.

Matray, James I. "Captive of the Cold War: The Decision to Divide Korea at the 38th Parallel." *Pacific Historical Review* 50, no. 2 (May 1, 1981): 145–68.

———. "Diplomatic History as a Political Weapon: An Assessment of Anti-Americanism in South Korea Today." *SHAFR Newsletter* 20 (March 1989): 1–14.

———. "The Failure of the Bush Administration's North Korean Policy: A Critical Analysis." *International Journal of Korean Studies* 17, no. 1 (Spring 2013): 140–77.

———. "The Hijacked War: Chinese POWs in the Korean War." *Journal of Cold War Studies* 22, no. 3 (Summer 2020): 268–71.

———, ed. *Historical Dictionary of the Korean War*. Westport CT: Greenwood, 1991.

———. "Irreconcilable Differences? Realism and Idealism in Cold War Korean-American Relations." *Journal of American-East Asian Relations* 19, no. 1 (January 2012): 1–26.

———. "Korea's War at 60: A Survey of the Literature." *Cold War History* 11, no. 1 (February 2011): 99–129.

———, ed. *Northeast Asia and the Legacy of Harry S. Truman: Japan, China, and the Two Koreas.* Vol. 8 of *The Truman Legacy Series.* Kirksville MO: Truman State University Press, 2012.

———. "Potsdam Revisited: A Prelude to a Divided Korea." *Journal of American-East Asian Relations* 24 (2017): 259–80.

———. *Reluctant Crusade: American Foreign Policy in Korea, 1941–1950.* Honolulu: University of Hawai'i Press, 1985.

———. "Revisiting Korea; Exposing Myths of the Forgotten War." *Prologue* 34, no. 2 (Summer 2002): http://www.archives.gov/publications/prologue/2002/summer/korean-myths-1.html.

———. "Someplace Else: The Tragedy of Korean-American Relations." *Diplomatic History* 28, no. 1 (January 2004): 159–63.

Matray, James I., and Donald W. Boose Jr., eds. *The Ashgate Research Companion to the Korean War.* Surrey, UK: Ashgate, 2014.

Maxwell, Jeremy P. *Brotherhood in Combat: How African Americans Found Equality in Korea and Vietnam.* Norman: University of Oklahoma Press, 2018.

May, Ernest R. *"Lessons" of the Past: The Use and Misuse of History in American Foreign Policy.* New York: Oxford University Press, 1973.

May, Lary. "Reluctant Crusaders: Korean War Films and the Lost Audience." In *Remembering the Forgotten War,* edited by Philip West and Suh Ji-moon, 110–36. Armonk NY: M. E. Sharpe, 2001.

Mayer, William E. "Communist Indoctrination: Its Significance to Americans." *Freedom Forum* 18 (April 15, 1957): 3–47.

———. "Why Did Many Captives Cave In?" *U.S. News & World Report* 40, no. 8 (February 24, 1956): 56–72.

Mayo, C. W. "Destroying American Minds: Russians Made It a Science." *U.S. News & World Report* 35 (November 6, 1953): 97–101.

McCann, David, and Barry S. Strauss. *War and Democracy: A Comparative Study of the Korean War and the Peloponnesian War.* Armonk NY: M. E. Sharpe, 2001.

McConnell, Malcolm. "Jonnie's List." *Reader's Digest* (January 1967): 49–55.

McCormack, Gavin. *Cold War, Hot War: An Australian Perspective on the Cold War.* Sydney: Hale & Iremonger, 1983.

McCormick, Thomas J. *America's Half-Century: United States Foreign Policy in the Cold War and After.* 2nd ed. Baltimore: The Johns Hopkins University Press, 1995.

McCullough, David. *Truman.* New York: Simon and Schuster, 1992.

McKnight, Brian D. *"We Fight for Peace": Twenty-Three American Soldiers, Prisoners of War, and "Turncoats" in the Korean War*. Kent OH: Kent State University Press, 2014.

McMaster, H. R. *Dereliction of Duty: Lyndon Johnson, Robert McNamara, the Joint Chiefs of Staff, and the Lies that Led to Vietnam*. New York: Harper Perennial, 1997.

McPherson, James. *Battle Cry of Freedom: The Civil War Era*. New York: Oxford University Press, 1988.

Meador, Daniel J., ed. *The Korean War in Retrospect: Lessons for the Future*. Lanham MD: University Press of America, 1998.

Melady, John. *Korea: Canada's Forgotten War*. Toronto: Dundum, 2011. First published 1983 by Macmillan (Canada).

Middleton, Harry J. *The Compact History of the Korean War*. New York: Hawthorn, 1965.

Millett, Allan R. "Captain James H. Hausman and the Formation of the Korean Army, 1945–1950." *Armed Forces and Society* 23, no. 4 (1997): 503–39.

———. *In Many a Strife: General Gerald C. Thomas and the U.S. Marine Corps, 1917–1956*. Annapolis: Naval Institute Press, 1993.

———. *The Korean War: The Essential Bibliography Series*. Washington DC: Potomac, 2007.

———. *Their War for Korea: American, Asian, and European Combatants and Civilians, 1945–1953*. Washington DC: Brassey's, 2002.

———. "Understanding Is Better than Remembering: The Korean War, 1945–1954." Lecture presented at the Dwight D. Eisenhower Lectures in War and Peace, No. 7, Department of History, Kansas State University, Manhattan KS, 1997.

———. *The War for Korea, 1950–51: They Came from the North*. Lawrence: University Press of Kansas, 2010.

Miscamble, Wilson. *From Roosevelt to Truman: Potsdam, Hiroshima, and the Cold War*. Cambridge: Cambridge University Press, 2007.

Mitchell, Arthur H. *Understanding the Korean War: A Ground Level View*. Jefferson NC: McFarland, 2013.

———. *Understanding the Korean War: The Participants, the Tactics, and the Course of Conflict*. Jefferson NC: McFarland, 2013.

Moise, Edwin E. *Tonkin Gulf and the Escalation of the Vietnam War*. Chapel Hill: University of North Carolina Press, 1996.

Moon, Katharine H. S. *Protesting America: Democracy and the U.S.-Korea Alliance*. Berkeley: University of California Press, 2012.

Morris, Seymour, Jr. *Supreme Commander: MacArthur's Triumph in Japan*. New York: Harper, 2021.

Morris-Suzuki, Tessa. *Exodus to North Korea: Shadows from Japan's Cold War*. Lanham MD: Rowman & Littlefield, 2007.

———. *The Past within Us: Media, Memory, and History*. New York: Verso, 2005.

———. "Remembering the Unfinished Conflict: Museums and Contested Memory of the Korean War." *Asia-Pacific Journal* 7, no. 4 (July 27, 2009): https://apjjf.org/-Tessa-Morris-Suzuki/3193/article.pdf.

———. "You Don't Want to Know About the Girls? The 'Comfort Women,' the Japanese Military and Allied Forces in the Asia-Pacific War." *Asia-Pacific Journal: Japan Focus* 13, no. 1 (August 3, 2015): https://apjjf.org/2015/13/31/Tessa-Morris-Suzuki/4352.html.

Morris-Suzuki, Tessa, Low Morris, Leonid Petrov, and Timothy Tsu. *East Asia beyond the History Wars: Confronting the Ghosts of Violence.* New York: Routledge, 2013.

Morrow, Sean. "Bridges at Panmunjom." *Wilson Quarterly* (Summer 2020): https://www.wilsonquarterly.com/quarterly/korea-70-years-on/bridges-at-panmunjom.

Moyn, Samuel. *Humane: How the United States Abandoned Peace and Reinvented War.* New York: Farrar, Straus & Giroux, 2021.

Mueller, John E. *War, Presidents and Public Opinion.* New York: Wiley, 1973.

Munro-Leighton, Judith. "A Post Revisionist Scrutiny of America's Role in the Cold War in Asia, 1945–50." *Journal of American East Asian Relations* 1, no. 1 (Spring 1992): 73–98.

Murphy, Edward R. *Second in Command: The Uncensored Account of the Capture of the Spy Ship* Pueblo. New York: Holt, Rinehart & Winston, 1971.

Myers, B. R. *The Cleanest Race: How North Koreans See Themselves (and Why It Matters).* Brooklyn: Melville House, 2010.

Na, Eunkyung, trans. *Historical Museum of Sexual Slavery by the Japanese Military.* Kyonggi-do Province, ROK: House of Sharing, n.d.

Neustadt, Richard E., and Ernest R. May. *Thinking in Time: The Uses of History for Decision Makers.* New York: Free Press, 1988.

Newman, John. *JFK and Vietnam: Deception, Intrigue, and the Struggle for Power.* New York: Warner, 1992.

Niebuhr, Reinhold. *The Irony of American History.* New York: Scribner's, 1952.

Novick, Peter. *The Nobel Dream: The "Objectivity Question" and the American Historical Profession.* Cambridge: Cambridge University Press, 1988.

Obama, Barack. "Remarks Following a Meeting with President Lee Myung-bak of South Korea in Toronto," June 26, 2010, *Public Papers of the Presidents of the United States, 2010*, Vol. 1 (Washington DC: GPO, 2010), 829.

Oberdorfer, Don, and Robert Carlin. *The Two Koreas: A Contemporary History.* Rev. 3rd ed. New York: Basic, 2014.

O'Connell, Aaron. *Underdogs: The Making of the Modern Marine Corps.* Cambridge: Harvard University Press, 2012.

Oh, Arissa. *To Save the Children of Korea: The Cold War Origins of International Adoption.* Palo Alto: Stanford University Press, 2015.

Oh, Kongdan, and Ralph C. Hassig. *North Korea in a Nutshell: A Contemporary Overview.* Lanham MD: Rowman and Littlefield, 2021.

———. *North Korea: Through the Looking Glass*. Washington DC: Brookings Institution, 2000.

Orwell, George. *1984*. New York: Signet, 1961.

Osgood, Kenneth, and Andrew K. Frank, eds. *Selling War in the Media Age: The Presidency and Public Opinion in the American Century*. Afterword by David Halberstam. Gainesville: University Press of Florida, 2010.

Oshinsky, David M. *A Conspiracy So Immense: The World of Joe McCarthy*. New York: Free Press, 1983.

Osins, Ted. *Nothing Is Impossible: America's Reconciliation with Vietnam*. New Brunswick: Rutgers University Press, 2020.

Paek, Nam-nyong. *Friend: A Novel from North Korea*. Translated by Immanuel King. New York: Columbia University Press, 2020.

Paige, Glen D. *The Korean Decision, June 24–30*. New York: Free Press, 1968.

Paik, Sun-yup. *From Pusan to Panmunjom*. Washington DC: Bassey's, 1992.

———. *Without My Country I Cannot Exist*. Seoul: M. Winners, 2010.

Park, Eugene Y. *Korea: A History*. Stanford: Stanford University Press, 2021.

Park, Jung H. *Becoming Kim Jung Un: A Former CIA Officer's Insights into North Korea's Enigmatic Young Dictator*. New York: Ballantine, 2020.

Park, Mi. *South Korea's Candlelight Revolution: The Power of Plaza Democracy*. Vancouver BC: Coal Harbour, 2018.

Park, Soojin. "Together Apart: Korea: 70 Years On." *Wilson Quarterly* (Summer 2020): https://www.wilsonquarterly.com/quarterly/korea-70-years-on/together-apart/.

Park, Tae Gyun. *An Ally and Empire: Two Myths of South Korea-United States Relations, 1945–1980*. Translated by Ilsoo David Cho. Seoul: Academy of Korean Studies Press, 2012.

Park, Therese. *When a Rooster Crows at Night: A Child's Experience in the Korean War*. New York: iUniverse, 2004.

Park, Yeon-mi, and Maryanne Vollers. *In Order to Live: A North Korean Girl's Journey to Freedom*. New York: Penguin, 2015.

Parritt, Brian. *Chinese Hordes and Human Waves: A Personal Perspective of the Korean War 1950–1953*. Barnsley, UK: Pen & Sword, 2011.

Pash, Melinda. *In the Shadow of the Greatest Generation: The Americans Who Fought the Korean War*. New York: NYU Press, 2012.

Pate, Soo Jin. *From Orphans to Adoption: U.S. Empire and Genealogies of Korean Adoption*. Minneapolis: University of Minnesota Press, 2014.

Pears, Maurice, and Fred Kirkland, comps. *Korea Remembered: The RAN, ARA, and RAAF in the Korean War of 1950–1953*. George Heights NSW: Combined Training and Development Centre, 1998.

Perov, Vladimir. "Soviet Role in the Korean War Confirmed: Secret Documents Declassified." *Journal of Northeast Asian Studies* 13, no. 3 (1994): 42–67.

Perry, John Curtis. *Sentimental Imperialists: The American Experience in Asia*. New York: Harper & Row, 1981.

Perry, Mark. *The Most Dangerous Man in America: The Making of Douglas MacArthur*. Philadelphia: Basic Books, 2014.

Peters, Richard, and Xiaobing Li. *Voices from the Korean War: Personal Stories of American, Korean, and Chinese Soldiers*. Lexington: University Press of Kentucky, 2004.

Phillips, Kimberly. *War! What's It Good For? Black Freedom Struggles and the U.S. Military from World War II to Iraq*. Chapel Hill: University of North Carolina Press, 2012.

Pickowicz, Paul G. "Revisiting Cold War Propaganda: Close Readings of Chinese and American Film Representations of the Korean War." *Journal of American-East Asian Relations* 17, no. 4 (2010): 352–71.

Piehler, G. Kurt. *Remembering War the American Way*. Washington DC: Smithsonian Institution Press, 1995.

Pierpaoli, Paul G., Jr. "Beyond Collective Amnesia: A Korean War Retrospective." *International Social Science Review* 76, nos. 3–4 (2001): 92–102.

———. *Truman and Korea: The Political Culture of the Early Cold War*. Columbia: University of Missouri Press, 1999.

Pinkham, Sophie. "Something Resembling Normal Life." *New York Review of Books* 67, no. 19 (December 3, 2020): 10–14.

Pompeo, Michael R. "Confronting Iran: The Trump Administration's Strategy." *Foreign Affairs* 97, no. 6 (November–December 2018): 60–70.

Pottinger, Matt. "Beijing's American Hustle: How Chinese Grand Strategy Exploits U.S. Power." *Foreign Affairs* 100, no. 5 (September–October 2021): 102–3.

Pound, Richard. *Five Rings Over Korea: The Secret Negotiations Behind the 1988 Olympics in Seoul*. Boston: Little Brown & Co., 1994.

Preston, Andrew. "Selling the Korean War: Propaganda, Politics, and Public Opinion in the United States, 1950–1953." *Cold War History* 9, no. 4 (November 1, 2005): 530–32.

Pritchard, Charles L. *Failed Diplomacy: The Tragic Story of How North Korea Got the Bomb*. Washington DC: Brookings Institution, 2007.

Public Papers of the Presidents: Harry S. Truman, 1945–1953. Washington DC: Government Publishing Office, 1963–1966.

Pubrick, Louise, Jim Allica, and Graham Dawson. *Contested Spaces: Sites, Representatives, and Histories of Conflict*. New York: Palgrave Macmillan, 2007.

Qing, Simei. *From Allies to Enemies: Visions of Modernity, Identity, and U.S.-China Diplomacy, 1945–1950*. Cambridge: Harvard University Press, 2007.

———. "The U.S.-China Confrontation in Korea: Assessment of Intentions in a Time of Crisis." In *Northeast Asia and the Legacy of Harry S. Truman: Japan,*

China, and the Two Koreas, ed. James I. Matray, 93–118. Vol. 8 of *The Truman Legacy Series*. Kirksville MO: Truman State University Press, 2012.

Radchenko, Sergey. *Sport and Politics on the Korean Peninsula: North Korea and the 1988 Seoul Olympics*. North Korea International Document Project. Washington DC: Woodrow Wilson Center, 2011.

Radchenko, Sergey, and David Wolff. "To the Summit via Proxy-Summits: New Evidence from the Soviet and Chinese Archives on Mao's Long March to Moscow, 1949." CWIHP *Bulletin* 16 (Fall 2007–Winter 2008): 105–12.

Rees, David. *Korea: The Limited War*. New York: St. Martin's, 1964.

Reiss, David S. M*A*S*H*: *The Exclusive, Inside Story of TV's Most Popular Show*. Foreword by Alan Alda. Indianapolis: Bobbs-Merrill, 1983.

"Report from Embassy of Hungary in North Korea: April 13, 1955." CWIHP *Bulletin* 14/15 (Winter 2003–Spring 2004): 107.

Rhyu, Sang-young, ed. *Democratic Movements and Korean Society: Historical Documents and Korean Studies*. Seoul: Yonsei University Press, 2007.

Rice, Richard B., and William Nimmo, eds. *The Korean War Veterans Memorial: A Tribute to Those Who Served*. Paducah KY: Turner, 1995.

———. "The Making of the Korean War Veterans Memorial in Washington DC." In *The Korean War Veterans Memorial: A Tribute to Those Who Served*. Paducah KY: Turner, 1995.

———. *The Occupation of Japan: The Impact of the Korean War*. MacArthur Memorial, 7th Annual Symposium, October 16–17, 1986. Norfolk VA: MacArthur Memorial, 1990.

Ridgway, Matthew B. *The Korean War*. Garden City NY: Doubleday, 1967.

———. *Soldier: The Memoirs of Matthew B. Ridgeway*. New York: Harper & Row, 1956.

———. *The War in Korea*. London: Crescent, 1967.

Rishell, Lyle. *With a Black Platoon in Combat: A Year in Korea*. College Station: Texas A&M University Press, 1993.

Robinson, Michael E. *Korea's Twentieth Century Journey*. Honolulu: University of Hawai'i Press, 1972.

Rockoff, Hugh. *America's Way of War: War and the U.S. Economy from the Spanish-American War to the First Gulf War*. Cambridge: Cambridge University Press, 2012.

Rohr, Stephanie, and Natalie Walker. *National Korean War Museum Collection Report*. HSTL working file, n.d.

Rolicka, M. "New Studies Disputing Allegations of Bacteriological Warfare during the Korean War." *Military Medicine* 160, no. 3 (March 1995): 97–100.

Rose, Gideon. *How Wars End: Why We Always Fight the Last Battle: A History of American Intervention from World War I to Afghanistan*. New York: Simon & Schuster, 2010.

Rosenzweig, Roy, and David Thelen. *The Presence of the Past: Popular Uses of American History in American Life*. New York: Columbia University Press, 1998.

Rovere, Richard H., and Arthur M. Schlesinger Jr. *The General and the President*. New York: Farrar, Straus & Young, 1951.

Rozman, Gilbert, ed. *Asia's Alliance Triangle: U.S.-Japan-South Korea Relations at a Tumultuous Time*. New York: Palgrave Macmillan, 2015.

Rubin, Steven J. *Combat Films: American Realism, 1945–2010*. Jefferson NC: McFarland, 2011.

Rusk, Dean. *As I Saw It*. New York: Norton, 1990.

Saldin, Robert P. *War: The American State and Policies Since 1898*. Cambridge: Cambridge University Press, 2011.

Salmon, Andrew. *Modern Korea: All that Matters*. New York: McGraw Hill, 2014.

———. *Scorched Earth, Black Snow: The First Year of the Korean War*. London: Aurum, 2012.

———. *To the Last Round: The Epic British Stand on the Imjin River, Korea 1951*. London: Aurum, 2009.

Sandler, Stanley. *The Korean War: No Victor, No Vanquished*. Lexington: University Press of Kentucky, 1999.

———. *Monument Wars: Washington DC, the National Mall, and the Transformation of the Memorial Landscape*. Berkeley: University of California Press, 2009.

Schleier, Merrill. "Fatal Attractions: 'Place,' the Korean War, and Gender in 'Niagara.'" *Cinema Journal* 51, no. 4 (Summer 2012): 26–43.

Schönherr, Johaness. *North Korean Cinema: A History*. Jefferson NC: McFarland, 2012.

Schrecker, Ellen. *Many Are the Crimes: McCarthyism in America*. Princeton: Princeton University Press, 1998.

Schwartz, Barry, and Todd Schwartz Bayma. "Commemoration and the Politics of Recognition: The Korean War Veterans Memorial." *American Behavioral Scientist* 42 (March 1999): 946–57.

Schwekendiek, Daniel. *Korean Migration to the Wealthy West*. New York: Nova Science, 2012.

Scott-Stokes, Henry, and Jai-eui Lee, eds. *The Kwangju Uprising: Eyewitness Press Accounts of Korea's Tiananmen*. Foreword by Kim Dae Jung. Armonk NY: M. E. Sharpe, 2000.

Scruggs, Jan, and Joel Swerdlow. *To Heal a Nation: The Vietnam Veterans Memorial*. Introduction by Howard K. Smith. New York: Harper & Row, 1986.

Seaton, Philip. "From Cultures of War to Cultures of Peace: War and Peace Museums in Japan, China, and South Korea by Takashi Yoshida (review)." *Monumenta Nipponica* 71, no. 1 (2016): 258–61.

Seed, David. *Brainwashing: The Fictions of Mind Control: A Study of Novels and Films*. Kent OH: Kent State University Press, 2004.

Seth, Michael J. *Korea: A Very Short Introduction*. Oxford: Oxford University Press, 2020.

Shaw, Tony. *Hollywood's Cold War*. Edinburgh: Edinburgh University Press, 2007.

Shen, Zhihua. "The Discrepancy between the Russian and Chinese Version of Mao's 2 October 1950 Message to Stalin on Chinese Entry into the Korean War: A Chinese Scholar's Reply." Translated by Chen Jian. *CWIHP Bulletin* 8/9 (Winter 1996–97): 237–42.

Sherman, Wendy. *Not for the Faint of Heart: Lessons in Courage, Power, and Persistence*. New York: Public Affairs, 2018.

Shimotomai, Nobuo. "Pyeongyang in 1956." *CWIHP Bulletin* 16 (Fall 2007–Winter 2008): 455–63.

Shin, Gi-wook, and Daniel C. Sneider, eds. *History Textbooks and the Wars in Asia: Divided Memories*. New York: Routledge, 2011.

———. *One Alliance, Two Lenses: U.S.-Korea Relations in a New Era*. Palo Alto: Stanford University Press, 2010.

Shin, Gi-wook, Daniel C. Sneider, and Rennie Moon. *Korea's Migrants: From Homogeneity to Diversity—An Asian Survey Special Section*. Palo Alto: APARC, Shorenstein Center, Stanford University, 2019.

Sinitiere, Phillip Luke. *Citizen of the World: The Late Career and Legacy of W. E. B. DuBois*. Evanston IL: Northwestern University Press, 2019.

Sloan, Bill. *The Darkest Summer: Pusan and Inchon 1950: The Battles that Saved South Korea—and the Marines—from Extinction*. New York: Simon & Schuster, 2009.

Snyder, Sarah B. *From Selma to Moscow: How Human Rights Activists Transformed U.S. Foreign Policy*. New York: Columbia University Press, 2018.

Sorensen, Ted C. *Kennedy*. Reprint. New York: Harper & Row, 1988.

Spock, Benjamin. "Are We Bringing Up Our Children Too 'Soft' for the Stern Realities They Must Face?" *Ladies Home Journal* (September 1950): 20.

Springer, Paul J. *America's Captives: Treatment of POWs from the Revolutionary War to the War on Terror*. Lawrence: University Press of Kansas, 2010.

Stairs, Denis. *Diplomacy of Constraint: Canada, the Korean War, and the United States*. Toronto: University of Toronto Press, 1974.

Stallard-Blanchette, Katie. "Past Present." *Wilson Quarterly* (Summer 2020): https://www.wilsonquarterly.com/quarterly/korea-70-years-on/past-present.

Stein, R. Conrad. *Korean War Veterans Memorial*. New York: Children's, 2002.

Steinberg, David I. *Foreign Aid in the Development of the Republic of Korea*. Washington DC: U.S. Agency for International Development, 1985.

———, ed. *Korean Attitudes toward the United States: Changing Dynamics*. Foreword by Robert L. Gallucci. Armonk NY: M. E. Sharpe, 2005.

Stevens, Mary. "Public Policy and the Public Historian: The Changing Place of Historians in Public Life in France and the UK." *Public Historian* 32, no. 3 (Summer 2010): 120–38.

Stoker, Donald. *Why America Loses Wars: Limited War and U.S. Strategy from the Korean War to Present*. New York: Cambridge University Press, 2019.

Stone, I. F. *The Hidden History of the Korean War, 1950–1951*. Preface by Bruce Cumings. New York: Open Road Integrated Media, 2014. First published 1988 by Little, Brown (London).

Straub, David. *Anti-Americanism in Democratizing South Korea*. Palo Alto: Shorenstein Asia-Pacific Research Centre, 2015.

Strausbaugh, John. "Meatball Surgery." *Wilson Quarterly* (Summer 2020): https:// www.wilsonquarterly.com/quarterly/_/the-mash-before-m-a-s-h.

Stueck, William. "The Korean War as History: David Rees' *Korea: The Limited War in Retrospect*." Paper presented at the Cold War International History Conference, College Park, Maryland, September 25–26, 1998. https://www.archives.gov /research/foreign-policy/cold-war/conference/stueck.html.

——. *The Korean War in World History*. Lexington: University of Kentucky Press, 2004.

——. *Rethinking the Korean War: A New Diplomatic and Strategic History*. Princeton: Princeton University Press, 2002.

——. "Revisionism and the Korean War." *Journal of Conflict Studies* 22, no. 1 (Spring 2002): 17–27.

——. *The Road to Confrontation: American Policy toward China and Korea, 1947– 1950*. Chapel Hill: University of North Carolina Press, 1981.

Sturken, Marta. *Tangled Memories: The Vietnam War, the AIDS Epidemic, and the Politics of Remembering*. Berkeley: University of California Press, 1997.

Suchman, Edward A., Rose K. Goldsen, and Robin M. Williams Jr. "Attitudes Towards the Korean War." *Public Opinion Quarterly* 17, no. 2 (Summer 1953): 171–84.

Suh, Jae-Jung, ed. *Truth and Reconciliation in South Korea*. New York: Routledge, 2012.

Suid, Lawrence H. *Guts and Glory: The Making of the American Military Image in Film*. Lexington: University of Kentucky Press, 2002.

Swartout, Robert, Jr. "American Historians and the Outbreak of the Korean War: A Historiographical Essay." *Asian Quarterly* 1 (1979): 65–77.

Szalontai, Balazs. "In the Shadow of Vietnam: A New Look at North Korea's Militant Strategy, 1962–1970." *Journal of Cold War Studies* 14, no. 4 (Fall 2012): 122–166.

——. "You Have No Political Line of Your Own: Kim Il-Sung and the Soviets, 1953–1964." *CWIHP Bulletin* 14/15 (Winter 2003–Spring 2004): 87–137.

Targ, Harry. "Cold War Revisionism Revisited: The Radical Historians of the U.S. Empire." *Monthly Review* 69, no. 7 (December 1, 2017): 31–37.

Taylor, Maxwell D. *The Uncertain Trumpet*. New York: Harper & Brothers, 1959.

Terry, Sue Mi. "North Korea's Nuclear Family: How the Kims Got the Bomb and Why They Won't Give It Up." *Foreign Affairs* 100, no. 5 (September–October, 2021): 115–27.

Tharp, Stephen M. *The Western* DMZ, *Paju: Tharp's Guidebooks to the Korean Front-lines*. Seoul: Cheolma, 2014.

Thomas, Evan. *Ike's Bluff: President Eisenhower's Secret Battle to Save the World*. New York: Little, Brown, 2012.

Thompson, Reginald. *Cry Korea: The Korean War: A Reporter's Notebook*. London: Reportage, 2009. First published 1951 by Macdonald (London).

Toland, John. *In Mortal Combat in Korea, 1950–1953*. New York: William Morrow, 1991.

Tomedi, Rudy. *No Bugles, No Drums: An Oral History of the Korean War*. New York: Wiley, 1993.

Trauschweizer, Ingo. *Maxwell Taylor's Cold War: From Berlin to Vietnam*. Lexington: The University Press of Kentucky, 2019.

Treatment of British Prisoners of War. London: Ministry of Defense, 1955.

Trip, Elise Forbes. *American Veterans on War: Personal Stories from World War II to Afghanistan*. Northampton MA: Olive Branch, 2011.

Truman, Harry S. *Memoirs*. Vol. 1, *Years of Decisions*. Garden City NY: Doubleday, 1955.

———. *Memoirs*. Vol. 2, *Years of Trial and Hope*. Garden City NY: Doubleday, 1956.

Truman, Margaret. *Harry S. Truman*. New York: William Morrow, 1973.

Tucker, Spencer C., ed. *Encyclopedia of the Korean War: A Political, Social, and Military History*. 2nd ed. Santa Barbara: ABC-CLIO, 2010.

Tudor, Daniel. *Ask a North Korean: Defectors Talk about Their Lives inside the World's Most Secretive Nation*. Translated by Elizabeth Jae, Nara Han, Ashely Cho, and Daniel Tudor. Rutland VT: Tuttle, 2017.

Updegrove, Mark K. *Indomitable Will: LBJ in the Presidency*. New York: Crown, 2012.

Utz, Curtis A. *Assault from the Sea: The Amphibious Landing at Inchon*. Washington DC: Naval Historical Center, 2000. First published 1994 as vol. 2 in the *U.S. Navy Modern World Series* by Naval Historical Center (Washington DC).

Valle, Edward. "Kim Family's 12-Year Devotion to Advancing Our Legacy." *Graybeards* 29 (November–December 2015): 26–27.

VanDeMark, Brian. *Into the Quagmire: Lyndon Johnson and the Escalation of the Vietnam War*. New York: Oxford University Press, 1991.

———. *Road to Disaster: A New History of America's Descent into Vietnam*. New York: HarperCollins, 2018.

Van Wagenen, Michael Scott. *Remembering the Forgotten War: The Enduring Legacies of the U.S.-Mexican War*. Amherst: University of Massachusetts Press, 2012.

Vatcher, William H. *Panmunjom: The Story of the Korean Armistice Negotiations*. New York: Praeger, 1958.

Vetter, Harold J. *Mutiny at Koje Island*. Rutland VT: Tuttle, 1965.

Voices from Another Place: A Collection of Works from a Generation Born in Korea and Adopted to Other Countries. St. Paul MN: Yeong & Yeong, 1999.

Wada, Haruki. *The Korean War: An International History*. Translated by Frank Baldwin. Lanham MD: Rowman & Littlefield, 2014.

Wang, Zheng. *Never Forget National Humiliation: Historical Memory in Chinese Politics and Foreign Relations*. New York: Columbia University Press, 2014.

———. "The Past's Transformative Power in China." *Wilson Quarterly* (Fall 2020): https://www.wilsonquarterly.com/quarterly/the-ends-of-history/the-pasts-transformative-power/.

Watson, Robert. "Their Place in History: The Rating Game." In *Leadership and Legacy: The Presidency of Barack Obama*, edited by Tom Lansford, Douglas M. Bratteboro, and Robert P. Watson, 1–22. Albany: State University of New York Press, 2021.

Weathersby, Kathryn. "Deceiving the Deceivers: Moscow, Beijing, Pyongyang, and the Allegations of Bacteriological Weapons Use in Korea." *Cold War International History Project Bulletin* no. 11 (1998): 176–99.

———. "An Exchange on Korean War Origins." *CWIHP Bulletin* 6/7 (Winter 1995): 120–22.

———. "The Korean War Revisited." *Wilson Quarterly* 23, no. 3 (Summer 1999): 91–95.

———. "New Evidence on North Korea: Introduction." *CWIHP Bulletin* 14/15 (Winter 2003–Spring 2004): 5–7.

———. "Should We Fear This?: Stalin and the Danger of War with America." North Korea International Documentation Project Working Paper 39, Woodrow Wilson International Center for Scholars, Washington DC, July 2002. https://www.wilsoncenter.org/sites/default/files/media/documents/publication/ACFAEF.pdf.

———. "Soviet Aims in Korea and the Origins of the Korean War, 1945–1950, New Evidence from the Russian Archives." Cold War International History Project Working Paper 8, Woodrow Wilson International Center for Scholars, Washington DC, November 1993.

———. "The Soviet Role in the Early Phase of the Korean War: New Documentary Evidence." *Journal of American East Asian Relations* 2, no. 4 (Winter 1993): 425–58.

———. "Stalin and the Cold War." In *Origins of the Cold War: An International History*, edited by Melvin P. Leffler and David S. Painter, 265–83. New York: Routledge, 2005.

———. "Stalin, Mao, and the End of the Korean War." In *Brothers in Arms: The Rise and Fall of the Sino-Soviet Alliance, 1945–1963*, edited by Odd Arne Westad, 96–116. Palo Alto: Stanford University Press, 1998.

———. "To Attack or Not Attack: Stalin, Kim Il Sung, and the Prelude to War." *CWIHP Bulletin* 5 (1995): 1–9.

Weintraub, Stanley. "How to Remember the Forgotten War." *American Heritage* 51, no. 3 (May–June 2000): 100–105.

———. *MacArthur's War: Korea and the Undoing of an American Hero*. New York: Free Press, 2000.

———. *War in the Wards: Korea's Unknown Battle in a Prisoner-of-War Hospital Camp*. New York: Doubleday, 1964.

Wells, Samuel F., Jr. *Fearing the Worst: How Korea Transformed the Cold War*. New York: Columbia University Press, 2020.

———. "Sounding the Tocsin: NSC 68 and the Soviet Threat." *International Security* 4 (Fall 1979): 116–58.

West, Philip. "Interpreting the Korean War." *American Historical Review* 94, no. 1 (February 1989): 80–96.

West, Philip, and Ji-moon Suh, eds. *Remembering the Forgotten War: The Korean War through Literature and Art*. Armonk NY: M. E. Sharpe, 2001.

West, Philip, Steven I. Levine, and Jackie Hiltz, eds. *America's Wars in Asia: A Cultural Approach to History and Memory*. Armonk NY: M. E. Sharpe, 1998.

Westad, Odd Arne, ed. *Brothers in Arms: The Rise and Fall of the Sino-Soviet Alliance, 1945–1963*. Palo Alto: Stanford University Press, 1998.

———. *The Cold War: A World History*. New York: Basic, 2017.

Westmoreland, William C. *A Soldier Reports*. New York: Dell, 1976.

Wetta, Frank J. "A Guide to Films on the Korean War." *Journal of Military History* 62, no. 1 (1998): 227–28.

White, Geoffrey M. *Memorializing Pearl Harbor: Unfinished Histories and the Work of Remembrance*. Durham NC: Duke University Press, 2016.

White, W. L. *The Captives of Korea: An Unofficial White Paper on the Treatment of War Prisoners: Our Treatment of Theirs; Their Treatment of Ours*. New York: Scribner's, 1957.

Whitney, Courtney. *MacArthur: His Rendezvous with Destiny*. New York: Knopf, 1956.

Williams, William J., ed. *A Revolutionary War: Korea and the Transformation of the Postwar World*. Chicago: Imprint, 1993.

Wills, Jenny Heijun. *Older Sister, Not Necessarily Related*. Toronto: McClelland and Stewart, 2019.

Wilson, Arthur W., and Norman L. Strickbine. *Korean Vignettes: Faces of War: 201 Veterans of the Korean War Recall that Forgotten War, Their Experiences and Thoughts and Wartime Photographs of that Era*. Portland OR: Artwork Publications, 1996.

Wiltz, John E. "The Korean War and American Society." *Wilson Quarterly* 2, no. 3 (Summer 1978): 127–34.

Wingrove, Paul. "Introduction: Russian Documents on the 1954 Geneva Conference." *CWIHP Bulletin* 16 (Fall 2007–Winter 2008): 85–104.

Winter, Jay. *Remembering War: The Great War between Memory and History in the 20th Century*. New Haven: Yale University Press, 1999.

Winter, Jay, and Emmanuel Sivan, eds. *War and Remembrance in the Twentieth Century*. Cambridge: Cambridge University Press, 1999.

Wittner, Lawrence S. *Rebels Against War: The American Peace Movement, 1933–1983*. Philadelphia: Temple University Press, 1984.

Woo, Susie. *Framed by War: Korean Children and Women at the Crossroads of U.S. Empire*. New York: New York University Press, 2019.

Wool-Rim Sjöblom, Lisa. *Palimpsest: Documents from a Korean Adoption*. Translated by Hanna Ströberg, Lisa Wool-Rim Sjöblom, and Richey Wyver. Montreal: Drawn and Quarterly, 2019. First published 2016 in Swedish by Ordfront (Stockholm).

Worland, Rick. "The Korean War Film as Family Melodrama: *The Bridges at Toko-Ri* (1954)." *Historical Journal of Film, Radio and Television* 19, no. 3 (August 1, 1999): 359–77.

Wright, Brendan. "Divided Nation, Divided Memories." In *Monumental Conflicts: Twentieth Century Wars and the Evolution of Public Memory*, edited by Derek R. Mallett, 111–29. London: Routledge, 2017.

———. "Memory of Politics, Politics of Memory." *Peace Tour* (2018): 52–62.

———. "Politicidal Violence and the Problematics of Localized Memory at Civilian Massacre Sites: The Cheju 4.3 Peace Park and the Kŏch'ang Incident Memorial Park." *Cross-Currents: East Asian History and Culture Review* no. 14 (March 2015): https://cross-currents.berkeley.edu/e-journal/issue-14/wright.

———. "Raising the Korean War Dead: Bereaved Family Associations and the Politics of 1960–1961." *Asia-Pacific Journal* 13, no. 2 (October 12, 2015): 1–19.

Wubben, W. W. "American Prisoners of War in Korea: A Second Look at the 'Something New in History' Theme." *American Quarterly* 22 (Spring 1970): 3–19.

Wylie, Philip. *A Generation of Vipers*. New York: Farrar and Rinehart, 1955. First published 1942 by Rinehart and Company (New York).

Yergin, Daniel. *Shattered Peace*. Boston: Houghton Mifflin, 1977.

Yonhap News Agency. *North Korea Handbook*. Translated by Monterey Interpretation and Translation Services. Armonk NY: M. E. Sharpe, 2003.

Yoo, Theodore Jun. *The Koreas: The Birth of Two Nations Divided*. Oakland: University of California Press, 2020.

Young, Benjamin. *Guns, Guerillas, and the Great Leader: North Korea and the Third World*. Stanford: Stanford University Press, 2021.

Young, Charles S. "Missing Action: POW Films, Brainwashing, and the Korean War, 1954–1968." *Historical Journal of Film, Radio and Television* 18, no. 1 (March 1, 1998): 49–74.

———. *Name, Rank and Serial Number: Exploiting Korean War POWs at Home and Abroad*. New York: Oxford University Press, 2014.

———. "Voluntary Repatriation and Involuntary Tattooing of Korean War POWs." In *Northeast Asia and the Legacy of Harry S. Truman: Japan, China, and the Two Koreas*, ed. James I. Matray, 145–67. Vol. 8 of *The Truman Legacy Series*. Kirksville MO: Truman State University Press, 2012.

Young, James V. *Eye on Korea: An Insider Account of Korean American Relations*, edited by William Stueck. College Station: Texas A&M University Press, 2003.

Young, Marilyn B. "Hard Sell: The Korean War." In *Selling War in a Media Age*, edited by Kenneth Osgood and Andrew Franks, 113–39. Gainesville: University Press of Florida, 2010.

———. *Making the Forever War: Marilyn B. Young on the Culture and Politics of American Militarism*, edited by Mark Philip Bradley and Mary L. Dudziak. Amherst: University of Massachusetts Press, 2021.

Yu, Young Ik. *The Making of the First Korean President: Syngman Rhee's Quest for Independence 1875–1948*. Honolulu: University of Hawai'i Press, 2014.

Yuen, Foong Khong. *Analogies at War: Korea, Munich, Dien Bien Phu, and the Vietnam Decisions of 1965*. Princeton: Princeton University Press, 1992.

Yuh, Ji-Yeon. *Beyond the Shadow of Camptown: Korean Military Brides in America*. New York: NYU Press, 2002.

Zakaria, Fareed. "The New China Scare: Why America Shouldn't Panic about Its Latest Challenger." *Foreign Affairs* 99, no. 1 (January–February 2020): 52–69.

Zubok, Vladislav M. *Failed Empire: The Soviet Union in the Cold War from Stalin to Gorbachev*. Chapel Hill: University of North Carolina Press, 2009.

Zubok, Vladislav M., and Constance Pleshakov. *Inside the Kremlin's Cold War: From Stalin to Khrushchev*. Cambridge: Harvard University Press, 1996.

Zweiback, Adam J. "The 21 'Turncoat GIs': Nonrepatriations and the Political Culture of the Korean War." *Historian* 60, no. 2 (1998): 345–62.

Index

Acheson, Dean, 28, 29–30, 55, 56, 84, 87, 96
Afghanistan, 46, 100, 156, 216
African Americans, 22, 35–36, 50, 59, 66–67, 85, 147
American Battle Monuments Commission (ABMC), 110, 141, 146, 147, 151
American Civil War, 53, 97, 139, 147, 213
American Revolutionary War, 108, 154

Banning, George C. (U.S. Army), 130–31
Banning, William (parent of war casualty), 130–31
Barker, Hal and Ted (sons of war veteran), 106–7, 141
Biden, Joseph, 153, 203
brainwashing: alleged use of, 5, 49, 64, 65, 68–69, 72, 100, 108, 180, 211, 212; origin of term, 9, 63–64
Bundy, McGeorge, 84, 89, 90, 91
Bush, George H. W., 76, 109, 145, 147
Bush, George W., 76, 109, 173, 195–96, 197, 198

Canada, 169, 181
Carter, Jimmy, 109, 191, 193
Center for the Study of the Korean War (CSKW) (Independence MO), 105–6, 133, 134
Central Intelligence Agency (CIA), 28–29, 64
Chiang Kai-shek, 21, 32, 80
China. See Peoples Republic of China (PRC)
Chosin Reservoir (DPRK), 34, 57, 127, 153
Chun Doo-hwan (ROK president), 98, 178–79, 190, 191
Churchill, Winston, 22, 180
Clark, Mark (UNC commander), 40, 73, 74
Clinton, William J. "Bill," 109, 149, 190, 194–95, 196
Cohen, William, 188–89. 189–90
Cold War: emergence, 4, 93, 94; end of, 108; expands, 10; influences public memory, 182; after Korean War, 65, 79, 81, 82; Korean War as first armed conflict of, 14, 16, 20, 31, 114, 118, 129, 149, 155, 207, 215; policy during, 6, 8, 55; stabilized, 44
Colombia, 180, 181
Communism: alliances between nations under, 6–7, 15, 16, 20, 29–30, 33, 34, 100, 101, 114, 160, 168, 182, 202, 213, 216; attempted

Communism (cont.)
indoctrination, 60, 62, 65, 68, 180; forces of seize Indochina, 41; opposition to, 11, 26, 45, 55, 56, 79, 80, 81, 83, 84, 85, 163, 181, 211; purge of in North Korea, 10, 42, 44; religious suppression under, 27; and reunification of Korea, 29; in South Korea, 39; as system of governance, 4, 6, 8, 13, 25, 27, 82, 88, 209; threat of, xii, xiii, 9, 11, 23, 49, 52, 57, 69, 72, 73, 74, 75, 76, 83–84, 91, 92, 102, 114, 126, 158, 172, 212; U.S. questions participation in, 11, 54, 55, 56, 81

Confucianism, xv, 96, 123

Cumings, Bruce, 94–99

CVID (complete, verifiable, irreversible denuclearization), 153, 200, 216

Daniel, Margaret Truman (president's daughter), xvi, 131

Demilitarized Zone (DMZ), 4, 11, 12, 16, 39, 42, 43, 50, 55, 66, 99, 100, 159, 160, 164, 168, 175, 177, 181, 183, 185, 190, 192, 193, 194, 200, 201, 205, 207, 214, 217

Democratic Party (U.S.), 11, 24, 55, 56, 76, 84, 115, 215

Democratic People's Republic of Korea (DPRK): additional threats from, 109; Agreed Framework, 193, 195, 196, 197; bombing of, 35, 42, 86, 87, 97, 176; communism in, 7, 8, 23, 42, 76, 114, 157, 159–60, 168, 187, 209, 211, 214; conflict with South Korea after armistice, 99–101, 214; creation of, 21, 26, 29; culture in, 164–65; cyberattacks by, 199; dictatorship in, 11, 159, 179, 209, 210; economy of, 44, 165, 176, 198; famine in, 170, 194; industrial sites in, 24; infiltrators in South Korea, 28, 66, 214; international relations, 43, 165, 168, 196, 199, 201, 204; invades South Korea, xii, xiii, 7, 12, 20, 30, 31, 32, 52, 55, 95, 162, 173, 209–10, 215, 217; isolation of, 6, 14, 101, 102, 138, 159, 160, 178; military forces of, 34, 36, 100, 126, 162, 189; nationalism in, 29, 160, 201; nuclear capabilities of, 16, 178, 183, 193, 194, 195, 197–98, 199, 200, 201, 216, 217, 218; orphans from, 122; oppose 1988 Summer Olympics, 101; prisoners of war from, 39, 41–42, 53; propaganda from, 13, 98, 161–63; public memory of Korean War in, xvii, 1–2, 3, 4, 6–7, 9–10, 14, 16, 159–60, 161–65, 182, 185, 187, 192–93, 200–202, 204–5, 213, 215, 217; refugees from, 27–28, 34–35, 66, 153, 172, 178; reunification with South Korea, 10, 25, 44, 76, 82, 98, 158, 170, 177, 178, 192–93, 194, 201, 216, 217; separated from South Korea, 22; signs Korean War armistice, 41; and Six-Party Talks, 197–98; supporters of, 5; suppresses elections, 26; treatment of prisoners of war in, 9, 34, 35, 58–59, 60, 61, 64, 65, 66, 73, 115; Victorious War Museum (Victorious Fatherland Liberation War Museum), 161–63, 213; Worker's Party of Korea, 164

Democratic Republic of Vietnam. See North Vietnam

DPRK. See Democratic People's Republic of Korea (DPRK)

Duncan, David Douglas (photographer), 74, 146

Eastwood, Clint, 69, 141–42

Edwards, Paul (U.S. Army), 105–6

Eisenhower, Dwight D.:

administration, 35, 41, 42, 44, 80, 81, 82–83; and communism, 81, 83; cuts veterans' benefits, 50; election, 38, 39–40, 56; and Korean War armistice, 73; memorial to, 145; and U.S. national security, 83; views of in South Korea, 158–59
Elsey, George (White House aide), xvi, 31
Ethiopia, 180, 181

France, 32, 80, 82, 83, 88, 92, 169, 179–80, 180–81, 196, 212

Gaylord, Frank (sculptor), 147, 149
Geneva Conference (1954), 82
Geneva Convention (1949), 39
Glenn, John (U.S. astronaut and senator), 51, 141
Graff, Henry (historian), 89–90, 91
Great Britain, 81, 92, 179–80, 181, 212
Gulf of Tonkin Resolution, 76, 85

Hansen, Robert (director of KWVAB, KWVMAB), 144, 146, 147, 149, 151
Harry S. Truman Library (HSTL) (Independence MO), xiv, xvi, 19, 47, 106, 130–34, 135, 170
Hawaiʻi, 26, 110–13, 121, 124, 173

Incheon, ROK, xi, xii, xiii, 13, 32, 33, 86, 157, 158, 176, 213
Independence MO, 19, 47, 105, 130–34
Indochina, 11, 32, 41, 80, 82, 180
International Atomic Energy Agency (IAEA), 193, 195
Iran, 31, 196
Iraq, 46, 76, 102–3, 156, 196, 200, 216

Japan: holds Korea as colony, 20, 23, 24, 25, 26, 27, 97, 121, 160, 162, 164, 171, 172–73, 179, 187, 192, 200, 204, 207, 209; holds territory in Manchuria, 23, 27, 165, 202; international relations, 203, 216; and Korean War, 67, 71, 168, 181; national security of, 21, 193, 198, 210; opposes communism, 81; post–World War II relations with U.S., 17, 32, 43, 80, 95, 203; snubbed for 1988 Summer Olympics, 101; and World War II, 7, 22, 23, 24, 46, 52, 54, 89, 95, 169, 203, 204, 209; mentioned, 72, 74, 77
Johnson, Lyndon B., 11, 55–56, 56–57, 76, 84–85, 86, 87, 89, 90, 91, 92, 93, 99
Juche. See Kim Il-sung (North Korean leader)

Kaesong, DPRK, 8, 38, 53, 73–74
Kansas, 114–16
Kennedy, John F., 11, 56–57, 83–84, 85, 173
Kim, Byong Moon, 125–29
Kim Dae-jung (ROK president), xvi, 95, 153, 169, 170, 175, 190, 194, 195, 197
Kim Il-sung (DPRK leader): and Communist allies, 21, 97, 167; cult of personality around, 42, 126, 159, 160–61, 214; death, 170; and Juche, 7, 98, 162, 213, 217; after Korean War, 48; before Korean War, 83; during Korean War, 32, 33, 171; leadership of, 7, 10, 16, 25, 27, 39, 42, 44, 96, 98, 101, 122, 159, 161, 162, 163, 165, 179, 193, 194, 210–11, 213; legacy, 159, 160, 161, 164, 165, 176, 194, 205, 217; purges Communist rivals, 10, 42, 44, 160, 213; and reunification of Korea, 28; relations with Soviet Union, 25, 41, 98; source of name, 26
Kim Jong-il (DPRK leader), 164–65, 194, 199
Kim Jong-un (DPRK leader), 154, 163–64, 199, 200

Kim Young-sam (ROK president), 149, 169

Korean Americans: adoptees, 122–24; Christianity among, 121, 127; communities, 15, 120–25, 129, 130, 133, 135, 153; involved in memorialization of Korean War, 105, 110, 113, 114, 116, 125, 127, 135–36, 138, 141, 149, 152, 153, 155, 212; Kansas City Korean Choir, 115, 128; Korean American Association of Greater Kansas City, 115, 128; and public memory of the Korean War, 126–29; survivors of Korean War, 158

Korean Augmentation to the United States Army (KATUSA), 122, 151, 153

Korean National Assembly. *See* Republic of Korea (ROK): Korean National Assembly

Korean People's Army (KPA), 126, 162, 189. *See also* North Korea (DPRK)

Korean War: armistice, xv, 3, 4, 9, 10, 11, 12, 14, 16, 19, 20, 21, 39, 40–41, 44, 45, 50, 73, 81, 91, 99, 110, 130, 138, 139, 160, 161, 166, 168, 190, 212, 213, 216, 218; deaths during, 111, 130, 148, 151, 153, 169, 176, 187, 188; documentaries about, 69; effects on civilian populations, 34–35; films about, 49, 66–69, 72, 119, 141; fiftieth anniversary of, 15, 113, 166; impacts U.S. immigration policy, 121; legacy of, 45–46, 77, 79, 82, 85, 185, 209, 217–18; officially designated "War" in U.S., 15; reassessment of, 12, 94; reporting on, 15; revisionist history of, 13, 80, 93–99, 175, 236–37n33, 238n47, 238n49; seventieth anniversary of, 203; summary of, 31–35, 37–41; survivors of, xiii, xv; television shows about, 70; veterans of in South Korea, xv, 151, 152, 158, 174, 176; veterans of in U.S., 15, 51–52, 58, 87, 91, 103, 106, 107, 111, 113, 116–17, 120, 127, 128, 129, 136, 140, 141, 142, 143, 145, 150, 151, 152, 155, 156, 175, 209, 212

Korean War Memorials: Boulder City NV, 119; Dayton OH, 119; *The Forgotten War* (Olympia WA), 116; Fort Wayne IN, 119; Harvard University, 126; Honolulu HI, 111–13; *Korean Cranes Rising* (Lawrence KS), 116, 135; Korean War Children's Memorial (Bellingham WA), 119; Massachusetts Institute of Technology (MIT), 125–26; Missouri Korean War Veterans Memorial (Kansas City MO), 116; Overland Park KS, 115, 116; Spokane WA, 119; Topeka KS, 116; Utah Korean War Memorial (Salt Lake City UT), 114; Vancouver, BC, 135; Vermillion County IL, 118–19; Wichita KS, 116; Williams College (Williamstown MA), 119; mentioned, 129–30, 134, 135, 148, 240n10, 247n43, 251n48. *See also* Korean War Veterans Memorial (KWVM)

Korean War Memorial Trust Fund, 141, 142

Korean War National Museum and Library (Springfield IL), 106, 133, 134–35

Korean War Project website, 107, 245n32

Korean War Veterans Advisory Board (KWVAB), 141, 142, 143–44, 145–46, 147, 148

Korean War Veterans Association (KWVA), 108, 109, 113, 137, 140, 142, 156

Korean War Veterans Memorial (KWVM), 1, 106, 109, 111, 137, 138–39,

141, 143, 147, 148, 149, 151, 154, 155, 156, 212

Korean War Veterans Memorial Advisory Board (KWVMAB), 147, 150

Korean War Veterans Memorial Foundation (KWVMF), 151, 152, 154

Lee Myung-bak (ROK president), 188, 199

MacArthur, Douglas (U.S. Army): admiration of, xii, 46, 51, 76–77, 157–58; attempts Republican nomination for U.S. presidential candidate, 56; autobiography, 74–75; commands U.S. and UN forces in Korean War, 31, 32–34, 37, 46–47, 87, 172, 177; dismissed, xii, 6, 8, 38, 51, 53, 74, 157–58; legacy of, 46–47, 76–77; meets with President Harry S. Truman, 33, 38, 74, 75; memorialized, 10, 141, 144, 145; plan for victory in Korean War, 40; statue of, xi, xii, 7, 13, 99, 158, 159, 176, 213; views on conduct of Korean War, 37–38, 55; vilified, 176

Mao Zedong: involvement in Korean War, 20–21, 33, 48, 98, 166, 171; leadership of, 10, 28, 33, 42–43, 157, 161, 167, 182, 202, 210, 211; relations with Soviet Union, 41; U.S. opposition to, 32

McCarthy, Joseph (U.S. senator), 11, 55, 56, 68, 81

missing in action (MIA), 108–9, 113, 143, 146, 148, 151, 200, 204

Moon Jae-in (ROK president), 153–54, 175, 179, 199, 203

National Capital Planning Commission (NCPC), 145, 147

National Cemetery of the Pacific (Honolulu HI), 110–11, 118

National Mall (Washington DC), 15, 106, 108, 109, 110, 111, 112, 118, 136, 137, 138, 140, 144, 147, 151, 154, 212

National Park Service (NPS), 148, 149, 151, 152

Native Americans, 36, 54, 67, 84, 147

New Zealand, 154, 181

Nixon, Richard M., 47, 56, 109, 167, 202

No Gun Ri, ROK, 13, 185, 188, 189–90

North Atlantic Treaty Organization (NATO), 7, 29, 30, 37, 44, 80, 210, 212

North Korea. See Democratic People's Republic of Korea (DPRK)

North Vietnam, 82, 85, 86, 88, 90

nuclear weaponry, 16, 20, 21, 22, 28, 36–37, 40, 41, 43, 44, 56, 73, 89, 183, 193, 196, 197, 199, 200, 201, 212, 216, 217, 218

Obama, Barack, 198–99

Olympia WA, 116–18

Olympic Games: 1980 Summer (Moscow), 100; 1984 Summer (Los Angeles), 10; 1988 Summer (Seoul), 6, 12, 100–102, 108, 129, 168; 2000 Summer (Sydney), 194; mentioned, 128

Paik Sun-yup (ROK general), xvi, 40, 169–70, 190

Panmunjom DMZ, xv, 8, 38, 50, 66, 74, 80, 110, 130, 164, 169, 200, 216

Park Chung-hee (ROK president), 12, 98, 99, 100–101, 169, 173, 174, 175, 178, 191, 199

Park Chung Hee Presidential Museum, xvi, 173–75

Park Geun-hye (ROK president), 179

Pennsylvania State University, 145, 146, 149

People's Liberation Army (PLA), xiii, 162. *See also* China

People's Republic of China (PRC): Chinese Communist Party in, 165, 167, 202–3; Chinese Military Museum (Beijing), 167; in Cold War, 8; communist government in, 28, 74, 76, 83, 157, 166, 202–3, 210; economy of, 16; industrial sites in, 24; international relations, 6, 12, 29, 43, 102, 154, 165, 166, 167, 168, 171, 192, 198, 216, 217; involvement in Korean War, 8–9, 16, 20, 33–34, 37, 38, 39, 42, 54, 58, 67, 73, 74, 77, 87, 96, 98, 116, 122, 127, 153, 159, 163, 167, 171, 181, 182, 207, 210, 211, 213, 218; involvement in Vietnam War, 88; Korean exiles in, 5; lessons learned from Korean War, 82; "loss of," 11, 52, 55, 84; Manchuria, 23, 27, 31, 91, 160; Memorial of the War to Resist U.S. Aggression and Aid Korea (Dandong), 166–67; military of, 16, 162; nationalism in, 203; Nationalist regime in, 10, 30, 32, 39, 44, 55, 168; and 1988 Summer Olympics, 101; orphans from, 123; prestige of, 10; prisoners of war from, 39, 53; public memory of Korean War in, xvii, 1–2, 4, 6–7, 165–68, 185, 187, 202, 204, 217; signs Korean War armistice, 41; and Six-Party Talks, 197–98; treatment of prisoners of war by, 9, 58–59, 60, 61, 64, 65, 73; veterans of Korean War in, 166; mentioned, xv, xvi

the Philippines, 46, 180, 181

Potsdam Conference, xii, 5, 22, 23, 177

prisoners of war (POWs): conditions in camps, 58, 60–61, 68; conduct of, 15, 49, 51, 57–58, 62, 63, 66, 69, 180, 212; deaths of, 9, 34, 58, 60–61, 64, 66, 96, 187; diversity among, 146; escape, 59, 64; false confessions of, 57, 64, 65, 74, 118; investigated, 59, 61–62, 100, 180; medals issued, 109; memories of, 100; missing, 41; mistreatment of, 5, 9, 34, 35, 58–59, 60–61, 64, 65, 211; names of, 148, 151; public perception of, 72, 108; refuse repatriation, 58; repatriation of, 8, 38–39, 53, 180, 229n20; research into, 106, 107; returned, 45, 59; and U.S. Progressive Party, 55

public memory: collective memory and, 2, 107–8; conflicting, 1, 20, 50, 185, 215, 217; contested, 4, 216, 217; and creation of national identities, 3; evolution of, 1; and forgetting, 2, 65, 77, 82, 96, 114, 179, 215; grassroots efforts toward, 107; imposed, 2; mistaken for history, 3, 107, 186; misuse of, 89; remembrance of wars, xvi, 3–4, 5, 6, 9, 12, 45, 46, 90, 107, 108, 109, 114, 129–30, 135, 137, 138, 139, 155, 179, 182, 186, 187, 215; subjective, 91; and veterans, 17, 103, 107, 108, 135, 138, 139

"Punchbowl Cemetery." *See* National Cemetery of the Pacific (Honolulu HI)

Pyongyang, DPRK, 27, 33, 34, 97, 98, 101, 160, 161, 163, 164, 166, 193, 194, 197

Rangel, Charles (U.S. representative), 51, 151

Reagan, Ronald, 66, 76–77, 101, 109, 140, 141, 142, 173

Republican Party (U.S.), 5–6, 11, 38, 39–40, 46, 50, 55, 56, 75, 76, 83, 84, 115

Republic of China (Taiwan), 10, 30, 32, 33, 39, 44, 80, 81, 168, 169, 204

Republic of Korea (ROK): Christianity

in, 163, 176, 190, 209; conflict with North Korea after armistice, 99–101, 214; corporate support for Korean War memorials, 15, 138, 142, 152, 180, 212; creation of, 21, 26, 29; culture in, 178; defense of, xii, 10; democracy in, 4–5, 12, 95, 102, 103, 109, 137, 138, 149, 154, 157, 168, 169, 173, 174, 176, 185, 186, 190, 193, 209, 211, 212, 213, 214, 216, 217, 218; dictatorship in, 11, 25–26, 45, 95, 137, 168, 173, 179, 185, 187, 190, 192, 200, 201, 213; economy in, 94, 109, 123, 138, 157, 168, 176, 179, 191, 192, 193–94, 201, 209, 211, 213, 217, 218; education in, xv, 133; emigrants from, 121–22; government support for Korean War memorials, 152–53; international relations, xvi, 5, 8, 17, 26, 27, 29, 30, 43, 75, 93, 102, 154, 155, 166, 168, 173, 175, 176, 178, 189, 192, 193, 195, 197, 203; invades North Korea, 12, 163; invasion of, xii, xiii, 20, 21, 30, 31, 32, 34, 52, 55, 95, 124, 162, 173, 209–10, 215, 217; Korean Ministry of Patriots and Veterans Affairs, 175; Korean National Assembly, 30; Korean War Memorial Foundation, 169; Korean War National Museum (KWNM; South Korea), 16; military forces of, 38, 39, 100, 122, 151, 157, 162, 167, 169; Ministry of National Defense, 189; Ministry of Unification, 193; nationalism in, 29, 201; 1988 Summer Olympics in, 6, 12, 100–102, 108, 129, 168; National Museum of Korean Contemporary History (Seoul, South Korea), 172; and North Korean infiltrators, 28, 187, 189; orphans from, 67, 71, 119, 121, 122, 123, 124, 125; People Power Party, 154; prisoners of war from,

39, 41, 59, 60; public memory of Korean War in, xvii, 1–2, 3, 4, 6, 7, 9–10, 13–14, 16, 98, 102, 108, 159, 168–78, 182, 185, 186–87, 192–93, 200–202, 213, 215, 217; recognized by UN, 16; refugees in, 172, 178, 189; reunification with North Korea, 10, 25, 44, 76, 82, 98, 158, 170, 177, 178, 192–93, 194, 201, 216, 217; separated from North Korea, 22; sites of conscience, 186–87; and Six-Party Talks, 197–98; war brides from, 121, 124, 125; War Memorial of Korea (Seoul, South Korea), 169–72

Republic of Korea Army (ROKA), 151, 169. *See also* Republic of Korea (ROK)

Republic of Vietnam. *See* South Vietnam

Rhee, Syngman (ROK president): Christianity of, 26; leadership of, 13, 25, 26, 27–28, 42, 44, 52, 87, 95, 96, 98, 158, 159, 168, 173, 174, 178, 187, 211, 214; opposes armistice, 39, 41, 42, 80, 213; and U.S., 10, 21, 25, 26–27, 28, 29, 30, 40, 43, 83, 121, 211

Rice, Condoleezza, 102–3, 195

Ridgway, Matthew (U.S. Eighth Army commander), 34, 36, 38, 73, 88–89

Roh Tae-woo (ROK president), 169, 176, 179, 187

ROK. *See* Republic of Korea (ROK)

Roosevelt, Franklin D., 21, 22, 23, 90

Rusk, Dean, 85, 87, 89, 90–91

Russia, 176, 197, 216. *See also* Soviet Union

Seoul, South Korea, xi, xiii, xv, 23, 34, 67, 99, 100, 101, 122, 126, 154, 164, 169, 170, 172, 173, 175, 176, 179, 188, 191, 194

South Africa, 181, 187

South Korea. *See* Republic of Korea (ROK)

South Vietnam, 11, 82, 83, 84, 93, 99, 154

Southeast Asia Treaty Organization (SEATO), 80–81

Soviet Union: blamed for brainwashing, 64, 65, 68; in Cold War, 8, 14, 44, 45, 94; culture in, 164; demise of, 97, 170, 176, 194; international relations, xii–xiii, 4, 5, 6, 12, 23, 29, 30–31, 32, 98, 102, 161, 168, 216; involvement in Korean War, 7, 8–9, 16, 20, 37, 39, 40–41, 42, 52, 53, 54, 55, 75, 77, 79, 86, 95, 96, 114, 160, 162, 163, 171, 182, 207, 210, 213, 217, 218; involvement in Vietnam War, 88; involvement in World War II, 22, 24, 209; and 1988 Summer Olympics, 101; nuclear weaponry possessed by, 28, 212; politics of, 10, 26, 157; public memory of Korean War in, 10, 217

Stalin, Joseph: death of, 40–41, 43; and end of World War II, 22, 23; involvement in Korean War, 20–21, 28, 29, 30–31, 33, 42, 48, 55, 80, 97, 98, 162, 171, 210, 211, 217; as originator of Cold War, 94

Stone, I. F. (journalist), 54, 94, 95

Taiwan. *See* Republic of China (Taiwan)

38th parallel: crossing of, 32–33, 34, 52, 182; established to divide North and South Korea, xii, 5, 23, 25, 177

Treaty on the Non-Proliferation of Nuclear Weapons (Non-Proliferation Treaty, NPT), 193, 197

Truman, Bess (president's wife), 22, 47, 131

Truman, Harry S.: approval ratings of, 12–13, 52, 53; chooses to not seek another term, 56; civil rights agenda, 132; criticism of, 55, 74–75, 76, 84, 93, 94; dismisses Gen. Douglas MacArthur, xii, 6, 8, 38, 51, 53, 74; expands U.S. military, 80; and immigration policy in U.S., 121; and Korean War, xiii, 5, 6, 7, 21, 22, 24, 25, 26, 28, 29, 30, 32, 36–37, 56, 75–76, 85, 87, 91, 92, 96, 170, 177, 210, 211, 218; legacy of, 45, 46, 47–48, 127–28, 177; meets with Gen. Douglas MacArthur, 33, 38, 74, 75; orders racial integration of U.S. Armed Forces, 35–36; after presidency, 19–20, 47, 73, 132; and prisoners of war, 39; reflects on Korean War, 19–20, 31, 73, 130–31; statue of, 177; views of in South Korea, xii, 158–59; after World War II, 23; mentioned, 90

Truman Institute for National and International Affairs, 128, 132–33, 134

Trump, Donald J., 153–54, 199–200, 202, 203

Truth and Reconciliation Commission, Korea (TRCK), 185, 187–88

Union of Soviet Socialist Republics (USSR). *See* Soviet Union

United Nations (UN): armistice negotiations, 73–74; credibility of, 21; danger to, 31; establishment of, 132; excludes China, 32, 44; and Korean War, 5, 7, 13, 16, 26, 53, 58, 74, 75, 87, 93, 118, 128, 129, 152, 168, 171, 172, 179, 209, 210; as peacekeeping organization, 54–55, 198; Security Council, 32, 199; support for war against Iraq, 76; Temporary Committee on Korea (UNTCOK), 26

United Nations Command (UNC):
armistice negotiations, 74; cemetery honoring, 7; included in
Korean War memorials, 117, 118;
and Korean War armistice, xv; military forces of, 1, 32, 33–34, 35, 38,
39, 40, 44, 52, 58, 122, 143, 144, 147,
149, 150, 157, 162, 163, 169, 170, 172,
175, 176, 181, 182, 188, 210, 211, 212,
214; public memory of Korean War
among nations of, 102, 179–82, 218;
prisoners of war from, 5, 39, 41, 57–
58, 61; support of Korean War, 6, 16;
supports South Korea, 10
United States: civil rights in, 22; in
Cold War, 8, 14, 44, 94; Commission of Fine Arts (CFA), 145, 147;
corporate support for Korean War
memorials, 115, 142, 152; as de facto
policeman for world, 43, 73, 76,
81, 215; Department of Defense,
106, 152, 153, 189; Department of
Housing and Urban Development,
115; Department of State (USDS),
97; Department of Treasury, 142;
immigration policy, 121; international relations, xvi, 5, 10, 11, 17,
23, 26, 27, 29–30, 55, 75, 95, 114,
195, 197, 201, 203; involvement in
Korean War, 7, 8, 19–20, 21, 36, 37,
39, 40, 74–75, 93, 94–95, 97, 98–99,
116, 159, 163, 164, 166, 172, 175, 176,
180, 207, 210, 213–14; involvement
in Vietnam War, 10–11, 45, 46, 57,
58, 71, 76, 80, 82–86, 87, 89, 90, 91,
92, 99–100, 137, 209; lessons from
Korean War, 82, 85, 91–92; Korean
exiles in, 5; military forces of, 1,
40, 176, 185, 191, 214, 216; national
security of, 83, 114; NSC-68, 32, 43,
80; opposes Mao Zedong, 32; Postal
Service, 109; prisoners of war from,

5, 39, 41, 45, 57, 58, 59–60, 61, 63,
64, 65, 68, 115; public memory of
Korean War in, xvi, 1, 2, 3, 4, 5, 6, 11,
13, 15–16, 44–45, 49–50, 65–73, 75,
77, 79, 82, 85, 88, 91–92, 96, 102, 107,
109, 120, 124, 137, 138, 139, 179, 181,
212, 215, 217, 218; signs Korean War
armistice, 41; and Six-Party Talks,
197–98; threatens use of nuclear
weaponry, 40, 41; views during
Korean War in, 8, 9, 15, 51–52, 53,
56, 57
U.S. Air Force (USAF), 34, 35, 36, 57, 65,
67, 99, 106, 120, 126, 143
U.S. Armed Forces, 14, 33, 35–36, 124–
25, 149, 151, 154, 202. See also specific
forces
U.S. Army: Corps of Engineers, 144;
Eighth Army, 34, 57, 86, 88, 143, 170;
Korean advisor to, 121; Inspector General, 189; 101st Airborne
Infantry Division, 86, 137; 181th
Airborne Regiment Combat Team,
143; racial integration in, 36; 24th
Infantry Regiment, 36; mentioned,
91, 105, 115
U.S. Congress, 15, 29, 30, 32, 38, 45, 50,
56, 76, 85, 110, 121, 140, 141, 144, 150,
151, 152, 153, 195, 197, 208
U.S. Marine Corps, 86, 127, 137, 143,
150, 153
U.S. Navy, 32, 36, 67, 79, 80, 85, 91, 99
USS Pueblo, 12, 99–100, 163
USSR. See Soviet Union

Vietnam, 204, 216. See also North Vietnam; South Vietnam
Vietnam Veterans Memorial, 15, 108,
109, 112, 118, 135, 136, 138, 140–41,
144, 145, 146, 147, 148, 151, 152, 154,
156
Vietnam War: deaths during, 111;

Vietnam War *(cont.)*
  impacts U.S. immigration policy,
  121; influenced by Korean War, 75,
  91, 93; *M*A*S*H* as allegory for,
  70, 71, 72; memorials to, 117, 118–
  19; opposition to, 55, 57, 71, 72, 79,
  90–91; public opinion of, 88; U.S.
  involvement in, 10–11, 45, 46, 57, 58,
  71, 76, 80, 82–86, 87, 88, 90, 91, 92,
  94, 99–100, 118, 137, 209, 215; veterans of, 15, 51, 108–9, 111, 113, 120, 138,
  155, 209, 212

Wake Island, 33, 38, 74, 75
Warner, John (U.S. senator), 51, 14
Washington DC, 15, 106, 108, 109, 110,
  111, 112, 118, 135, 136, 137, 138, 140,
  153, 154, 155, 212
Weathersby, Kathryn, 97, 223n23
Weber, William (U.S. Army), 143–44, 152

World War I, 3, 24, 109, 139, 154
World War II: conduct of, 56; deaths
  during, 110; effects on U.S. population, 29; end of, 8, 20, 21, 43, 53, 202,
  208; international relations after,
  14, 23, 80, 93, 209, 210; memorials to, 118, 145, 154; as precursor to
  Cold War, 4; prosperity after, 45;
  public memory of, 9, 19, 31, 38, 46,
  90, 92, 203, 213, 215; racial integration during, 36; recovery from, 180;
  veterans of, 5, 8, 45, 50, 51, 57, 87, 91,
  120, 137, 155, 162, 169, 174; victory in,
  15, 38, 53, 54, 94, 208; mentioned, 27,
  42, 55, 79, 88, 89

Yalu River, 33, 46, 59, 60, 122, 165, 166,
  209, 211
Yonsei University (South Korea), xv,
  122, 175

STUDIES IN WAR, SOCIETY, AND THE MILITARY

Military Migration and State Formation: The British Military Community in Seventeenth-Century Sweden
Mary Elizabeth Ailes

Managing Sex in the U.S. Military: Gender, Identity, and Behavior
Edited by Beth Bailey, Alesha E. Doan, Shannon Portillo, and Kara Dixon Vuic

The State at War in South Asia
Pradeep P. Barua

Marianne Is Watching: Intelligence, Counterintelligence, and the Origins of the French Surveillance State
Deborah Bauer

Death at the Edges of Empire: Fallen Soldiers, Cultural Memory, and the Making of an American Nation, 1863–1921
Shannon Bontrager

An American Soldier in World War I
George Browne
Edited by David L. Snead

Beneficial Bombing: The Progressive Foundations of American Air Power, 1917–1945
Mark Clodfelter

Fu-go: The Curious History of Japan's Balloon Bomb Attack on America
Ross Coen

Imagining the Unimaginable: World War, Modern Art, and the Politics of Public Culture in Russia, 1914–1917
Aaron J. Cohen

The Rise of the National Guard: The Evolution of the American Militia, 1865–1920
Jerry Cooper

The Thirty Years' War and German Memory in the Nineteenth Century
Kevin Cramer

Political Indoctrination in the U.S. Army from World War II to the Vietnam War
Christopher S. DeRosa

The Korean War Remembered: Contested Memories of an Unended Conflict
Michael J. Devine

In the Service of the Emperor: Essays on the Imperial Japanese Army
Edward J. Drea

American Journalists in the Great War: Rewriting the Rules of Reporting
Chris Dubbs

America's U-Boats: Terror Trophies of World War I
Chris Dubbs

The Age of the Ship of the Line: The British and French Navies, 1650–1815
Jonathan R. Dull

American Naval History, 1607–1865: Overcoming the Colonial Legacy
Jonathan R. Dull

Soldiers of the Nation: Military Service and Modern Puerto Rico, 1868–1952
Harry Franqui-Rivera

You Can't Fight Tanks with Bayonets: Psychological Warfare against the Japanese Army in the Southwest Pacific
Allison B. Gilmore

A Strange and Formidable Weapon: British Responses to World War I Poison Gas
Marion Girard

Civilians in the Path of War
Edited by Mark Grimsley and Clifford J. Rogers

A Scientific Way of War: Antebellum Military Science, West Point, and the Origins of American Military Thought
Ian C. Hope

Picture This: World War I Posters and Visual Culture
Edited and with an introduction by Pearl James

Indian Soldiers in World War I: Race and Representation in an Imperial War
Andrew T. Jarboe

Death Zones and Darling Spies: Seven Years of Vietnam War Reporting
Beverly Deepe Keever

For Home and Country: World War I Propaganda on the Home Front
Celia Malone Kingsbury

I Die with My Country: Perspectives on the Paraguayan War, 1864–1870
Edited by Hendrik Kraay and Thomas L. Whigham

North American Indians in the Great War
Susan Applegate Krouse
Photographs and original documentation by Joseph K. Dixon

Remembering World War I in America
Kimberly J. Lamay Licursi

Citizens More than Soldiers: The Kentucky Militia and Society in the Early Republic
Harry S. Laver

Soldiers as Citizens: Former Wehrmacht Officers in the Federal Republic of Germany, 1945–1955
Jay Lockenour

Deterrence through Strength:
British Naval Power and Foreign
Policy under Pax Britannica
Rebecca Berens Matzke

Army and Empire: British Soldiers
on the American Frontier, 1758–1775
Michael N. McConnell

Of Duty Well and Faithfully
Done: A History of the Regular
Army in the Civil War
Clayton R. Newell and
Charles R. Shrader
Foreword by Edward M. Coffman

The Militarization of Culture in
the Dominican Republic, from the
Captains General to General Trujillo
Valentina Peguero

A Religious History of the
American GI in World War II
G. Kurt Piehler

Arabs at War: Military
Effectiveness, 1948–1991
Kenneth M. Pollack

The Politics of Air Power:
From Confrontation to
Cooperation in Army Aviation
Civil-Military Relations
Rondall R. Rice

Andean Tragedy: Fighting the
War of the Pacific, 1879–1884
William F. Sater

The Grand Illusion: The
Prussianization of the Chilean Army
William F. Sater and
Holger H. Herwig

Sex Crimes under the Wehrmacht
David Raub Snyder

In the School of War
Roger J. Spiller
Foreword by John W. Shy

Empire between the Lines: Imperial
Culture in British and French Trench
Newspapers of the Great War
Elizabeth Stice

On the Trail of the Yellow
Tiger: War, Trauma, and Social
Dislocation in Southwest China
during the Ming-Qing Transition
Kenneth M. Swope

Friendly Enemies: Soldier
Fraternization throughout
the American Civil War
Lauren K. Thompson

The Paraguayan War, Volume 1:
Causes and Early Conduct
Thomas L. Whigham

Policing Sex and Marriage
in the American Military:
The Court-Martial and the
Construction of Gender and
Sexual Deviance, 1950–2000
Kellie Wilson-Buford

The Challenge of Change:
Military Institutions and
New Realities, 1918–1941
Edited by Harold R. Winton
and David R. Mets

To order or obtain more information on these or other University
of Nebraska Press titles, visit nebraskapress.unl.edu.

CPSIA information can be obtained
at www.ICGtesting.com
Printed in the USA
LVHW041153170623
750068LV00004B/26